Building Blocks for Learning: Occupational Therapy Approaches

Building Blocks for Learning: Occupational Therapy Approaches

Practical Strategies for the Inclusion of Special Needs in Primary School

Jill Jenkinson
*Senior Children's Occupational Therapist, Children's Centre,
Dorset County Hospital, Dorchester*

Tessa Hyde
*Senior Children's Occupational Therapist, Children's Centre,
Royal United Hospital, Bath*

and

Saffia Ahmad
*Senior Children's Occupational Therapist, Avon
and Wiltshire Mental Health Partnership NHS Trust;
Wiltshire Locality*

John Wiley & Sons, Ltd

This edition first published 2008
© 2008 John Wiley & Sons Ltd

Wiley-Blackwell is an imprint of John Wiley & Sons, formed by the merger of Wiley's global Scientific, Technical and Medical business with Blackwell Publishing.

Registered office
John Wiley & Sons Ltd, The Atrium, Southern Gate, Chichester, West Sussex, PO19 8SQ, United Kingdom

Editorial office
John Wiley & Sons Ltd, The Atrium, Southern Gate, Chichester, West Sussex, PO19 8SQ, United Kingdom

For details of our global editorial offices, for customer services and for information about how to apply for permission to reuse the copyright material in this book please see our website at www.wiley.com/wiley-blackwell.

The right of the authors to be identified as the author of this work has been asserted in accordance with the Copyright, Designs and Patents Act 1988.

Wiley also publishes its books in a variety of electronic formats. Some content that appears in print may not be available in electronic books.

Designations used by companies to distinguish their products are often claimed as trademarks. All brand names and product names used in this book are trade names, service marks, trademarks or registered trademarks of their respective owners. The publisher is not associated with any product or vendor mentioned in this book. This publication is designed to provide accurate and authoritative information in regard to the subject matter covered. It is sold on the understanding that the publisher is not engaged in rendering professional services. If professional advice or other expert assistance is required, the services of a competent professional should be sought.

Library of Congress Cataloging-in-Publication Data

Jenkinson, Jill.
  Building blocks for learning, occupational therapy approaches : practical strategies for the inclusion of special needs in primary school / Jill Jenkinson; Tessa Hyde and Saffia Ahmad.
     p. cm.
  Includes bibliographical references and index.
  ISBN 978-0-470-05857-2 (hbk. : alk. paper)
1. Special education.   2. Occupational therapy
for children.   I. Hyde, Tessa.   II. Ahmad, Saffia.   III. Title.
  LC3965.J457 2008
  371.9'0472—dc22

                                                                                    2008002752

A catalogue record for this book is available from the British Library.

Set in 12 pt and Scala-Regular by Integra
Printed in Singapore by Markono Print Media Pte Ltd

2 2010

Contents

vii

Foreword

Over the past decade, there have been several positive shifts in social policy that have encouraged us to accept difference and embrace diversity. As a consequence, approaches to learning have also changed, and there has been a marked shift in emphasis from the segregation of children who have different learning needs to differentiating the needs of *all* children within a mainstream classroom. This has led to us thinking about differences rather than deficiencies; abilities rather than limitations; and viewing children as individuals with unique learning needs rather than children with a series of symptoms which make up a recognised syndrome or condition.

This paradigm shift has influenced how paediatric occupational therapists practice, and also how educationalists address the diverse motor, cognitive, sensory, language and/or perceptual needs of children now included in the mainstream education system. The two systems at work, education and health, must converge their different yet not disparate methods of meeting special educational needs to support this positive movement, in order to enable children to achieve their potential within the constraints of the educational curriculum.

Occupational therapy facilitates a child's engagement in purposeful activities such as play, educational activities such as handwriting and physical education (PE), and activities for daily living, including dressing and undressing before and after PE. In addition, they are concerned with productivity which, when related to children, focuses on organisation, motivation, attention and application. The professional education of occupational therapists provides an understanding of child development in respect to biological, physiological, sensory and psychological processes, enabling them to understand internal constraints, while appreciating the importance of motivation, on a child's occupational performance.

Teachers facilitate learning within the context of a structured educational curriculum. The term 'education' originates from the Latin *educare*, meaning to 'draw forth'. This can be seen in their professional education, which provides the background for enabling children to learn, by providing the tools, explanations and resources from which they explore and understand their world. Teachers are equipped in planning and preparing the learning experience based on their understanding of the scaffolding of children's development.

The successful inclusion of children with special educational needs (SEN) can only be achieved by the sharing of this expertise. *Building Blocks for Learning* is a text that aims to do this by informing teachers and parents alike about the influences on children's engagement and success in education, by providing some understanding as to why children may respond in the way they do. This information will add to the body of knowledge about children's development. The practical elements provide possible strategies in addressing certain issues that have arisen in the classroom and have been developed in collaboration with teachers.

The *foundation skills* of early sensory development are described in detail in order that there may be an understanding of how these underpin many educational activities. For example, the skill of handwriting not only requires complex manipulative skills, but also intact visuo-spatial processing, visual discrimination, proprioceptive regulation, symbol recognition and literacy skills. Practical strategies are suggested where a child has been unable to establish these fundamental foundation skills.

The effects of constraints in acquiring foundation skills are then discussed in relation to selected *subject areas*. These address several aspects of the educational curriculum, for example literacy, numeracy, ICT, art, science and PE. These help the reader to embed information in the appropriate context rather than see the child as having a deficit. The teacher therefore ascertains whether a differentiated teaching approach is needed or whether the environment or context of learning can be adapted to address the specific learning need. For example, if a child is struggling to attend due to the overwhelming visual material in the classroom, can the classroom environment be adjusted to accommodate this? If a child cannot participate in the PE lesson can the whole or part of the lesson be adapted to accommodate her needs?

The introduction of the *International Classification of Function, Disability and Health* (ICF) by the World Health Organisation in 2001 challenged the use of diagnostic labels to classify individual need. By shifting the focus from cause to functional impact, intended to reduce the premise that the needs of children with SEN could be explained in terms of a 'medical' or 'biological' dysfunction, this ICF framework appreciates that contextual factors as well as body functions and structures can restrict an individual's participation and learning. However, in many local authorities additional educational resources to support the child with SEN are allocated on the basis of dysfunction. Therefore, the section entitled *medical conditions* gives the teacher and/or therapist some insight into terminology still used by many health care and educational practitioners.

Reference to medical diagnosis should, in time, reduce as we move away from using recognised terms to describe a group of symptoms towards an emphasis on individual profiles with functional abilities and functional restrictions. During this transitory period, this section can provide teachers, parents and new health care practitioners with an overview of the diagnostic criteria for many childhood conditions seen in mainstream schools today.

The final section of this immensely practical manual entitled *occupational therapy approaches* provides a wealth of workable strategies for enabling the busy teacher to individualise and differentiate learning resources to enable each child to maximise his potential. It also advises on occasions where the classroom itself should be restructured or altered. It helps the practitioner to see the unique needs of all children and to adjust materials accordingly; as such, it demonstrates how inclusive practice is a continuous process involved in breaking down the barriers to learning for *all* children.

Lois M. Addy
Senior Lecturer
Faculty of Health and Life Sciences
York St John University

Acknowledgements

Our interest and motivation in attempting this second book initially arose through encouragement from teachers and occupational therapists who were using our previous book *Occupational Therapy Approaches for Secondary Special Needs: Practical Classroom Strategies*. In preparing this second manuscript we have sought the views and experience of occupational therapists, teachers and teaching assistants and other educational and medical specialists.

We wish to thank our family and friends who have provided endless supplies of patience, support, encouragement, and practical help, wondering if this task would ever end. In particular, John Hyde for his unstinting patience designing and formatting the subject tables and Dennis Jenkinson for his endless patience and perseverance in classifying and finding references, formatting the condition tables and responding to cries for help.

We are most grateful to colleagues who have given us their expertise, advice and support in their specialist areas, often at short notice within their busy schedules: Rosemary Blundell for her detailed proof reading and suggestions on grammar; our occupational therapy colleagues Naomi Floyd, Gill Pocock and Emma Puttock for their ongoing ideas, support and editing; Catherine Catterall, a speech and language therapy colleague, for her time and contribution writing the communication and language sections; Johanna Gates for her educational advice and constructive editing; Keith Holland for his contribution to the visual processing and vision and ocular motor control section and Jane Taylor for proof reading the handwriting section.

The ideas and activities within this book have been tried and tested over many years of occupational therapy practice in a variety of settings. We would like to acknowledge our colleagues who have shared their skills and expertise with us and are grateful for the many ways they have enriched our working lives. None of this would have been possible without the children and their families who have taught us so much.

The authors acknowledge that the teaching observations and practical strategies are not exhaustive and they cannot take any responsibility for their use. They have also used most, but not all, of the equipment listed and cannot accept any responsibility for its use. Web addresses cited throughout the book were last accessed in March 2008.

Introduction

Building Blocks for Learning is a highly practical guide to activities and approaches that will assist teachers to help children who are experiencing difficulties within the curriculum progress through Foundation Stage and Key Stages 1 and 2, from their entry in reception to secondary school transition.

Building Blocks for Learning was initially modelled on our previous book, *Occupational Therapy Approaches for Secondary Special Needs: Practical Classroom Strategies*, after feedback from both teachers and occupational therapists that a similar book targeting the primary years would be an invaluable resource. However, it soon became apparent that the emphasis for the primary years would need to be changed to enable classroom teachers to address the developmental needs of younger children.

The need for early intervention, pupil and parental involvement and working in partnership with other agencies is current good practice as well as being clearly identified in existing legislation including: *Every Child Matters; Change for Children* (DfES, 2003); *The National Service Framework for Children, Young People and Maternity Services* (DoH, 2004); and the *Disability Discrimination Act* (TSO, 1995). As a result of the strategic implications of national special educational needs policy, more and more children with a wide range of special needs are being educated within mainstream classes.

This book has been written by occupational therapists in consultation with primary teachers and other specialists in this area. Occupational therapists are trained in physical medicine and mental health and are able to apply this specialist knowledge when looking at the physical, psychological and social aspects of children's development using assessment, problem solving and activity analysis. They are therefore in a strong position to identify a child's strengths and weaknesses and how these may impact upon classroom performance.

This book explores the links between a teacher's observation of a child within the school environment and the possible reasons for the difficulties the child is experiencing. It highlights practical strategies within the context of the child's age and cognitive development to help overcome their difficulties.

All the evidence suggests that early intervention is essential to help children reach their potential. The emphasis of support and intervention change as a child moves through school. Initially, new skills need to be taught to support the child's development, with minimal emphasis on coping strategies. However, if the child continues to find tasks challenging the introduction of coping strategies and modifications to the environment may become more appropriate. See Figure 1.

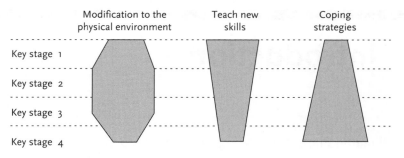

Figure 0.1   Varying emphasis on interventions through key stages.
Source: Ripley 2001 with permission

Given the increasing demands placed upon teachers and support staff to develop the curriculum and achieve results, the resources presented in this book are intended to offer straightforward and practical ways to assist teachers to help a child who is having difficulties accessing the curriculum. There will, however, be some children who require further specialist input and advice, such as occupational therapy. Occupational therapy referral routes vary from area to area but can generally be clarified by contacting the local education authority (LEA) or occupational therapy department at the local hospital.

▷   How to use this book

This book is designed as a reference manual to be 'dipped into' rather than read from 'cover to cover'. It will give a quick and easy way of identifying children's problems by observing their behaviour, providing alternative strategies for enhancing their classroom performance and suggesting activities to improve their skills.

Paediatric occupational therapists observe and assess the foundation skills that become the building blocks for learning, so this is the central theme throughout the book and each section relates back to these skills. The book can be used in several ways:

- *For a child displaying specific difficulties acquiring age appropriate skills, refer to the* **Foundation Skills** *chapter.* This chapter locates specific skill areas and identifies possible behaviours that the teacher may observe, provides advice and ideas on classroom management and suggests activities for individual or small group work.
- *For a child having difficulties accessing a particular classroom task, refer to the* **Subject Areas** *chapter.* This chapter allows the teacher to link classroom observations with the skill areas that comprise the foundation building blocks for learning that task. By identifying the most likely skill areas both main and secondary, which could be impacting upon the child's ability to perform the task, an individual profile of the child can be compiled. The foundation skills of the areas identified will help in planning a programme to work on these areas.
- *For a child with a recognised medical condition, refer to the* **Medical Conditions** *chapter.* This chapter gives an overview of the condition and identifies areas that link the teacher's observations of the child's

behaviour with practical strategies that can be implemented within school. Further advice and additional resources are also identified.

- *The **Occupational Therapy Approaches** are cross-referenced within the text.* They give further information and practical ideas for activities to help children master the basic skills required for learning, and are designed to augment any existing occupational therapy programme.
- *The **Appendices** contain checklists, proformas, programmes, resources and work systems* to target specific deficit skill areas and implement strategies.
- *The **Equipment Resources** are cross-referenced in the text* and give details of equipment and suppliers.
- *The **Glossary** explains terms* used in this book.

▷ Icons

Throughout the book you will find a number of icons to help you spot information quickly. They are:

  Teacher observations

  Strategies

  Activities

  Resources, including useful address, references, further reading, websites etc.

▷ References

Ayres A. J. (1979) *Sensory Integration and the Child: Understanding Hidden Sensory Challenges.* Los Angeles, CA, Western Psychological Services.

Department for Education and Skills (2003) *Every Child Matters: Change for Children.* Green Paper. London, Department for Education and Skills.

Department of Health (2004) *The National Service Framework for Children, Young People and Maternity Services*. London, Department of Health.

Office of Public Sector Information (1995) *Disability Discrimination Act*. London, Stationery Office.

Ripley, K. (2001); *Inclusion for Children with Dyspraxia /DCD; A Handbook for Teachers*. London; Fulton.

Online resources

The following resources are available to download from
www.blackwellpublishing.com/jenkinson

Foundation Skills

 Introduction to foundation skills

Foundation skills are the developmental building blocks for learning and are essential for establishing firm foundations for everyday tasks. They enable children to acquire age appropriate life skills and function successfully. In essence, children learn the skills to:

- Look after themselves
- Work effectively in school
- Play

Occupational therapists have expertise in assessing foundation skill development and identifying the link between acquisition of a foundation skill and classroom performance. Occupational therapists use a variety of approaches and interventions depending on the theoretical model used. A 'top down' approach uses task analysis, modification and adaptation to enable children to achieve functional tasks to enhance learning. 'Bottom up' approaches are based on the assumption that, if foundation motor skills are developed, motor control will emerge and task performance will be improved. Occupational therapists may use either approach or a combination of both, but generalisation is considered the key to learning.

Throughout their early years, children experience a range of activities that promote the development of individual building blocks. The 'foundation skills for learning' (Figure FS 0.1) shows the range of skills involved in the learning process that are essential for establishing firm foundations for every day tasks. Since all skills are interrelated, the delay in acquiring one skill will have a knock-on effect for many others and children will find performing activities of daily living, work and play extremely challenging.

Foundation skills continue to develop as a natural process whilst working through Foundation Stage and Key Stage 1 and 2 curricula. The primary years provide many opportunities for foundation skills to be developed and enhanced. Children use these skills throughout the school day and many experiences occur which provide opportunities for foundation skills to be consolidated and enhanced. For example:

- To use scissors accurately to cut along a line children need to have developed postural stability, manual dexterity, visual motor integration, visual spatial relationships, motor planning and bilateral integration.

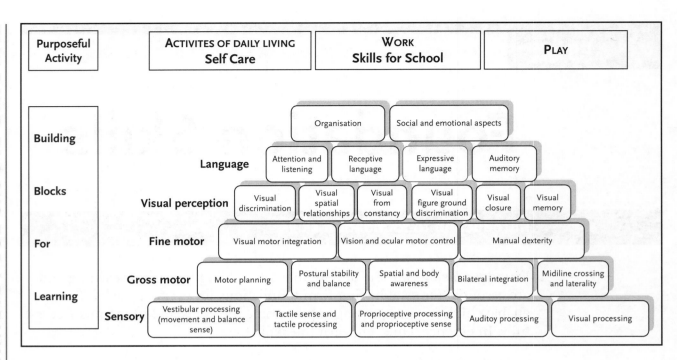

Purposeful Activity	ACTIVITES OF DAILY LIVING Self Care		WORK Skills for School		PLAY	

Building Blocks For Learning

		Organisation	Social and emotional aspects			
Language	Attention and listening	Receptive language	Expressive language	Auditory memory		
Visual perception	Visual discrimination	Visual spatial relationships	Visual from constancy	Visual figure ground discrimination	Visual closure	Visual memory
Fine motor	Visual motor integration		Vision and ocular motor control		Manual dexterity	
Gross motor	Motor planning	Postural stability and balance	Spatial and body awareness	Bilateral integration	Midline crossing and laterality	
Sensory	Vestibular processing (movement and balance sense)	Tactile sense and tactile processing	Proprioceptive processing and proprioceptive sense	Auditoy processing	Visual processing	

Figure FS 0.1   Foundation Skills for Learning.

- To catch a ball, children need to have developed postural stability and balance, spatial and body awareness, bilateral integration, midline crossing, visual motor integration and ocular motor control.

By the time children leave primary school it is essential that all necessary foundation skills are fully established in preparation for transition into secondary school. The foundation skills are:

- Sensory processing
- Gross motor coordination
- Fine motor control
- Perception
- Language
- Organisation
- Social and emotional aspects

The foundation skills are adapted from our previous book *Occupational Therapy Approaches for Secondary Special Needs*, as follows:

- *What it is*—defines the specific skill area
- *Why is it important?*—explains why the child needs to acquire the skill
- *What are the implications*—suggests what the class teacher may observe when the skill is not in place
- *Teaching strategies*—provides advice and ideas on classroom management
- *Activities to improve the skill*—suggests activities for individual or small group work
- *Resources for further information and advice*—gives further ideas for resources and additional reading/information

▶▶▶ References

Jenkinson, J., Hyde, T. and Ahmad, S (2002) *Occupational Therapy Approaches for Secondary Special Needs*. London, Whurr.

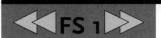

Introduction to sensory processing

 ## What is it?

'Sensory processing involves the registration and modulation of sensory information, as well as the internal organisation of the sensory input, so human beings can execute successful adaptive responses to situational demands and thus engage meaningfully in daily occupations (Humphrey, 2002). Adaptive behaviours are purposeful and goal-directed and enable individuals to overcome challenges and to learn new skills' (Prudhomme White *et al.*, 2007); such as when you touch something extremely hot you withdraw your hand; a baby sees something attractive and reaches out, ultimately leading to crawling and more complex movement patterns and skills.

 ## Why is it important?

Sensory processing is considered to be an internal process of the nervous system which helps us receive, organise and understand sensory information from both the environment (auditory and visual input as well as taste and smell) and from within our bodies (touch, movement and joint receptors). This then helps us know how to respond to environmental demands. Efficient sensory processing is needed to enable us to participate fully in everyday life and adequately engage in our daily routines and roles.

Each individual responds differently to sensory information as the nervous system has 'thresholds' for acting. We can respond easily to sensory input if we have a 'low threshold' and this is said to be 'hyper-responsive'; or we can take a long time to respond and be 'hypo-responsive'. Children in the first category tend to avoid situations which increase their sensory input and children in the latter category seek sensory input. The basic patterns of high and low threshold responses to sensory input are:

- *Sensory seeking*, e.g. may be on the move touching everything
- *Sensory avoiding*, e.g. may seem withdrawn, reluctant to move, climb, etc., avoid touching things, getting messy, etc.
- *Sensory sensitivity*, e.g. oversensitive to sound and/or touch, and easily irritated (Dunn, 1999)

It is possible to have a low threshold for one sensory input and a high threshold in another, e.g. become distracted by lots of noise but not notice lots of colour and visual 'clutter'. Threshold levels and our ability to cope with sensory information are dependent on a variety of factors and vary from day to day as well as throughout the day. We may be competent drivers and be able to drive around familiar places with the radio on and children chatting in the car, but if we are in an unfamiliar place and it starts to rain heavily we may ask the children to stop chatting and turn the radio off to enable us to process the increased sensory information and focus, in order to successfully carry out the familiar task.

Self-regulation or modulation is the way we manage the sensory input available to us through the ability to attain, maintain and change arousal level/alertness appropriately to match the demands of the environment. Problems occur when there is 'difficulty responding to sensory input with behaviour that is graded relative to the degree, nature or intensity of sensory information. Responses are inconsistent with the demands of the situation, and inflexibility adapting to sensory challenges encountered in daily life is observed' (Miller *et al.*, 2007).

We all have sensory preferences in everyday life; some of us choose to wear bright clothing and chunky jewellery, to decorate our homes with strong bright colours and to have lots of clutter, while others prefer softer plain colours and clutter free spaces in order to feel calm. Some people enjoy fairground rides or adventure sports, while others prefer activities that are more sedentary. It is only when an extreme response interferes with everyday life that there is cause for concern.

It is important that class teachers consider their own sensory preferences and how these are evident in their classroom and style of teaching, as this may not be 'in sync' with a child with sensory needs and, as such, any strategies implemented must work for both teacher and child. It can be a challenge to balance the needs of all the children within the class.

 ## What are the implications?

Parham and Mailloux (2005) reported that sensory processing problems are often associated with decreased social skills, immature play skills, impaired self-concept, decreased fine and gross motor skills, and difficulties performing daily living skills. There may be many other reasons for children to show these characteristics, but where sensory processing difficulties may be the cause, it is likely that sensory seeking, sensory avoidance or sensory sensitivity is causing the behaviour.

In the classroom, children with these difficulties may present with:

- Some challenges performing daily living skills
  - difficulty wearing certain clothing
  - being a messy eater or having a rigid diet
  - difficulty organising oneself

- Decreased social skills
  - a tendency to invade another's personal space
  - appearing not to listen to others
  - a tendency to butt into conversations

- Immature play skills
  - a tendency to avoid messy play
  - flitting from one task to another
  - a narrow choice of activities

- Impaired self-concept
  - impaired self-esteem
  - a reluctance to take part in class activities
  - unrealistic expectations of self and task

- Decreased fine and gross motor skills
  - poor pencil skills, impaired grasp
  - frequently bumping into others or furniture
  - constantly on the go

The identification of sensory processing difficulties and needs should be made by a specialist in this area, so if a teacher is concerned about a child, advice needs to be sought from a person trained in this area, e.g. an occupational therapist.

Within this section, sensory processing has been broken down into:

- Vestibular processing (movement and balance sense)
- Tactile sense and tactile processing
- Proprioceptive processing/sense
- Auditory processing
- Visual processing

 References

Dunn, W. (1997) The impact of sensory processing abilities on the daily lives of young children and their families: a conceptual model. *Infants and Young Children,* **9** (4), 23–35.

Dunn, W. (1999) *Sensory Profile, User's Manual.* San Antonio, Texas, Psychological Corporation.

Dunn, W. (2001) The sensations of everyday life: theoretical, conceptual and pragmatic considerations. *American Journal of Occupational Therapy,* **55**, 608–620.

Millar, L.J. & Lane, S.J. (2000) Toward a consensus in terminology in sensory integration theory and practice: part 1, taxonomy of neurophysiological processes. *Sensory Integration Special Interest Section Quarterly*, **23** (2). Rockville, Maryland, American Occupational Therapy Association.

Miller, L.J., Anzalone, M.E., Lane, S.J., Cermak, S.A. & Osten, E.T. (2007) Concept evolution in sensory integration: a proposed nosology for diagnosis. *American Journal of Occupational Therapy*, **61** (2), 135–140.

Parham, L.D. & Mailloux, Z. (2005) Sensory integration. In: J. Case-Smith (ed.), *Occupational Therapy for Children* (5th edn). St Louis, MO, Moseby.

Prudhomme White, B., Mulligan, S., Merrill, K. & Wright, J. (2007) An examination of the relationships between motor and process skills and scores on the sensory profile. *American Journal of Occupational Therapy*, **61** (2), 154–160.

Further reading and resources

Ayres, J.A. (1979) *Sensory Integration and the Child: Understanding Hidden Sensory Challenges*. Los Angeles, CA, Western Psychological Services.

Bhreathnach, E. (1995) *Your Child's Sensory Needs*. Belfast, BTRS.

Bissell, J., Fisher, J., Owens, C. & Polcyn, P. (1998) *Sensory Motor Handbook: a Guide for Implementing and Modifying Activities in the Classroom*, 2nd edn. San Antonio, Texas, Therapy Skill Builders.

Brown, C. & Dunn, W. (2002) *Adolescent/Adult Sensory Profile User's Manual*. San Antonio, Texas, The Psychological Corporation.

Bundy, A.C., Murray, E.A. & Lane, S.J. (2002) *Sensory Integration: Theory and Practice*, 2nd edn. Philadelphia, FA Davis Company.

Cribbin, V., Lynch, H., Bagshawe, B. & Chadwick, K. (2003) *Sensory Information*—information booklet a resource for parents and therapists. Dublin, Sensory Integration Network, UK and Ireland.

Fink, B.E. (1989) *Sensory Motor Integration Activities*. Tucson, AZ, Therapy Skill Builders.

Fisher, A.G., Murray, E.A. & Bundy, A.C. (1991) *Sensory Integration Theory and Practice*. Philadelphia, F.A. Davis Company.

Humphrey, R. (2002) Young children's occupations: explicating the dynamics of developmental processes. *American Journal of Occupational Therapy*, **56**, 171–179.

Jeffries, J.A. & Jeffries, R. (2001) *Auditory Processing Activities: Materials for Clinicians and Teachers*. Perth, Western Australia, Unicom International.

Koomar, J. & Friedman, B. (1998) *The Hidden Senses Your Muscle Sense*. Hugo, Minnesota, PDP Press.

Kranowitz, C.S. (1998) *The Out of Sync Child—Recognising and Coping with Sensory Integration Dysfunction*. New York, Perigee.

Newton Inamura, K. (ed.) (1998) *SI for Early Intervention: a Team Approach*. San Antonio, Texas, Therapy Skill Builders.

Oettter, P., Richter, E. & Frick, S. (1995) MORE: *Integrating the Mouth with Sensory and Postural Functions*, 2nd edn. Hugo, MN, PDP Press Inc.

Trott, M.C. (2002) *Oh Behave! Sensory Processing and Behavioural Strategies: a Practical Guide for Clinicians, Teachers and Parents.* Tucson, AZ, Therapy Skill Builders/ Psychological Corporation.

Tupper, L. & Miesner, K. (1995) *School Hardening, Sensory Integration Strategies For Class and Home.* San Antonio, Texas, Therapy Skill Builders.

Williams, M. & Shellenberger, S. (1996) *'How Does Your Engine Run?': a Leader's Guide to the Alert Program for Self-regulation.* Albuquerque, Therapy Works Inc.

Young, S. (1988) *Movement is Fun. A Preschool Movement Program.* Torrance, Sensory Integration International.

Websites

www.alertprogram.com
www.besmart.org.uk
www.out-of-sync-child.com
www.ot-innovations.com
www.sensoryintegration.org.uk
www.sinetwork.org
www.sifocus.com
www.spdnetwork.org
www.sensory-processing-disorder.com
www.sensorystories.com

Further resources

Refer to Foundation Skills

- FS 1A, 1B, 1C, 1D, 1E within this area pages 11–27

Refer to Occupational Therapy Approaches

- OTA 1 Building firm foundations for spatial and body awareness page 249
- OTA 8 Sensory strategies page 323

Refer to Appendix

- A 1 Ages and stages of development page 361
- A 7 Movement programmes and gross motor resources page 381
- A 9 Resources for developing social, emotional and behavioural skills page 389

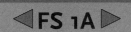

Vestibular processing (movement and balance sense)

▷ What is it?

'The vestibular sense is our sense of movement. Our movement system enables us to stay upright, to adjust our position, to balance, and to detect motion. Through movement we also develop our sense of direction and appreciation of spatial relationships. The sensation of movement influences our muscle tone in that we tense our muscles if we are on something which moves in order to keep our balance. If we relax our muscles on a moving object we fall off. We adjust our body in relation to the speed and force of the movement. The vestibular system links with our visual system in that we sense movement through merely seeing something move' (Bhreathnach, 1995). The vestibular system is activated by the proprioceptive system during movement to modify balance response.

▷ Why is it important?

The vestibular system is important for effective posture and balance in relation to the activity being performed. In order to achieve and maintain a calm, alert state, well-modulated vestibular processing is essential. 'We feel the calming effects of slow vestibular stimulation when we rock in a rocking chair and feel the arousing effects of fast vestibular stimulation when riding in a roller coaster. The vestibular system also helps keep the level of arousal of the nervous system well balanced.' (Ayres, 1979).

▷ What are the implications?

Sensation avoiding

Children who are oversensitive to vestibular input tend to avoid movement, they may:

- Have a rigid posture and be overwhelmed by movement
- Avoid playing on playground equipment, such as swings, slides, merry-go-rounds

- Be fearful of heights and any activities 'off the ground', e.g. wall bars, beam/bench, kerbs, PE apparatus
- Dislike stairs and escalators—rely on the handrail longer than others of the same age
- Become disorientated when bending over
- Become car/motion sick easily
- Avoid rough and tumble play
- Dislike being up side down, e.g. forward rolls, handstands, cart wheels

Sensation seeking

Children who have an undersensitive vestibular system tend to seek vestibular input and may:

- Have no sense of limits or control when in potentially dangerous situations, showing no fear
- Crave movement, playground/fairground rides—are 'thrill seekers' and do not feel dizzy or sick when other children do
- Seek constant movement, e.g. rocking, spinning, running, balancing on two legs of a chair, and are always 'on the go'
- Like sudden movements—will often 'throw' themselves at equipment/mats/floor
- Enjoy climbing high and do not think of the consequences

▷ **Teaching strategies for sensation avoiding**

- Prepare the child in advance of changes in position; break down the task into achievable steps.
- Grade the activity to build up the child's tolerance of movement gradually.
- Allow the children to lead the activity at their own pace to prevent adverse reactions.

▷ **Teaching strategies for sensation seeking**

- Incorporate movement activities into the child's daily life, e.g. trampolining, running, football.
- Give the child regular movement breaks throughout the day.
- Allow the child to regularly change position (floor sitting, sitting on a chair, standing, lying on the floor, kneeling) if it helps her.
- Sit the child on a movin'sit cushion, a therapy ball or place one chair leg through a hole in a tennis ball so that the chair rocks.

▷ Activities to improve vestibular processing

It is important with all vestibular activities that the child is in control and must be allowed to stop or slow down on request, as some children are extremely sensitive to movement and may become dizzy, pale and sick very quickly. Precautions should be taken to reduce the chance of a child putting himself at risk. After completing activities children often require resistive/deep pressure sensory input to modulate and calm themselves.

The following ideas are graded so that the most challenging vestibular tasks, e.g. spinning, are presented at the end of the list.

- *Crawling*—in crawling position (on hands and knees) ask the child to pretend to be a rocking horse, lying on his tummy commando crawl along a mat.
- *Rocking*—Lay the child over a large ball or a barrel with hands on the floor and rock backwards and forwards from hands to knees. Use rocking chairs or wobble cushions such as movin'sit.
- *Bouncing*—space hoppers, trampolines, car inner tubes, etc.
- *Sliding*—playground slides, move in different ways.
- *Rolling*—log/pencil rolling across the floor with arms above head, trying to keep in a straight line. Close eyes to make the task easier. Increase difficulty by asking the child to hold a beanbag in hands or between knees. Roll on cushions or on sloped surfaces.
- *Spinning*—encourage the child to be a helicopter or spinning top. Try spinning different ways, e.g. both feet, one foot flat, on bottom, on back, in/on commercial spinning equipment.
- *Swinging*—playground swings, monkey bars, adventure playground, ropes/tyres.

Kinaesthesia is the term commonly used to describe a combination of tactile, proprioceptive and vestibular processing (see Glossary page 423).

▷ References

Ayres, J.A. (1979) *Sensory Integration and the Child: Understanding Hidden Sensory Challenges.* Los Angeles, CA, Western Psychological Services.

Bhreathnach, E. (1995) *Your Child's Sensory Needs.* Belfast, BTRS.

DeGangi, G.A. (1994) *Documenting Sensorimotor Progress.* Tucson, AZ, Therapy Skill Builders.

Fisher, A.G., Murray, E.A. & Bundy, A.C. (1991) *Sensory Integration Theory and Practice.* Philadelphia, F.A. Davis Company.

Kranowitz, C.S. (1998) *The Out of Sync Child—Recognising and Coping with Sensory Integration Dysfunction.* New York, Perigee.

Williams, M. & Shellenberger, S. (1996) *'How Does Your Engine Run?' A Leaders Guide to the Alert Program for Self-regulation.* Albuquerque. Therapy Works Inc.

▷ Further reading

See introduction to section page 5.

▷ Further resources

Refer to Foundation Skills

- FS 1B Tactile/sense and tactile processing page 15
- FS 1C Proprioceptive processing/sense page 19
- FS 3B Vision and ocular motor control page 63
- FS 7 Social and emotional aspects page 113

Refer to Occupational Therapy Approaches

- OTA 1 Building firm foundations for spatial and body awareness page 249
- OTA 8 Sensory strategies page 323
- OTA 10 Consolidating foundation skills through group activities page 333

Refer to Appendix

- A 7 Movement programmes and gross motor resources page 381
- A 9 Resources for developing social, emotional and behavioural skills page 389

Refer to Equipment Resources page 407

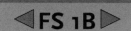

Tactile sense and tactile processing

◀ FS 1B ▶

▷ What is it?

'The skin has many different kinds of receptors for receiving sensations of touch, pressure, texture, heat or cold, pain and movement of the hairs on the skin. Although we may not think much about the role of touch in our lives, the tactile system is the largest sensory system and it plays a vital role in human behaviour, both physical and mental' (Ayres, 1979).

▷ Why is it important?

It is through the tactile system, that we first receive information about the world. Until language, motor skills and cognitive processes develop, we are highly dependent on our sense of touch. Receiving and processing this information effectively allows us to feel safe, calmed, and to develop both socially and emotionally. Touch can be both protective and discriminative, helping to alert our bodies to potential danger and allowing us to identify where and what is being touched. When the child's protective function is working, the level of arousal is high and the discrimination function will be less efficient.

▷ What are the implications?

Sensation avoiding

Children who are oversensitive to touch have an overactive protective function and this is seen in the tendency to avoid tactile sensation (known as being tactile defensive) in order to remain calm. They may:

- Dislike messy activities/play, e.g. having glue, paint, chalk, sand, food on hands/face
- Flinch away or be fearful/anxious of unexpected touch or light touch or prefer firm touch
- Become distressed when standing close to peers in a line and/or push others away or isolate themselves

- Over react when responding to texture, touch or injury, e.g. minor cuts, may hit out or bite others
- Show distinct likes and dislikes with texture of activities/objects and so develop a limited repertoire
- Have a rigid diet or a limited range of acceptable foods, e.g. 'white' food, sliced bread, yoghurt
- Explore objects with fingertips, but seldom explore with whole hand— may react defensively by touching everything
- Dislike wind, rain or taking showers and cleaning teeth
- Dislike tight/restrictive clothing or specific textures, may choose long sleeves and trousers in the summer and minimal clothing in the winter

Sensation seeking

Children who are undersensitive to touch are less aware of being touched and therefore have diminished protective responses. They may also seek tactile sensation in order to discriminate and therefore learn. They may:

- Seek out messy play/activities/textures; be unaware of food/paint on hands/ face and have difficulty keeping clean and tidy
- Have an untidy dishevelled appearance—will not notice if clothing is crumpled or inside out
- Show a preference for tight clothing and items that are too small
- Have limited awareness of personal space of self and that of others— tend to invade personal space of others, touch people and items, seek physical contact, sit too close to other children at carpet time or play with other children's hair or clothing
- Lack awareness of injury—may not notice cuts/bruises
- Be unaware of touch from others or objects unless intense, frequently hurt other children when playing, e.g. can stand on someone's foot without noticing
- Fumble and lack dexterity with making and doing activities
- Prefer intense flavours and textures of food, e.g. spicy, sweet, salty, and sour
- Put things in mouth—may mouth items and chew sleeves/pencils or bite self

▷ Teaching strategies

- Avoid light touch, use firm pressure when touching the child and approach from the front.
- Regulate the child's environment to suit the child's need, e.g. limit or increase the amount of items in a working space.
- Place the child at the end of the line.
- Position the child in the classroom away from the main thoroughfare so the child is not accidentally knocked or touched.

- Use fiddle toys to provide 'legitimate fiddling', permit biting an object such as a tube on the end of pencil.
- Consider the texture of work surfaces/equipment/toys, e.g. table, paper, maths equipment, if these cause distress to the child. Wrap tape around a piece of chalk.
- Discuss the child's clothing with parents—removal of labels may help.

▷ **Activities to improve tactile discrimination**

It is important to remember that for children who avoid tactile sensation (tactile defensive) some textures and touch can be distressing. It is therefore essential to approach activities sensitively, starting with less challenging textures and building from this to allow the child to control the level of contact and stop when she needs to. For children who are less aware of touch and may be touch seeking, there is a need to help develop discriminative ability. Professionals who specialise in these areas may be able to offer advice to help provide an environment in which the child can develop, e.g. occupational therapists.

- *Water play*—play in water that is different temperatures and with or without bubbles. Use a variety of toys, containers, shells, kitchen utensils to pour and measure.
- *Play dough activities*—making dough, rolling, modelling, etc. Texture can be added with lentils/sand, etc.
- *'Drawing'* in a variety of substances, e.g. sand, paint, rice, chopped jelly, cornflour and water, shaving foam.
- *Encourage the child to explore different textures* on his skin, e.g. paint brushes, scrubbing brush, pot scourers, soft cloths, fur, liquid soap.
- *Dress up* in different clothing, e.g. silk, fur, hats, false beards, bangles.
- Play with different textured objects and ask the child to identify different features, e.g. hard/soft, warm/cold, rough/smooth.
- *Feely box*—hide objects in rice/sand/pasta/polystyrene pieces and ask the child to find them.
- *Feely bag*—place a variety of objects into a bag and ask the child to feel them and identify before taking them out of the bag. Ask the child to find a specific item; if there are two identical sets one can be visible for the child to compare with.
- *'Draw'* letter/shapes on the hand or back of the child and ask her to identify.

Kinaesthesia is the term commonly used to describe a combination of tactile, proprioceptive and vestibular processing (see Glossary page 423).

▷ References

Ayres, J.A. (1979) *Sensory Integration and the Child: Understanding Hidden Sensory Challenges.* Los Angeles, CA, Western Psychological Services.

Bissell, J., Fisher, J., Owens, C. & Polcyn, P. (1998) *Sensory Motor Handbook: a Guide for Implementing and Modifying Activities in the Classroom,* 2nd edn. San Antonio, Texas, Therapy Skill Builders.

Fisher, A.G., Murray, E.A. & Bundy, A.C. (1991) *Sensory Integration Theory and Practice.* Philadelphia, F.A. Davis Company.

Kranowitz, C.S. (1998) *The Out of Sync Child—Recognising and Coping with Sensory Integration Dysfunction.* New York, Perigee.

▷ Further reading

See introduction to section page 5.

▷ Further resources

Refer to Foundation Skills

Refer to Occupational Therapy Approaches

Refer to Appendix

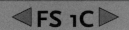

Proprioceptive processing/sense

▷ What is it?

Proprioception is our innate sense of 'position'. We receive information from our muscles and joints through muscle contraction/activation, which helps us know how our body is moving *and that our body can do what we need it to*. This sense allows us to know our body position without looking—if we close our eyes, we know that our feet are on the floor or we are able to move an arm behind us. It makes us aware of our precise body position in space and enables us to judge grading (speed and force) of movements. This system has been described as our 'internal sense of vision' (Bhreathnach, 1995). Proprioception is closely linked with our other senses, particularly tactile and vestibular, and is a prerequisite for balance, posture, motor planning and coordination.

▷ Why is it important?

'Proprioception helps us move. With poor proprioception our body movements would be slower, clumsier, and involve more effort. If the proprioception from your hands were not sufficient to tell you what your hands were doing, it would be very difficult to button clothes, take something out of a pocket, screw a lid on a jar, or remember which way to turn a water faucet [tap].Without adequate proprioception from the trunk and legs, you would have a very hard time getting in or out of an automobile [car], walking down steep stairs, or playing sport. You tend to rely upon visual information by looking closely at what your body is doing. Children with poorly organised proprioception usually have a lot of trouble doing anything when they cannot see it with their eyes' (Ayres, 1979).

▷ What are the implications?

Children with poor proprioceptive processing may:

- Be constantly 'on the go' and fidgeting, rock on a chair and balance on two legs of the chair
- Have low muscle tone and poor posture, so 'flop/prop' and become tired easily

- Become easily frustrated
- Stamp when walking (heavy footed), grind teeth and speak too loudly
- Be more over reactive with other systems, e.g. emotional responses
- Seek out physical contact/ hugs
- Press too hard or too lightly with a pencil when writing
- Drop things or overshoot when pouring
- Use too much or too little force with actions, always seems to break things and may hurt others unintentionally during play
- Bump into others/furniture/doorframes, etc., frequently and trip over 'thin air'

▷ Teaching strategies

'Heavy muscle work' or activities against resistance are the key way of providing calming and organising through proprioceptive input.

- Provide activities against resistance or involving more than usual pressure which will enable the child to become more aware of her body position, e.g. rolling and squashing play dough in her hands while standing.
- Encourage the child to walk to school carrying a backpack.
- Provide opportunities for the child to carry a full backpack or heavy tray between lessons or to the school office at times when becoming particularly restless.
- Build movement breaks into the child's day.
- Sit on movin'sit cushion to raise sensory awareness and concentration.
- Teach child to use visual and cognitive strategies to help plan and carry out movements.

▷ Activities to improve proprioception

- *Dressing up* in heavy clothes, especially hats, shoes, necklaces.
- *Drawing/painting* on a large scale, in different planes (horizontal and vertical) and on textured surfaces such as corrugated card, tree bark, sand paper, sugar paper.
- *Games involving some resistance* when taking toys apart, e.g. stickle bricks, lego, popoids.
- *PE activities*—pulling along a bench, bunny jumps, hopping, push-ups against the wall or from kneeling position.
- *Any push/pull activities*, e.g. tug of war.
- *Trampolines*, space hoppers and skipping.
- *Animal walks*—ask the child to move like an animal, e.g. elephant, snake, rabbit, kangaroo, frog, crocodile.
- *'Pressure sandwich/roll'*; make the child into a hot dog or sandwich by rolling him in a mat or blanket and then applying pressure to different parts of his body.

- *Get the child to help to carry* shopping/school bags, move chairs, mats, gym equipment.
- *When sitting,* ask the child to place her hands on the sides of her chair, palm down and lift her body off the seat.

Kinaesthesia is the term commonly used to describe a combination of tactile, proprioceptive and vestibular processing (see Glossary page 423).

▷ References

Ayres, J.A. (1979) *Sensory Integration and the Child: Understanding Hidden Sensory Challenges.* Los Angeles, CA, Western Psychological Services.

Bhreathnach, E. (1995) *Your Child's Sensory Needs.* Belfast, BTRS.

Bissell, J., Fisher, J., Owens, C. & Polcyn, P. (1998) *Sensory Motor Handbook: a Guide for Implementing and Modifying Activities in the Classroom,* 2nd edn. San Antonio, Texas, Therapy Skill Builders.

Newton Inamura, K. (1998) *SI for Early Intervention a Team Approach.* San Antonio, Texas, Therapy Skill Builders.

Tupper, L. & Miesner, K. (1995) *School Hardening: Sensory Integration Strategies For Class and Home.* San Antonio, Texas, Therapy Skill Builders.

Williams, M. & Shellenberger, S. (1996) *'How Does Your Engine Run?' a Leaders Guide to the Alert Program for Self-regulation.* Albuquerque, Therapy Works Inc.

▷ Further reading

See introduction to section page 5.

▷ Further resources

Refer to Foundation Skills

- FS 1A Vestibular processing page 11
- FS 1B Tactile sense and tactile processing page 15
- FS 2B Postural stability and balance page 39
- FS 2C Spatial and body awareness page 43
- FS 7 Social and emotional aspects page 113

Refer to Occupational Therapy Approaches

Refer to Appendix

Refer to Equipment Resources page 407.

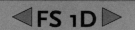

Auditory processing

▷ What is it?

'Auditory processing is the ability to perceive and understand what is heard in the environment. This involves more than the sense of hearing. Understanding auditory information requires intricate processing. Discriminating, associating and interpreting sounds; remembering and comprehending what is heard; and relating words in a meaningful way are all parts of auditory processing' (Bissell, 1988). It is important to be able to inhibit background sounds to focus on the specific sounds or voices that require attention.

▷ Why is it important?

'Good auditory processing is an important foundation for the development of language skills and plays an important role in children's classroom performance and peer relationships. Children who experience difficulty with processing what they hear may at times appear confused or inattentive. They may haphazardly rush into tasks and may take a long time to respond to directions and to complete tasks. They may over respond to competing noise in the environment' (Bissell, 1988). Children may have difficulty following several instructions or these will require extra effort. They are likely to be visual learners.

▷ What are the implications?

Sensation avoiding

Children who are oversensitive to sound tend to avoid auditory input and may:

- Dislike unexpected noises such as fire bells, loud bangs and may respond with anxiety or fear
- Avoid loud noises or certain sounds, as these may feel painful
- Frequently ask children and adults to be quiet when they are talking
- Dislike background noise such as the hum of an interactive whiteboard projector, fans, children chatting, noisy heaters, chairs scraping on the floor, clock ticking

- Find it hard to focus on work when there is a lot of noise
- Dislike noisy places such as a swimming pool or dining hall
- Be distractible and have poor concentration
- Cover their ears or scream at certain noises

Sensation seeking

Children who are undersensitive to sound tend to either seek auditory input or appear passive. They may:

- Not respond to voices, even in a quiet environment
- Appear not to hear
- Appear oblivious to what is going on around them
- Need instructions to be repeated
- Talk aloud to themselves, make noises with their body or objects
- Love excessively loud noises
- Show poor phonological awareness and difficulty with literacy

▷ Teaching strategies

- Make eye contact with the child before speaking.
- Give one instruction at a time.
- Speak slowly and clearly, repeat instructions to child and ensure he has understood by asking him to repeat.
- Ensure the child does not move away until the instruction is finished.
- Wait for the child to process the information and respond; this is likely to take her longer than her peers.
- Use visual timetables/work systems/ prompt sheets to back up instructions, give physical demonstration if necessary.
- Prepare the child for predictable loud noises such as school bell.
- Be aware of background noises such as interactive whiteboard projectors, fluorescent lights, and turn these off if possible, for some of the time.
- Reduce auditory distraction both inside and outside the room.
- Provide headphones/earplugs for the child to wear when he needs to focus on work, or in particularly noisy situations, or allow child to work in a workstation or a quiet area.
- Talk to the child and parent about use of music if this will help her focus, either soothing background music or more alerting music depending on need.

▷ Activities to improve auditory processing

If a child shows a marked sensitivity to noise, a referral to a speech and language therapist or occupational therapist is recommended.

- *Memory games* such as 'I went to the market and bought . . .'
- *Action rhymes* such as 'head shoulders, knees and toes'.

- *Repeating well-known sequences*, e.g. days of the week, months of the year, numbers. Vary this by asking which part of the sequence is out of order.
- *Feely bag games*—place a variety of objects in a bag and ask the child to find a specific item or something hard/soft/ fluffy, etc., without looking.
- *Give directions* using locations on a map.
- Before reading a story to a child, ask him to listen for a particular word, character or phrase. Then read the story to him and when the story is finished, ask him to recall and elaborate on the original question.
- *Circle games* such as 'duck, duck goose', 'Hokey Cokey'.
- Gross motor games following auditory instructions, e.g. 'Simon Says', 'Captain's Coming'.
- *Play games* which involve identifying specific everyday noises from background noise, e.g. clock ticking, door closing.
- *Commercially available games* such as 'sound lotto'.

▷ References

Bissell, J. (1988) *Sensory Motor Handbook a Guide to Implementing and Modifying Activities in the Classroom*. San Antonio, Texas, Therapy Skill Builders.

Chu, S. (1999) *Assessment and Treatment of Children with Developmental Perceptual Dysfunction* (course handbook, self-published). London, West London Healthcare NHS Trust.

Newton Inamura, K. (ed.) (1998) *SI for Early Intervention: a Team Approach*. San Antonio, Texas, Therapy Skill Builders.

▷ Further reading

See introduction to section page 5.

Evamy, B. (2003) *Auditory and Visual Discrimination Exercises—a Teacher's Aid*. Bridlington, Yorkshire, BJE Publications; email Barbaraevamy@aol.com; available from Dyslexia Action.

Jeffries, J.A. & Jeffries, R. (2001) *Auditory Processing Activities: Materials for Clinicians and Teachers*. Perth, Western Australia, Unicom Publications.

Moseley, J. (2005) *Circle Time for Young Children*. London, Routledge.

▷ Further resources

Refer to Foundation Skills

- FS 5 Introduction to language page 101
- FS 5A Attention and listening page 103

- FS 5B Receptive language page 105
- FS 5C Expressive language page 107
- FS 5D Auditory memory page 109

Refer to Occupational Therapy Approaches

- OTA 8 Sensory strategies page 323

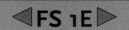

Visual processing

▷ What is it?

Visual processing is a general term that refers to all those skills needed to use the visual sense. The skills include:

- Acquiring of information through the eyes—including focus, eye teaming, eye movement or tracking and awareness of periphery
- Transporting of information to the visual cortex and sharing (or integration) of visual information with other systems—such as hearing, touch and balance
- The interpretation of what we see and the use of this to promote actions

▷ Why is it important?

Over 80% of our learned knowledge is visual. Inefficient visual processing will seriously affect how efficiently we can interact with our surroundings and develop new memories and knowledge of the world around us.

▷ What are the implications?

Children with poor visual processing will find the simple act of living harder work, and will be less efficient in a range of areas, generally, for example:

- Hand-eye coordination tasks will be harder—affecting sport and movement.
- They may find it harder to recall information, or rely more heavily on verbal skills, making creativity challenging.
- At more extreme levels, they may become insecure in their surroundings due to poor spatial awareness. This can influence confidence in a whole range of ways—affecting their social interactions.

Sensation avoiding

Children who avoid visual input may:

- Frequently rub their eyes
- Become distracted by lots of visual stimuli
- Dislike fluorescent lights or bright sunshine
- Prefer to work in dim lighting or dark environments
- Be unable to find what they are looking for
- Have difficulty copying from the board
- Be inconsistent writing on lines

Sensation seeking

Children who seek visual input may:

- Like bright lights or sunshine
- Enjoy 'busy' displays and classrooms
- Like bright colours
- Have difficulty telling the difference between similar pictures or colours
- Lose their place when reading
- Become easily fatigued with school work
- Forget spacing, or have poor spacing when writing

▷ Teaching strategies

- Provide work station/privacy board so child can work in an area without visual distractions.
- Try to avoid placing the child under fluorescent light for work.
- Ensure work area is uncluttered.
- Work on an angled work surface.
- Be aware of visual distractions such as wall displays, teacher's jewellery, interactive whiteboard.
- Use visual organisers/schedules.
- Use mirror for the child to check appearance.
- Use different colours for different lines on whiteboard/interactive whiteboard.
- Use highlighters or dark pen to underline work and emphasise salient points.
- Wear sunglasses in bright sunshine.

▷ **Activities to improve visual skills**

Refer to FS 3B Vision and ocular motor control (page 63).

▷ **References**

Personal correspondence with Keith Holland.

▷ **Further resources**

Refer to Foundation Skills

- FS 3A Visual motor integration page 59
- FS 4 Introduction to perception page 73

Refer to Occupational Therapy Approaches

- OTA 4 Building firm foundations for handwriting page 271
- OTA 8 Sensory strategies page 323

Refer to Appendix

- A 4 Handwriting self-evaluation checklist page 373
- A 5 Handwriting programmes and fine motor resources page 375
- A 10 Teacher's checklist for visual signs page 395
- A 13 Visual perception materials page 403

Refer to Equipment Resources page 407.

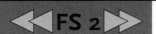

Introduction to gross motor coordination

 What is it?

Gross motor coordination is the ability to perform large movements with fluency, accuracy and precision. In order to achieve efficient gross motor coordination, children must have developed and integrated foundation component skills. Sensory processing of information which is received and then processed through receptors in the joints, skin, eyes, ears and mouth, needs to be automatic to enable higher-level skills to develop. Gross motor movements are then dependent on coordinated and well-integrated skills that include motor planning, postural stability and balance, spatial and body awareness, bilateral integration, midline crossing and laterality.

 Why is it important?

Gross motor coordination provides the postural control necessary for the acquisition of mature gross and fine motor skills. It is essential for the development of fine manual dexterity, since controlled and coordinated large gross motor movements must be in place before smaller movements can be refined.

 What are the implications?

Children with gross motor problems may have difficulties with:

- Organising body movements, being aware of 'personal space', sitting on the carpet without causing a disturbance and getting up and down from the floor
- Changing for PE and taking part in lessons, e.g. using apparatus, music and movement sessions, drama

- Joining in playground activities and games, e.g. skipping, hula hoops, running games
- Moving around the classroom without bumping into objects or people, turn-taking and waiting in line
- Staying still, alert and focused
- Maintaining a functional working position, working on vertical surfaces, e.g. interactive whiteboard
- Opening heavy fire doors and undertaking tasks requiring stamina/standing tolerance
- Collecting and carrying equipment
- Participating in practical lessons, especially when required to use both hands together
- Maintaining stamina during extended periods of writing, producing an acceptable quantity of written work

Within this section, gross motor coordination has been broken down into:

- Motor planning
- Postural stability and balance
- Spatial and body awareness
- Bilateral integration
- Midline crossing and laterality

 References

Chu, S. (2003) *Occupational Therapy for Children with Developmental Coordination Disorder*, 5th edn (course handbook, self-published). London, Ealing Primary Care Trust.
Levin, K.J. (1991) *Fine Motor Dysfunction, Therapeutic Strategies in the Classroom*. Tucson, AZ, Therapy Skill Builders.

 Further reading

See Appendix A 7 Movement programmes and gross motor resources page 381.

Further resources

Refer to Foundation Skills within this area

- FS 2A, 2B, 2C, 2D, 2E within this area page 35–51

Refer to Occupational Therapy Approaches

- OTA 3 Building firm foundations for fine motor control—warm-up for the upper limb page 259
- OTA 8 Sensory strategies page 323
- OTA 10 Consolidating foundation skills through group activities page 333

Refer to Appendix

- A 1 Ages and stages of development page 361

Refer to Equipment Resources page 407.

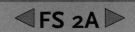

Motor planning

▷ What is it?

Motor planning is the first step in complex new skills, or those requiring sequencing, as it involves praxis (planning). Praxis is a unique human skill, which requires conscious thought 'enabling the brain to conceptualise, organise and direct purposeful interaction with the physical world' (Ayres *et al.*, 1987). It involves:

- Ideation—knowing what to do
- Motor planning/programming—knowing how to do it
- Execution—knowing how to complete it successfully

▷ Why is it important?

Every activity undertaken, however simple, demands motor planning, since a child needs to have an idea of the task, what it involves and then how to achieve it. Organisation, planning and then execution of new or old unpractised motor tasks are required throughout the child's day. For good motor planning to be achieved, the brain needs essential information from all the sensory systems as well as integrating body awareness and perception of movement. It can then utilise sensory impulses to plan, organise, time and sequence an unfamiliar task.

▷ What are the implications?

Children with motor planning problems may have difficulties with:

- Mastering a new skill—may struggle and appear clumsy, accident prone or messy
- Starting a task—cannot fathom out what to do
- Performing task—may rush, be clumsy producing messy, haphazard work
- Finishing work on time—unable to work out a strategy of completion
- Handwriting tasks—organisation of words on a line, thoughts on a page, may perform a task in a jerky or fragmented way lacking the spontaneity, which comes from sequence planning
- Practical tasks/art and craft/construction/topic work

- Manipulating equipment—using paintbrush, glue stick, scissors, ruler, compass, protractor
- Organising body movements, being aware of their 'personal space', sitting on the carpet without causing a disturbance, thinking up movement sequence in PE, e.g. different ways of travelling along a bench
- Self-care tasks—dressing, using cutlery, cleaning self
- Undertaking tasks requiring stamina/standing tolerance

▷ Teaching strategies

- Help the child to break down task, repeat instructions and record steps on paper.
- Ask what/when/where/why/how/questions to get the child to think about task.
- Provide visual cues, schedules.
- Encourage verbalisation whilst doing task, if necessary helping the child physically move through action.
- Set small achievable targets and plan method of recording when completed.
- Give one direction at a time, when task completed add another.
- Minimise visual distractions, aim for clutter free environment.
- Review rules of games before actually playing it—explain verbally as well as demonstrating.
- Mark boundaries of a game—use tape, carpet square, hoop.
- Rehearse what the child has learnt on a regular basis, give demonstration with instructions.
- Get the child to plan changes of sequence and remember and implement those changes, so that the skill becomes generalised.

▷ Activities to improve motor planning

- *Obstacle courses* using different positions (over, under, through), directions (clockwise, anti-clockwise, always turning right or left, forwards, backwards, sideways), postures (crawling, commando crawling, tiptoe, lying on scooter board), heights, textures (hard, soft, uneven, wobbly)
- *Stepping stones*—planning route across the room
- *Spatial orientation work*—moving through a room or obstacle course blindfolded, following instructions
- *'Twister' game/*'Simon Says'—imitating posture, sequence of movements
- *Playground games*—skipping, hopscotch, space hoppers, ball games
- *Maze drawings*, art and craft activities, junk modelling, origami, collage
- *Map reading*, from basic pictorial representations to OS maps
- *Cutting with scissors*, pasting into position, art projects or tasks that require assembling parts to make a whole
- *Construction tasks*—following instructions
- *Practising tying laces*, tying school tie, tying bows in aprons

▷ **References**

Ayres, A.J., Mailloux, Z.K. & Wendler C.L. (1987) Developmental dyspraxia: is it a unitary function? *Occupational Therapy Journal of Research*, **7**, 93–110.

Chu, S. (2003) *Occupational Therapy for Children with Developmental Coordination Disorder*, 5th edn (course handbook, self-published). London, Ealing Primary Care Trust.

Levine, K.J. (1991) *Fine Motor Dysfunction, Therapeutic Strategies in the Classroom*. Tucson, AZ, Therapy Skill Builders.

▷ **Further reading**

See introduction to section page 31.

Drew, S. (2005) *Including Children with Developmental Coordination Disorder (Dyspraxia) in the Foundation Stage*. Lutterworth, Featherstone Education Limited.

Kirby, A. & Drew, S. (2003) *Guide to Dyspraxia and Developmental Coordination Disorders*. London, Fulton.

Ripley, K. (2001) *Inclusion for Children with Dyspraxia/DCD—a Handbook for Teachers*. London, Fulton.

Ripley, K., Daines, B. & Barrett, J. (1997) *Dyspraxia—a Guide for Teachers and Parents*. London, Fulton.

▷ **Further resources**

Refer to Foundation Skills

- FS 1C Proprioceptive processing/sense page 19
- FS 2B Postural stability and balance page 39
- FS 2C Spatial and body awareness page 43
- FS 2D Bilateral integration page 47
- FS 3A Visual motor integration page 59

Refer to Occupational Therapy Approaches

- OTA 3 Building firm foundations for fine motor control—Hand gym page 263
- OTA 4 Building firm foundations for handwriting—Pre-writing patterns page 286, Multi-sensory approaches page 288
- OTA 6 Building firm foundations for dressing skills page 315
- OTA 7 Building firm foundations for scissor development page 319
- OTA 9 Self-organisation approaches page 327
- OTA 10 Consolidating foundation skills through group activities page 333

Refer to Appendix

- A 7 Movement programmes and gross motor resources page 381
- A 11 Thinking skills page 397

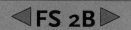

Postural stability and balance

▷ What is it?

Postural stability is the ability to maintain and change the position of the trunk and neck so that the spine provides a stable base for positioning and movement of the extremities, while the head is maintained in the optimal position for effective visual function. Balance can be divided into static (holding a posture whilst still) and dynamic (controlling postures whilst on the move).

▷ Why is it important?

Good postural stability is required for efficient movement control. All gross motor movements originate from working out of a central axis or core. Stability at the pelvic and shoulder girdles (core stability) allows a wide range of movement of the arms and legs. Arm control and therefore all fine manual dexterity and stamina is greatly reduced when the trunk is not stabilised.

It provides the postural control necessary for the acquisition of mature gross and fine motor skills. It is essential for the development of fine manual dexterity, since controlled and coordinated large gross motor movements must be in place before smaller movements can be refined.

▷ What are the implications?

Children with postural stability and balance problems may have difficulties with:

- Hopping, skipping, jumping/moving fluently/changing direction, joining in playground games
- Walking over uneven ground/along a rope or bench/going upstairs
- Team games/bat and ball games/obstacle courses
- PE activities/working with equipment or on apparatus off the ground
- Sitting on a chair or the floor without fidgeting, slouching or falling
- Maintaining a functional working position, writing on interactive board, and having stamina for task, school day and school term
- Opening heavy doors

- Inaccuracy when building with bricks, construction tasks, stabilising equipment
- Self-care—dressing, eating, personal care, putting lunch box on high shelf, hanging up coat
- Waiting in line/maintaining personal space/not leaning on peers or furniture

▷ Teaching strategies

- Use visual cues, e.g. coloured mats.
- Provide chair, rather than sitting on the carpet or standing for a demonstration.
- Teach compensatory movements, e.g. fix elbows into side or rest on table when accuracy required for hand movements, eye fixing to maintain balance.
- Provide angled writing surface and wedge cushion, e.g. movin'sit cushion.
- Ensure the child has clear vision of teacher and board without moving body.

▷ Activities to improve postural stability and balance skills

- *Stand with one foot* on a low box to sing/clap, play throw/catch games or pick up objects from floor.
- *Work on an uneven surface*, e.g. stand on wobble board or with one foot on football to challenge child with above activities. Repeat activities standing on one leg.
- *Heel-toe walking* between two ropes or along a line forwards, backwards, sideways on floor or along a bench.
- *Stepping stones*, using coloured mats or hoops, varying size, distance and direction.
- *Hopping games* in straight line, backwards, forwards, sideways or weaving in and out of skittles/poles, balancing on different body parts, later incorporating bean bag/target games.
- *Statue game*, keeping still when signal given, or trying to stay in statue position when partner tries to move statue.
- *Activities incorporating lying on tummy* (prone extension), lying on back and bending knees to chest, (supine flexion) and turning (rotation).
- *Commando crawling*, crab walking, press ups, bunny jumps, coffee grinder.
- *Stilt walking*, scooter board games, climbing frame apparatus, adventure playground equipment.
- *Obstacle courses* incorporating different apparatus, textures, heights, directions, orientation.

▷ References

Chu, S. (2003) *Occupational Therapy for Children with Developmental Coordination Disorder*, 5th edn (course handbook, self-published). London, Ealing Primary Care Trust.

Levine, K.J. (1991) *Fine Motor Dysfunction, Therapeutic Strategies in the Classroom.* Tucson, AZ, Therapy Skill Builders.

▷ Further reading

See introduction to section page 31.

▷ Further resources

Refer to Foundation Skills

- FS 1A Vestibular processing page 11
- FS 2 Introduction to gross motor coordination page 31
- FS 2A Motor planning page 35
- FS 2C Spatial and body awareness page 43
- FS 2D Bilateral integration page 47
- FS 2E Midline crossing and laterality page 51

Refer to Occupational Therapy Approaches

- OTA 4 Building firm foundations for handwriting—Ergonomics page 281
- OTA 10 Consolidating foundation skills through group activities page 333

Refer to Appendix

- A 7 Movement programmes and gross motor resources page 381

Refer to Equipment Resources page 407.

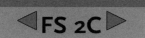

Spatial and body awareness

▷ What is it?

Spatial awareness is the ability to interpret spatial information and use it in an organised, systematic way for planning movement. It provides us with information about our environment and the relationship of one's body to an external space. Body awareness is a subconscious skill of knowing where each part of the body is and how it is moving, without relying on vision. This information is interpreted through muscles, joints and skin receptors, after which visual information can be integrated. It is reliant upon good proprioceptive, tactile and vestibular processing.

▷ Why is it important?

'As infants develop awareness of their ability to control their own movements and to act on the environment, they learn to perceive distance and direction between objects and their own body parts. Early spatial judgements are made using the self as reference (intra-personal space). Children gradually develop awareness of objects and external space as separate from themselves, and they apply the information learned in reference to their body to objects in extra-personal space' (Levine, 1991).

Children develop through the following stages using physical exploration and movement:

- Spatial relationships of body parts
- Judgement of size, shape and distance between body parts and objects
- Relationships between one object and other objects in space

Children with poor spatial and body awareness tend to rely heavily on visual information since they may only have a vague awareness of their position in space. They may not be able to move fluently if they cannot see their arms and legs. They may also have problems with visual attention, laterality, right/left discrimination, crossing the body midline and spatial concepts of the body (up/down, front-side-back).

▷ What are the implications?

Children with spatial and body awareness problems may have difficulties with:

- Identifying, locating and recalling body parts on themselves and others
- Recognising right/left sides of their body and using right/left awareness in relation to people, objects and handwriting
- Moving in space—not bumping into people or objects, joining in PE activities, team games, running in the right direction, dance/drama improvisation, moving legs in swimming
- Self-care—clothes on correctly, buttons aligned, shoes on correct feet, wiping bottom, brushing hair, cleaning teeth, using cutlery, spreading butter on bread, pouring
- Organising themselves and their belongings
- Staying within their personal boundaries without invading another's space, safely crossing the road, judging moving traffic
- Following directions which include spatial concepts and prepositions, vertical and linear scanning, symmetry and tessellations, understanding geometry
- Handwriting—size, shape and spacing of letters, writing on a line, setting work out on a page
- Pencil and paper activities—copying pictures, drawing plans, labelling diagrams, tracking mazes
- Completing puzzles, constructing things either from a model (3D-3D) or from a picture (2D-3D)

▷ Teaching strategies

- Provide verbal reinforcement of position and direction.
- Teach to scan work/activity left to right, top to bottom.
- Use cue cards to help the child talk through an activity.
- Use colour coding to organise work and space.
- Concentrate on movement activities that motivate the child.
- Use carpet squares for defining sitting area.
- Use mouse mat or desk mat to define work area.

▷ Activities to improve spatial and body awareness

It is essential that children move around and experience their body position in space rather than initially try to learn through doing puzzles and sedentary activities.

- *Name and touch different body parts* with eyes open and then shut; reproduce body movements, initially copying adult, then mirrored and later following diagrams.

- *'Simon Says'*, Follow-the-leader, Twister, Dance Sacs (Lycra® bags to climb into and make shapes).
- *Body wrestling* using tactile feedback, e.g. sitting back to back with knees bent and elbows linked, try to force partner sideways onto the floor in a chosen direction.
- *Shine a torch* onto various parts of the child's body and get them to identify where it is shining.
- *Draw round child* and make collage—use stickers to label and refer to this when child draws own picture.
- *Use body or face puzzles*, finish an incomplete drawing of a person, copy pictures of different characters.
- *Rolling on different surfaces* and textures—carpet, mat, wood, grass; weight bearing activities—carry heavy load, handprints on wall/floor, pushing down.
- *Pulling/pushing along a bench*, crawling through tunnels, bouncing on a trampette, cycle or road safety activities.
- *Obstacle courses* involving moving into, out of, through, over, under, between and around objects.
- *Target activities* with balls or bean bags, gradually reducing size of targets and increasing distance to throw/hit.

▷ **References**

Chu, S. (2003) *Occupational Therapy for Children with Developmental Coordination Disorder*, 5th edn (course handbook, self-published). London, Ealing Primary Care Trust.

Levine, K.J. (1991) *Fine Motor Dysfunction, Therapeutic Strategies in the Classroom*. Tucson, AZ, Therapy Skill Builders.

▷ **Further reading**

See introduction to section page 31.

▷ **Further resources**

Refer to appropriate Foundation Skills

- FS 1A Vestibular processing page 11
- FS 2 Introduction to gross motor coordination page 31
- FS 2A Motor planning page 35

- FS 2D Bilateral integration page 47
- FS 2E Midline crossing and laterality page 51

Refer to Occupational Therapy Approaches

Refer to Appendix

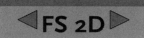

◄ FS 2D ►

Bilateral integration

▷ What is it?

Bilateral integration is the ability to coordinate both sides of the body together, in an effective manner to accomplish an activity, enabling movements of the right and left sides as well as top and bottom to become coordinated in a skilful manner. These movements may be:

- Symmetrical (the same movements both sides of the body), e.g. star jumps
- Alternating/reciprocal (the same movements performed by one side of the body and then the other), e.g. crawling
- Performing different functions (one side of the body doing one thing and the other side doing something completely different), e.g. tying shoe laces

▷ Why is it important?

Bilateral integration forms the 'foundation for the development of coordination between right and left sides of the body, mature hand dominance and effective two- handed coordination. It also contributes to the communication between the right and left sides of the brain for the development of specialisation of perceptual function and cognitive function for learning' (Chu, 2003).

▷ What are the implications?

Children with bilateral integration problems may have difficulties with:

- Managing stairs using one foot after the other (reciprocal pattern)
- PE activities, apparatus work, crawling, hopping, star jumps, skipping, tug of war
- Swimming, riding a bicycle, adventure playground equipment, climbing
- Bat and ball games, throwing and catching, kicking and dribbling
- Self-care—doing up buttons, using knife and fork, tying laces, tying a tie, making a drink
- Learning and playing musical instruments

- Using scissors, doing cut and stick activities, general art and craft, topic work
- Construction tasks, puzzles, form boards, model making, paper folding
- Practical tasks—using tools and stabilising equipment, sewing, cooking, woodwork, gardening
- Pencil and paper tasks—stabilising the paper, using a stencil, ruler, protractor, templates

▷ Teaching strategies

- Use visual cues to mark starting and stopping position.
- Start with activities that are unilateral/ipsilateral, then progress to symmetrical, asymmetrical and alternating.
- Break down each task into small achievable stages and practise individual parts.
- Help the child to use verbal prompts/cues.
- Work with the child to pre-plan task using thinking strategies, e.g. goal, plan, do, check/stop, think, do.
- Modify the task, e.g. use curly laces rather than standard that require tying.
- Use magnetic maths equipment/ruler.

▷ Activities to improve postural stability and balance skills

- *Marching on the spot* or around room, eyes open/eyes shut, commando crawling, obstacle courses.
- *Jumping feet together*, star jumps—legs only then arms and legs, bunny jumps.
- *Skipping with rope*, jumping side to side across rope, hopscotch with hoops.
- *Ball games*—bouncing, throwing or catching using two hands together, kicking, dribbling.
- *Cycling*, swimming, roller-skating/blading, stilt walking.
- *Sand and water play*, pouring, filling bottles, making sandcastles, bubble blowing and clapping.
- *Art and craft activities*:
  - paper: scrunching, folding, tearing, collage, weaving, templates, stencils, sticking and glueing
  - scissor activities: cutting, making, assembling
  - painting: finger painting, shaving foam, marble painting, lino cuts, potato cuts
  - cooking: mixing, rolling, beating, stirring, spreading, cutting, pouring
  - sewing and bead work: lacing, threading, Hamma beads
  - string work: cats cradle, macramé, Scooby doos, knitting, crochet, French knitting

- woodwork: measuring and marking, sawing, sanding, hammering, assembling
- gardening: digging, planting, tending, harvesting
- *Construction activities*: model making: play dough, clay, papier mâché, using junk, art straws, pipe cleaners, puppets; lacing, threading, Lego®, K'nex, Sticklebricks, Popoids, peg boards
- *Practising using school equipment*: rulers, compass, protractor, set square, underlining
- *Commercially available games*: Jenga, Labyrinth, Bop it, speed balls, Velcro™ bat and ball, computer/Playstation® games
- *Playing musical instruments*: drums, triangle, shakers, tambourine, maracas, wind and string instruments, piano

▷ **References**

Chu, S. (2003) *Occupational Therapy for Children with Developmental Coordination Disorder*, 5th edn (course handbook, self-published). London, Ealing Primary Care Trust.

Levine, K.J. (1991) *Fine Motor Dysfunction, Therapeutic Strategies in the Classroom*. Tucson, AZ, Therapy Skill Builders.

▷ **Further reading**

See introduction to section page 31.

▷ **Further resources**

Refer to Foundation Skills

- FS 1 Introduction to sensory processing page 5
- FS 2A Motor planning page 35
- FS 2C Spatial and body awareness page 43
- FS 2E Midline crossing and laterality page 51
- FS 3A Visual motor integration page 59
- FS 3C Manual dexterity page 69

Refer to Occupational Therapy Approaches

- OTA 1 Building firm foundations for spatial and body awareness page 249
- OTA 2 Building firm foundations for left/right awareness page 253

- OTA 3 Building firm foundations for fine motor control—Hand gym page 263
- OTA 7 Building firm foundations for scissor development page 319
- OTA 10 Consolidating foundation skills through group activities page 333

Refer to Appendix

- A 7 Movement programmes and gross motor resources page 381

Refer to Resources Equipment page 407.

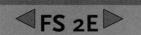

Midline crossing and laterality

▷ What is it?

Midline crossing is the ability to move hand, foot and eye(s) across the centre of the body. Laterality is the awareness that the body has two distinct sides and to have established a preferred dominance; right/left discrimination is an advanced form of laterality.

▷ Why is it important?

Midline crossing enables different activities to be performed without too much energy and effort. Children unable to cross midline may have ipsilateral hand use, preferring to use their left hand for activities on the left side of their body and their right hand for activities on the right side of their body. This is seen when a child transfers a crayon into his other hand to complete writing on the other side; as a result full functional dexterity may not develop in either hand.

▷ What are the implications?

Children with midline crossing and laterality problems may have difficulties with:

- Deciding which hand to use for a task—may alternate them
- Maintaining a functional position for table top work—may tend to turn their body to avoid writing or drawing across midline; in extreme cases, they may write from the body in a forward direction, instead of left to right across the body
- Two-handed tasks, e.g. stabilising paper when writing
- Drawing people
- Handwriting—drawing diagonal lines, changing stroke direction when writing, thus impairing fluency, writing letters and numbers without some reversals
- Writing across the body from left to right, may write from the body in a forward direction or move across chair as write on page, so may fall off chair
- Practical tasks, e.g. holding and turning paper when cutting

- Following grid games, map work
- Bat and ball games, hitting across the body
- Using a knife and fork

▷ Teaching strategies

- Mark the page with start and stop, e.g. green dot on top left and red on top right.
- Use visual cues to indicate where the child should stand for activities, e.g. in middle of board when drawing rainbow.
- Sit the child in 'side sitting' position (knees bent and feet to one side of body) and encourage weight bearing through one arm, so the child has to use the other arm across the body.
- Check the child is sitting on the correct height chair with feet supported, use angled work surface and position paper correctly with non-dominant hand, stabilising paper on base of page.
- Position equipment and toys on opposite side of body to dominant hand and encourage the child to reach across and pick up with dominant hand.

▷ Activities to improve midline crossing and laterality

NB it is essential that the child uses his eyes, hands and feet in a wide range of movements right across his body and does not compromise by swivelling his body or changing his hand

- *Draw a large rainbow on paper* on the wall or floor while kneeling; in four point kneeling draw an arc around self, draw simple shapes in air or on blackboard using both hands together.
- *Eye games*—follow the beam of a torch, marbles, balls, small objects, etc., keeping body still and tracking with eyes in horizontal, vertical and circular movements.
- *'Simon Says'* (using instructions that cross midline of body), hand clapping games.
- *Bean bag/ball games*—sorting bean bags from box on left to box on right (whilst in sitting or kneeling), passing beanbag around body, throwing bean bags across body (pick up with left hand to throw into container on right side), roll or bounce ball around body (keeping feet still), catch small ball in paper cone (encouraging reaching across midline).
- *French cricket*, tug-of-war, skittles (played side onto skittles) and balloon games.
- *Roll or bounce ball* around body keeping feet still.
- *Hammer games* requiring crossing the midline.
- *Tracking games*, e.g. taking a wand along a wire.

- Cross crawling and any brain gym warm ups.
- Commercially available games, such as Twister.

▷ References

Chu, S. (2003) *Occupational Therapy for Children with Developmental Coordination Disorder*, 5th edn (course handbook, self-published). London, Ealing Primary Care Trust.

Levine, K.J. (1991) *Fine Motor Dysfunction, Therapeutic Strategies in the Classroom*. Tucson, AZ, Therapy Skill Builders.

▷ Further reading

See introduction to section page 407.

▷ Further resources

Refer to Foundation Skills

- FS 1 Introduction to sensory processing page 5
- FS 2A Motor planning page 35
- FS 2B Postural stability and balance page 39
- FS 2C Spatial and body awareness page 43
- FS 2D Bilateral integration page 47
- FS 3B Vision and ocular motor control page 63

Refer to Occupational Therapy Approaches

- OTA 1 Building firm foundations for spatial and body awareness page 249
- OTA 2 Building firm foundations for left/right awareness page 253
- OTA 3 Building firm foundations for fine motor control—Hand gym page 263
- OTA 4 Building firm foundations for handwriting—Pre-writing patterns page 286, Multi-sensory approaches page 288
- OTA 10 Consolidating foundation skills through group activities page 333

Refer to Appendix

■ A 7 Movement programmes and gross motor resources page 381

Refer to Equipment Resources page 407.

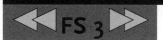

Introduction to fine motor control

 What is it?

Fine motor control, which is the ability to perform arm and hand movements with fluency and accuracy, depends not only on the control of the trunk, shoulder, arms and hands but also on ocular motor control, visual motor integration, visual perception and cognitive development.
Initially, a young or immature child will use large, inaccurate movements before refining them to achieve specialised skills. 'To control fine movements, children must be able to hold some body parts steady (stabilise) while moving others' (Levine, 1991). Accurate reach and controlled grasp and release are all required for the development of manipulation skills.

 Why is it important?

Fine motor control facilitates participation and independence in all areas of a child's life through play, self-care and learning.

 What are the implications?

 Children with fine motor control problems may have difficulties with:

- Exploratory play
- Cutting with scissors, drawing, writing, colouring (as they use whole arm movement instead of increased control achieved from finer movements of the wrist and fingers)
- Holding and manipulating tools, e.g. scissors, pencil, paintbrush, ruler
- Pencil and paper tasks, e.g. painting, drawing, handwriting
- Using writing tools—awkward grasp, slow manipulation, reducing speed of output

- Drawing on a vertical surface—unable to move hand to make smooth up/down movements
- Turning pages of a book
- Self-care, e.g. dressing, using cutlery, hand washing, using the toilet
- Confidence—acutely aware of their lack of ability compared to their peer group; often opt out
- Frustration—give up easily, opt out, destroy games/work

Within this section, fine motor control has been broken down into:

- Visual motor integration
- Vision and ocular motor control
- Manual dexterity

▷▷ References

Chu, S. (2003) *Occupational Therapy for Children with Developmental Disorder*, 5th edn (course handbook, self-published). London, Ealing Primary Care Trust.

Erhardt, R. (1993) *Developmental Hand Dysfunction, Theory, Assessment and Treatment.* Oxford, Harcourt Assessment.

Levine, K.J. (1991) *Fine Motor Dysfunction, Therapeutic Strategies in the Classroom.* Tucson, AZ, Therapy Skill Builders.

▷▷ Further reading

Benbow, M. (1992) *Neuro-kinaesthetic Approaches to Hand Function and Handwriting*, Chicago, IL, Advanced Rehabilitation Institutes.

Case Smith, J. & Pehoski, C. (1992) *Development of Hand Skills in the Child.* Bethesda, MD, American Occupational Therapy Inc.

Henderson, A. & Pehoski, C. (1995) *Hand Function in the Child—Foundations for Remediation.* St Louis, Missouri, Moseby.

Hill, M. & Hill, K. (2002) *Cutting Skills. Photocopiable Activities to Improve Scissor Technique.* Cambridge, LDA.

Hill, M. & Hill, K. (2006) *Fine Motor Skills. Photocopiable Activities to Improve Motor Control* Cambridge, LDA.

Lear, R. (1999) *Fingers and Thumbs—Toys and Activities for Children with Hand Function Problems.* Oxford, Butterworth Heinemann.

Mahoney, S. & Markwell, A. (2004) *Developing Scissor Skills—a Guide for Parents and Teachers.* Dunmow, Peta UK.

Miller Knight, J. & Gilpin Decker, M. (1994) *Hands at Work and Play. Developing Fine Motor Skills at Home and School.* Tucson, AZ, Therapy Skill Builders.

Further resources

Refer to Foundation Skills

- FS 3A, 3B, 3C within this area page 59–69
- FS 1B Tactile sense and tactile processing page 15
- FS 2D Bilateral integration page 47
- FS 2E Midline crossing and laterality page 51

Refer to Occupational Therapy Approaches

- OTA 3 Building firm foundations for fine motor control page 259
- OTA 4 Building firm foundations for handwriting page 271
- OTA 5 Building firm foundations for alternative methods of recording page 305
- OTA 6 Building firm foundations for dressing skills page 315
- OTA 7 Building firm foundations for scissor development page 319
- OTA 10 Consolidating foundation skills through group activities page 333

Refer to Appendix

- A 1 Ages and stages of development page 361
- A 2 Alphabet ABC sentences page 369
- A 3 Fine motor circuit page 371
- A 4 Handwriting self-evaluation checklist page 373
- A 5 Handwriting programmes and fine motor resources page 375
- A 12 Twelve rules of legibility page 401

Websites

- www.abcteach.com (good certificates)
- www.activityvillage.co.uk (lots of projects—origami/printables)
- www.colouringbookfun.com (colouring pictures)
- www.coloringcastle.com (range of colouring pictures)
- www.dltk-kids.com (crafts, etc.)
- www.enchantedlearning.com (lots of print outs and crafts)
- www.everythingpreschool.com (different activities)
- www.ltscotland.org.uk/earlyyears/resources/illustrations (good pictures)
- www.preschoollearners.com (handwriting patterns)
- www.printables4kids.com (printable)
- www.under5s.co.uk (various information)

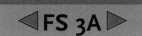

Visual motor integration

▷ What is it?

'Visual motor integration is the degree to which visual perception and finger-hand movements are well coordinated' (Beery, 2004). Children translate what they see into a motor movement. Those with weak visual motor integration know what they want to do, but are unable to complete the task satisfactorily as they have difficulty producing the accuracy of movement.

▷ Why is it important?

Visual motor integration is an essential component for the development and refinement of all practical skills including handwriting and drawing. Efficient visual motor integration is needed to catch a ball, thread a needle, colour within boundaries, use visual guidelines for cutting or write on lines. It is important that visual motor integration is developed adequately and is therefore automatic, so that attention can be focused on the content, not the execution of the task.

▷ What are the implications?

Children with visual motor integration problems may have difficulties with:

- Construction tasks, e.g. posting, jigsaws, threading, Lego®, building models
- Self-care, e.g. dressing, using cutlery
- Holding and manipulating tools, e.g. underlining with ruler, cutting along a line with scissors
- Pencil and paper tasks, e.g. tracing, colouring within lines, drawing, learning letter formation, designs needing directional changes
- Presentation—spacing, staying within lines, consistent sizing of writing
- Copying from book to paper, or board to paper
- Performing practical tasks
- Copying and reproducing shapes/designs especially when orientation, spatial placement and direction are involved
- PE, e.g. ball skills, team games, apparatus work
- Sustaining motivation for handwriting tasks

▷ **Teaching strategies**

- Break down activity into observation/planning/execution.
- Use large movements to reinforce spatial concepts, e.g. prepositions, direction, orientation.
- Simplify visual motor activities, so less accuracy is needed.
- Allow more time to complete task.
- Provide tactile, visual or auditory cues to help guide movements, e.g. increase width of line to be cut or size of space to be coloured.
- Provide verbal feedback when the child is struggling with task.
- Allow the child to focus on content of creative writing task rather than presentation.
- Consider alternative methods of recording.

▷ **Activities to improve visual motor integration**

- *Tearing/cutting/sticking* activities/paper folding/craft.
- *Graded scissor activities*—initially making small snips before cutting along lines and around shapes (see OTA 7 page 319).
- *Tracing activities*, colouring, stencil and template work.
- *Maze activities*, in shaving foam or sand before drawing on paper.
- *Imitating and copying lines*, shapes, letters and numbers using different materials, e.g. play dough, Plasticene®, lolly sticks, pipe cleaners.
- *Writing patterns* in different media before using lined paper, identify how many times child stays within line (see OTA 4 page 271), alphabet awareness work (see A 2 page 369).
- *Threading activities* starting with large equipment and progressing to smaller.
- *Peg patterns*, dot-to-dot, copying patterns drawn on square or circle grids, word searches, completing symmetry patterns and tessellations.
- *Using a torch in a darkened room* child traces over outline of door, window or pre-writing patterns drawn on board or wall.
- *PE activities*—practise throwing and catching using scarves, balloons, scratch ball, etc., target games; ask child to go to named place in the hall and complete a movement sequence, walking along a raised bench or line/pattern on the ground.
- *Introduce laptop* in conjunction with touch typing software to improve typing skills for recording work.

▷ References

Beery, K.B. (2004) *Developmental Test of Visual; Motor Integration, VMI.* New Jersey, USA, Modern Curriculum Press

Chu, S. (1999) *Assessment and Treatment of Children with Developmental Perceptual Dysfunction* (course handbook, self-published). London, West London Health Care Trust.

Levine, K.J. (1991) *Fine Motor Dysfunction, Therapeutic Strategies in the Classroom.* Tucson, AZ, Therapy Skill Builders.

▷ Further reading

See introduction to section page 55.

▷ Further resources

Refer to Foundation Skills

Refer to Occupational Therapy Approaches

Refer to Appendix

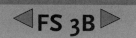

Vision and ocular motor control

▷ What is it?

Vision is the act or power of sensing with the eyes. It refers to the total system that allows an individual to see, and to experience, objects and images in space. A small part of this system is the eye; the rest includes all of the complex neurological processes that go to convert light impulse reaching the eye into a meaningful mental image of the world we are in (Holland, 1995a). To achieve ocular motor control the six muscles of each eye must coordinate effortlessly to obtain a single unified and clear image for transmission via the optic nerves to the visual cortex.

▷ Why is it important?

Life experiences help us acquire vision and since most of our knowledge of the world around us is obtained through vision, correct operation of the system is crucial for efficient functioning. Links between the ocular motor system and the tactile and proprioceptive systems also provide accurate spatial information to allow correct and efficient body posturing and motor control. Children need to be able to:

- Keep their head still whilst moving their eyes
- Keep their eyes still whilst moving their head
- Move both their head and eyes independently in a coordinated way whilst staying still or moving

Good ocular motor control is a precursor for developing efficient eye-hand coordination. The need to improve visual tracking and ocular motor control is frequently overlooked when trying to improve other gross and fine motor and perceptual skills.

▷ What are the implications?

Children with ocular-motor problems may:

- Show visual stress (headaches and eye strain), discomfort, avoidance with close work; typically, however, young children prefer to avoid the task, rather than experience headaches, and this as a symptom will often not be reported

- Be fatigued, tired, lose concentration, or be distractible when working; young children, especially, show loss of attention and distractible behaviour, which can sometimes be mistaken for hyperactivity
- Screw up their eyes, squint and close or cover one eye when working; young children who appear very sensitive to bright light may well be suffering from binocular vision problems and should always be checked for this by an optometrist
- Have an abnormal posture when reading or writing, often leaning down towards the paper with a very short working distance
- Have a problem keeping place and/or line when reading unless using a marker; small children will rapidly give up if place keeping is an issue, and may become quite resistant to close work as a result
- Have difficulties with copying, either from book to paper or from board to paper
- Skip or re-read lines or words/read slowly/complain of print 'running together or jumping'/use finger or marker as a pointer
- Have difficulties drawing—orientating and spacing drawings on a page
- Demonstrate handwriting problems—poor spacing, erratic use of lines, losing place when copying, frequently omitting words, writing up or downhill on paper, fatigue quickly
- Show poor coordination and balance in games or PE—either in ball games or team games/immature ball control and poor following flight of ball/clumsiness/fall over and bump into things

▷ Teaching strategies

- *Visual breaks are essential* and may need to be scheduled every five minutes for some children, to reduce fatigue.
- Reduce amount of time spent on close work, intersperse practical session with close work.
- Schedule a few moments to close and relax eyes between classroom tasks.
- Alternate board activities with less visually demanding tasks.
- Keep board clean with only current information; circle/highlight word to be copied.
- Limit peripheral distractions—consider use of a workstation.
- Ensure good posture and check whether angled surface is beneficial.
- Check book/paper position to find optimum working distance (i.e. equal to the distance from the elbow to the knuckle).
- Sit facing the board to eliminate need to turn body.
- Ensure as much natural lighting as possible.
- Provide paper copy when information on board.
- Enlarge worksheets to ease focus demands.
- Use computers to reduce amount of handwriting required.
- Try using line trackers or guidelines on clear acetate to keep place in text.

- Reinforce working left to right, top to bottom when scanning and use margin as a reference point, use ruler/paper guide/sticker.
- Experiment with different coloured overlays to minimise visual stress.
- Use noisy or light-up toys to maintain visual attention and focus.

> ### ▷ Activities to enhance visual tracking and ocular motor control

Initially, start gross motor activities lying down, before progressing to sitting with back supported, sitting with back unsupported, then standing with a wall close behind, before finally being able to stand in the middle of a large space.

- *Look up, down, left and right*, with the eyes only, whilst keeping head still—possibly to the four corners of a room (ten times at the start of a lesson will stimulate simple tracking).
- *Lie under a suspended ball* that the child should be able to reach up and touch. It should be directly above the child's chest when stationary. Try to stop the swinging ball with one hand, gently poke it as it swings past, catch it, strike ball with one hand, then use a small bat until able to strike ball continuously.
- *Track moving objects* (e.g. torch, quoit, car, balloon) horizontally, vertically, diagonally and in circular directions, play 'chase' with two torches, follow marbles rolled around a large tray or down marble racer.
- Play 'swing ball', practise bouncing balloons, throw bean bags into rolling barrel, throw and catch bean bags/balls, stop a bounced power ball.
- *Write a sequence of letters*, numbers, pictures, etc., in rows horizontally across page, get child to scan from left to right, line by line, reading or circling particular letters/numbers/pictures.
- *Draw numbers in a random order* over a blackboard/whiteboard and get child to draw a continuous line to connect them, trying to avoid head movements.
- *Read first and last letters* on every line of a page of text or the first letter of every word, to develop saccadic eye movements needed for reading.
- *Read aloud whilst moving* the material in and out and in circles, to help develop stable focus, only for a few words at a time.
- *Shift focus* between two objects placed either side by side, or at different distances away by following verbal instructions in quick succession.
- *Encourage pattern-copying*, using increasingly complex shapes to develop visual analysis skills, word searches, pattern games, e.g. Battleships, Tangrams.
- *Encourage visualisation*, e.g. day dreaming and then describe the dreams with as much sensory detail as possible.
- *Play a piece of music* and picture the scene being portrayed whilst listening with eyes closed, e.g. *Peter and the Wolf*.

▷ References

Holland, K. (1995a) *Visual Skills for Learning in Topic*, Spring 1995, Issue 13. London, NFER-Nelson.

Holland, K. (1995b) *Vision for Writing, Handwriting Review*, Vol. 9. pp. 92–98. Bicester, Oxon, Handwriting Interest Group (now National Handwriting Association).

Information taken from study day 'Visual Factors and Occupational Therapy' by Keith Holland, Behavioural Optometrist, 1996, and personal correspondence.

▷ Further reading

Wachs, H. & Frith, H. (1975) *Thinking Goes to School*. New York, Oxford University Press.

Willows, D., Kruk, R. & Corcos, E. (1993) *Visual Processes in Reading and Reading Disabilities*. London, Lawrence Earlbaum Associates.

British Association of Behavioural Optometrists—see Useful Addresses page 417.

▷ Further resources

Building Auditory and Visual Perceptual Skills. Cambridge, Learning Development Aids (LDA) out of print.

Refer to Foundation Skills

- FS 1A Vestibular processing page 11
- FS 1E Visual processing page 27
- FS 2C Spatial and body awareness page 43
- FS 2D Bilateral integration page 47
- FS 3A Visual motor integration page 59

Refer to Occupational Therapy Approaches

- OTA 1 Building firm foundations for spatial and body awareness page 249
- OTA 2 Building firm foundations for left/right awareness page 253
- OTA 4 Building firm foundations for handwriting page 271
- OTA 5 Building firm foundations for alternative methods of recording page 305
- OTA 7 Building firm foundations for scissor development page 319
- OTA 10 Consolidating foundation skills through group activities page 333

Refer to Appendix

Refer to Equipment Resources page 407.

Manual dexterity

▷ What is it?

Manual dexterity is the ability to perform intricate and precise movements of the hands with fluency, accuracy and speed commensurate with developmental age. Fine manual dexterity skills mature according to recognised developmental patterns. The foundation skills necessary for mature hand function are generally considered to be in place by the time a child enters school.

Hand skills develop in sequence:

- Isolation of index finger to point
- Pinch/pincer grasp
- Tripod grasp
- Counter-balance of two sides of the hand—stabilising with ring and little finger whilst being able to move thumb, index and middle fingers
- In-hand manipulation—moving objects within the hand

▷ Why is it important?

Mature hand function is reliant upon precise, accurate and fluid movements of the hand. This enables a child to learn new skills and perform tasks efficiently without using excess effort.

▷ What are the implications?

Children with manual dexterity problems may have difficulties with:

- Construction and posting tasks, e.g. Lego®, Stickle bricks, modelling, play dough
- Doing up buttons, zips, tying laces, using knife and fork, opening packaging for packed lunch, operating soap dispenser
- Grasping, releasing, pinching and manipulating objects with the fingers
- Turning objects in one hand with fingers, e.g. use both hands when needing to rotate pencil to use eraser
- Grasp—constantly shifting pencil position, awkward hold on scissors
- Pencil and paper tasks—colouring; drawing; stencils; tracing; developing pencil control when learning to form letter with neatness, fluency and speed

- Manipulating objects—using whole hand grasps and possibly two hands together instead of using refined finger grasp and movements
- Handling practical equipment—number fan, multi-link, phonics equipment, mouse, ruler, protractor, compass, set square
- Fine motor tasks requiring accuracy and precision—DT projects, science experiments, art and craft
- In-hand manipulation—picking up a number of counters one at a time and keeping hold of them in the same hand (squirrelling)

▷ Teaching strategies

- Allow the child to write on whiteboard, wide lined paper, raised lines or paper with minimal resistance.
- Allow the child to use alternative positions for writing (on stomach, propped on elbows) at times.
- Self-care—adapt clothing with Velcro®, allow the child to wear elasticated trousers, polo shirts, tie with elastic band; use cutlery with enlarged handles.
- Consider alternative scissors, ruler with raised ridge or handle for holding.
- Improve stability whilst completing task by using non-slip mat, magnetic tape on tools, Blu-Tack or bulldog clip to secure paper, key guard and wrist support for ICT.
- Use alternative pens or pencils that require less effort, e.g. felt tip pens, roller ball, gel pens, soft pencil, writing tool with larger barrel.
- Provide pencil grips, consider extra time for writing task and focus on legibility rather than neat presentation.
- Provide adult or peer support when task becomes frustrating.
- Differentiate work.

▷ Activities to improve manual dexterity

Activities need to be graded to reflect the child's developing skills. Start with larger items that require little pressure, then gradually decrease size of equipment and increase resistance to build up strength. These activities can either be done on an individual or group basis.

- *Continue to use activities* commonly seen in reception classes to consolidate and reinforce fine motor development.
- *Dressing up games*; toys and boards involving fastenings, tying laces.
- Constructional toys and games requiring increasing strength and dexterity.
- *Art and craft projects* involving tearing, scrunching, pulling, poking, pushing, threading, etc., in a variety of materials.
- *Modelling with play dough*, Plasticene®, clay—pinching, poking, rolling out, etc., using fingers and clay tools.

- *Model making* and paper folding.
- *Practise scissor skills* (see OTA 7 page 319).
- *Set up a timed circuit* of fine motor activities to encourage improvement in precision and speed (See OTA 3 Hand gym page 263).
- *Practise using equipment,* e.g. ruler, compass, protractor through art projects and games.
- *Squirrelling activities*—picking up small objects with thumb and index finger, holding them between ring and little finger whilst continuing to pick up more. See how many items can be held in the hand. Place same objects into small container one at a time.

▷ **References**

Addy, L. (2006) *Speed Up—A Kinaesthetic Programme to Develop Fluent Handwriting.* Wisbech, LDA.

Chu, S. (1998) *Assessment and Treatment of Children with Handwriting Difficulties* (course handbook, self-published). London, West London Health Care Trust.

Erhardt, R. (1993) *Developmental Hand Dysfunction, Theory, Assessment and Treatment.* Tucson, AZ, Therapy Skill Builders.

Levine K.J. (1991) *Fine Motor Dysfunction, Therapeutic Strategies in the Classroom.* Tucson, AZ, Therapy Skill Builders.

▷ **Further reading**

See introduction to section page 55.

▷ **Further resources**

Refer to Foundation Skills

- FS 1B Tactile sense and tactile processing page 15
- FS 1C Proprioceptive processing/sense page 19
- FS 2A Motor planning page 35
- FS 2B Postural stability and balance page 39
- FS 2D Bilateral integration page 47
- FS 2E Midline crossing and laterality page 51
- FS 3A Visual motor integration page 59
- FS 4 Introduction to perception page 73

Refer to Occupational Therapy Approaches

Refer to Appendix

Refer to Equipment Resources page 407.

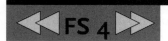

Introduction to perception

Each of our senses opens a different aspect of the world to us. The skills that develop through the efficient use of our senses are called perceptual skills. These become the building blocks for healthy development and the foundation for our cognitive and reasoning skills. The following comes from our previous book *Occupational Therapy Approaches for Secondary Special Needs*.

 Visual perception

Visual perceptual skills develop from the first weeks of life through to adolescence, by which time the full range of basic skills should be consolidated. The normal developmental growth patterns of early childhood establish the essential concepts through experiences of vertical and horizontal axes, depth, speed and directional judgements, both at rest and in motion. Upon this foundation, skills in both two-dimensional (2D) and three-dimensional (3D) perception develop. Two-dimensional skills can be formally assessed in categories such as visual discrimination, visual memory, visual sequential memory, visual spatial relationships, visual figure-ground, visual form constancy and visual closure. Three-dimensional perception can also be formally assessed by tasks such as block construction, but difficulties may also be evident in functional skills such as road safety, moving smoothly through a busy environment, or packing assorted items into a school bag. Further information on visual perceptual skills is given in the following pages in this section. Occupational therapists, in conjunction with educational psychologists, are able to assess these skills.

 Tactile perception

It is easy to underestimate the importance of our *tactile* system and the problems that inadequate or distorted perceptions can cause. External stimuli such as heat or cold, light or heavy pressure, texture and pain have to be sorted and assimilated. Upon this foundation, discrimination of shape, size, weight and density develop. As the child learns to seek information by touch, inhibition of unwanted sensory stimulation must also take place if she is not to be confused and distracted by sensory overload. For example, tactile figure-ground awareness of clothing during dressing allows her to put on her clothing comfortably, but sensory inhibition then permits her to move on to other activities undistracted by sensory arousal from her clothes.

Proprioception is an additional and inter-linked area of tactile perception, which relates to the awareness of the body in space. Information is gained from muscles, tendons and joints, gravitational pull and balance receptors. *Vestibular* skills relate specifically to our posture and balance mechanisms. The awareness of the body in motion is our *Kinaesthetic* sense and repetition of planned movements establishes motor memories. Visual motor activity needs to be integrated into postural balance and fluency of movement.

The stability and control we have over body posture and movement, and the control we are able to exercise in adapting to our environment, have enormous significance on our ability to learn. Occupational therapists and physiotherapists are able to assess these skills.

 ## Auditory perception

As with other senses, a wide range of essential skills develops through efficient integration of auditory stimulation. Figure-ground skills enable us to listen to a particular sound undistracted by background noise. Short and long-term memory is fundamental to learning. Sounds, rhythms and intonation must be discriminated, distance and direction interpreted. Correct sequencing also underpins effective communication. Speech and language therapists are able to assess auditory perceptual development, sometimes in conjunction with occupational therapists.

Management of perceptual deficits

The benefit of a good assessment of perceptual development is that it enables *identification* of specific areas of difficulty so that therapy or educational programmes can be targeted more accurately.

Since visual perceptual skills peak during puberty, remediation is most effective *during the primary years*. Teaching should be through a multi-sensory approach, whereby children are encouraged to verbalise what they are doing, look carefully whilst undertaking the task and try to feel what their body is doing. This provides auditory, visual, tactile and kinaesthetic feedback, which in turn reinforces more efficient performance.

Within this section, visual perception has been broken down into:

- Visual discrimination
- Visual spatial relationships
- Visual form constancy

- Visual figure ground discrimination
- Visual closure
- Visual memory

Further reading

Refer to A 13 Visual perception resources page 403.

Further resources

Refer to Foundation Skills

- FS 4A, 4B, 4C, 4D, 4E, 4F in this section page 77–97
- FS 1E Visual processing page 27
- FS 3A Visual motor integration page 59
- FS 3B Vision and ocular motor control page 63

Refer to Occupational Therapy Approaches

- OTA 1 Building firm foundations for spatial and body awareness page 249
- OTA 2 Building firm foundations for left/right awareness page 253

Refer to Appendix

- A 1 Ages and stages of development page 361
- A 10 Teacher's checklist for visual signs page 395

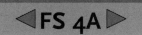

Visual discrimination

▷ What is it?

Visual discrimination is the ability to identify similarities or differences of a given shape or object. It is the first perceptual skill to develop and therefore when in place children can begin to match and sort objects by size, shape, colour, position, number and detail.

▷ Why is it important?

Children need this skill as it provides a foundation for all visual perceptual development. Without it, they are unable to identify objects by their features and therefore cannot make quick, accurate and refined interpretations of visual information. They may go on to have difficulties recognising numbers and letters, which may then affect their ability to read and write, since the key element of discrimination is the ability to register change.

▷ What are the implications?

Children with discrimination problems may experience difficulty with:

- Sorting and categorising toys, puzzles, objects
- Recognising variations in size of toys, puzzle pieces, objects
- Finding similar objects regardless of size
- Spotting similarities/differences
- Completing practical tasks, e.g. jigsaw puzzles, inset trays, posting toys, construction toys
- Matching or recognising differences in numbers, letters, shapes, words or objects
- Writing may have reversals or inversions when the child is writing numbers or letters, past the age when this is normal
- Using capital letters appropriately
- Concentration, appearing inattentive and disorganised
- Changing for PE, they may be slower than their peers

▷ **Teaching strategies**

- Teach strategies to learn orientation of letters—Letterland, arrows, alphabet.
- Trace over letters using directional cues when describing letters.
- Use visual cues, e.g. making hands in shape on 'b', 'd', 'L'.
- Encourage verbalisation whilst doing task.
- Provide clear, concise work sheets.
- Ensure concrete examples are available when further explanation is required.

▷ **Activities to improve visual discrimination**

- *Odd one out*/spot the difference games.
- *Finding and sorting activities*, categorising into sets, colours, shapes.
- *Finding shapes* in room or pictures—pick out all square, round, oblong things, etc.
- *Inset puzzles*, posting games, construction toys, bead and peg pattern.
- *Making shapes* with pipe cleaners, sticks, straws, identifying shapes drawn on child's back and copy on paper.
- *Familiar objects game*—get the child to indicate objects that can be eaten, objects used to clean the house, objects used in the garden, etc., make up scavenger hunt using similar ideas.
- *Card games*—Happy Families, Snap, Lotto, memory pairs, picture and shape dominoes.
- *'Feely' games*—recognising shapes, objects, toys by feeling with eyes closed and describing them in detail (circle, square, long, short, hard, soft, thick, thin, big, little, top, middle, side, etc.).
- *Finding the same letter*, shape, object/circling designated letter, word, ending (-ed, -ing) on page, in story; use a newspaper and circle/highlight all the 't's or other designated letter, a designated word such as 'and', the first word in every sentence, the last word in every sentence, all the double letters in various words.
- *Activities using shapes* painted on the floor or playground—moving in and out of named shapes, running, walking, hopping, jumping.

▷ **References**

Chu, S. (1999) *Assessment and Treatment of Children with Developmental Perceptual Dysfunction* (course handbook, self-published). London, West London Health Care Trust.

Levine, K.J. (1991) *Fine Motor Dysfunction, Therapeutic Strategies in the Classroom.* Tucson, AZ, Therapy Skill Builders.

> ## Further reading

See A 13 Visual perceptual resources page 403.
See introduction to section page 73.

> ## Further resources

Refer to Foundation Skills

- FS 4B, 4C, 4D, 4E, 4F within this section page 81–97
- FS 2C Spatial and body awareness page 43
- FS 3A Visual motor integration page 59
- FS 3B Vision and ocular motor control page 63
- FS 5A Attention and listening page 103

Refer to Occupational Therapy Approaches

- OTA 1 Building firm foundations for spatial and body awareness page 249
- OTA 2 Building firm foundations for left/right awareness page 253
- OTA 4 Building firm foundations for handwriting—Pre-writing patterns page 286, Multi-sensory approaches page 288
- OTA 10 Consolidating foundation skills through group activities page 333

Refer to Appendix

- A 4 Handwriting self-evaluation checklist page 373
- A 5 Handwriting programmes and fine motor resources page 375
- A 10 Teacher's checklist for visual signs page 395
- A 13 Visual perceptual resources page 403

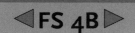

Visual spatial relationships

▷ What is it?

Visual spatial perception provides us with information about our environment and the relationship of one's body to an external space. It begins with knowing spatial concepts and where an object is in relation to oneself. Later, a child will perceive the relationship of two or more objects to themselves or each other. This will include whether an object is on top of another or underneath, in front or behind, up or down, inside or outside, etc. 'Vision needs to be combined with an interpretation of the physical environment to gain meaning from what we see' (Chu, 1999). Through the first years of life, as a child learns to sit, crawl, stand and walk, an innate awareness of vertical, horizontal and diagonal planes develops, which forms the foundation of judgements estimating size, distance and direction between objects and self.

▷ Why is it important?

Some children experience difficulty in appreciating and processing spatial information from their environment, which can affect their gross motor skills and classroom performance. On entering school, a child may bump into people and furniture, often finding it difficult to find adequate space when sitting beside others on the carpet. In later years, there may be problems with acquiring spatial judgements and interpreting page layout.

▷ What are the implications?

Children with visual spatial relationship problems may experience difficulty with:

- Knowing where their body is in space; often knocking over things for no apparent reason
- Moving around in classroom or playground without bumping into things or people, climbing stairs with one foot in front of the other
- Awareness of personal space, leading to problems lining up or sitting down on carpet

- PE activities when travelling through space, riding a bike, pushing a scooter and crossing a road
- Dressing—getting clothes on inside out/upside down/back to front
- Learning left/right, top/bottom in vertical and horizontal plane
- Handwriting in comparison with peer group—orientation of letters/numbers, size, shape, spacing of letters, placement on the line, messy work
- Setting out work on a page, developing mature drawing skills, copying pictures, drawing diagrams, following and keeping place on paper, board or book, copying from vertical to horizontal plane
- Playing with construction toys, constructing a model (3D-3D or 2D-3D) or drawing a diagram from a model (3D-2D)
- Sorting and organising personal belongings, keeping within personal boundaries

▷ Teaching strategies

- Use large movements to reinforce body awareness and spatial concepts, e.g. body parts, prepositions, direction, orientation.
- Encourage the child to experience the movement themselves before progressing to developing an understanding of position, space and placing of objects.
- Work on 3D-3D before attempting 2D-3D.
- Trace through maze or worksheet with finger before using writing tool.
- Use coloured lines and visual cues to clarify shape, size, position and placement of letters on line.
- Place green dot on top left side of page to indicate margin and where to start, place red dot on right hand side of page to indicate where to stop.

▷ Activities to improve visual spatial relationships

- *Outside playground* equipment/hopscotch/obstacle courses—in/ under/out/through/round, walking on stepping stones, hoop games stepping through, over, jumping in/out; use carpet squares or hoops to move around or step into, e.g. musical statues.
- *Ball skills*—throwing and catching, target games, bat and ball games, kicking ball into goal, throwing bean bags into different height boxes, balloon play.
- *Blindfold games* following verbal instructions—walk forward, stop, jump right, stop, jump left, stop, jump back.
- *Orienteering*, interpreting grid references, reading a map or plan.
- *Constructional play*—making a model based on an object, peg patterns, junk modelling, jigsaws, form boards, model making (3D-3D) and (2D-3D).

- *Activity book*—colouring, mazes, dot-to-dot, complete picture, find the difference, copying a picture.
- *Multi-sensory* pre-writing activities in variety of media—paint, shaving foam, sand, cornflour.
- *Craft activities*—cutting, sticking, paper folding, threading, weaving, sewing.
- *Board games*, Connect 4, Snakes and Ladders, Draughts, 'boxes' drawn on a grid.
- *Games to develop form* and shape, e.g. Dime Solids, Build Up, Tangrams, symmetry, tessellations, computer games.

▷ **References**

Chu, S. (1999) *Assessment and Treatment of Children with Developmental Perceptual Dysfunction* (course handbook, self-published). London, West London Health Care Trust.

▷ **Further reading**

See A 13 Visual perception resources page 403.
See introduction to section page 73.

▷ **Further resources**

Refer to Foundation Skills

- FS 4A, 4C, 4D, 4E, 4F within this section page 77–97
- FS 1 Introduction to sensory processing page 5
- FS 2C Spatial and body awareness page 43
- FS 2D Bilateral integration page 47
- FS 3A Visual motor integration page 59
- FS 3B Vision and ocular motor control page 63
- FS 6 Organisation approaches page 111

Refer to Occupational Therapy Approaches

- OTA 1 Building firm foundations for spatial and body awareness page 249
- OTA 2 Building firm foundations for left/right awareness page 253

- OTA 4 Building firm foundations for handwriting page 271
- OTA 5 Building firm foundations for alternative methods of recording page 305

Refer to Appendix

- A 4 Handwriting self-evaluation checklist page 373
- A 5 Handwriting programmes and fine motor resources page 375
- A 10 Teacher's checklist for visual signs page 395

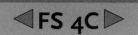
Visual form constancy

▷ **What is it?**

Visual form constancy is the ability to recognise that a shape or object remains the same despite changes in size, position, direction, orientation and distance, e.g. an object is still the same whether it is seen from the top, side or underneath.

Visual memory, visual figure ground and visual discrimination skills may all contribute to establishing form constancy. Form constancy develops from early years. It matures and refines in complex forms in association with visual closure, e.g. a continuous and increasingly complex development from 2D to 3D and depends on conceptual thought. There is considered to be a strong link between visual form constancy and visual figure ground, therefore it is advisable to work on both areas at the same time. 'Form constancy develops at about seven years of age and becomes relatively mature by eleven years' (Chu, 1999).

▷ **Why is it important?**

It enables the child to interpret the environment consistently and accurately, regardless of changes in presentation. Where constancy of shape is concerned, the child recognises that both two-dimensional and three-dimensional forms belong to certain categories of shape, regardless of their size, texture, colour, means of representation or angle from which they are seen, e.g. a cube is a cube.

▷ **What are the implications?**

Children with form constancy problems may experience difficulty with:

- Performing age appropriate daily activities, e.g. dressing, imaginative/role play, road safety, riding tricycles/bicycles, using adventure playground equipment
- Sorting and matching objects, shapes, materials when orientation and size vary
- Construction tasks where the child is required to copy from given information

- Recognising properties of shape and being able to generalise
- Acquiring early drawing and writing skills, understanding and using upper and lower case letters, making reversals and orientating letters correctly
- Reading material written in different fonts, e.g. italic, cursive
- Changing writing styles from printed to cursive writing
- Copying from a book or board which is in a vertical plane onto paper on a desk which is orientated horizontally
- Judging height, width, depth, size, distance, orientation of an object, estimation tasks
- Practical subjects and developing concepts, e.g. maths, science, design technology, art, topic work, PE

▷ Teaching strategies

- Use appropriate language to describe orientation and position of an object or objects.
- Verbalise and talk through properties and orientation of objects to help the child form concept.
- Demonstrate how horizontally presented material looks when presented vertically.
- Trace letter shapes on palm or tabletop.
- Practice upper/lower case in relation to a line, e.g. 'J' and 'j'.
- Break task down into practical steps, physically exploring the properties of an object, e.g. table, box.

▷ Activities to improve visual form constancy

- *Practical activities*, e.g. sorting objects by shape, size, texture, colour, category or orientation (horizontal, vertical, tilted at an angle), teach same/different, differentiate between objects, upper and lower case letters and shapes with obvious differences, gradually introducing smaller differences.
- *Identify different objects* in a room, which are a given shape, e.g. everything that is square.
- *Show child an object* (lorry, brick, teddy) and get them to guess what it is when they only see the front, back, side, bottom. Order objects in relation to size, e.g. biggest to smallest.
- *Posting/threading activities*, puzzles, large construction/junk modelling investigating shapes in different orientation and size.
- *Match 2D shapes* on card with 3D objects in sorting box, make models from pictures or diagrams—(2D-3D).
- *Dressing-up games* where child has to identify clothing when its appearance varies, e.g. an upside down shoe, a helmet.

- *Obstacle courses* using the same shape in different sizes or orientation, activities to help children understand height and distance, adventure playgrounds walking on uneven ground.
- *Art and craft activities*, making/overlapping shapes in different orientations and media—potato cuts, lino cuts, finger paints, shaving foam, pipe cleaners, play dough, straws. Cut out the same shape, but in different sizes and use for collage.
- *Practise tracing*, drawing and colouring different shapes in various orientations, find geometric shapes that are reversed or rotated and match.
- *Write the same letter* or word in many different styles, colours, and size. Encourage child to underline the same word presented in many different fonts.

▷ **References**

Chu, S. (1999) *Assessment and Treatment of Children with Developmental Perceptual Dysfunction*, 8th edn (course handbook, self-published). London, West London Health Care Trust.

Levine, K.J. (1991) *Fine Motor Dysfunction: Therapeutic Strategies in the Classroom*. Tucson, AZ, Therapy Skill Builders.

▷ **Further reading**

See A 13 Visual perception resources page 403.
See introduction to section page 73.

▷ **Further resources**

Refer to Foundation Skills

- FS 4A, 4B, 4D, 4E, 4F within this section page 77–97
- FS 1 Introduction to sensory processing page 5
- FS 2A Motor planning page 35
- FS 2C Spatial and body awareness page 43
- FS 3A Visual motor integration page 59
- FS 3B Vision and ocular motor control page 63

Refer to Occupational Therapy Approaches

- OTA 1 Building firm foundations for spatial and body awareness page 249

- OTA 4 Building firm foundations for handwriting—Pre-writing patterns page 286, Multi-sensory approaches page 288
- OTA 6 Building firm foundations for dressing skills page 315
- OTA 10 Consolidating foundation skills through group activities page 333

Refer to Appendix

- A 4 Handwriting self-evaluation checklist page 373
- A 5 Handwriting programmes and fine motor resources page 375
- A 10 Teacher's checklist for visual signs page 395

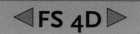

Visual figure ground discrimination

▷ What is it?

Visual figure ground discrimination is the ability to identify and distinguish an object or relevant information from a background/context that contains irrelevant or distracting information. Children need to be able to visualise before looking and so this skill is dependent on their ability to form concepts. There is a strong link between visual form constancy and visual figure ground; therefore, it is advisable to work on both areas at the same time. 'Children between the ages of eight and thirteen acquire a marked refinement of figure ground ability' (Chu, 1999).

▷ Why is it important?

Children need to be able to discriminate objects in everyday life. On entering school, a child may be unable to find things, see things in pictures or negotiate their way around a room without stepping on things. They may frequently appear disorganised and distractible. Training in this area should help children to shift attention appropriately, concentrate on the relevant stimuli whilst ignoring irrelevant stimuli, scan adequately and have more organised behaviour.

▷ What are the implications?

Children with figure ground discrimination problems may experience difficulty with:

- Preparing and settling into task, attending to task and concentrating when surrounded by a lot of visual stimulus
- Finding objects in tray, on table, on floor, on coat peg; finding a particular piece to build a model from a pile of construction toy materials
- Performing practical tasks, e.g. jigsaw puzzles, inset trays, posting toys, construction toys, sorting
- Colouring and tracing tasks, dot-to-dot activities, finding the hidden object
- Changing for PE, finding own kit and dressing appropriately
- Negotiating route around the classroom, playground, to and from school

- Organising themselves and their work area, laying out work on a page, finding own book from a selection of books on a table
- Keeping place when reading, completing a worksheet or copying work from book or board, scanning adequately to find required information (skim and scan skills)
- Finding details in a picture or specific place in worksheet, text, map, multiple choice test/interpreting and labelling diagrams, drawings, graphs, spreadsheets
- Noticing all the relevant words in question, identifying keywords, completing all sections in written assignments, proof reading and editing work

▷ Teaching strategies

- Encourage the child to visualise the named object before searching and starting task.
- Practice dressing skills, give prompts and cues to simplify tasks.
- Provide opportunities to experience moving in, on, or around equipment safely.
- Keep visual field uncluttered, provide organisation 'helps', e.g. boxes for finished work.
- Ensure desk position is free from distractions—up at front of class and near board, limit amount of items on it.
- Limit amount of information on page or board to keep work free of 'visual clutter'.
- Use tactile and visual cues—darkening/thickening lines for cutting, sticker at margin.
- Use 'windows' or 'boxes' to isolate work and provide line tracker when reading text.
- Encourage use of highlighter pen to emphasise text or important points.
- Enlarge fonts when typing and use bold, clear print, use wider lines and larger spacing when writing.
- Colour contrast when writing on whiteboard or workbook.

▷ Activities to improve visual figure ground discrimination

- *Finding and sorting activities* by colour, shape, size, texture, etc., 'I Spy' games.
- *Tracing and colouring*, trace or colour round a particular shape in a picture.
- *Jigsaw puzzles*, inset puzzles, posting games, construction toys, What's in a Square? mosaics, parquetry, complex cube patterns.
- *Bead and peg patterns*, lacing cards, threading activities.
- *Art and craft activities*, collage, mosaics, paint by numbers, Spiro graph.

- *Finding the same letter*, shape, object/circling designated letter, word, ending (-ed, -ing) on page, in story; use a newspaper and circle/highlight all the 't's or other designated letter, a designated word such as 'and', the first word in every sentence, the last word in every sentence, all the double letters in various words.
- *Activity books*—find all the 'hidden' objects, find all the . . . , find the odd one out, find the difference/word searches, word hunts, mazes, 'Where's Wally?'
- *Explore and talk* about the content of pictures, photographs.
- *Exploratory/imaginative play*, e.g. dressing-up, playing with dolls' house, farm, home corner, sand and water play.
- *Snakes and ladders*, Monopoly®, Ludo, computer games.

▷ References

Chu, S. (1999) *Assessment and Treatment of Children with Developmental Perceptual Dysfunction* (course handbook, self-published). London. West London Health Care Trust.

Levine, K.J. (1991) *Fine Motor Dysfunction: Therapeutic Strategies in the Classroom*. Tucson, AZ, Therapy Skill Builders.

▷ Further reading

See A 13 Visual perception resources page 403.
See introduction to section page 73.

▷ Further resources

Refer to Foundation Skills

- FS 4A, 4B, 4C, 4E, 4F within this section page 77–97
- FS 1 Introduction to sensory processing page 5
- FS 1E Visual processing page 27
- FS 2C Spatial and body awareness page 43
- FS 3A Visual motor integration page 59
- FS 3B Vision and ocular motor control page 63
- FS 6 Organisation page 111

Refer to Occupational Therapy Approaches

Refer to Appendix

Refer to Equipment Resources page 407.

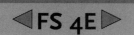

Visual closure

▷ What is it?

Visual closure is the ability to see 'in the mind's eye' the whole of an object when part of it is hidden. It involves manipulating and transposing visual information. It allows accurate judgements to be made from familiar, but partial information. 'Early in development the child focuses on the whole, whereas later in development he focuses on the parts, and in particular, on the parts as they make up a whole. Five-year-olds centre on one aspect of the stimulus figure, whereas generally whole-part relationships are mature in nine-year-olds (75%)' (Chu, 1999). Visual closure is often the last visual perceptual skill to develop, as it is closely inter-linked with cognitive ability and development of concepts.

▷ Why is it important?

It is a foundation skill for fluency and speed in reading and spelling. Efficient reading relies on visual closure because with each fixation of the eye only some of the letters of a word or phrase are actually perceived. As a child becomes more competent in reading, her eye fixations become fewer and she must 'fill in' more material and encompass a wider area of print.

▷ What are the implications?

Children with visual closure problems may experience difficulty with:

- Identifying a visual object (e.g. shoe) when only part of it is visible, so it may be hard for them to find what they are looking for
- Initiating and organising unfamiliar tasks
- Putting parts together to form a whole for construction tasks, jigsaws, peg and mosaic patterns, activity books—complete the picture, dot- to-dot, what is missing?
- Visualising the completed task, given the component parts, e.g. following a recipe, assembling a construction from a picture, completing a jigsaw by searching for matching parts
- Reading and spelling fluently—may be slow as cannot recognise words or groups of words without studying every individual letter

- Acquiring sound blends and spelling patterns, putting letters together to make a word although they may be able to read the individual letters
- Precision of letter/shape formation—letters/shapes often not fully closed or spaced accurately
- Mathematical calculations, problem solving and multiplication tables, mental maths
- Work involving tessellation, symmetry and rotation of object
- Whole day planning and working within time constraints, categorising time and space, identifying whether a worksheet has been completed, or a task finished

▷ **Teaching strategies**

- Reinforce rules of letter formation to encourage accuracy.
- Emphasise the need to work from left hand margin.
- Set time limits for some tasks and record result so the child can improve.
- Increase number of pieces in puzzle as skills improve.
- Verbalise about shape/letter/number to be drawn, using directions, size and other descriptions to help create a visual picture.
- Use tactile letters to trace over and reinforce shape.

▷ **Activities to improve visual closure**

- *Dot-to-dot*, paint by numbers—ask child to identify picture as soon as the image is apparent.
- *Colouring*, stencils, finishing incomplete pictures (woman with hand missing), gradually reducing prompt.
- *Model making*—building 3D models from cubes, Lego®, K'nex, Octons, etc., copying from a picture, finishing incomplete jigsaws, mix the pieces of two puzzles together and get child to complete.
- *Matching* complete and incomplete shapes, making patterns with matchsticks, cutting out pictures and sticking them together again, making collages.
- *Drawing/writing* in variety of media—sand, cornflour, shaving foam, paint, chalk on blackboards, play dough, pipe cleaners, felt tip pens—emphasising shape, orientation; closure—make a shape/letter/number and then make another with one part missing and ask child to complete.
- *Manipulating and rotating* shapes/objects when discussing their properties—use positional referents, drawing a picture/shape/object then rotating it through 90 °—drawing it upside down, highlighting lower half.

- *Transferring a design* shape from one grid to another, symmetry and tessellations—completing the other half of a picture, design.
- *Worksheets*—filling in letters to complete words or fill in words to complete sentences.
- *Covering up objects* and slowly revealing them a bit at a time. Start with familiar objects and ask child to guess before the object is totally revealed.
- *Computer*, board and pencil and paper games, e.g. Scrabble®, hangman, noughts and crosses, boxes, Tangrams.

▷ References

Chu, S. (1999) *Assessment and Treatment of Children with Developmental Perceptual Dysfunction* (course handbook, self-published). London, West London Health Care Trust.

Levine, K.J. (1991) *Fine Motor Dysfunction: Therapeutic Strategies in the Classroom.* Tucson, AZ, Therapy Skill Builders.

▷ Further reading

See A 13 Visual perception resources page 403.
See introduction to section page 73.

▷ Further resources

Refer to Foundation Skills

- FS 4A, 4B, 4C, 4D, 4F within this section page 73–99
- FS 1 Introduction to sensory processing page 5
- FS 1D Auditory processing page 23
- FS 1E Visual processing page 27
- FS 2A Motor planning page 35
- FS 2C Spatial and body awareness page 43
- FS 3A Visual motor integration page 59
- FS 3B Vision and ocular motor control page 63

Refer to Occupational Therapy Approaches

- OTA 1 Building firm foundations for spatial and body awareness page 249
- OTA 6 Building firm foundations for dressing skills page 315
- OTA 9 Self-organisation approaches page 327
- OTA 10 Consolidating foundation skills through group activities page 333

Refer to Appendix

- A 4 Handwriting self-evaluation checklist page 373
- A 5 Handwriting programmes and fine motor resources page 375
- A 10 Teacher's checklist for visual signs page 395

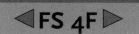
Visual memory

▷ What is it?

Visual/sequential memory is the ability to remember what is seen and to recall visual images of objects, shapes, symbols and movements both individually and in sequence. It is the term used to describe how memory activity processes visual information from short-term recall to long-term store. Efficient visual memory requires organised storing of information to enable rapid recall. It is dependent upon concentration and attention, good motivation, keen observation and speed.

▷ Why is it important?

It is a foundation skill for all learning, closely related to other forms of memory (hearing, touch and movement) and is essential for accuracy in copying tasks. The role of language in labelling and fixing a visual experience in the memory, together with the development of visual imagery and visualisation is also fundamental to achieving this skill.

The ordering of letters in words, and words in sentences, is part of the visual decoding process in reading and the encoding process in spelling. Children who are experiencing difficulties with reading and spelling may have problems with visual sequential memory.

▷ What are the implications?

Children with visual/sequential memory problems may experience difficulty with:

- Construction toys when following a model or picture instruction, form boards, puzzles
- Daily activities, e.g. dressing, organisation of self for tasks, initiating and settling down for activity, recognising people, places and equipment
- Staying on task and finding it hard to complete work
- Learning and visualising writing patterns and letter formation
- Remembering visual sequences, pattern work and recalling information apparently learnt previously

- Sequencing pictures to tell a story, sequencing the alphabet from sight, reading and spelling
- Orientation of letters and numbers, copying information from board or book and making notes
- Maths—recalling basic shapes, number sequences, methods for problem solving and learning multiplication tables
- Remembering the sequence from a practical demonstration—maths, science, art, design technology
- Recalling and reproducing sequences of movements in PE, games, dance, often appearing one step behind peers

▷ Teaching strategies

- Use visual approaches to learning, e.g. look, cover, spell, check.
- Ensure visual memory is being practised and not auditory memory, when working individually with the child.
- Use memory joggers—symbols or simple drawings.
- Encourage the child to give herself verbal cues when attempting task, e.g. big blue peg, little round bead.
- Allow the child to use physical prompt (trace with finger or touch item) when appropriate.
- Use mind mapping and spidergram to aid memory.
- Use mnemonics for learning sequences/spellings

▷ Activities to improve visual/sequential memory

- *Practise dressing* in the correct sequence, provide visual prompts.
- *Provide visual strategy/timetable* and overview of the day, encourage child to draw pictures or mind map of day's events, ask parents to talk to child about day's events. Use home school diary to provide overview.
- *Games to encourage recall*—'Simon Says', Kim's game (with objects, letters shapes or numbers) 'I went shopping and I bought . . .', using objects, I Spy. Ask child to look out of the window and recall three things they can see. Use memory pairs, flash card Bingo, Stare game, auditory approaches for multiplication tables, e.g. rap CD.
- *Remove an object* from a room or article of clothing and ask child 'what is missing?' show a 'busy' picture and ask child to list details, ask child to describe what the person next to him is wearing.
- *Create an obstacle course* and ask child to recall/repeat layout; practise movement sequences in 'chunks'.
- *Copying patterns* with beads, bricks, pegs, Lego®, etc., change sequence and get child to replace correctly, draw and copy a repeated sequence of shapes and sequence stories.

- *Show abstract shapes* briefly and ask child to repeat pattern once it has been covered.
- *Activity books*—word searches/find the differences, highlight the word or object to be found
- *Underlining letter*/number combinations in given text.
- *Timed exercises* copying from board to paper.

▷ References

Chu, S. (1999) *Assessment and Treatment of Children with Developmental Perceptual Dysfunction* (course handbook, self-published). London, West London Health Care Trust.

Levine, K.J. (1991) *Fine Motor Dysfunction: Therapeutic Strategies in the Classroom.* Tucson, AZ, Therapy Skill Builders.

▷ Further reading

See A 13 Visual perception resources page 403.
See introduction to section page 73.

▷ Further resources

Refer to Foundation Skills

- FS 4A, 4B, 4C, 4D, 4E within this section page 77–93
- FS 1D Auditory processing page 23
- FS 1E Visual processing page 27
- FS 2A Motor planning page 35
- FS 3B Vision and ocular motor control page 63

Refer to Occupational Therapy Approaches

- OTA 2 Building firm foundations for left/right awareness page 253
- OTA 6 Building firm foundations for dressing skills page 315
- OTA 9 Self-organisation approaches page 327
- OTA 10 Consolidating foundation skills through group activities page 333

Refer to Appendix

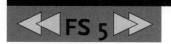

Introduction to language

Whilst this book predominantly focuses on developing the motor, perceptual and cognitive skills required for learning, the important role of language development in enabling a child to access the curriculum cannot be overlooked. In many children a combination of factors will contribute to the difficulties they are experiencing and therefore an overview of the main areas of language development have been included to enable a more holistic approach when supporting a child in school. If a child's difficulties are primarily speech and language-based specific advice should be sought from a speech and language therapist.

The areas covered in this section are:

- Attention and listening
- Receptive language
- Expressive language
- Auditory memory

 Further reading and resources

Consult with your local speech and language therapist.

Beales, G. (1995) *Oral Language Upper—Promoting Confidence in Speaking and Listening*. Coventry, Primary Education.

Beales, G. (1996) *Oral Language Lower—Promoting Confidence in Speaking and Listening*. Coventry, Primary Education.

Beales, G. (1996) *Oral Language Middle—Promoting Confidence in Speaking and Listening*. Coventry, Primary Education.

Edwards, J. (1998) *Look! Listen! Think!* Coventry, Primary Education.

Evamy, B. (2003) *Auditory and Visual Discrimination Exercises—a Teacher's Aid*. Bridlington, Yorkshire, BJE Publications; email BarbaraEvamy@aol.com; available from Dyslexia Association.

Frost, L. & Bondy, A. (2002) *PECS the Picture Exchange Communication System*. Brighton, Pyramid Educational Consultants; email pyramid@pecs.co.uk; www.pecs.co.uk

Mosely, J. (2005) *Circle Time for Young Children*. London, Routledge.

Pie Corbett (2006) *Speak Out! Great Ideas for Speaking and Listening. Ages 7–9*. London, A & C Black Publishers.

Pie Corbett (2006) *Speak Out! Great Ideas for Speaking and Listening. Ages 9–11*. London, A & C Black Publishers.

Warren, C. (2004) *Speaking and Listening Games: New Bright Ideas; Ages 5–11*. London, Scholastic.

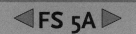
Attention and listening

▷ What is it?

Attention and listening is the ability to focus on sound that carries meaning.

▷ Why is it important?

Attention and listening skills are important prerequisites for speech and language development. Attention and listening skills are needed in all situations where the child must listen to and act in response to spoken words. Children who experience difficulties with listening do not necessarily have a hearing impairment.

▷ What are the implications?

Children who have difficulties with attention and listening are likely to:

- Fidget and experience difficulty sitting still
- Appear 'naughty' because they have not listened to instructions
- Experience difficulty 'listening' and 'doing' at the same time
- Be easily distracted and distract others
- Appear to daydream
- Have difficulty maintaining eye-contact

▷ Teaching strategies

- Say the child's name to gain her attention before speaking to her.
- Ensure the child has stopped what she is doing to listen.
- Use visual prompts to remind the child to listen.
- Use visual material to support spoken language.
- Give instructions and information in short 'chunks' in the sequence they are to be carried out.

- Help the child to succeed with attention and listening by keeping tasks short and rewarding the child for completed tasks.
- Try to seat the child close to the teacher and remove possible distractions.
- Introduce class guidelines or rules for good listening and incorporate these into reward schemes.

▷ Activities to improve attention and listening

- *Ready, Steady, Go* games, especially activities in PE.
- *Music activities*, e.g. copying rhythm, guessing which instrument is being played.
- *Musical games*—musical chairs/musical statues/musical bumps.
- *Listening for a target word* in a story, and responding with agreed action, e.g. holding up corresponding object.
- *Locating sound activities*—hide an object, e.g. alarm clock or timer, in the room and ask child to listen and find it.
- *Sound lotto*, available from LDA, Duke Street, Wisbech, Cambridgeshire, PE13 2AE; Website www.LDAlearning.com
- *Curriculum listening activities*, e.g. *Letters and Sounds: Principles and Practice of High Quality Phonics* (2007) DfES.
- *Developing Baseline Communication Skills*, Catherine Delamain and Jill Spring (2003) Brackley, Speech Mark Publishing Ltd.

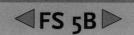

Receptive language

▷ **What is it?**

Receptive language is the ability to understand the content and structure of spoken language.

▷ **Why is it important?**

Children need to develop receptive language skills in order to access the curriculum successfully and to develop relationships with adults and peers. Children need to:

- Understand a range of vocabulary relevant to a variety of situations
- Be able to process information presented in the form of sentences in order to understand instructions and explanations
- Be able to relate new information learnt, to previously gained information in order to learn
- Understand how the meaning of an utterance can change according to the context and the way it is said

▷ **What are the implications?**

Children with receptive language difficulties may:

- Only carry out part of an instruction
- Copy the actions of children around them
- Be dominant in conversation so that they are not faced with a question or topic change which they do not understand
- Show avoidance or challenging behaviours when language levels become more complex
- Appear 'naughty' because they have not understood instructions
- 'Switch off' when information is presented verbally
- Carry out instructions in the wrong sequence because they have not understood concepts such as 'before', 'after', 'if' and 'when'
- Respond to questions with unusual answers
- Echo words used in questions and instructions without showing understanding

▷ **Teaching strategies**

- Use visual material to support spoken language.
- Give instructions and information in short 'chunks' in the sequence they are to be carried out.
- Give the child time to process spoken information.
- Use unambiguous language.
- Pre-teach important curriculum vocabulary.
- Repeat instructions in one-to-one or small group situation.

▷ **Activities to improve receptive language**

- *Derbyshire Language Scheme*—W. Knowles and M. Masidlover, Amber Valley and Erewash Area, 'Market House', Market Place, Ripley, Derbyshire DE5 3BR. www.derbyshire-language-scheme.co.uk
- *Language Steps*—Amanda Armstrong (2000) STASS Publications, 44 North Rd, Ponteland, Northumberland NE20 9UR.
- *Understanding and Using Spoken Language: Games for 7–9 year olds.* Catherine Delamain and Jill Spring (2003) Brackley, Speech Mark Publishing Ltd.

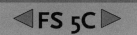

Expressive language

▷ **What is it?**

Expressive language is the ability to communicate using words and sentences.

▷ **Why is it important?**

Children need to develop expressive language skills to enable them to:

- Communicate with other people
- Express their views
- Request items to meet their needs and wants
- Reject something they do not want, like or need

Expressive language skills allow children to develop social relationships and to demonstrate their understanding of situations and curriculum material.

▷ **What are the implications?**

Children with expressive language difficulties may:

- Find it hard to explain their thoughts and ideas
- Be unable to express their needs and wants
- Make grammatical errors
- Use language with a 'telegrammatic' style or use short sentences
- Have difficulty thinking of specific words; children may describe words or use substitute words such as 'this', 'that', 'there'
- Become frustrated at their inability to communicate effectively
- Find it hard to participate in conversation and discussion
- Be unable to retell a story or talk about an event in the correct sequence
- Use fillers such as 'um', 'er' and learnt phrases
- Have difficulty with written language

▷ Teaching strategies

- Use home/school book to support child during news/circle time.
- Get teaching staff to ask targeted questions and support the child to give the answer.
- Practise using important curriculum vocabulary in sentences.
- Model correct use of language rather than correcting the child.
- Expand on the child's language by modelling how to add another word.
- Allow time for the child to formulate her response without fear of being interrupted.
- Use pictures, story boards, spider diagrams and word webs to generate ideas for creative writing and practical activities.
- Give choices if the child is experiencing difficulty thinking of a word.

▷ Activities to improve expressive language

- *Cambridge Language Activity File*—Sadie Bigland and Jane Speake (2000) STASS Publications, 44 North Rd, Ponteland, Northumberland NE20 9UR.
- *Derbyshire Language Scheme*—W. Knowles and M. Masidlover, Amber Valley and Erewash Area, 'Market House', Market Place, Ripley, Derbyshire DE5 3BR. www.derbyshire-language-scheme.co.uk
- *Language Steps*—Amanda Armstrong (2000) STASS Publications, 44 North Rd, Ponteland, Northumberland NE20 9UR.
- *Speaking, Listening and Understanding—Games for Young Children (5–7 year olds)* Catherine Delamain and Jill Spring (2004) Brackley, Speech Mark Publishing Ltd.
- *Understanding and Using Spoken Language: Games for 7–9 year olds.* Catherine Delamain and Jill Spring (2003) Brackley, Speech Mark Publishing Ltd.
- *Speaking and Listening Through Narrative: a Pack of Activities and Ideas.* Becky Shanks and Helen Rippon (2000) Black Sheep Press, Keighley, W. Yorks. www.blacksheep-epress.com

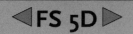

Auditory memory

▷ What is it?

Auditory memory is the ability to remember information received in the form of sound.

▷ Why is it important?

Auditory memory is a vital skill in being able to remember lists of items, instructions and information when it is presented verbally without visual or kinaesthetic information. Children with auditory memory deficits may make errors that can lead to them storing inaccurate information in the long-term memory that will be accessed in the future.

▷ What are the implications?

Children with auditory memory difficulties may:

- Be unable to remember a list of instructions given verbally
- Experience difficulty retaining new vocabulary
- Find it hard to rote learn information including songs and rhymes
- Find it hard to remember telephone numbers
- Be unable to retell a story or paraphrase information given verbally
- Experience difficulty understanding long sentences; children may forget information given at the beginning of the sentence, which may be referred to again at the end of the sentence
- Have difficulty using skills of prediction in stories due to poor recall of outcomes in previously encountered stories

▷ Teaching strategies

- Use visual material to support information presented verbally.
- Teach the child strategies, such as using fingers to represent items in a list.

- Give instructions and information in short 'chunks' in the sequence they are to be carried out.
- Repeat spoken instructions and ask the child to repeat what he has been asked to do.
- Give the child a password to remember to allow them to access an activity. As the child's skills improve increase the number of instructions.

▷ **Activities to improve auditory memory**

- *'I went to market* and I bought . . .' game.
- *Taking messages* around school.
- *Remembering a sequence* of instructions in PE, music, dance.
- *Remembering telephone number.*
- *Rote learning songs* and rhymes.
- *Give children a password* to allow access to an activity. Increase the amount of time the word must be remembered.

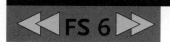
Organisation

 What is it?

Essential components of organisation are planning, body awareness and timing. Every new task involves motor planning when the brain has to conceive, organise and carry out a sequence of unfamiliar actions.

 Why are they important?

Organisational skills enable the child to function effectively in daily and learning activities.

 What are the implications?

Children with organisational problems may have difficulties with:

- Being aware of their 'personal space' when joining in gross motor activities
- Manoeuvring themselves around the classroom, participating as member of a team and being in confined spaces
- Working alongside other children or participating in a group activity
- Changing for PE and maintaining a tidy appearance, e.g. tucking in clothes after using toilet
- Getting ready for a lesson and starting work promptly, gathering belongings at the end of the day, putting letters, books, etc., into book bag
- Having the right equipment for the task, organising work area, often encroaching on others' workspace
- Following visual and/or auditory instructions for given task, particularly if a sequence of instructions are given
- Planning and organising school work
- Recording and completing homework
- Performing practical tasks
- Using ICT
- Time keeping, as forgetful and often in the wrong place at the wrong time
- Poor self-esteem and vulnerability to teasing

Activities to improve organisation skills

OTA 1 Building firm foundations for spatial and body awareness page 249.
OTA 6 Building firm foundations for dressing skills page 315.
OTA 9 Self-organisation approaches page 327.

References

Benson, B., Cuff, C. & Elkin, P. (1984) *Cambridge Primary Language Level 1 Study Skills.* Cambridge, Cambridge University Press.

Benson, B., Cuff, C. & Elkin, P. (1984) *Cambridge Primary Language Level 2 Study Skills.* Cambridge, Cambridge University Press.

Benson. B., Cuff, C. & Elkin, P. (1984) *Cambridge Primary Language Level 3 Study Skills.* Cambridge, Cambridge University Press.

Benson, B., Cuff, C. & Elkin, P. (1984) *Cambridge Primary Language Level 4 Study Skills.* Cambridge, Cambridge University Press.

Davis, L., Soirotowitz, S. & Parker, H. (1996) *Study Strategies Made Easy, a Practical Plan for School Success.* Plantation, Florida, Speciality Press Inc.

Kirby, A., Peters, L. & Baudinette, K. (2007) *Organisational Skills at Home* (Dyscovery series). Cardiff, Dyscovery Press.

Naglleri, J. & Pickering, E. (2003) *Helping Children Learn: Intervention Handouts for use in School and at Home.* Baltimore, MD, Brookes Publishing Co.

Stein, S. & Chowdhury, U. (2006) *Disorganised Children—a Guide for Parents and Professionals.* London, Jessica Kingsley Publishers.

Further resources

Refer to Foundation Skills

- FS 2A Motor planning page 35
- FS 2C Spatial and body awareness page 39

Refer to Appendix

- A 11 Thinking skills page 397

Social and emotional aspects

 What is it?

'Social and emotional aspects of learning' is one of many terms used within the school setting to describe the concept of emotional health and well-being. Other frequently used terms include social and emotional competence, emotional literacy, emotional intelligence, and social, emotional and behavioural skills.

A range of social, emotional and behavioural skills are thought to constitute the foundation blocks for emotional health and well-being, including:

- Making and sustaining friendships
- Working and playing cooperatively
- Dealing with and resolving conflict fairly
- Understanding, valuing and respecting the differences between people
- Being able to solve problems alone and with others
- Being an effective and successful learner
- Managing feelings such as anxiety, frustration, anger

Why is it important?

Children's emotional health and well-being can be considered as the strength and capacity of children to grow and develop with confidence those skills necessary to participate fully in all aspects of everyday life, and to recognise their own special talents. It consists of the capacity to learn from experience and to overcome difficulty (adversity).

Social, emotional and behavioural skills are considered to underpin almost every aspect of home, school and community life and are key aspects of effective learning. It is recognised that schools have a direct influence on the emotional health of children and that this in turn impacts on acaedemic and other school achievements.

Social, emotional and behavioural skills are used to:

- Manage a range of feelings that may interfere with learning, such as frustration, sadness, disappointment, anger and anxiety

- Promote a state of mind that enable tasks to be carried out
- Manage the social and emotional components that accompany an activity

The evidence available demonstrates that by fostering children's social, emotional and behavioural skills the following are all positively affected:

- Educational and work success
- Improvements in behaviour
- Increased inclusion
- Improved learning
- Greater social cohesion
- Mental health

Weare & Gray (2003)

A primary factor in building and maintaining social, emotional and mental well-being is considered to be healthy self-esteem. Children with healthy self-esteem are more able to handle anxiety, hurt and anger in positive and constructive ways.

It is acknowledged that some children who experience delay and disorder in developing their foundation building blocks, e.g. gross motor coordination, fine motor control, may have difficulties performing school activities. Similarly, difficulties establishing social, emotional and behavioural skills may impact on the development of foundation building blocks and in turn on school performance.

Children with developmental coordination disorder, attention deficit hyperactivity disorder, autistic spectrum disorder or those with physical disabilities and sensory impairments are particularly vulnerable to associated social, emotional and behavioural problems.

⯈⯈ What are the implications?

Children whose social, emotional and behavioural development is of concern may experience difficulty with:

- Preparing and settling into task
- Maintaining concentration throughout task—appear off task, have excessive tiredness, daydreams and appear preoccupied
- Organisational skills—remembering information and equipment needed for an activity, wandering around class, becoming disruptive
- Listening skills—remembering instructions, attending to information, participating in activities previously enjoyed, opting out of activity
- Social skills—establishing friendships, maintaining relationships with peers, working effectively with others in groups
- Cooperating with adults and peers/coming into conflict with peers and/or adults
- Working independently, requiring adult attention and interaction
- Dealing with and resolving conflicts, emotional regulation, becoming tearful, having temper tantrums and outbursts

- Managing a range of feelings, becoming irritable and showing frustration
- Attending school regularly, refusing school

Children will often use their behaviour to show how they feel and to communicate their underlying emotional needs.

Activities to promote social, emotional and behavioural skills

Schools promote children's development through initiatives such as circle time, self-esteem approaches, peer support programmes, mentoring and buddy schemes, and commercially available programmes for developing social, emotional and behavioural skills, such as Social and Emotional Aspects of Learning (SEAL) (DfES, 2005).

In many cases, improvements in children's behaviour will be evident through:

- *Participation in initiatives* aimed at developing self-esteem and emotional well-being
- *Developing a foundation building block*, e.g. body and spatial awareness, expressive language, which has been identified as impacting on the child's social, emotional health and well-being
- *Working in collaboration* with parents and family

Seeking further advice and support

If feelings and behaviour causing concern continue for months, to a point where they interfere with day-to-day living, extra support may be needed. Parents, carers and school staff may need to seek advice and support from agencies such as school nurse, doctor, educational psychologist, educational welfare officer, general practitioner, primary mental health worker and social services. The Common Assessment Framework (CAF) pre-assessment checklist can assist services in deciding whether a child is in need of additional help.

A variety of services are available which provide help for children. This additional support will enable the child, family and school to find ways to help understand and deal with the feelings behind the behaviour. Concerns indicating need for further help include:

- Excessive fatigue
- Deterioration in appearance, unkempt
- Frequent wetting or soiling, inappropriate to child's age
- Social withdrawal
- School refusal
- Depression
- Eating problems

- Anxiety
- Increase in intensity and severity of aggression
- Emotionally labile
- Putting themselves in danger, risk-taking behaviours

If concerns continue and there is further impact on the child's ability to engage in day-to-day living or there is a sudden deterioration in a child's appearance, then further advice may need to be sought from specialist services such as Child and Adolescent Mental Health Services (CAMHS). Specialist CAMHS provide a range of interventions for children where there are emotional, behavioural, relationship problems and mental health concerns.

 ## References

Colby-Trott, M. (2002) *Oh Behave! Sensory Processing and Behavioural Strategies*. Tucson, AZ, Therapy Skill Builders.

Cooper, P. & Tiknaz, Y. (2007) *Nurture Groups in School and at Home— Connecting with Children with Social, Emotional and Behavioural Difficulties*. London, Jessica Kingsley.

Cummins, A., Piek, J. & Dyck, M. (2005) Motor coordination, empathy and social behaviour in school-aged children. *Developmental Medicine and Child Neurology*, **47** (7), 437–42.

Department for Children, Schools and Families (2005) *Developing Children's Social, Emotional and Behavioural Skills: Guidance* (September). Department for Children, Schools and Families. Available at www.standards.dfes.gov.uk/primary

Department for Education and Skills (2003) *Excellence and Enjoyment: a Strategy for Primary Schools*. London, Department for Education and Skills, Crown.

Department for Education and Skills (2004) *Promoting Emotional Health and Well-being: Through the National Healthy School Standard*. London, Department for Education and Skills/Department of Health.

Department for Education and Skills (2005a) *Excellence and Enjoyment: Social and Emotional Aspects of Learning: Guidance: Primary National Strategy*. London, Department for Education and Skills, Crown.

Department for Education and Skills (2005b) *Every Child Matters: Change for Children, Aims and Outcomes*. London, Department for Education and Skills. Available at www.everychildmatters.gov.uk/aims

Lougher, L. (2001) *Occupational Therapy for Child and Adolescent Mental Health*. London, Harcourt Publishers Limited.

Plummer, D. (2007) *Helping Children to Build Self-esteem*. London, Jessica Kingsley.

Rae, T. (2003) *Dealing With Some More Feelings: an Emotional Literacy Curriculum*. Bristol, Lucky Duck Publishing.

The Royal College of Psychiatrists information service has produced a series of leaflets on common mental health issues for the general public. Available at www.rcpsych.ac.uk

Weare, K. (2000) *Developing Mental, Emotional and Social Health Needs in Schools.* London, Routledge.

Weare, K. & Gray, G. (2003) *What Works in Developing Children's Emotional and Social Competence and Well-being?* DfES Research Report 456. Southampton, The Health Education Unit, Research and Graduate School of Education, University of Southampton.

Young Minds is a national charity committed to improving the mental health of all children and young people and produces range of leaflets which can be ordered or downloaded. Available at www.youngminds.org.uk

Further resources

Refer to Foundation Skills

- FS 1 Introduction to sensory processing page 5
- FS 2 Introduction to gross motor coordination page 31
- FS 3 Introduction to fine motor control page 55
- FS 4 Introduction to perception page 73
- F5 Introduction to language page 101

Refer to Occupational Therapy Approaches

- OTA 8 Sensory strategies page 323

Refer to Appendix

- A 9 Resources for developing social, emotional and behavioural skills page 389
- A 11 Thinking skills page 397
- A 14 Work system page 405

Subject Areas

 Introduction to subject areas

During the course of a day, a primary classroom teacher presents the curriculum in a variety of ways. When learning new skills, children need to build on previous achievements. Foundation skills are building blocks enabling children to move from one skill to the next. If they have deficits in any area, it will impact on classroom performance.

In this book, the foundation building blocks for learning are categorised as:

- Sensory processing
- Gross motor coordination
- Fine motor control
- Perception
- Language
- Organisational approaches
- Social and emotional aspects

The subject areas have been chosen to cover the broad range of tasks which children have to complete in primary years. Occupational therapists are skilled in functional analysis and look at the performance components of everyday skills. Using these principles the core subjects of the curriculum (literacy, numeracy and science) as well as more practical areas (art/design, PE and ICT) have been analysed by considering the general behaviours that are observed by the classroom teacher and then linked to the foundation building blocks which are most likely to be causing the difficulty.

It should be noted that if a child has generalised learning difficulties it will show on the tables as relating to many specific foundation skill areas; however, it is likely to be due to underlying immaturities rather than a specific difficulty. When considering these tables relating to a specific child it will be important to consider the child's academic abilities.

Each subject area has been presented in a table, which is cross-referenced to specific foundation skill areas. For each teacher observation, the four most likely (primary) skill areas underpinning the task have been identified by a diamond (◆); additional skills (secondary) that could also be impacting on the child's performance have been identified by an open square (□). The information on the tables naturally clusters into the foundation areas that underpin the curriculum area requirements. When the table is completed for an individual child, it is likely that the difficulties the child is showing in the classroom will crystallise into a few foundation skill areas and this will provide the basis for planning the child's individual programme. The number of symbols for each teacher observation has been limited to a maximum of eight.

The table may be used to identify an individual child's profile:

- *Read down the list of observations* to identify relevant difficulties and highlight across each row.
- *Scan the foundation blocks* vertically, highlighting columns containing ◆
- *Add up all the* ◆ *in each column* and record each score in 'Primary Totals' at the bottom of the table.
- *Repeat the procedure for the* □ and record each score in 'Secondary Totals' at the bottom of the table.
- *Look at the total scores* for ◆ and identify the foundation blocks with the three highest scores.
- Look at the total scores for □ and identify the foundation blocks with the three highest scores.
- *Refer to the relevant foundation* skills in the Foundation Skills chapter and select appropriate activities to target in the child's individual programme.
- *Use the proforma* provided to produce the child's individual programme and, if appropriate, transfer information to the Individual Education Plan (IEP)/Pupil Inclusion Plan (PIP).
- *Review the child's progress* at agreed intervals.
- *Referral to specialist services* should be considered if the child continues to show more difficulty than peers.

Teacher Observations of Child

MOTOR CO-ORDINATION		
Unable to sit down on carpet without causing a disturbance		
Inability to maintain correct sitting posture for task		
Slouches/falls off chair		
Cannot maintain a functional working position		
Constant movement/fidgety/on the go		
Trips and falls/bumps into people and things		
Flops or props against wall, apparatus or children		
Cannot stay within personal boundaries		
Unable to organise body movements		
Problems participating in team sports		
Difficulty waiting turn in line		
Low energy levels/poor stamina/gives up easily		
FINE MOTOR CONTROL		
Dropping equipment/knocking things over		
Difficulty handling equipment age appropriately, e.g. ruler, scissors		
Inaccurate cutting and sticking		
Poor mouse control		
Unable to do up buttons and fastenings		
Poor manipulation when attempting two handed tasks, e.g. construction		
CLASSROOM SKILLS		
Unable to trace accurately		
Cannot hold pencil correctly/awkward, immature grip		
Letters and numbers poorly formed		
Immature writing for age		
Slow speed for written tasks		
Smudges work		
Difficulty copying work from board or book		
Difficulty recording ideas		
Untidy work/lots of crossing or rubbing out		
Problems interpreting shape and form		
Cannot copy models (3D-3D)		
Cannot make model from a picture (2D-3D)		
Poor reading fluency		
Poor spelling		
Poor at researching topic information		
Difficulty finding way around computer		
Unable to research information using ICT		
Incomplete homework		
	MAIN TOTALS	
	SECONDARY TOTALS	

122

	FS 1 Sensory Processing					FS 2 Gross Motor					FA 3 Fine Motor			FS 4 Visual Perception						FS 5 Language					
Foundation Blocks	Vestibular processing	Tactile/kinaesthesia	Proprioception	Auditory processing	Visual processing	Motor planning	Postural stability and balance	Spatial and body awareness	Bilateral integration	Midline crossing/laterality	Visual motor integration	Vision and ocular motor	Manual dexterity	Discrimination	Spatial relationships	Form constancy	Figure ground	Closure	Memory/sequential memory	Attention and listening	Receptive language	Expressive language	Auditory memory	Organisation	Social and emotional aspects
	FS 1A	FS 1B	FS 1C	FS 1D	FS 1E	FS 2A	FS 2B	FS 2C	FS 2D	FS 2E	FS 3A	FS 3B	FS 3C	FS 4A	FS 4B	FS 4C	FS 4D	FS 4E	FS 4F	FS 5A	FS 5B	FS 5C	FS 5D	FS 6	FS 7
	□	□	◆			◆	◆	◆												□					□
	□	□	◆			◆	◆	◆	□	□															
	□	□	◆				◆	◆		□										◆					□
	□	□	◆			□	◆	◆	□	◆															
	◆	◆	◆				□	◆				□								□					□
	◆	□	□		□	◆	◆	◆				□													
	◆	□	◆				◆	◆												□					
	□	◆	◆			□	◆	◆			□														◆
		◆	□			◆	□	◆	□		◆	□													
	□	□				◆		◆	□			◆								□					◆
	□	◆	□			◆	◆	◆												□					□
	◆	□				□	◆	◆					□							□					◆
		□	◆			◆	◆	◆	□		□	□													
		□				◆		◆	□	◆	□		◆							□	□				
						□		◆	□	◆	□	◆	◆	◆		□									
		□				◆	□			◆	□	◆	◆	◆		□									
	◆	□				◆			◆		◆		□		□	□									
	□	◆				◆		□	◆	□	□		◆												
		◆				◆			□	◆	□		□	□		◆									
		◆		◆		◆	□			□		◆		□				□							
		◆		□			◆		□	◆				□				◆	□						
		□	◆		◆	◆		□	◆	◆															
		□		◆					□	◆		◆	□	◆		◆	□	◆	□					◆	
				◆				□	◆	□	◆			□	◆			□	◆	◆	□				
			◆			◆		□	◆	□	□		◆	◆				□			□				□
		◆				◆			◆			□	◆		□		◆				□				□
			□				◆			◆		□	□	◆	□						□				
				◆			□		□		◆			◆	◆	□		□			□				□
						□		□		◆			□	◆	◆	◆	◆			□			◆		□
			◆					◆			◆					◆	□		◆			□		□	□
			◆	□				◆		□			□			◆		◆		□					□
			◆	□				◆		□			□			◆		□		◆		□			
			□			◆			◆		□					□				◆	◆				□
◆																									
□																									

Teacher Observations
of Child

GETTING READY TO WORK		
Takes many trips to collect necessary equipment		
Difficulty planning and organising approach to task		
Poor organisation of work on page/untidy presentation		
Unable to start task independently		
Appears disorganised when attempting task		
Easily distracted/frequently off task		
Slow, rarely completes work		
Careless and slapdash approach		
Takes a long time changing for PE		
LISTENING		
Unable to listen/understand verbal instructions		
Cannot follow a sequence of verbal instructions		
Takes a long time responding to instructions and completing task		
Unable to listen to others		
Finds turn taking and listening to others hard		
Does not participate in group discussions		
Starts task before instructions completed		
Finds noisy environments distressing		
BEHAVIOUR		
Unaware of safety issues		
Impulsive/rushes all tasks and activities		
Distractable/unable to attend		
Appears in a world of their own		
Difficulty sharing equipment/taking turns		
Socially isolated/preference for working alone		
Lacks confidence/overly confident in social situations		
Silly behaviour/acts as class 'clown'		
Gives up easily in task/uses negative self talk		
Temper tantrums/frustrated		
Difficulty understanding boundaries/following rules		
Emotionally reactive – cries/gets upset quickly/hits out		
	MAIN TOTALS	
	SECONDARY TOTALS	

Legend for cell markers: ◆ = filled diamond, □ = open square.

Foundation Blocks	FS 1A Vestibular processing	FS 1B Tactile/kinaesthesia	FS 1C Proprioception	FS 1D Auditory processing	FS 1E Visual processing	FS 2A Motor planning	FS 2B Postural stability and balance	FS 2C Spatial and body awareness	FS 2D Bilateral integration	FS 2E Midline crossing/laterality	FS 3A Visual motor integration	FS 3B Vision and ocular motor	FS 3C Manual dexterity	FS 4A Discrimination	FS 4B Spatial relationships	FS 4C Form constancy	FS 4D Figure ground	FS 4E Closure	FS 4F Memory/sequential memory	FS 5A Attention and listening	FS 5B Receptive language	FS 5C Expressive language	FS 5D Auditory memory	FS 6 Organisation	FS 7 Social and emotional aspects
				□	□	◆	◆													□	□		◆	◆	
				□	□	◆							◆				□			□	◆			◆	
						□		□			◆	◆	□	◆		□								◆	
				□	□	◆													◆	◆	◆	□	◆		□
				◆	□	◆										□		□		◆	◆				□
	□	□	◆	□	◆															◆	◆				□
			□	◆	◆	◆	□		□											◆					□
			□	□	□	◆					◆		□							◆					◆
		□				◆	□	◆	◆		□		◆							□					◆
				◆				□												◆	◆		□		◆
				◆			□													◆	◆		◆	□	
				□			◆		□											□	◆		□		◆
				◆				□												◆	◆		□		◆
				◆																◆	◆	□	□		◆
			□	□		◆														◆	◆	◆	□		◆
		◆	◆		◆							□								◆	◆		◆		◆
					◆															◆	◆		◆		□
			□	□	◆	◆		□												□	◆				◆
	□		◆		◆					□			□							◆	□				◆
			□	◆	◆										□	□				◆	◆				□
	□	□	□	□																◆	◆		◆		◆
			◆	◆	◆																				◆
	□					◆		□												◆					◆
	□			□	□	◆														◆	◆				◆
						◆	◆	◆											◆	□	□			◆
						◆	□	□		□	□									◆	◆				◆
						◆	□	□		□	□									◆	◆				◆
						◆		□												◆					◆
	◆		□			◆														◆	□				◆
◆																									
□																									

Teacher Observations
of Child

WRITING		
Does not hold pencil in same hand consistently		
Cannot hold pencil correctly – immature/awkward grasp		
Poor letter formation		
Inconsistent slant		
Variable sizing of letters		
Poor or no spacing		
Poor placement of letters on line		
Reversal/inversion of letters		
Writing lacks fluency/spidery writing		
Reduced quantity of work incomplete/unfinished		
Incomplete homework		
Slow speed for written tasks		
Slouches/falls off chair		
Fidgets on chair/cannot sit still		
Unable to trace accurately		
Untidy work/lots of crossing out/rubbing out		
Smudges work		
Heavily reliant on visual prompt		
Difficulty copying from book/board		
Unable to sequence events and recount in relevant detail		
Difficulty using word banks and dictionaries		
Difficulty developing cursive script when printing established		
Inability to choose appropriate handwriting for task		
Poor spelling		
Difficulty recognising usual patterns in words		
Problems drafting work		
Problems planning work		
Unable to start creative writing task		
Unable to recall and present relevant points		
Inconsistent ability to work left to right		
Poor organisation of work on page		
Unable to start task independently		
Incorrect sentence structure		
Ideas scrambled in haste to put thoughts down on paper		
Unable to use a clear structure to start writing		
Difficulty organising thoughts to put down on paper		
		MAIN TOTALS
		SECONDARY TOTALS

Building Blocks for Learning. © 2008 John Wiley & Sons Ltd.

Foundation Blocks	FS 1 Sensory Processing					FS 2 Gross Motor					FA 3 Fine Motor			FS 4 Visual Perception						FS 5 Language					
	Vestibular processing	Tactile/kinaesthesia	Proprioception	Auditory processing	Visual processing	Motor planning	Postural stability and balance	Spatial and body awareness	Bilateral integration	Midline crossing/laterality	Visual motor integration	Vision and ocular motor	Manual dexterity	Discrimination	Spatial relationships	Form constancy	Figure ground	Closure	Memory/sequential memory	Attention and listening	Receptive language	Expressive language	Auditory memory	Organisation	Social and emotional aspects
	FS 1A	FS 1B	FS 1C	FS 1D	FS 1E	FS 2A	FS 2B	FS 2C	FS 2D	FS 2E	FS 3A	FS 3B	FS 3C	FS 4A	FS 4B	FS 4C	FS 4D	FS 4E	FS 4F	FS 5A	FS 5B	FS 5C	FS 5D	FS 6	FS 7
	□								◆	◆	◆	□	◆												
		◆	◆			◆	□						◆												
		◆						◆		□	◆			□		□		□	◆						
		□									◆		□	◆	□	◆									
		□	◆								◆	□		□	◆	◆			□						
		□				◆			□			◆				◆		□	◆						
		◆	□			□					◆	◆			◆	□	□								
		□								◆	◆	◆		◆	◆	□		□							
		◆	□					◆			◆	□	◆		□			□							
				□		◆	◆				◆				□					◆		□			□
				□		◆					◆			□						◆	◆				□
		◆						□			◆	□					◆	□				□		◆	
	□	□	◆			◆	◆		□											◆	□				
	□	□	◆			◆	◆					□								◆	□				
	◆					◆			□	◆	□		□	□		◆									
		◆				◆				◆		□		◆		□	□							□	
		□	◆			◆	◆	□		◆	□	◆													
		◆				◆				□								◆	□	◆		□		□	
	□				◆				□	◆				◆	□	◆		◆	□						
				□		□											◆	◆		◆	□	◆	◆	◆	
				□						◆				□	□	◆		◆	□		□			□	
		◆	□			□			◆	□	◆		◆					□							
						◆				□		◆	◆	◆	◆				□				□	□	
				□						□		□		□	◆	◆			◆	□	◆	◆			
										□	◆			◆	□	◆			◆						
						◆			□									◆		◆	◆	◆	□		□
						◆									◆	□		◆		◆	◆	◆	□		
				□	□	◆														□	◆	◆			◆
				□										◆	□					□	◆	◆	◆	◆	
						□		◆	◆	◆	◆	□	□												
						□		□		◆	◆		◆		□				◆						◆
				□	□	◆													◆	□		□		□	
						□								◆	□	◆	◆	□	◆	◆	□		◆	
						◆							◆	□		□	◆	◆			□			
						◆								□	◆	□	◆	◆						
						◆									□	◆	□	□					□	
◆																								
□																								

Teacher Observations of Child

SPEAKING AND LISTENING	
Unable to follow instructions in the correct order	
Seldom offers correct answer to questions	
Unable to get the gist of an account	
Unable to identify sound patterns in language	
Unable to recall relevant points	
Poor understanding of the spoken word	
Difficulty participating in drama sessions	
Unable to understand another person's viewpoint	
Switches off	
Starts task before instructions completed	
Appears disorganised when attempting task	
Easily distracted/frequently off task	
Inattentive/in a 'world of their own'	
Unable to ask relevant questions to clarify understanding	
Jumbled speech patterns/muddled thoughts	
Poor clarity of speech	
Limited vocabulary/poor word finding	
Reluctant to speak in front of class	
Off topic when speaking	
Unable to use speech appropriately in different contexts	
READING	
Poor phonic recognition	
Unable to match sound to letter	
Poor reading fluency	
Reluctance to read aloud	
Unable to recognise words with common spelling patterns	
Unable to identify patterns of rhythm/rhyme/sounds	
Dependent on physical prompt for following text	
Lack of fluency when scanning text	
Slow when reading from board/book	
Misses words/substitutes words when reading	
Loses place on page/board/computer screen	
Difficulty recognising letters/words in different fonts	
Difficulty searching alphabetically, e.g. index, dictionary	
Difficulty understanding text	
Discrepancy between reading ability and reading comprehension age	
Difficulty extracting information from text	
Difficulty responding imaginatively to what is read	
Poor at researching information	

MAIN TOTALS

SECONDARY TOTALS

FS 1 Sensory Processing · FS 2 Gross Motor · FA 3 Fine Motor · FS 4 Visual Perception · FS 5 Language

Foundation Blocks	FS 1A Vestibular processing	FS 1B Tactile/kinaesthesia	FS 1C Proprioception	FS 1D Auditory processing	FS 1E Visual processing	FS 2A Motor planning	FS 2B Postural stability and balance	FS 2C Spatial and body awareness	FS 2D Bilateral integration	FS 2E Midline crossing/laterality	FS 3A Visual motor integration	FS 3B Vision and ocular motor	FS 3C Manual dexterity	FS 4A Discrimination	FS 4B Spatial relationships	FS 4C Form constancy	FS 4D Figure ground	FS 4E Closure	FS 4F	FS 5A Memory/sequential memory	FS 5B Attention and listening	FS 5C Receptive language	FS 5D Expressive language	FS 6 Organisation	FS 7 Social and emotional aspects
				◆		☐														◆	◆		◆	☐	☐
				◆																◆	◆	◆		☐	
				◆																◆	◆		◆		
				◆																◆	◆		◆		
				☐																◆	◆	◆	◆		
				◆																☐			☐		◆
				☐	☐	☐		◆												◆	◆	◆			☐
				☐																◆	◆		◆		◆
	☐	☐	◆	◆	☐															◆	◆				☐
				◆			☐													◆	◆	☐	◆		
				◆	☐	◆		☐									☐			◆	◆				☐
			◆	☐	◆		☐		☐											◆	◆				☐
		☐		☐	☐															◆	◆	☐	◆		
	☐			☐	☐																◆		◆		◆
						◆														☐	◆	◆	◆	☐	◆
						☐														☐	◆	◆			◆
				☐																	◆	◆	◆		◆
	☐																				◆	◆	◆		◆
				☐	☐	☐														◆	◆	◆	☐		◆
				◆																◆	☐	◆	☐		

Foundation Blocks	FS 1A	FS 1B	FS 1C	FS 1D	FS 1E	FS 2A	FS 2B	FS 2C	FS 2D	FS 2E	FS 3A	FS 3B	FS 3C	FS 4A	FS 4B	FS 4C	FS 4D	FS 4E	FS 4F	FS 5A	FS 5B	FS 5C	FS 5D	FS 6	FS 7
				☐																◆	◆		◆	◆	
											☐		☐	☐				◆		◆			◆		
					◆					☐		◆				☐	◆	◆			☐				
			☐	☐						◆					◆	◆				◆				◆
					☐						☐			◆	◆	◆			◆					
		◆		☐						☐				☐	◆			◆			◆	◆		
		☐		☐	◆					◆		☐						☐						◆
				◆		☐		☐	☐	◆				◆	◆						☐			☐
	☐			☐	☐		☐			◆				◆	◆	◆								
				☐						◆				◆	◆			◆		☐				☐
				◆				☐	◆	◆		◆		◆		☐					☐			
				☐						◆			◆	☐	◆	☐	◆							
			☐	☐	☐					◆				◆	☐	◆			◆	☐				
										☐			◆	◆			◆	◆			☐		☐	
																	◆	◆			◆	☐		☐
				◆					☐	◆				◆	◆			☐						◆
				◆													◆	☐			◆			
					◆									◆	☐			◆				☐		
◆																								
☐																								

Teacher Observations of Child

NUMBER		
Poor number formation		
Reversal/inversion of numbers in comparison with peers		
Inconsistent number size affecting layout of work		
Immature number calculations compared with peers		
Poor spacing of numbers in square/on line		
Misalignment of numbers in square/on line		
Poor at mental maths		
Difficulty solving maths problems		
Unable to develop rapid recall of number facts		
Unable to grasp mathematical rules e.g. +, −, ×, ÷		
Problems when counting		
Lack of number recognition		
Inability to learn or retain multiplication tables		
Unable to create and describe number patterns		
Difficulty making predictions		
Inability to recognise sequences		
Unable to explain reasoning for task		
Problems with sorting/classifying/organising data or information		
Difficulty marking numeral on number line		
Problems when completing mental maths tasks		
Difficulty recognising/ordering number patterns		
		MAIN TOTALS
		SECONDARY TOTALS

Foundation Blocks	FS 1A Vestibular processing	FS 1B Tactile/kinaesthesia	FS 1C Proprioception	FS 1D Auditory processing	FS 1E Visual processing	FS 2A Motor planning	FS 2B Postural stability and balance	FS 2C Spatial and body awareness	FS 2D Bilateral integration	FS 2E Midline crossing/laterality	FS 3A Visual motor integration	FS 3B Vision and ocular motor	FS 3C Manual dexterity	FS 4A Discrimination	FS 4B Spatial relationships	FS 4C Form constancy	FS 4D Figure ground	FS 4E Closure	FS 4F Memory/sequential memory	FS 5A Attention and listening	FS 5B Receptive language	FS 5C Expressive language	FS 5D Auditory memory	FS 6 Organisation	FS 7 Social and emotional aspects
		◆				□		◆		□	◆		□	◆					□						
									□	◆	◆	□		◆	◆	□			□						
		□	◆					□			◆	□		□	◆	◆									
								□			□				◆	□			◆		◆	□	◆		
		◆	□			□		□			◆	◆			◆		□								
						□	□				◆	◆		□	□		◆							◆	
								□									◆	□	□	◆		◆	□		
								□								◆	□	◆	□	◆	◆	□			
				◆															□	◆	◆	◆	◆	□	
															◆	□	◆	□	◆	◆	□	□			
												□		◆	□	◆			□	◆	◆	□			
		□						◆						◆		□			◆	□	◆		□		
			□		□											◆		□	◆		◆	□	◆		
															◆	◆		□		□	□	◆	◆	□	
			□		□	◆								□	◆		◆			□			◆		
						□								◆	◆	□	□		◆		◆				
						◆									□	□	□			◆	◆	◆	□		
						◆								◆	□	◆	□				◆	□	□		
						◆					◆	□	□	□	◆		◆				□				
				◆	□															□	◆	◆	◆		
										□				◆		◆		◆			□	□		□	
◆																									
□																									

Teacher Observations of Child

SHAPE, SPACE AND MEASURE		
Unable to correctly name shapes, spaces and measures		
Difficulty recognising simple spatial patterns/relationships		
Unable to describe properties of shape		
Problems estimating length, depth, height, volume		
Unable to obtain measurements, e.g. reading scales		
Problems understanding and interpreting scale		
Problems with linear and vertical scanning, e.g. reading graphs		
Difficulty drawing adjacent/overlapping/interlocking shapes		
Poor handling of maths equipment		
Inability to copy 3D-3D to make a model		
Unable to interpret 2D picture to make 3D model		
Inaccurate copying of 2D shapes		
Unable to recognise and reproduce 2D symmetry		
Poor understanding of position and movement of objects		
HANDLING DATA		
Unable to select, sort and sift relevant information presented in written form		
Unable to select, sort and sift relevant information presented verbally		
Difficulty interpreting data to solve problem		
Problems generalising mathematical principles across the curriculum		
Difficulty recognising what changes need to be made to reach correct conclusion		
Inflexible approach to working out solutions		
Unable to recognise/understand that solution to problem is unreasonable		
Poor organisation of information on page		
Inability to present information in a variety of styles		
Slow acquisition of mathmatical language/terminology		
Difficulty explaining and justifying their reasoning		
Unable to find data in table/chart/list		
Problem making sense of information recorded on table/list/chart		
Difficulty drawing and completing table/chart/list		
Poor organisation of work on page/untidy presentation		
Unable to start task independently		
Inability to present similar data using a variety of styles		
Lack of awareness/understanding of possible ways to display information		
Unable to present results using ICT		
Difficulty constructing tables/graphs/pictograms using ICT		
Inability to find relevant information on screen		
Poor mouse control		
Poor understanding of discrete terms, e.g. fair, unfair, certain		
		MAIN TOTALS
		SECONDARY TOTALS

Foundation Blocks	FS 1 Sensory Processing					FS 2 Gross Motor					FA 3 Fine Motor			FS 4 Visual Perception						FS 5 Language					
	Vestibular processing	Tactile/kinaesthesia	Proprioception	Auditory processing	Visual processing	Motor planning	Postural stability and balance	Spatial and body awareness	Bilateral integration	Midline crossing/laterality	Visual motor integration	Vision and ocular motor	Manual dexterity	Discrimination	Spatial relationships	Form constancy	Figure ground	Closure	Memory/sequential memory	Attention and listening	Receptive language	Expressive language	Auditory memory	Organisation	Social and emotional aspects
	FS 1A	FS 1B	FS 1C	FS 1D	FS 1E	FS 2A	FS 2B	FS 2C	FS 2D	FS 2E	FS 3A	FS 3B	FS 3C	FS 4A	FS 4B	FS 4C	FS 4D	FS 4E	FS 4F	FS 5A	FS 5B	FS 5C	FS 5D	FS 6	FS 7
								◆							◆		□		□	◆	◆	□			
				□				◆							◆	◆		◆	□						
								◆			◆			□		◆		□	□	□	◆			
								◆							◆	◆	◆		□					
				□					◆		◆	□			◆		□		□					
			□	□											◆	◆			◆	□				
			□	□							□	◆	◆		◆		□							
											◆	□	□	□	◆	◆	□							
						◆		◆	◆	□	◆				□		□		□					
						◆		□			□		◆		◆		□							
						□					□		□		◆	◆	◆							
											◆	□	◆		◆	◆								
						◆					◆		□	□	□	◆	□	◆						
	◆	□				□		◆				□		□						◆	◆			
				□		◆						◆		◆	□		◆		□	□				
		◆																	◆	◆	□	◆		
			□	□							◆					◆	□		◆	◆		□		
						◆												◆	◆	□	□			□
						◆											◆	□		◆	◆	□		□
			□	□		◆														◆	□		□	◆
						◆														◆	□			◆
				□		□					◆	◆		◆		□		□					◆	
						◆					◆		□		◆		□	◆		□				□
			□	□													□		◆	◆	□			
						◆					□									◆	◆			□
											□	◆		◆		◆	□							
		◆	◆											◆		◆							□	
						◆					◆	□				◆		□					□	
						◆					◆	□	□	◆		◆		□					□	
						◆					◆								◆	◆				□
				□		◆					◆			◆		◆	□		◆			□		
						◆												◆	◆	□				◆
				□								□	◆	□		◆		□	◆			◆		
						◆					◆	□	□	□		◆	◆							
				◆							□	◆				◆	◆					□		
						◆		□			◆		□	◆										
																			◆	◆	◆	◆		
◆																								
□																								

Teacher Observations
of Child

SCIENTIFIC ENQUIRY		
Problems asking appropriate questions		
Inability to think about what may happen before attempting task		
Cannot follow sequence of auditory instructions		
Reluctant to talk about own work in front of group		
Muddled explanation when explaining result of task		
Difficulty planning/organising ideas		
Takes many trips to collect necessary equipment		
Difficulty developing ideas from initial instructions		
Impaired investigative skills, e.g. evaluating, analysing		
Finds making graphs to represent outcomes challenging		
Poorly controlled or impulsive movements resulting in reduced safety		
Difficulty with practical aspects of task		
Immature drawing skills		
Difficulty recording ideas/observations		
Finds predicting outcomes challenging		
Problems thinking and doing simultaneously		
Problems estimating length, depth, height, width		
Difficulty generalising principles		
Difficulty analysing simple patterns/associations		
Over/under reaction to sensory exploration, e.g. sight, hearing, smell, touch, taste		
Fixated by one particular aspect of science		
LIFE PROCESSES AND LIVING THINGS		
Difficulty recognising body part on self, others or animals		
Reluctance to try new foods		
Difficulty making links between life processes in familiar animals and plants		
Problems recognising material/objects in different forms to enable classification		
Inability to visualise a complete lifecycle/circuit		
Unable to understand abstract concepts to complete task		
Unable to predict outcome		
	MAIN TOTALS	
	SECONDARY TOTALS	

Building Blocks for Learning. © 2008 John Wiley & Sons Ltd.

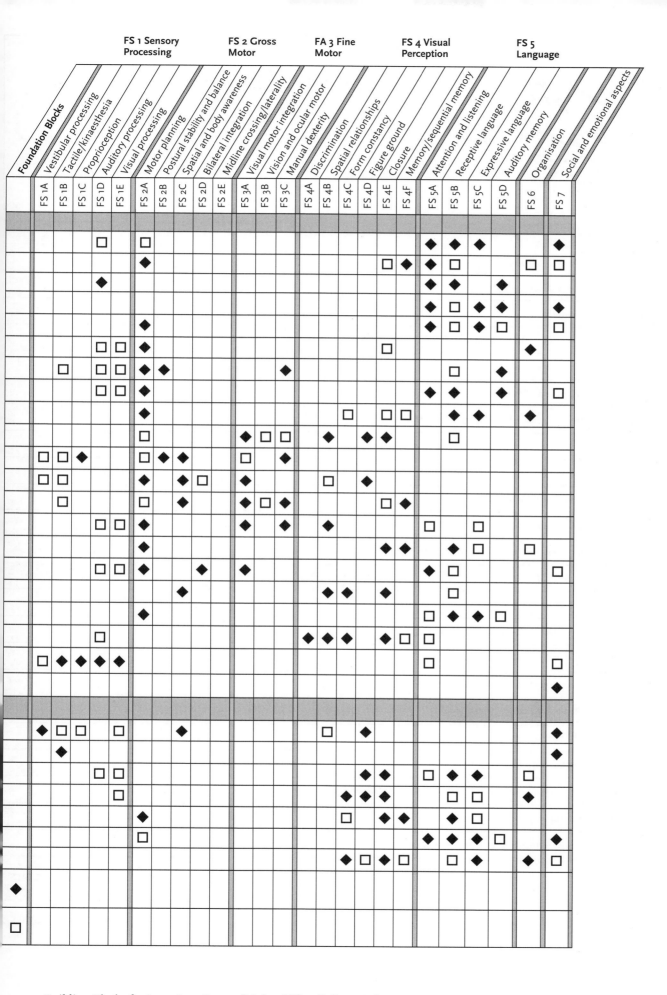

Teacher Observations
of Child

MATERIALS AND THEIR PROPERTIES		
Reluctant to touch, taste or smell certain materials		
Unable to cope with some noises		
Difficulty discriminating textures		
Poor sensory feedback – heavy handed or not enough pressure		
Problems sorting and classifying objects		
Unable to recognise and name common types of material		
Mismatch between academic ability and practical work		
Immaturity and poor quality of finished work compared with peers		
Careless and slapdash approach		
Finds all practical work hard		
Difficulty handling materials		
Poor accuracy when measuring, cutting, drawing		
PHYSICAL PROCESSES		
Inability to link cause and effect		
Unable to understand basic concepts, e.g. push/pull		
Cannot interpret 2D to make a 3D circuit		
Difficulty drawing representation of 3D model		
Problems when using scale or measuring		
Difficulty with linear or vertical scanning		
Cannot remember conventional symbols		
Unable to use and remember appropriate scientific language and terms		
Unaware of personal space (own and others)		
Excessive body movements when completing tasks		
		MAIN TOTALS
		SECONDARY TOTALS

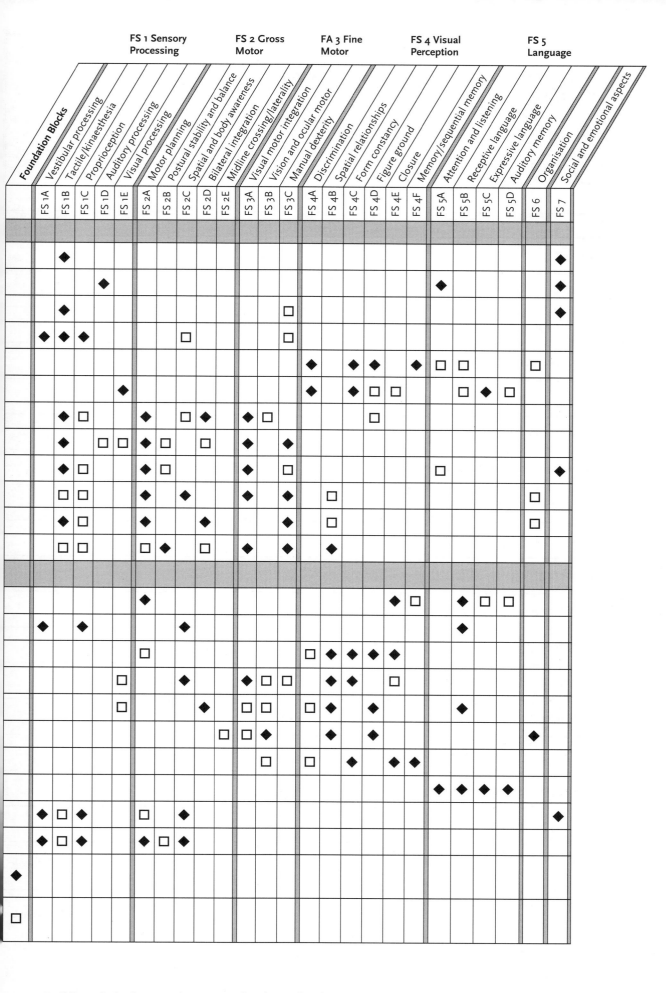

Teacher Observations
of Child

EXPLORING & DEVELOPING IDEAS		
Unable to be imaginative		
Unable to link ideas		
Difficulties asking appropriate questions		
Unable to grasp concept to complete task		
Cannot follow sequence of auditory instructions		
Difficulty planning ideas		
Unable to select ideas and materials to use in his work		
Limited ability to collect and sift materials needed for project		
Difficulty with practical aspects of task		
Difficulty recording ideas		
Unable to imagine simple sketch/prototype		
Poor observational skills		
Difficulty developing ideas from initial instructions		
Dislikes certain textures		
Fixated on one particular colour, shape or texture		
Reluctant to try new art media/materials		
Finds noisy environments distressing		
		PRIMARY TOTALS
		SECONDARY TOTALS

Foundation Blocks	FS 1A	FS 1B	FS 1C	FS 1D	FS 1E	FS 2A	FS 2B	FS 2C	FS 2D	FS 2E	FS 3A	FS 3B	FS 3C	FS 4A	FS 4B	FS 4C	FS 4D	FS 4E	FS 4F	FS 5A	FS 5B	FS 5C	FS 5D	FS 6	FS 7
						◆														☐	☐	☐			◆
						◆												◆		☐	☐			☐	◆
						◆															◆	◆	☐		◆
				☐		◆														☐	◆			☐	◆
				◆		☐														☐	◆		◆	☐	
						◆								◆	◆		◆				☐			☐	☐
					☐	◆								◆		☐	◆		☐	◆				☐	
					☐	☐								◆			◆		☐	◆	☐			◆	
		☐	☐			◆		☐	◆		◆		☐	◆										☐	
						◆			☐		◆	☐	◆	◆			◆			☐		☐			
						◆								◆	☐		◆							☐	◆
					◆						◆					☐		◆	◆		☐				
		◆				◆						◆							☐	☐	☐	☐			◆
		◆			◆																				◆
		◆			◆																				◆
		◆			◆																				◆
				◆															◆	◆	☐	◆			
◆																									
☐																									

Teacher Observations of Child

INVESTIGATING AND MAKING ART, CRAFT AND DESIGN	
Finds all practical work hard	
Difficulty handling tools	
Poor accuracy when measuring, cutting, drawing etc.	
Constantly swopping hands when using tools	
Only using one hand in activities when two are needed	
Unable to draw anything recognisable	
Immature drawing skills	
Inability to stabilise equipment efficiently	
Immature drawing of people	
Dislikes messy activities	
Difficulties identifying tactile/sensory qualities of materials	
Heavy handed or poor control of pressure	
Reduced awareness of personal space (own and others)	
General clumsiness with 2 handed tasks	
Forgets verbal instructions and practical demonstration	
Careless and slapdash approach	
Excessive body movements when completing tasks	
Rushes all tasks/activities/starts without thinking	
Impulsive movements compromising safety	
Unable to select appropriate material for task	
Takes many trips to collect necessary equipment	
Poor quality of finished work compared with peers	
Discrepancy between cognitive ability and performance skills	
Cannot understand scale	
Unable to construct 3D models	
Cannot interpret 2D to make a 3D model	
Difficulty drawing 3D objects	
Problems when copying 2D to 2D	
Difficulties analysing patterns/exploring specific details from artifacts	
Problems estimating length, depth, height	
Problems understanding and generalising common properties of object	
	PRIMARY TOTALS
	SECONDARY TOTALS

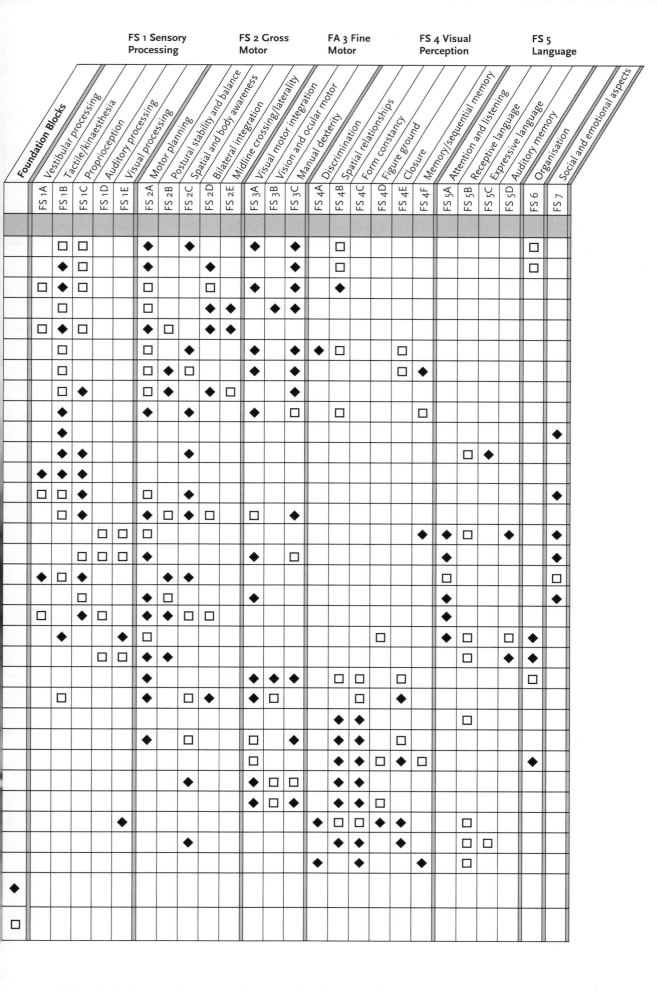

Teacher Observations
of Child

EVALUATING AND DEVELOPING WORK	
Difficulty listening to verbal instructions	
Difficulty listening to others	
Reluctant to talk about own work in front of group	
Finds turn-taking and listening to others hard	
Unable to be focussed and contribute to discussions	
Difficulties following sequence of written instructions	
Difficulties following sequence of verbal instructions	
Little awareness of cause and effect	
Unable to predict outcome	
Problems developing ideas	
Very fixed and rigid in their ideas	
Resistant to ideas from others	
Unable to see what changes could be made	
KNOWLEDGE AND UNDERSTANDING	
Little understanding of shape, size, space	
Unable to link one shape to another	
Problems analysing repeating patterns	
Difficulty interpreting subtle similarities/differences in colour, tone, design, style etc.	
Difficulty comparing and contrasting different styles, mediums and cultures	
Difficulty conceptualising completed design	
Problems understanding and generalising common properties of object	
	PRIMARY TOTALS
	SECONDARY TOTALS

Foundation Blocks mapping grid — SA 5 Art and Design

	FS 1 Sensory Processing					FS 2 Gross Motor					FA 3 Fine Motor			FS 4 Visual Perception						FS 5 Language					
	Vestibular processing	Tactile/kinaesthesia	Proprioception	Auditory processing	Visual processing	Motor planning	Postural stability and balance	Spatial and body awareness	Bilateral integration	Midline crossing/laterality	Visual motor integration	Vision and ocular motor	Manual dexterity	Discrimination	Spatial relationships	Form constancy	Figure ground	Closure	Memory/sequential memory	Attention and listening	Receptive language	Expressive language	Auditory memory	Organisation	Social and emotional aspects
	FS 1A	FS 1B	FS 1C	FS 1D	FS 1E	FS 2A	FS 2B	FS 2C	FS 2D	FS 2E	FS 3A	FS 3B	FS 3C	FS 4A	FS 4B	FS 4C	FS 4D	FS 4E	FS 4F	FS 5A	FS 5B	FS 5C	FS 5D	FS 6	FS 7
				♦			□													♦	♦		□		♦
				♦			□													♦	♦		□		♦
				□	□															♦	□	♦	□		♦
				♦																♦	♦	□	□		♦
				♦			□													♦	♦	♦	□		□
					□	♦					□	♦					□		♦	□	♦				
				♦		□														♦	♦		♦		♦
						♦											♦					□			
																	♦					□			♦
			♦	♦		♦																□		□	♦
																									♦
																					□				♦
																									♦
											□			♦	♦	♦		♦							
											♦				♦	♦			♦						
														♦	♦		♦		♦						
					♦									♦			♦		♦						
											♦			♦		□	□		♦						
						♦									♦			♦	♦						
														♦		♦			♦		□				
	♦																								
	□																								

143

Teacher Observations of Child

GENERAL SKILLS	
Poor mouse control	
Difficulty depressing correct key	
Problems finding cursor on screen	
Problems locating specific icons/tools	
Cannot remember icon tool function	
Difficulty remembering and following verbal instructions	
Problem transferring material given via an interactive whiteboard to own computer	
Cannot remember sequences when using pathways, e.g. to open a file	
FINDING THINGS OUT	
Difficulty using databases and spread sheets	
Problem with vertical and linear scanning	
Difficulty reading information presented in different font styles and sizes	
Problems understanding and interpreting information	
Cannot recognise and interpret computer graphics particularly when orientation is altered	
Inability to relate control input to turtle movement	
Difficulty incorporating sound into presentation	
DEVELOPING IDEAS AND MAKING THINGS HAPPEN	
Problems identifying relevant information on the screen when lots of irrelevant information is presented e.g. on internet pages	
Difficulty recognising uniformity or differences in font size	
Unable to interpret and produce a range of layouts, e.g. spreadsheets/pie charts/posters	
Difficulty understanding and using 3D representations on the screen	
Problem reorganising information in order to present it in a different format	
Difficulty understanding what pictograms represent	
Inability to link mouse movement to direction on screen, e.g. using Flair programme	
Unable to insert graphics within text	
EXCHANGING AND SHARING INFORMATION	
Unable to participate in group work	
Inability to recognise differing needs of others when communicating information	
Difficulty sharing information through email	
Difficulty understanding and using new programme, e.g. Powerpoint	
Problems inserting information into programmes	
Inability to use appropriate tools to enhance presentation, e.g. using several different transitions between slides	
Cannot produce presentation notes to go with slides	
Difficulty in giving verbal presentation to audience	
REVIEWING, MODIFYING AND EVALUATING WORK AS IT PROGRESSES	
Inability to incorporate other people's ideas into own work	
Problem evaluating own work	
Difficulty understanding what improvements could be made	
Unwillingness to edit work	
Lack of understanding how to edit	
Problems questioning plausibility of researched information	
	MAIN TOTALS
	SECONDARY TOTALS

	FS 1A	FS 1B	FS 1C	FS 1D	FS 1E	FS 2A	FS 2B	FS 2C	FS 2D	FS 2E	FS 3A	FS 3B	FS 3C	FS 4A	FS 4B	FS 4C	FS 4D	FS 4E	FS 4F	FS 5A	FS 5B	FS 5C	FS 5D	FS 6	FS 7
Column label	Vestibular processing	Tactile/kinaesthesia	Proprioception	Auditory processing	Visual processing	Motor planning	Postural stability and balance	Spatial and body awareness	Bilateral integration	Midline crossing/laterality	Visual motor integration	Vision and ocular motor	Manual dexterity	Discrimination	Spatial relationships	Form constancy	Figure ground	Closure	Memory/sequential memory	Attention and listening	Receptive language	Expressive language	Auditory memory	Organisation	Social and emotional aspects
	□					◆	□				◆	□	◆		◆		□								
		◆	◆					□			◆	□	□				◆		□						
					◆						□	◆	□	□	◆		◆		□						
						◆					◆	◆	□	□		□	◆		◆		□				
					◆														◆		◆			◆	
				◆		□														□	◆		◆		◆
					◆							◆			◆		◆	□	□		□			□	
				□		◆						□							◆	◆	□			◆	
					◆							◆			□	□	◆		◆	□				□	
			□	◆							□	◆			◆	◆	◆				□				
				□								□			◆	◆	◆	◆		□	◆	◆	□	◆	
				□								□				◆		◆			□				
						◆		□			◆		◆						□		□			□	
			◆		◆							□				◆	□		◆		□			□	
					◆						□		□		□	◆	◆		◆	□	◆				
					□						◆		◆	□	◆	◆	□								
				◆		□									◆	◆	◆	□	□	□	◆	□			
											□	□			◆	◆			◆						
			□	◆									◆			◆		◆	◆	□	□	□			
				□								□		◆				◆		◆				□
	◆						□	◆		◆	□	□		◆											
				□	◆						◆			□		◆	◆		□	□					
		◆	□		□														◆	◆	◆	□			□
		◆																	◆	□	◆	◆			◆
				◆													◆		◆	□	◆	◆			
				◆				◆	□					□				◆	◆	◆	◆				
			□										□	◆		◆	◆			□	□		◆		
			□										□	◆	◆	◆	□	◆		◆			◆		
				◆											□	□	□		◆			◆			
		□		◆													□	◆	◆	◆	◆	□		◆	
				□															□	◆	◆	□	◆	◆	□
				◆				□		□									□	◆	◆		□	◆	
									□											◆	◆		□	◆	
																			□			◆		◆	
				◆			□		□							◆		◆	◆		□		◆	
				□													□		◆	◆	□		◆	
◆																								
□																								

Teacher Observations of Child

MOTOR CO-ORDINATION		
Lack of stamina		
Inability to sustain movement		
Poor balance		
Reduced fluency when moving		
Bumps into things/trips and falls over		
Ungainly/awkward movement walking and running		
Flops or props against apparatus, children or wall		
Poor grading of movement, e.g. too much/too little force		
Heavy footed/'earthbound' movements		
Slower than peers in acquiring skills		
Slow to change for PE		
Difficulty with buttons, zips, laces		
Reluctance to participate due to anticipated difficulties		
Difficulty maintaining control of movement		
Constant movement to give self stability		
Reduced ability when hopping		
Difficulty co-ordinating both sides of body together, e.g. swimming		
Reduced spatial awareness		
Constant movement/fidgety/on the go		

DANCE/GYMNASTICS		
Unaware of own position in relation to others		
Poor sense of rhythm and timing		
Difficulty with quick directional changes		
Lacks fluency of movement		
Ungainly, awkward and exaggerated movements		
Uses speed in an attempt to overcome poor balance/control		
Unable to accurately recall sequences of movement		
Unable to change from one movement pattern to another		
Difficulty copying or imitating patterns		
Difficulty with synchronisation work		
Difficulty executing precise controlled movement		
Dislikes or anxious of being off the ground		
Difficulty learning to skip and hop		
Problems co-ordinating arms and legs together		
Fearful of unstable equipment, e.g. ropes		
Difficulty creating and performing own movement patterns		
Poor judgement of height, depth, distance		

MAIN TOTALS

SECONDARY TOTALS

Foundation Blocks	FS 1 Sensory Processing: Vestibular processing FS 1A	Tactile/kinaesthesia FS 1B	Proprioception FS 1C	Auditory processing FS 1D	Visual processing FS 1E	FS 2 Gross Motor: Motor planning FS 2A	Postural stability and balance FS 2B	Spatial and body awareness FS 2C	Bilateral integration FS 2D	Midline crossing/laterality FS 2E	FA 3 Fine Motor: Visual motor integration FS 3A	Vision and ocular motor FS 3B	Manual dexterity FS 3C	FS 4 Visual Perception: Discrimination FS 4A	Spatial relationships FS 4B	Form constancy FS 4C	Figure ground FS 4D	Closure FS 4E	Memory/sequential memory FS 4F	FS 5 Language: Attention and listening FS 5A	Receptive language FS 5B	Expressive language FS 5C	Auditory memory FS 5D	Organisation FS 6	Social and emotional aspects FS 7
	◆	□	◆			□	◆	◆					□												□
	□	□	□			◆	◆	◆	◆		□														
	◆		◆			□	◆	◆	□			□								□					
	◆	□	◆			◆	◆	□	□		□														
	◆	□	□		□	◆	◆	◆				□													
	◆	□	◆			□	◆	◆	□		□														
	◆	□	◆				◆	◆												□					□
	□	◆	◆			◆	◆	□					□												□
	◆	□	◆				◆	◆																	□
	□	□	□			◆	□	◆	◆		◆														
		□				◆	□	◆	◆		□		◆							□					
		◆				□			◆		◆	□	◆				□			□					
	◆		□	□	□	◆	◆				□														◆
	◆		□			□	◆	◆		□	◆	□													
	◆	□	◆				◆	◆																	
	◆	□	◆			□	◆	◆	□																
	□	□	◆			◆		◆	◆	□															
	□	□	◆					◆				◆				□									◆
	◆	◆	◆				□	◆												□					□
	□	□	◆			□		◆				□			◆										◆
	◆	□	◆	◆	□	□			◆											□					
	◆		□			◆	◆			□									□	◆	□				
	◆	□	◆			◆	◆	□	□		□														
	◆	□	◆			□	◆	◆	□		□														
	◆	◆	◆				◆	□												□					□
				□	□	◆									□				◆	◆	□		◆		
	□	◆	□			◆		◆												□	□				◆
		□	◆			◆		□		□		□							◆	◆					
		◆	□			◆		◆	◆	□									□	□					
	□	□	◆			◆	◆	◆	□	□															
	◆	□	◆				□	◆				◆				□									□
	□	□	□			◆	◆	◆	◆	□															
	□	◆	□			□	□	◆	◆	◆															
	◆	◆	◆				◆		□			□													□
	◆	□	□			◆	□	◆		□															◆
	◆	□	□				□	◆				◆			□	◆									
◆																									
□																									

Teacher Observations of Child

GAMES/ATHLETICS		
Difficulty with ball skills/poor accuracy		
Does not track flight of ball		
Inability to hit target/throw at target		
Immature catching and throwing		
Flinches when ball comes towards self		
Waits for ball to hit body before responds		
Difficulty holding equipment		
Unable to keep position in team/in the wrong place at the wrong time		
Reluctance to participate in games		
Last to be chosen for team		
Always wants to be team captain		
Slow response to instructions in team situations		
Inappropriate social behaviour in team sports		
Difficulty finding, maintaining and relocating correct position on pitch/court/field		
Reduced awareness of team roles/team working		
Failure to initiate interaction with others		
Inattentive/unable to listen to instructions/needs to have instructions repeated		
Problems understanding rules/tactics/strategies of team games		
OUTDOOR AND ADVENTURE ACTIVITIES		
Difficuilty orientating, reading and interpreting maps		
Poor problem solving skills		
Fearful of new experiences		
Slow and hesitant when attempting new activities		
Unable to accurately judge, height and depth		
Unable to shift weight accurately		
Unstable on uneven ground, trips over stationary objects, e.g. roots		
		MAIN TOTALS
		SECONDARY TOTALS

Foundation Blocks	FS 1 Sensory Processing					FS 2 Gross Motor					FA 3 Fine Motor			FS 4 Visual Perception						FS 5 Language					
	Vestibular processing	Tactile/kinaesthesia	Proprioception	Auditory processing	Visual processing	Motor planning	Postural stability and balance	Spatial and body awareness	Bilateral integration	Midline crossing/laterality	Visual motor integration	Vision and ocular motor	Manual dexterity	Discrimination	Spatial relationships	Form constancy	Figure ground	Closure	Memory/sequential memory	Attention and listening	Receptive language	Expressive language	Auditory memory	Organisation	Social and emotional aspects
	FS 1A	FS 1B	FS 1C	FS 1D	FS 1E	FS 2A	FS 2B	FS 2C	FS 2D	FS 2E	FS 3A	FS 3B	FS 3C	FS 4A	FS 4B	FS 4C	FS 4D	FS 4E	FS 4F	FS 5A	FS 5B	FS 5C	FS 5D	FS 6	FS 7
		◆	□					□	◆	□	◆	◆					□								
	□				◆		□	□		◆	□	◆					◆								
			◆			□	□		□		◆	◆		□			◆								
		□	◆			□		◆	◆		◆	□	□												
		◆	□			□		◆	□		□	◆													◆
	□	□				◆		◆	◆	□	◆														
		◆	◆			□			◆	□	□		◆												
	□	□				□		◆								□	◆			◆					◆
	□		□	□		◆	□								◆			◆							◆
	◆			□	□	◆		◆				□					□								◆
		□		□	□	◆																			◆
	□			□	□	◆	□	◆												◆	◆				
	□	□	□			◆														◆	◆				◆
						◆		□				□					◆		□	◆	◆				□
																		◆						◆	◆
																						□			◆
	□	□	□	◆	□															◆	◆		◆		
			□	□		◆														◆	◆		◆		□
						□					□		◆	◆		◆	◆	□							
						◆											◆			□	◆	□	□	□	□
	◆	◆		□	□	◆												□							◆
	◆	□				◆														□	◆	□	□		◆
	◆		□				□	◆			◆			□	◆										
	◆	◆	◆			◆	□																		
	◆		◆				◆	◆			□			□	□	□									
	◆																								
	□																								

Subject areas teacher observation summary chart

Child............................

Class............................

Teacher............................

Date............................

	Foundation Blocks	FS 1 Sensory Processing					FS 2 Gross Motor					FS 3 Vision			FA 3 Fine Motor						FS 4 Visual Perception				FS 5 Language				FS 5	
		Vestibular processing	Tactile/kinaesthesia	Proprioception	Auditory processing	Visual processing	Motor planning	Postural stability and balance	Spatial and body awareness	Bilateral integration	Midline crossing/laterality	VMI/eye/hand co—ordination	Vision and ocular motor	Manual dexterity	Discrimination	Spatial relationships	Form constancy	Figure ground	Closure	Memory/sequential memory	Attention and listening	Receptive language	Expressive language	Auditory memory	Organisation	Social and emotional aspects		
		FS 1A	FS 1B	FS 1C	FS 1D	FS 1E	FS 2A	FS 2B	FS 2C	FS 2D	FS 2E	FS 3A	FS 3B	FS 3C	FS 4A	FS 4B	FS 4C	FS 4D	FS 4E	FS 4F	FS 5A	FS 5B	FS 5C	FS 5D	FS 6	FS 7	Main Totals	Secondary Totals
General																												
Literacy																												
Numeracy																												
Science																												
Art/Design																												
ICT																												
PE																												

Main Totals ◆

Secondary Totals ☐

Building Blocks for Learning. © 2008 John Wiley & Sons Ltd.

Personalised profile for child

Child............. Age.............

Class............. Teacher............. Date.............

Teacher Observations on Child

Legend: ◆ = Main Totals □ = Secondary Totals

Teacher Observations on Child	FS 1 Sensory Processing					FS 2 Gross Motor					FS 3			FA 3 Fine Motor						FS 4 Visual Perception				FS 6	FS 7
	FS 1A Vestibular Processing	FS 1B Tactile/kinaesthesia	FS 1C Proprioception	FS 1D Auditory processing	FS 1E Visual processing	FS 2A Motor planning	FS 2B Postural stability and balance	FS 2C Spatial and body awareness	FS 2D Bilateral integration	FS 2E Midline crossing/laterality	FS 3A Visual motor integration	FS 3B Vision and ocular motor	FS 3C Manual dexterity	FS 4A Discrimination	FS 4B Spatial relationships	FS 4C Form constancy	FS 4D Figure ground	FS 4E Closure	FS 4F Memory/sequential memory	FS 5A Attention and listening	FS 5B Receptive language	FS 5C Expressive language	FS 5D Auditory memory / Organisation	FS 6	FS 7 Social and emotional aspects
unable to sit down on carpet without causing disturbance	□	□	◆																	□					□
difficulty waiting turn in line	□	◆	□			◆	◆	◆												□					□
dropping equipment/knocking things over	◆	◆	◆			◆	◆	◆	□		◆	□	□												
smudges work			◆			□	◆	◆	□		◆	□	◆							◆					
takes a long time changing for PE		□	◆			◆	□	◆	◆		□	□	□	□						□	□				
impulsive/rushes all tasks and activities	□		◆			◆											◆			◆					◆
Main Totals ◆		1				5	4	4	1		2	2	1	1			1			1					1
Secondary Totals □	4	3	1			1	1	4	2		2	2	1	1						3	1				2

Building Blocks for Learning. © 2008 John Wiley & Sons Ltd.

Personalised profile for child

Child........................

Class............... Teacher................ Age............... Date.........

Teacher Observations on Child		

Foundation Blocks								

FS 1 Sensory Processing
- FS 1A — Vestibular processing
- FS 1B — Tactile/kinaesthesia
- FS 1C — Proprioception
- FS 1D — Auditory processing
- FS 1E — Visual processing

FS 2 Gross Motor
- FS 2A — Motor planning
- FS 2B — Postural stability and balance
- FS 2C — Spatial and body awareness
- FS 2D — Bilateral integration
- FS 2E — Midline crossing/laterality

FA 3 Fine Motor
- FS 3A — Visual motor integration
- FS 3B — Vision and ocular motor
- FS 3C — Manual dexterity

FS 4 Visual Perception
- FS 4A — Discrimination
- FS 4B — Spatial relationships
- FS 4C — Form constancy
- FS 4D — Figure ground
- FS 4E — Closure
- FS 4F — Memory/sequential memory

FS 5 Language
- FS 5A — Attention and listening
- FS 5B — Receptive language
- FS 5C — Expressive language
- FS 5D — Auditory memory
- FS 6 — Organisation
- FS 7 — Social and emotional aspects

Main Totals ◆

Secondary Totals ☐

Medical Conditions

Occupational therapists work with children who present in a wide variety of ways in primary schools. Some children will have already received a diagnosis, others will be under going a diagnostic assessment, and for some, who are causing concern in school, the exact nature of their difficulties remains uncertain.

Experience has shown that for most children their strengths and weaknesses are clarified during their primary years. As children become older and the demands of the curriculum increase, the way in which they present in the classroom may enable a specific diagnosis to be made. However, there will be a proportion of children who do not meet all the criteria for a specific diagnosis but still present with many features of recognised conditions and struggle in school. These children find school very challenging and their ability to access the national curriculum is impaired. As many conditions are of a developmental nature, a diagnosis may only be made shortly before children transfer to secondary school.

Having a diagnosis can help clarification of the teaching approaches and intervention suitable to support children in class. It is now acknowledged many conditions co-exist alongside each other, so children can present with behaviour that may be attributed to more than one diagnosis. This is known as co-morbidity and can be particularly evident in children displaying behaviours commonly seen in attention deficit hyperactivity disorder, autistic spectrum disorders and developmental coordination disorder.

A child can be supported appropriately within school regardless of whether a formal diagnosis has been given. There are occasions where a diagnosis can help clarification of the approaches and resources needed to support a child. However, the way in which the child presents within the classroom is not affected by diagnosis.

The local primary school is the preferred option for many parents of children with a specific diagnosis. It is likely, therefore, that within any class a primary school teacher will have children with a wide variety of needs. Occupational therapists work with teachers and support staff to integrate students during their primary years.

This book expands on the most common medical conditions seen by occupational therapists working in school, detailed in our earlier publication entitled *Occupational Therapy Approaches for Secondary Special Needs: Practical Classroom Strategies*. The conditions discussed are:

- Attention deficit disorder/attention deficit hyperactivity disorder (ADD/ADHD)
- Autistic spectrum disorders including Asperger's syndrome
- Cerebral palsy (CP)
- Developmental coordination disorder (DCD), including dyspraxia
- Physical disabilities

The overview sheets summarise the conditions and are presented as follows:

- *How does the condition impact on the child?*
- *What is the condition?*
- *Why did it start?*
- *What are the main forms?*
- *What treatment could be offered?*
- *How will the child be affected in future?*
- *Further information and reading.*

The table format summarises each condition by:

- Linking teacher observations of the child
- Suggesting practical strategies to be implemented within school
- Giving further resources of information and resources

Teachers will be aware of children who have other medical conditions. Details of these conditions should be available from the school doctor, school nurse and information sources such as the 'Contact a Family Directory'.

Treatment procedures and the personnel referred to in the text will vary, depending on the medical, educational and social services networks in the local area. To ensure that a consistent approach is maintained throughout the school it is advisable that any request for further advice from outside agencies is discussed with the special educational needs coordinator (SENCO). These sheets are based on material from our previous book *Occupational Therapy Approaches for Secondary Special Needs: Practical Classroom Strategies*.

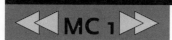

Attention deficit disorder/attention deficit hyperactivity disorder

 How does the condition impact on the child?

Specific characteristics and behaviour may include:

Inattention

The child:

- Has difficulty sustaining attention and focus on task, leading to mistakes
- Is unable to follow instructions accurately through to completion of task
- Fails to complete school work and homework
- Has a disorganised approach to work, often has little sense of time and priorities
- Loses equipment, books, PE kit, etc., frequently
- Has poor selective attention and is easily distracted by everyday sensory stimuli, background noise, 'busy' display boards
- Shifts from one uncompleted task to another
- Becomes forgetful in daily activities
- Is easily bored so will find something to do rather than be bored

Hyperactivity

The child:

- Tends to fidget and fiddle
- Finds sitting still difficult—is constantly 'on the move'
- Leaves seat often when in classroom
- Becomes restless in self/has inner restlessness
- Talks excessively and is demanding in group situations
- Has difficulty settling to any task

Impulsiveness

The child:

- Tends to make decisions hastily without considering alternatives/ consequences
- Is an avid risk taker—will accept any dare

- Has difficulty waiting his turn, frequently interrupts, is desperate to share his thoughts
- Lacks self-control and ability to stop and think or wait with rest of the class
- Fails to analyse problems before he rushes into an activity

Other possible associated features

Cognitive

The child:

- Often appears to be off task, although may have processed some of the information, i.e. 'learning by osmosis'; she may be listening whilst appearing distracted
- Has immaturity, or appears to have delays in acquiring early learning skills, has lots of ideas but is unable to be selective to complete task successfully
- Processes written or spoken information slowly
- Is able to remember information but cannot always accurately select the most relevant part on request
- Finds it hard to listen, think, process and carry out tasks at the same time
- Has word finding difficulties

Social/emotional

The child:

- Displays immature behaviours
- Finds friendships hard to develop and maintain, can have difficulty turn taking, sharing and listening to others
- Is unable to conform to social rules
- Behaves as 'class clown' as a way to get social approval or distract from his educational difficulties
- Is considered to be the naughty child in class
- Becomes frustrated by his difficulties, often gives up tasks
- Lacks confidence and may be withdrawn—this often develops as insight into difficulties increases
- Fears failure, affecting his ability to attempt tasks
- Has inappropriate social behaviours, can become antisocial or seek social approval from an unsuitable peer group
- Has difficulties or is unable to follow social rules in group situations
- Exhibits poor sleeping patterns affecting behaviour at school
- Reacts to sensory stimulation with an over or under sensitive response
- Is unable to filter out extraneous noises, movements, visual stimuli and may respond adversely
- Becomes easily distracted by everyday sensory stimulation
- Over reacts to situations with emotional volatility due to emotional dysregulation

What is the condition?

Attention deficit disorder/attention deficit hyperactivity disorder (ADD/ADHD) may be diagnosed in children where behaviour appears impulsive, overactive and/or inattentive to an extent that is unwarranted for their developmental age and is a significant hindrance to their social and educational successes (British Psychological Society, 1996). In order to be given a clinical diagnosis of ADD/ADHD the child must be formally assessed by specialist medical practitioners and meet certain diagnostic criteria in two or more settings. The practitioner will collect information from the parents, school and others involved with the child. They will take into account whether there are any other medical reasons for the behaviour and what else may be going on in the child's life. Two major diagnostic instruments are currently used by clinicians—the *Diagnostic and Statistical Manual of Mental Disorders* (DSM-IV/V) and *International Classification of Diseases,* 10th edition (ICD-10).

Why did it start?

The precise cause of ADD/ADHD cannot yet be specified. However, it is thought that a number of different factors may be at work. Hypotheses include that it is a neurologically based condition, resulting in a shortage of brain chemicals that help a child concentrate, plan and carry out their activities and control their emotions. Other theories suggest that there is a known strong genetic inheritance; that some children have difficulties forming relationships with their main carers in early years and certain foods/food additives can play a part. It is thought that up to 20% of children with ADHD have a parent with the condition.

What are the main forms of ADHD?

The three main features of ADHD are identified as inattention, hyperactivity and impulsivity. Some children display predominately inattentive/sluggish behaviour, whilst others show hyperactivity/impulsive behaviour. In a few instances these features may be combined. Girls often have a diagnosis of ADHD without hyperactivity (ADD or ADHD-H), whereas boys often have both aspects of the problem. 'ADHD can put a child at risk of other emotional and behavioural problems, such as conduct disorder, oppositional and defiant behaviours, mood and anxiety problems and alcohol or drug misuse' (AAP Clinical Practice Guidelines, 2000). It can often be seen with other co-existing conditions such as Asperger's syndrome, developmental coordination disorder, attachment disorder or specific learning difficulties.

The intensity of the core features can differ significantly from child to child and from one situation to another. This inconsistency of behaviour is often very puzzling for parents, teachers and peers. This unevenness of features may affect the child's performance within the classroom, depending on the subject, the teaching method used, the time of day and the timing of medication, if prescribed. Behaviour at home may vary according to normal demands of family life, social interaction, roles within the family and timing of medication, if prescribed.

What treatment could be offered?

No treatment has yet been proved to cure ADD/ADHD; all provide symptomatic relief or can help alleviate some features. However, as children get older and learn to live with and manage this condition improvement is often noticed.

Common types of intervention include:

- Psychosocial/behaviour management—home and school
- Advice on learning approaches in school—an appropriate structure with flexibility
- Medication
- Social skills training
- Self-control monitoring and calming techniques
- Manipulation of the environment
- Sensory processing advice
- Dietary advice
- Managing emotions; anger, anxiety, coping strategies

How will the child be affected in future?

Some children grow out of their problems; however, for some the features continue to persist into adult life, but they continue to benefit from medication and can learn strategies to help them modify their behaviour.

Further information

Attention Deficit Disorder Information and Support Service (ADDISS)
2nd Floor, Premier House, 112 Station Road, Edgeware, Middlesex HA8 7BJ. Tel 0208 952 2800; Email info@addiss.co.uk; Website www.addiss.co.uk

Young Minds—for Children's Mental Health
48–50 St John Street, London EC1M 4DG. Tel 0207 336 8445; Email enquiries@youngminds.org.uk; Website www.youngminds.org.uk; Parent information service 0800 0182138.

ADH Training
www.adhtraining.co.uk; provides training and support for clinicians

References

Association of Accessibility Professionals (2000) Clinical practice guideline: diagnosis and evaluation of the child with ADHD. *Pediatrics*, **105**, 1158–1170.

British Pyschological Society (1996) *Attention Deficit Hyperactivity Disorder (ADHD): a Psychological Response to an Evolving Concept.* Leicester, England, The British Psychological Society.

Gillberg, C. (1983) Perceptual motor and attention deficits in Swedish primary school children: some child psychiatric aspects. *Journal of Child Psychology and Psychiatry*, **24**, 337–403.

Reed, C.L. (2001) *Quick Reference Guide to Occupational Therapy.* 2nd edn. Gaithersburg, MD, Aspen Publishers.

Further reading

Alban-Metcalfe, J. and Alban-Metcalfe, J. (2001) *Managing ADHD in the Inclusive Classroom—Practical Strategies for Teachers.* London, Fulton.

Barkley, R.A. (1995) *Taking Charge of ADHD—the Complete, Authoritative Guide for Parents.* New York, Guilford Press.

Barkley, R.A. (2006) *ADHD in the Classroom; Strategies for Teachers.* New York, Guilford Press.

Cooper, P. & Ideus, K. (1996) *ADHD—a Practical Guide for Teaching.* London, Fulton.

Cooper, P. & O'Regan, F. (2001) *Educating Children with AD/HD: a Teacher's Manual.* London, Routledge.

Goldstein, S. & Goldstein, M. (1990) *Managing Attention Disorders in Children: a Guide for Practitioners.* New York, John Wiley and Sons.

Green, C. & Chee, K. (1997) *Understanding ADHD—a Parent's Guide to ADHD in Children.* London, Vermillion.

Jones, C.B. (1991) *Sourcebook for Children with ADD—a Management Guide for Early Childhood Professional and Parents.* Tucson, AZ, Communication Skill Builders.

Jones, C.B. (1994) *Attention Deficit Disorder—Strategies for School Age Children.* Tucson, AZ, Communication Skill Builders.

Kewley, G. (2001) *ADHD Recognition, Reality and Resolution.* London, Fulton.

Kewley, G. (2006) *Attention Deficit Hyperactivity Disorders: What Teachers Can Do.* London, Fulton.

Moss, D. (1998) *Shelley the Hyperactive Turtle.* Bethesda, MD, Woodbine House Inc.

Reimers, C. & Brunger, B. (1999) *ADHD and the Young Child—Driven to Redirection—a Guide for Parents and Teachers of Young Children with ADHD.* North Branch, MN, Speciality Press/ADD Warehouse.

Zeigler D.C.A. (2005) *Teenagers with ADD and ADHD: a Guide for Parents and Professionals.* Bethesda, MD, Woodbine House Inc.

Teacher observations of the child	Practical strategies	Further advice
Children diagnosed with ADD/ADHD will present with varying degrees of need depending on the severity of their condition. The teacher observations mentioned below may not all be relevant.	*Practical strategies should be targeted for the individual child after analysis of the teacher's observations. It will then be important to decide whether the behaviour needs to be managed or changed.*	*To implement the further advice it may be necessary to discuss the concerns and issues with the special educational needs coordinator*

OBSERVED BEHAVIOURS

Impulsive:
    Blurts out answers/interrupts
    Starts activity before listening to full instructions
    Acts without thinking
    Bumps into others/knocks things over
	Provide behaviour management programme
	 Help and encourage child to pre-plan task—stop/think/do
	 Provide 'time out' cards/system
	 Heighten teacher's and peers' awareness of child's difficulty
	 Consider adult support for group situations
	 Implement calming/relaxation techniques provided by occupational therapist
		Seek advice from behavioural support team, educational psychologist
		
		 Refer to A 11 page 397
		
		 Refer to OTA 8 page 323

Has fluctuating performance:
    Is easily distracted during study
    Is frequently off task
    Has difficulty sustaining attention
    Lacks persistence in activities
    Has difficulty initiating task
	Provide frequent positive teacher feedback and redirection
	 Set short attainable goals in collaboration with child
	 Use work systems and visual schedules
	 Give one-to-one encouragement at start of task
	 Arrange paired working
	 Have regular breaks in task, consider movement breaks
	 Allow 'fiddle' items
	 Trial use of movin'sit cushion
	 Limit distractions—only essential items in work area
	 Consider position in class
	 Implement behaviour management programme
		Seek advice from educational psychologist, behavioural support team, occupational therapist
		 Refer to A 14 page 405, A 11 page 397
		
		 Refer to OTA 8 page 323
		 Refer to Equipment Resources page 407
		
		 Refer to A 9 page 389

Teacher observations of the child	Practical strategies	Further advice
OBSERVED BEHAVIOURS (Continued)		
Does not conform to rules or understand the consequences of his behaviour	Consider behaviour management/ social skills programme Provide clear, concise and consistent expectations as to desired behaviour Reward child when behaving well	Refer to A 9 page 389
Shows changeable/unpredictable behaviour	Ensure any medication is taken as prescribed Consider behaviour management programme Provide clear, concise and consistent expectations as to desired behaviour	Ask parents to discuss with child's doctor whether altering timing and dosage of medication could help to optimise performance

Responds inappropriately to sensory input (auditory, tactile, visual):
    Has difficulty filtering out inputs and then refocusing on task
    Is unable to ignore irrelevant background noises
	Heighten staff awareness that child may under or overreact to normal sensory input, e.g. the buzz of equipment/interactive whiteboard
	
	Prepare child in advance of predictable noises, e.g. bell
	
	Reduce distracting stimuli, e.g. background noise, pencils on desk, crowded wall displays
	
	Consider child's position in class, place child so distraction is obscured from view
		Seek advice from occupational therapist
		Refer to FS 1 page 5, OTA 8 page 323

Fails to complete work	Use home/school book daily to check with teaching staff Clarify expectations, e.g. provide structured information detailing what the child is to achieve	Refer to OTA 9 page 327 Refer to A 11 page 397, A 14 page 405

Displays risk taking behaviours and shows reduced sense of dangers:
    Has limited awareness of danger/no sense of danger
    Seeks and needs movement activity
	Heighten staff awareness
	
	Raise child's awareness to potential danger, provide an exciting but safer alternative activity
	
	Arrange paired working and/or adult support
	
	Use safety checklists
	
	Undertake risk assessment
		Refer to school health and safety policy

Teacher observations of the child	**Practical strategies**	**Further advice**
GROSS MOTOR COORDINATION		*Refer to Gross motor coordination Foundation Skills FS 2, FS 2A—FS2E page 31, 35–51*
Shows impulsivity: Has inability to sustain controlled movements Fluctuates in quality of movement Executes slow rhythmical movements with difficulty Has poor listening skills when instructions given before starting task Finds awaiting his turn hard Interferes during team games Has reduced sense of danger Shows poor sequencing and organising of movements	Encourage/practise slow controlled movements Encourage child to repeat back to adult to ensure she has understood task Help child to pre-plan movements required for task Implement calming techniques provided by occupational therapist Heighten awareness of safety issues and undertake risk assessments as appropriate Provide opportunities for individual/partner sports Consider adult support to maintain awareness of safety Provide regular breaks in task, consider movement breaks and use of 'time out' cards	Seek advice from occupational therapist, physiotherapist Refer to A 11 page 397 Refer to OTA 8 page 323 Refer to school health and safety policy Refer to OTA 8 page 323
Finds static balance activities challenging: Has difficulty executing slow precise/controlled movements Shows reduced ability to sustain balance postures	Encourage stop/think/do strategy Break down activity into achievable stages and practice individual component parts, giving positive feedback throughout Give child adequate space to allow for excessive/uncoordinated movement	Refer to A 11 page 397 Refer to OTA 10 page 333, A 7 page 381
Is unable to coordinate eye/hand/foot movements: Has difficulty catching/kicking ball	Identify specific difficulty and practice skill Heighten awareness of teacher and peers to child's difficulty	Refer to OTA 10 page 333, A 7 page 381
Demonstrates poor ability to sustain posture: Is constantly on the move Slouches Fidgets and fiddles	Provide regular breaks in task at agreed times, consider 'time out' cards Build in regular movement breaks, give child a task which allows for movement, e.g. handing out books, running errand Provide specific spot/area, e.g. on mat, in hoop, to 'earth' child Allow child to 'fiddle' with an agreed object, e.g. Blu-Tack, stress ball	Seek advice from physiotherapist/occupational therapist Refer to OTA 8 page 323, FS 1 page 5 Refer to OTA 4 page 271

Teacher observations of the child	Practical strategies	Further advice
GROSS MOTOR COORDINATION (Continued)		*Refer to Gross motor coordination Foundation Skills FS 2, FS 2A—FS2E page 31, 35–51*
	Check seating posture—chair/table size/height Encourage child to sit rather than stand in activities when appropriate	Refer to OTA 4 page 271
FINE MOTOR CONTROL		*Refer to Fine motor control Foundation Skills FS 3, FS 3A—FS 3C page 55, 59–69*
Rushes all fine motor tasks affecting/compromising accuracy: E.g. cutting, pouring liquids Has untidy and poor presentation of written work	Consider behaviour management programme	Seek advice from occupational therapist Refer to A 11 page 397
	Set attainable goals—encourage child to slow down and monitor results	
	Allow short breaks to refocus during tasks	
	Heighten awareness of safety issues and undertake risk assessment as appropriate	Refer to school health and safety policy
	Teach self-checking skills	Refer to A 11 page 397
	Use specific handwriting schemes, e.g. Write from the Start, Write Dance, Handwriting Without Tears	Refer to A 5 page 375
	Use visual prompts, e.g. coloured lines, traffic lights to mark start and finish line	Refer to A 11 page 397, OTA 4 page 271
	Consider alternative recording methods, e.g. ICT, part prepared worksheets	Refer to OTA 5 page 305, A 6 page 379
Has difficulty developing age appropriate manipulative skills	Provide regular practice session to acquire manipulative skills, practice skill at the child's level of ability	Refer to A 1 page 361, OTA 4 page 271, OTA 7 page 319, A3 page 371
	Implement hand gym activities	Refer to OTA 3 page 259
	Use of alternative/adapted equipment	Refer to Equipment Resources page 407
Produces variable quantity of written work	Clearly reward quality and effort put into achieving task rather than just quantity	Refer to OTA 4 page 271, A 12 page 401, A 4 page 373
	Set attainable goals—encourage child to slow down and monitor results, teach self-checking skills	
	Allow short breaks to refocus during tasks	
	Use specific handwriting schemes, e.g. Write from the Start, Write Dance, Handwriting Without Tears	Refer to A 5 page 375

Building Blocks for Learning. © 2008 John Wiley & Sons Ltd.

Teacher observations of the child	Practical strategies	Further advice
ORGANISATION		*Refer to Organisation Foundation Skills FS 6 page 111*
Is unable to organise self and task: Acts before thinking Prepares inadequately for school day Makes several journeys to collect equipment in preparation for classroom task Starts task without all necessary equipment available	Use behavioural/star charts Liaise with family/carers regarding consistent strategies to help develop routines Consider behaviour management programme Consider use of work system Provide checklist/cue cards identifying required equipment Help and encourage child to pre-plan task—stop/think/do Ensure all equipment easily accessible for task Encourage child to self-check and self-monitor Use timers/timed checklists to aid pacing Encourage separate sets of equipment in alternative places, e.g. a spare PE kit at school	Seek advice from educational/clinical psychologist, behavioural support team Refer to OTA 9 page 327 Refer to A 14 page 405 Refer to A 11 page 397 Refer to Equipment Resources page 407
Is unable to recognise personal space when sitting on the carpet, lining up, etc.	Use visual cue, e.g. cushion, mat to mark child's area Use movin'sit cushion or place child on edge of circle, at beginning or end of line to minimise disruption Work on body and spatial awareness	 Refer to Equipment Resources page 407 Refer to OTA 1 page 249, FS 2C page 43
Finds organising work area challenging	Use checklists to ensure only essential items are in work area Help and encourage child to pre-plan task to ensure all equipment is available for task Consider providing a visual cue on table, e.g. pencil pot Consider use of work system and visual checklists	Refer to OTA 9 page 327 Refer A 14 page 405, A 11 page 397
Submits incomplete homework: Does not fully understand task before going home Records task inaccurately in homework diary Takes much longer than allocated time to complete task	Discuss reason with child and parents Check timing of medication as effect of medication may have worn off	

Building Blocks for Learning. © 2008 John Wiley & Sons Ltd.

Teacher observations of the child	Practical strategies	Further advice
ORGANISATION (Continued)		Refer to Organisation Foundation Skills FS 6 page 111
Finds concentrating difficult as effects of medication may have worn off Works in a distractible environment at home	Set realistic goals and agree expectations with child and parent, agree on a maximum amount of time to be spent on homework each day, draw up a contract Consider use of system for recording homework Discuss strategies with child and parent, e.g. use of computer, parent to scribe, dictaphone, quality versus quantity Use work system Use the homework club in school Allow time for out of school activities	Refer to OTA 9 page 327 Refer to A 6 page 379, OTA 5 page 305 Refer to A 14 page 405

Demonstrates risk taking behaviours:
  Has limited awareness of danger/ no sense of danger
  Seeks and needs movement activity
	Heighten staff awareness
	Raise child's awareness to potential danger, provide an exciting but safe alternative
	Arrange paired working and /or adult support
	Use safety checklists
	Undertake risk assessment
		Refer to A 11 page 397, OTA 8 page 323
		
		Refer to school health and safety policy

Has reduced concept of time	Plan/check weekly timetable with adult support Monitor unstructured situations Teach coping strategies, e.g. use alarm on watches, timers, timed checklist Use work system, visual timetable Introduce behavioural strategies, e.g. star chart Liaise with parents to promote consistent management	Refer to Equipment Resources page 407 Refer to A 14 page 405, A 11 page 397
Becomes anxious, upset, agitated, over active when coping with changes in routine	Use visual timetable to inform child of predicted change Encourage child to pre-plan for change and reinforce plan by talking it through, rehearse changes to routine and what might happen next Prepare child for known change before it happens Adhere to established routines as much as it is possible	Refer to A 11 page 397, A 9 page 389

Teacher observations of the child	Practical strategies	Further advice
SENSORY PROCESSING		*Refer to Sensory processing Foundation Skills FS 1, FS 1A–FS 1E page 5, 11–27*
Auditory Becomes easily distracted with noise Is unable to identify relevant information through background noise Has difficulty understanding and responding to instructions	Limit unnecessary background noise if possible Provide quiet area where child can work Reinforce verbal instructions with visual reminders/timetable Use headphones if appropriate Heighten staff awareness	Seek advice from speech and language therapist, occupational therapist Refer to FS 5A page 103
Visual Becomes distracted by extraneous visual information, e.g. wall display, own or other children's work on table, cloakroom Is unable to identify relevant visual information from background	Limit distractions, ensure desk area is as uncluttered as possible Provide worksheets/books with small amounts of key information clearly presented/highlighted Provide designated work area/station, e.g. booth with enclosed sides and no visual distractions Heighten staff awareness	Seek advice from occupational therapist
Tactile Seeks or withdraws from physical contact Wriggles excessively as unable to tolerate clothing, materials Dislikes getting messy/does not notice mess on hands or face	Increase child's sensory input by providing 'fiddle' items, or warm up exercises before starting activity Be aware that deep pressure is more easily tolerated than light touch Respect child's personal space and be aware of consequences of personal contact Build up tolerance for messy activities gradually Heighten awareness of food around mouth, paint on hands	Seek advice from occupational therapist Refer to OTA 8 page 323
Oral Needs to constantly seek out something to chew, e.g. cuff/collar of sweater, finger nails, thumbs, pencils, water bottle tops Is overly sensitive/has reduced tolerance to certain smells	Be aware that child is seeking oral input to help him organise himself and concentrate Discuss with child appropriate and acceptable strategies Provide and allow child to have something suitable to chew throughout the day, e.g. tubing on pencil, sports water bottles, tubing, wrist band	Seek advice from occupational therapist Refer to OTA 8 page 323

Teacher observations of the child	Practical strategies	Further advice
SENSORY PROCESSING (Continued)		*Refer to Sensory processing Foundation Skills FS 1, FS 1A–FS 1E page 5, 11–27*
Proprioception Constantly fidgeting and moving to enhance his awareness of body position Slumps over table/desk Has poor body awareness Knocks into peers or furniture Unable to grade her movements and judge force	Give opportunities to have regular movement breaks Acknowledge need for physical movement at playtimes to enable her to sit and concentrate more readily later Allow plenty of opportunity for 'heavy' work Provide movin'sit cushion Consider implementing body awareness programme	Seek advice of occupational therapist Refer to OTA 8 page 323 Refer to Equipment Resources page 407 Refer to OTA 1 Page 249
PERCEPTION		*Refer to Visual perception Foundation Skills FS 4, FS 4A–FS 4F page 73, 77–97*
Has specific difficulties with certain aspects of perceptual tasks	Refer to specific sheet in Foundation Skills chapter once visual perceptual area has been identified	Refer to A 13 page 403
VISION AND OCULAR MOTOR CONTROL		*Refer to Vision and ocular motor control FS 3B page 63 and Visual processing FS 1E page 27*

Has difficulty with visual tracking and controlling eye movements:
 	
  Is unable to maintain focus on teacher/board
 	
  Finds copying from board hard
 	
  Has difficulty following text in book/paper
 	
  Is unable to make directional changes quickly
 	
  Perceives print as fuzzy/blurred
	Sit centrally in class facing front
	
	Give individual paper copy of instructions/work written on board
	
	Use reading guide or ruler below line of print/figures in columns
	
	Consider use of individual coloured overlay
	
	Provide regular breaks
	
	Consider providing extra time for child to complete task
		Seek advice from behavioural optometrist, occupational therapist
		
		Refer to A 10 page 395

COGNITIVE	Where possible ensure child works on a task which motivates, is achievable and provides opportunities for success When differentiating work ensure children are learning with their cognitive peer group	Seek advice from educational psychologist, advisory teacher Refer to A 1 page 361
Finds it hard to listen, think and carry out tasks at the same time	Heighten staff awareness and encourage adult mentoring	

Teacher observations of the child	Practical strategies	Further advice
COGNITIVE (Continued)		
	Help child to break task down into manageable/achievable chunks that he can think about planning and doing	Refer to A 11 page 397
	Ensure child has understood instructions accurately before he begins task	
	Use visual check list	
	Use thinking strategies, e.g. stop/think/do	
	Provide writing frames, mind mapping	
	Gain child's attention before starting task	
Has poor attention span: Appears distracted whilst listening	Break task down into small attainable targets	
	Provide visual cues/timetable, work system	Refer to A 14 page 405
	Use thinking skills/strategies	Refer to A 11 page 397
	Consider sensory issues, movement breaks	Refer to OTA 8 page 323
Has difficulty with short-term memory and sequencing tasks: Is able to remember information but cannot always select accurately the most relevant part on request	Use visual timetable/schedule	Refer to A 11 page 397
	Implement stop/think/do type strategies	
	Pre-plan task and provide adult support	
	Encourage mind mapping, writing frames	
	Use multi-sensory approaches to learning	Refer to OTA 4 page 271
Has immaturity of early learning skills: Has lots of ideas but finds it difficult to successfully complete task by being selective	Assess which foundation skills are in place	Seek advice from speech and language therapist, occupational therapist, educational psychologist
	Allow plenty of time to practice skills in small group or individual sessions	
	Ensure that child has learnt one stage before moving onto the next	Refer to A 1 page 361
	Be aware of need for constant reinforcement and over learning	

Teacher observations of the child	Practical strategies	Further advice
SELF-CARE		

Dresses slowly:
  Appears inattentive
  Shows poor organisation
  Rushes task
  May have a dishevelled appearance
	Use visual timetable to identify sequence for dressing
	Remind child to check appearance after changing
	Provide help when necessary
	Use timers
		Seek advice from occupational therapist
		Refer to OTA 6 page 315
		
		Refer to Equipment Resources page 407

Is unaware of road safety implications	Heighten awareness of adults and child, particularly at beginning and end of day, school trips Reinforce thinking skills such as think/plan/do Consider reinforcing Highway Code through multi-sensory learning	Refer to A 11 page 397

Rushes mealtimes:
  Becomes restless standing in lunch queue
  Appears inattentive with aspects of task
  Is unaware of having a messy mouth/hands/clothing after meals
	Consider behaviour management programme
	Ask child to stand at front/back of queue
	Heighten awareness of child's need for lunch time assistance
	Encourage child to routinely check that face/hands are clean
	Encourage child to use facecloth and wash hands after every meal
		Seek advice from behaviour support team, occupational therapist

Has difficulty telling the time and understanding the concept of time	Agree with child amount of work to be completed in given time frame Use visual support to show time concepts and sequences, e.g. visual timetables, work system, egg timers, digital timers, timed checklist, now/next boards Introduce behavioural strategies, e.g. star chart, reward charts Use large plastic clock with moveable hands	Refer to A 11 page 397, Equipment Resources page 407 Refer to Equipment Resources page 407
COMMUNICATION		*Refer to Auditory processing Foundation Skills FS 1D page 23 and Language Foundation Skills FS 5, FS 5A–FS 5D page 103–109*
Receptive language Has a range of difficulties in the area of understanding spoken language: Has problems focusing on and	Give clear concise instructions in small steps and check child has understood,	Seek advice from speech and language therapist, educational psychologist

Teacher observations of the child	Practical strategies	Further advice
COMMUNICATION (Continued)		*Refer to Auditory processing Foundation Skills FS 1D page 23 and Language Foundation Skills FS 5, FS 5A–FS 5D page 101, 101–109*
responding to relevant auditory information Does something different to what has been asked to do Starts activity but soon becomes distracted, may have heard first or last part of the instruction Appears disorganised, has difficulty selecting priorities for work Watches other children as a visual aid/reminder Has problems understanding grammatical structures Language/auditory processing difficulties may become more evident as the child gets older	Provide written prompts Use visual cues/timetables, break down activity into small steps	Refer to A 11 page 397
Expressive language Has a range of difficulties in the area of using spoken language: Speaks before she thinks Has fast/jumbled thoughts when speaking/writing Gives random introduction of topics and ideas Has word-finding difficulties Displays poor vocabulary	Teach child to stop and think before speaking, encourage child to self-check Encourage child to slow down and take time before speaking or writing Teach self-checking skills, encourage child to stop and think before speaking Encourage child to make notes of key points to help with sequencing and to maintain focus Pre-teach new vocabulary and teach new words in multi-sensory way to improve recall	Refer to A 11 page 397
Attention and listening Has difficulty focusing on spoken language when required to listen: Is unable to focus on spoken language in the presence of background noise and other distractions Has difficulty focusing on spoken language for prolonged amounts of time	Teach strategies to improve listening skills Keep tasks short to enable success Reduce extraneous background noises, consider withdrawing child to quiet area and give simplified instructions Heighten awareness of child's difficulty with focusing Provide adult support to aid with focusing and keeping on task Allow child to 'fiddle' with an agreed item Teach strategies to improve thinking skills	Refer to OTA 8 page 323 Refer to A 11 page 397

Building Blocks for Learning. © 2008 John Wiley & Sons Ltd.

Teacher observations of the child	Practical strategies	Further advice
SOCIAL AND EMOTIONAL ASPECTS		*Refer to Social and emotional aspects Foundation Skills FS 7 page 113*
Has difficulty forming and maintaining peer relationships: 　Does not recognise or acknowledge emotions in self and others 　Is unable to read non-verbal cues and emotional expressions	Use friendships as a topic in circle time Encourage friendship groups Facilitate Circle of Friends scheme and foster mentoring schemes Discuss situation with parent Facilitate attendance at after school clubs Implement initiatives to foster emotional literacy and social skills Use verbal reinforcement to explain non-verbal communication, e.g. I am feeling cross/sad Use social story™	Refer to A 9 page 389
Finds unstructured/unfamiliar situations difficult	Establish clear boundaries Ensure environment and task are as structured as possible Prepare child in advance for predictable changes, unstructured situations Consider adult/paired working Provide photos of new people/ places Use social story™	Refer to A 9 page 389
Has problems when working with others, e.g. team games, group work: 　Does not understand or follow social rules 　Is unable to share, take turns and listen to others	Implement social skills training programme and enhance emotional literacy Consider carefully choice of partner/group members Heighten staff awareness Foster mentoring schemes, Circle of Friends Facilitate attendance at after school clubs Use social story™	Refer to A 9 page 389
Displays inappropriate behaviour: 　May hum, tap, fiddle, fidget excessively 　Shows immature behaviours 　Can become antisocial or seek approval from unsuitable peer group	Undertake behaviour analysis to identify reasons for behaviour Consider using a behaviour management programme	Seek advice from educational psychologist, behavioural support, child and adolescent mental health, occupational therapist

Teacher observations of the child	Practical strategies	Further advice
SOCIAL AND EMOTIONAL ASPECTS (Continued)		*Refer to Social and emotional aspects Foundation Skills FS 7 page 113*
	Enhance emotional literacy	
	Allow child to 'fiddle' with an agreed object, e.g. Blu-Tack, stress balls and/or chew a pencil	Refer to OTA 8 page 323
	Use 'time out cards' and movement breaks	
	Implement social skills programme, model interactions, use role play	Refer to A 9 page 389
	Use social story™	

Displays low confidence/poor self-esteem as insight into difficulties develop:
 	
  Is shy and appears isolated from peers
 	
  Becomes unwilling to volunteer for tasks
 	
  Fears failure
	Implement initiatives to foster self-esteem
	
	Implement positive praise systems
	
	Facilitate Circle of Friends scheme, circle time approaches, foster friendship groups
	
	Liaise with parents
	
	Provide frequent opportunities for child to experience success and personal improvements
	
	Set realistic, attainable goals in tasks and praise for effort as well as achievement
	
	Discuss situation with parents
	
	Investigate clubs and groups which are prepared to accommodate child's need
		Refer to A 9 page 389

Uses diversion techniques in an attempt to avoid difficult tasks, e.g. going out to use toilet, forgetting equipment: Becomes class clown to cover up fact that skills are not at similar level with peers	Break down task into achievable steps and practice stages Discuss with child and parent, agree on goals and produce a contract Implement system for praising effort Discuss with child and parent alternative coping techniques Choose peers carefully when planning group work Facilitate Circle of Friends, use circle time approaches Implement initiatives to develop emotional literacy and social skills	Refer to A 9 page 389

Building Blocks for Learning. © 2008 John Wiley & Sons Ltd.

Teacher observations of the child	Practical strategies	Further advice
SOCIAL AND EMOTIONAL ASPECTS (Continued)		Refer to Social and emotional aspects Foundation Skills FS 7 page 113
Has mood swings—may be related to medication and sleep difficulties	Liaise with parents Heighten awareness of staff and child/peers as appropriate Reduce potential frustrations and anxieties Liaise with parents regarding situation Implement initiatives to develop anger/anxiety management and self-esteem Introduce use of time out cards when stressed or overwhelmed	Seek advice from school nurse, doctor involved, child and adolescent mental health service, educational psychologist Refer to A 9 page 389

Shows emotional difficulties:
  Experiences frustration, anger, anxiety and lowering of mood
  Has poor emotional regulation
	Discuss with parents and child
	
	Provide safe environment for child to discuss issues, have regular contact with designated member of staff
	
	Lessen potential frustrations and anxieties
	
	Enhance emotional literacy and social skills
	
	Implement initiatives to foster self-esteem, mood management and friendships
	
	Facilitate Circle of Friends scheme, circle time activities
	
	Implement initiatives to develop anger/anxiety management
	
	Introduce use of time out cards when stressed or overwhelmed
	
	Set up 'whole school environment' to enable child to achieve
		Seek advice from school nurse, doctor involved, child and adolescent mental health service, educational psychologist
		
		Refer to A 9 page 389

Difficulty regulating emotional responses:
  Becomes emotionally labile
  Cries easily, is easily hurt
  Over reacts to other children
  Uses physical force sometimes to express pent-up emotions
	Discuss management with parents
	
	Heighten staff awareness
	
	Facilitate Circle of Friends scheme, circle time activities
	
	Implement initiatives to foster self-esteem, mood management and friendships
		Refer to A 9 page 389

173

Teacher observations of the child	Practical strategies	Further advice
SOCIAL AND EMOTIONAL ASPECTS (Continued)		*Refer to Social and emotional aspects Foundation Skills FS 7 page 113*
	Enhance emotional literacy and develop social skills Identify tasks which motivate and are achievable and practise skills to facilitate integration with peers	
FURTHER CONSIDERATIONS		
Relationships within the family and parenting approaches can also influence how a child is performing within the school setting. It is therefore essential to consider all aspects of the child's life rather than just seeing school life in isolation. Children may be reluctant to take part in activities due to anticipated difficulties based on past failure. Often a parent will also have elements of the condition—they too may be disorganised and impulsive.	Provide regular contact with designated pastoral support/mentor so that family and school have consistent approach and can review priorities together. Ensure family have sufficient support and advice from key professionals.	

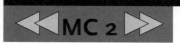
Autistic spectrum disorders, including Asperger's syndrome

The autistic spectrum disorders cover a broad range of behaviours. Many children diagnosed with autistic spectrum disorder seen in mainstream primary schools are likely to have Asperger's syndrome.

 How does the condition impact on the child?

The intensity of the core features can differ significantly from child to child and from one situation to another. The unevenness of features may affect a child's performance within the classroom to varying degrees, depending on the subject, the teaching methods used and the classroom environment. In addition, behaviour at home may vary, according to normal demands of family life, social relationships within the family and the environment. Children's behaviour and their ability to cope with everyday situations will vary within the day, from day to day and throughout the different stages of their life.

Children with Asperger's syndrome may have some of the following features in varying degrees of severity. Although the symptoms listed below are categorised, it is important to note these are interrelated and should not be considered in isolation.

Main presenting features

The child:

- Behaves inappropriately due to lack of understanding of social rules
- Fails to initiate contact with others
- Has difficulty establishing relationships with peers
- Prefers to be a loner or dominates play situations
- Lacks empathy
- Lacks spontaneity and flexibility
- Fails to share experiences
- Is considered 'odd' by teachers or peers
- Lacks insight of cause and effect
- Has superficial perfect expressive language but shows pedantic/ stereotypical speech

- Has abnormal intonation
- Uses abnormal/inappropriate language
- Understands things literally
- Lacks facial expression
- Has an abnormal gaze/gestures and 'odd' posturing
- Has difficulty with abstract concepts
- Concentrates intensely when engaged in his specialist interest/passion or certain topics
- Becomes obsessional about interests
- Has problems managing transitions and change

 Other possible associated features

Motor

The child:

- Looks awkward when walking, running, hopping, skipping, due to motor clumsiness
- Has problems joining in PE activities or pronounced difficulty with bat and ball games
- Writes with slow, untidy and laborious handwriting which is often late to develop and lacks flow or is meticulous with writing
- Has delays in developing self-care skills, e.g. using cutlery, fastening buttons, tying laces
- Manipulates tools poorly, e.g. scissors, rulers, compass

Organisation

The child:

- Loses equipment, books, letters, PE kit, etc., frequently
- Has difficulty with thinking flexibly, planning ahead and altering 'plan' in response to seemingly unpredictable or unexpected changes
- Is unable to learn instinctively/has difficulty generalising learnt skills to other areas
- Is unable to organise herself or organise work within her own environment
- Has little sense of time and priorities

Sensory

The child:

- Reacts adversely to a range of sensory stimulation
- Is unable to filter out extraneous noises, movements, excessive visual stimuli and may respond adversely
- Becomes easily distracted by everyday sensory stimulation

Cognitive

The child:

- Has a specific learning difficulty with a particular activity, e.g. reading, writing, drawing
- Memorises factual information with remarkable ease
- Has an excellent rote memory recollection of patterns
- Performs poorly when required to sequence
- Has average or above average intelligence
- Has a learning difficulty (mild, moderate, severe) making learning slower

Social/emotional

The child:

- Is prone to teasing by other children
- Becomes socially isolated
- Has difficulty waiting for turn, frequently interrupts
- Displays anxiety; has difficulty managing stress and frustration
- Is inclined towards depression
- Develops temper tantrums and rages, has mood swings/poor emotional regulation
- Has destructive behaviour arising from anger/frustration, not understanding the world around them

▷▷ What is the condition?

Asperger's syndrome is an autistic spectrum disorder and individuals with Asperger's syndrome are commonly described as having a triad of impairment in:

- Reciprocal social interaction/relationships
- Social communication
- Restricted activities and lack of flexibility

In order to be given a medical diagnosis of Asperger's syndrome the child needs to present with four features from the six categories listed below:

- Theory of mind
- Peer/social relationships
- Emotional regulation/recognition
- Rigidity of thought/routines/behaviours
- Sensory issues
- Motor clumsiness

Asperger's syndrome can often be seen with other co-existing conditions, such as attention deficit hyperactivity disorder (ADHD), developmental coordination disorder (DCD), Tourette's syndrome and specific learning difficulties. It can also put a child at risk of other emotional and behavioural problems such as mood and anxiety problems.

What causes it?

The precise cause of autistic spectrum disorder cannot yet be specified. Many experts believe that the pattern of behaviour from which an autistic spectrum disorder is diagnosed may not result from a single cause. It is considered to be a developmental disorder and a possible cause may include genetic fragility. 'Boys are three times more likely to be affected than girls, but it is not known why' (Gibson, 2004).

 ## What treatment could be offered?

No treatment has yet been proved to cure the condition of autistic spectrum disorder. Children may be offered different types of intervention to manage the 'non-understandable world'. The most common approaches are:

- Social skills training, understanding emotions
- Psychosocial/behaviour management—home and school
- Sensory processing advice/sensory programmes including sensory diets
- Adaptation of the environment
- Social Stories™; Comic Strip Conversations (Gray)
- Specific approaches, e.g. TEACCH, applied behavioural analysis
- Advice on learning approaches in school
- Understanding and managing emotions—anxiety, anger
- Specific skill teaching

 ## How will the child be affected in future?

Although the symptoms persist, children, can learn strategies to help modify their behaviour which parents and teachers can reinforce. Long-term effects on anxiety and reduced self-esteem may result in:

- Dropping out of school (school failure)
- Becoming socially isolated
- Limited life experiences

 ## Further information

The National Autistic Society Headquarters
393 City Road, London EC1V 1NG. Tel 0207 833 2299; Email nas@nas.org.uk; Website www.nas.org.uk; Helpline 0845 070 4004.

NAS Cymru, 6–7 Village Way
Greenmeadow Springs Business Park, Tongwynlais, Cardiff CF15 7NE. Tel 02920 629312; Email wales@nas.org.uk; Website www.nas.org.uk; Helpline 0845 070 4004.

NAS Scotland, Central Chambers
First floor, 109 Hope Street, Glasgow G2 6LL. Tel 0141 221 8090; Email scotland@nas.org.uk; Website www.nas.org.uk; Helpline 0845 070 4004.

NAS Northern Ireland
57a Botanic Avenue, Belfast BT7 1JL. Tel 028 902 36235; Email northern. ireland@nas.org.uk; Website www.nas.org.uk; ASD Teacher Resource Pack available on request. Information sheets/library/drop-in service available.

References

Attwood, T. (1998) *Asperger's Syndrome: a Guide for Parents and Professionals.* London, Jessica Kingsley.

Attwood, T. (2006) *Complete Guide to Asperger's Syndrome.* London, Jessica Kingsley.

Gibson, J. (2004) *Understanding Autistic Spectrum Disorders.* London, MIND.

National Autistic Society (2003) *What is Asperger's Syndrome?* London, National Autistic Society.

Schopler, E., Mesibor, G.B. & Hearsey, K. (1995) Structured Teaching in the TEACCH System. In: Schopler, E. and Mesibor, G.B. (eds) *Learning and Cognition in Autism.* New York, Plenum Press.

Vermeulen, P. (2000) *I am Special.* Jessica Kingsley, London.

Wing, L. & Gould, J. (1979) Severe impairments of social interaction and associated abnormalities in children: epidemiology and classification. *Journal of Autism and Childhood Schizophrenia,* 9, 11–29.

Further reading

Beswick, C. (2004) *Including Children with Autistic Spectrum Disorders (ASD) in the Foundation Stage.* Lutterworth, Featherstone Educational Limited.

Beswick, C. (2005) *Including Children with Asperger's Syndrome in the Foundation Stage.* Lutterworth, Featherstone Education Limited.

Bogdashina, O. (2003) *Sensory Perceptual Issues in Autism and Asperger Syndrome: Different Sensory Experiences- Different Perceptual Worlds.* London, Jessica Kingsley.

Clements, J. and Zarkowska, E. (1998) *Behavioural Concerns and Autistic Spectrum Disorders.* London, Jessica Kingsley.

Cumine, V., Leach, J. & Stevenson, G. (1998) *Asperger's Syndrome—a Practical Guide for Teachers.* London, Fulton.

Godwin Emmons, P. & McKendry Anderson, L. (2005) *Understanding Sensory Dysfunction, Learning Development and Sensory*

Dysfunction in Autism Spectrum Disorders ADHD, Learning Disabilities and Bipolar Disorder. London, Jessica Kingsley.

Grandin, T. (1995) *Thinking in Pictures.* New York, Doubleday.

Jordan, R. and Jones, G. (1999) *Meeting the Needs of Children with Autistic Spectrum Disorders.* London, Fulton.

Jordan, R. and Powell, S. (1995) *Understanding and Teaching Children with Autism.* Chichester, Wiley.

Nazeer, K. (2006) *Send in the Idiots: Stories from the other side of Autism.* London, Bloomsbury Publishing plc.

Reed, C.L. (2001) *Quick Reference to Occupational Therapy*, 2nd edn. Maryland, USA, Aspen Publishers.

Sainsbury, C. (2000) *Martian in the Playground.* Bristol, Lucky Duck Publishing.

Smith Myles, B. & Southwick, J. (1999) *Asperger Syndrome and Difficult Moments.* Kansas, USA, Autism Asperger Publishing Company.

Smith-Myles, B. (2000) *Asperger Syndrome and Sensory Issues—Practical Solutions for Making Sense of the World.* Shawnee Misson, Kansas, Autism Asperger Publishing Co.

Yack, E., Aquilla, P. & Sutton, S. (2002) *Building Bridges Through Sensory Integration—Therapy for Children with Autism and other Pervasive Developmental Disorders.* Las Vegas, Sensory Resources.

>> Further resources

Team Asperger (2000) *Gaining Faces.* CD-ROM for teaching people to interpret facial expression. Appleton, WI, USA, Team Asperger. Gaining Face has been purchased by Stone Mountain Software of Bel Aire, KS, and is available from public@StonemountainSoftware.com

Dixon, J. (2006) *ISPEEK at Home.* Over 1300 Visual Communication Images. London, Jessica Kingsley.

Dixon, J. (2006) *ISPEEK at School.* Over 1300 Visual Communication Images. London, Jessica Kingsley.

The Transporters(™) (DVD) (2006) *Transporters Discover the World of Emotions.* Ashton-under-Lyne, UK, Catalyst Pictures Ltd. Commissioned by Culture Online, produced by Catalyst Pictures with the Autism Research Centre at Cambridge University.

>> Useful websites

www.do2learn.com
www.grodencenter.com
www.ispeek.co.uk
www.sensorystories.com
www.socialthinking.com
www.teacch.com
www.thegraycenter.org
www.tonyattwood.com.au

![Teacher observations icon] Teacher observations of the child	![Practical strategies icon] Practical strategies	![Further advice icon] Further advice
Children diagnosed with autistic spectrum disorder will present with varying degrees of need, depending on the severity of their condition. The teacher observations mentioned below may not all be relevant.	Practical strategies should be targeted for the individual child after analysis of the teacher's observations. It will then be important to decide whether the behaviour needs to be managed or changed.	To implement the further advice it may be necessary to discuss the concerns and issues with the special educational needs coordinator.
OBSERVED BEHAVIOURS		
Tends towards routines, rituals and obsessions	Consider behaviour management programmes/strategies Use social skills training programme	Seek advice from advisory team for Asperger's syndrome, clinical psychologist Refer to A 9 page 389
Has difficulty coping with changes in routine: Becomes anxious, upset and agitated Has temper tantrums, as unable to predict new task Becomes rigid in outlook, unwilling to 'give it a go'	Prepare child for change before it happens Adhere as much as possible to established routines, and where not possible give extra preparation Rehearse changed routines, e.g. how to get to new location in advance Use visual timetable to inform child of predicted changes Encourage child to pre-plan change and reinforce by talking it through Build in flexibility to system	Seek advice from advisory team for Asperger's syndrome, child and adolescent mental health service, educational psychologist Refer to A 9 page 389, A 11 page 397
Has inappropriate behaviour due to lack of understanding of social rules	Use social story™ Heighten staff and peers awareness	Refer to A 9 page 389
Has difficulty coping with unstructured and/or unfamiliar situations	Provide a clear structure and inform child of changes in advance Use work system and visual schedule Provide photos of new people/places, etc.	Refer to A 9 page 389, A 14 page 405
Does not always respond to sanctions	Provide clear, concise, consistent and visual expectations of desired behaviour Use social story™	Seek advice from advisory team for Asperger's syndrome Refer to A 9 page 389
Becomes off task, distractible and has difficulty sustaining attention	Implement behaviour management programme, e.g. star charts, behaviour charts Recognise the need for frequently providing positive praise Set short, attainable goals and give regular breaks Negotiate and agree on a time span for working on specific tasks, e.g. use timers	Seek advice from educational psychologist, advisory team for Asperger's syndrome, child and adolescent mental health service, occupational therapist, specialist speech and language therapist

Teacher observations of the child	Practical strategies	Further advice
OBSERVED BEHAVIOURS (Continued)		
	Limit distractions—only essential items in work area	Refer to FS 5A page 103
	Use work systems and visual schedules	
	Consider using an individual work station	
	Give frequent teacher feedback and redirection	
	Obtain child's attention by using agreed non-verbal cues	
	Use time out card/system/work system including start/finish boxes	Refer to A 11 page 397, A 14 page 405

Fluctuates in performance:
   Is distractible during study
   Becomes frequently off task
   Has difficulty sustaining attention
   Lacks persistence in activities
   Has problems initiating task
	Give frequent positive teacher feedback and redirection	Seek support from educational psychologist, child and adolescent mental health service, occupational therapist

	Consider behaviour management programme	
	Set short attainable goals in collaboration with child	
	Give one-to-one encouragement at start of task	
	Limit distractions—only essential items in work area/work stations	Refer to FS 1E page 27, FS 5A page 103
	Consider child's position in class	
	Use work systems and visual schedules	Refer to A 14, page 405 A 11 page 397
	Give realistic targets of quantity of work expected	
Has inappropriate responses to sensory input (auditory, visual, tactile, taste, smell): Has difficulty filtering out inputs and then refocusing on task, e.g. unable to ignore irrelevant background noise	Undertake behavioural observation/ analysis to determine sensory needs, agree clear behavioural guidelines for appropriate use	Seek advice from occupational therapist, advisory team for Asperger's syndrome
	Discuss with parent sensory issues and implement sensory strategies/diet after discussion with occupational therapist	Refer to FS 1 page 5, OTA 8 page 323
	Heighten staff awareness that child may over or under-react to 'normal' auditory, visual, tactile, taste, smell, e.g. the buzz of equipment, fluorescent lighting, room with echo, school bell, textures, materials and touch	
	Reduce distracting background stimuli, e.g. background noise, pencils on desk, crowded wall displays	Refer to FS 5A page 103, FS 1D page 23, FS 1E page 27

	Practical strategies	Further advice
OBSERVED BEHAVIOURS (Continued)		
	Negotiate and agree on a time within child's work schedule for 'sensory session' or 'fiddle' items to be used, use sensory stories	Refer to OTA 8 page 323, FS 1 page 5
	Prepare child in advance of predictable noises, e.g. bell	
	Consider position in class	
Tends to interrupt	Use social skills training programme	Refer to FS 5 page 101, A 9 page 389
	Consider behaviour management programme	
	Undertake behavioural observation/ analysis to determine reason, agree clear behavioural guideline	
	Place visual guide on desk	
	Use comic strip conversations	
Has inappropriate movements which often become more pronounced under stress or excitement: Displays stereotyped movement patterns, handclapping, rocking	Consider behaviour management programme, reduce stress	Seek advice from advisory team for Asperger's syndrome
	Use social skills training programme	Refer to A 9 page 389
	Provide clear, concise and consistent expectations of desired behaviour	
	Negotiate and agree on a time within child's work schedule for 'inappropriate movements'	Refer to OTA 8 page 323
Has difficulty starting work and cannot stop until completely finished	Clarify expectations, e.g. structured information on what child to achieve, use work systems, visual schedules	Refer to A 9 page 389, A 11 page 397, A 14 page 405
	Set short, attainable goals and give regular breaks	
	Use timers	Refer to Equipment Resources page 407
GROSS MOTOR COORDINATION		*Refer to Gross motor coordination Foundation Skills FS 2, FS 2A–FS 2E page 31, 35–51*
Has poor or unusual posture, e.g. slouching or rigid	Encourage appropriate seating— check table/chair size/height	Refer to OTA 4 page 271
Lacks fluent movements/may be rigid	Break down task and practice individual stages	Refer to A 7 page 381, OTA 10 page 333
	Work on developing and putting rhythm into tasks	
	Consider implementing a programme for body awareness	OTA 1 page 249

Teacher observations of the child	Practical strategies	Further advice
GROSS MOTOR COORDINATION (Continued)		*Refer to Gross motor coordination Foundation Skills FS 2, FS 2A–FS 2E page 31, 35–51*
Unable to judge distances and speed due to poor spatial concepts	Explore alternative PE/games options which can be systematically taught, e.g. swimming	Refer to OTA 1 page 249, OTA 10 page 333, A 7 page 381
Has difficulty participating in team games, e.g. interpreting rules, social interaction, varying nature of games, turn taking	Explore alternative PE/games options which can be systematically taught, e.g. swimming Give clear and precise explanation of the expectation of the players and rules of the game Explore alternative PE/games options which are more predictable and not team based	Refer to OTA 1 page 249, OTA 10 page 333, A 7 page 381 Refer to A 9 page 389
Dislikes physical contact or has reduced awareness of physical space	Use social skills training programme Give guidance on personal space 'rules'	Refer to A 9 page 389
Has poor coordination of eye/hand/foot, has difficulty catching/kicking	Identify specific difficulty and practice skill Heighten awareness of teacher and peers to child's difficulty	Refer to A 7 page 381, OTA 10 page 333

Unable to sequence and organise movements:
  Unable to plan tasks
  Unable to anticipate, plan and respond whilst participating in any activity
  Has fixed ideas of how to approach task
	Encourage child to pre-plan task
	Provide verbal and physical prompts.
	Reduce amount of prompts as child's abilities improve
	Use visual supports—stop/think/do work system
	Heighten staff awareness to importance of giving clear, detailed yet concise instructions
		Refer to OTA 9 page 327
		
		Refer to A 11 page 397, A 14 page 405

FINE MOTOR CONTROL		*Refer to Fine motor control Foundation Skills FS 3, FS 3A–3C page 55, 59–69*

Finds handwriting challenging:
  Has impaired pen grasp and uses variable pressure which hampers sustained written output
  Takes longer than his peers to learn basic skills
  Has undecided hand dominance
  Has difficulty acquiring basic letter formation
  Reverses and inverts letters or forms them poorly
  Writes letters in variable size with poor spacing and positioning
	Use specific handwriting schemes, e.g. Write from the Start, Handwriting Without Tears, Write Dance and practise daily to establish pattern
	Teach correct pencil grasp/use pen grips but may need to accept 'awkward' pen grasps and reduced speed
	Teach through a multi-sensory approach
		Refer to OTA 4 page 271, A 4 page 373, A 5 page 375, A 12 page 401
		
		Refer to Equipment Resources page 407

Teacher observations of the child	Practical strategies	Further advice
FINE MOTOR CONTROL (Continued)		*Refer to Fine motor control Foundation Skills FS 3, FS 3 A–3C page 55, 59–69*
Does not sit letters on the line Has untidy work, due to excessive crossing out and correcting Puts variable pressure on writing tool Has not fully established hand-writing as an automatic skill	Use visual prompts, e.g. coloured lines, traffic lights to mark start and finish of line Ensure 'building blocks' are fully learnt, before moving onto next stage of writing Accept that quantity of written work will be reduced, so set attainable goals Consider alternative recording methods, e.g. ICT, part prepared worksheets Teach touch typing and provide regular daily practice	Refer to A 6 page 379, OTA 5 page 305 Refer to Equipment Resources page 407
Has not developed age appropriate manipulative skills, e.g. scissors, compass	Break down task and practise specific skill Provide regular practice session to develop mature manipulative skills Practice skill at child's level of ability Trial alternative equipment, adapt grasp as necessary Heighten awareness of safety issues and undertake risk assessment as appropriate	Refer to A 1 page 361, OTA 7 page 319, OTA 3 page 259, OTA 10 page 333 Refer to Equipment Resources page 407
Unable to share equipment	Explain which items to be shared and by whom Use social skills training programme	Refer to A 9 page 389
ORGANISATION		*Refer to Introduction to organisation Foundation Skills FS 6 page 111*
Cannot negotiate way around school or outside in playground	Practise route to new classrooms/ subject areas prior to year transition Provide child with map Allow child to leave class early to miss crowded corridors, provide appropriate supervision	Refer to OTA 9 page 327, A 9 page 389

Has poor ability to organise self and task:
 	
   Unaware of expectations
 	
   Misconstrues the meaning of instructions
 	
   Has limited problem solving skills
	Give clear expectations and ensure child understands them
	
	Consider use of work system, visual timetable/schedules
		Refer to A 11 page 397, A 14 page 405

⟨⟨Teacher observations of the child⟩⟩	⟨⟨Practical strategies⟩⟩	⟨⟨Further advice⟩⟩
ORGANISATION (Continued)		*Refer to Organisation Foundation Skills FS 6 page 111*
	Break down task and set attainable goals	
	Use strategies, e.g. personal time-tables, schedules, checklists, calendars, pictorial clues	Refer to OTA 9 page 327
	Use checklists to ensure only essential items in work area	
	Set up colour coded filing system within school bag	
	Clearly label job, e.g. homework, to do, finished	
	Help and encourage child to pre-plan task to ensure all equipment is available for task	
	Use behaviour management programmes, behaviour star charts	
	Liaise with family/carers regarding consistent strategies to help develop routines	
Difficulty completing homework: 　Does not fully understand task before going home 　Does not record task properly in homework diary 　Takes much longer than allocated time to complete task 　Has excessive tiredness once home due to extra physical exertion at school for all tasks 　Has unrealistic task set by teacher	Discuss reason with child and parents Set realistic goals and agree expectations with child and parent, agree on a maximum amount of time to be spent on homework each day, draw up a contract Consider use of system for recording homework, explain expectations to child and parents Discuss strategies with child and parent, e.g. use of computer, parent to scribe, dictaphone, quality versus quantity Use work system Use school homework club Allow time for out of school activities	Refer to OTA 9 page 327, A 11 page 397 Refer to A 6 page 379, OTA 5 page 305 Refer to A 14 page 405
Has reduced concept of time and urgency: 　Becomes absorbed in activity and finds it hard to stop 　Needs to complete task before doing next activity	Teach coping strategies, e.g. use alarms on watches, timer, timed checklists Plan/check weekly timetable with adult support	Refer to Equipment Resources page 407 Refer to OTA 9 page 327

Building Blocks for Learning. © 2008 John Wiley & Sons Ltd.

Teacher observations of the child	Practical strategies	Further advice
ORGANISATION (Continued)		*Refer to Organisation Foundation Skills FS 6 page 111*
	Use work system, thinking strategies/skills Monitor working in unstructured situations	Refer to A 11 page 397, A 14 page 405
Changes slowly for PE	Allow extra time; start before rest of class Discuss with parents possibilities for alternative clothing within constraints of uniform policy Use visual timetable to identify sequence of clothing and raise child's awareness if clothes are on back to front/inside out Practise self-care skills	Refer to OTA 6 page 315 Refer to A 11 page 397
Has difficulty hanging coat on peg, placing books in bag, clearing lunch box away	Provide peg on end of row, pack books in class, develop routine for lunch time Use visual timetable, cue cards Practice specific tasks, use over learning techniques	 Refer to A 11 page 397
Has inappropriate sense of danger/ no sense of danger.	Raise child's awareness of danger concerns Heighten staff awareness and undertake risk assessment if appropriate Use paired working/adult support Consider use of safety checklists Get adult to monitor unstructured situations	Refer to A 9 page 389, A 11 page 397 Refer to school health and safety policy

Unable to generalise skills:
 	
  Unable to transfer skills to competently achieve similar task
 	
  Becomes very frustrated and aware that they are unable to keep up with their peers although cognitively able
 	
  Requires longer to learn skill for task, but once learnt able to competently perform, e.g. catching a ball
	Break down task and work on specific skill areas then link them with similar tasks
	
	Encourage pre-planning
	
	Provide extra adult support to practise skill
	
	Teach each new task separately
	
	Teach 'splinter skills'
	
	Ensure child works on a task which motivates her
		
		Refer to A 11 page 397, OTA 9 page 327

Teacher observations of the child	**Practical strategies**	**Further advice**
ORGANISATION (Continued)		*Refer to Organisation Foundation Skills FS 6 page 111*

Has difficulty in formulating a plan of action when attempting new task:
 	
   Knows what is required, but unable to complete task
 	
   Is unsatisfied with end result
 	
   Is slow to start task and often work is incomplete
 	
   Becomes muddled and frustrated with own performance
	Use activity analysis approach and breakdown task into easy stages, use work system
	
	 Provide written or visual step-by-step instructions
	
	 Encourage child to pre-plan activity before she starts task
	
	 Talk through ideas
	
	 Give written plan as well as verbal instructions
	
	 Formulate a plan of action
		Refer to A 11 page 397, OTA 9 page 327

Has difficulty managing equipment, materials, books, etc., needed for school day	Use checklists; liaise with parents	Refer to OTA 9 page 327
SENSORY PROCESSING		*Refer to Sensory processing Foundation Skills FS 1, FS 1A–FS 1E page 5, 11–27*
Auditory Unable to identify relevant information through background noises Has difficulty understanding and responding to instructions Becomes distractible with noise Reacts adversely to noise	Consider providing a quiet area where child can work Use headphones if appropriate Speak more slowly and use simple phrases Limit unnecessary background noises Allow extra time when communicating with child Prepare child in advance of predictable loud noise Allow child to 'fiddle' with agreed item	Seek advice from speech and language therapist, occupational therapist, advisory team for Asperger's syndrome Refer to FS 5A page 103, FS 1D page 23 Refer to OTA 8 page 323
Visual Unable to identify relevant visual information from background Becomes distracted by extraneous visual information within her field of vision, e.g. wall displays, other children's work on table, children walking across room Has difficulty working in certain lighting conditions, e.g. fluorescent lighting, glare from sun, interactive whiteboard	Heighten staff awareness Provide books/worksheets with small amounts of information clearly presented Ensure desk area is uncluttered Provide designated work station, e.g. booth with no distracting visual information and enclosed sides	Seek advice from occupational therapist, advisory team for Asperger's syndrome Refer to FS 1E page 27

Teacher observations of the child	Practical strategies	Further advice
SENSORY PROCESSING (Continued)		*Refer to Sensory processing Foundation Skills FS 1, FS 1A–FS 1E page 5, 11–27*
Tactile Hates getting messy/does not notice mess on hands or face Dislikes being touched Wriggles constantly as unable to tolerate clothing/materials/textures	Gradually build up tolerance for messy activities Heighten awareness of food around mouth, paint on hands, etc. Respect child's personal space and be aware of consequences of personal contact Be aware that deep pressure is more easily tolerated than light touch	Seek advice from occupational therapist Refer to OTA 8 page 323, A 9 page 389
Oral Needs to constantly seek out something to chew, e.g. cuff/collar of sweater, finger nails, thumbs, pencils Has soreness around mouth due to constantly licking lips	Be aware that child is seeking oral input to help organise and concentrate Discuss with child appropriate and acceptable strategies	Seek advice from occupational therapist Refer to OTA 8 page 323
Proprioception Constantly fidgeting and moving to enhance his awareness of body position Slumps over table/desk Has poor body awareness Knocks into peers or furniture Unable to grade his movements and judge force	Give opportunities to have regular movement breaks Acknowledge need for physical movement at playtimes to enable him to sit and concentrate more readily later Allow plenty of opportunity for 'heavy' work Provide movin'sit cushion Consider implementing body awareness programme	Seek advice of occupational therapist Refer to OTA 8 page 323 Refer to Equipment Resources page 407 Refer to OTA 1 page 249
PERCEPTION		*Refer to Visual perception Foundation Skills FS 4, FS 4A–FS 4F page 73, 77–97*
Has specific difficulties with certain aspects of perceptual tasks	Refer to specific sheet in Foundation Skills chapter once visual perceptual area has been identified	
VISION AND OCULAR MOTOR CONTROL		*Refer to Vision and ocular control Foundation Skills FS 3B and Visual processing Foundation Skills FS 1E page 27*
Has difficulty with visual tracking and controlling eye movements: Is unable to maintain focus on teacher/board	Provide regular breaks Consider providing extra time for child to complete task	Seek advice from behavioural optometrist, occupational therapist

Teacher observations of the child	Practical strategies	Further advice
VISION AND OCULAR MOTOR CONTROL (Continued)		*Refer to Vision and ocular control Foundation Skills FS 3B page 63 and Visual processing Foundation Skills FS 1E page 27*
Finds copying from board hard Cannot follow text in book/paper Is unable to make directional changes quickly Perceives print as fuzzy or blurred	Sit child centrally, directly facing teacher/board Check if child has glasses and should be wearing them Enlarge print Provide visual breaks Give paper copy or use small individual whiteboard on desk Use overlay with window or line tracker to minimise visual text	Refer to A 10 page 395 Refer to Equipment Resources page 407
COGNITIVE	Ensure child works on a task which motivates, is achievable and provides opportunities for success, whenever possible Differentiate work to ensure child is learning with others of similar age and ability	Seek advice from educational psychologist, advisory teacher Refer to A 1 page 361
Has an uneven cognitive profile	Heighten awareness of child's difficulty when demonstrating her knowledge on paper Use writing frames, part prepared worksheets and mind mapping techniques Give table top copy of information written on interactive whiteboard/ board with key information highlighted	Seek advice from educational psychologist Refer to A 11 page 397 Refer to OTA 4 page 271
SELF-CARE		
Has difficulty with daily living tasks: Has poor grasp and cutting action when using cutlery Dresses slowly, difficulty with fastenings, has a dishevelled general appearance Eats a restricted diet, inclined to be messy Has problems standing in lunch queue	Provide help where necessary Stand at front/back of queue or go early for lunch Raise awareness of need for child to cut up own food where possible Use plate with lip and non-slip mat Trial Caring Cutlery Implement social skills/life skills training programme Allow extra time to complete activity, e.g. changing for PE	Seek advice from occupational therapist Refer to Equipment Resources page 407 Refer to A 9 page 389

![Teacher observations icon] Teacher observations of the child	![Practical strategies icon] Practical strategies	![Further advice icon] Further advice
SELF-CARE (Continued)		
	Check shoes on correct feet, clothes right way round and tucked in, remind child to check appearance after changing, adapt fastenings, discuss with parents and child the possibility of wearing alternative clothing, e.g. polo shirts	Refer to OTA 6 page 315, Equipment Resources page 407
	Use visual timetable to identify sequence of clothing and raise child's awareness, if clothes on back to front or inside out	Refer to A 11 page 397
	Practise individual skills, e.g. buttons, tying laces, tying tie	
	Use visual schedules/social story™	Refer to A 9 page 389
Is reluctant to undertake personal hygiene routines, e.g. toileting, due to ritual obsessions	Consider behaviour management programme Provide visual system, sequencing cues Implement social skills training programme Use social story™	Seek advice from advisory team for Asperger's syndrome, clinical psychologist, school nurse/doctor Refer to A 9 page 389
Eats a restricted diet due to being a 'faddy' eater	Discuss situation with parents Encourage a balanced diet	Seek advice from dietician, speech and language therapist, occupational therapist, CAMHS
Has poor road safety awareness	Heighten awareness of adults and child, particularly at beginning and end of day, school trips	Seek advice from advisory team for Asperger's syndrome
	Reinforce thinking strategies, such as stop/think/do	Refer to A 11 page 397
	Consider reinforcing Highway Code through multi- sensory learning	
COMMUNICATION		*Refer to Auditory processing Foundation Skills FS 1D page 23 and Language Foundation Skills FS 5, FS 5A–FS 5D page 101, 103–109*

Receptive language
Has a range of difficulties in the area of understanding spoken language:
  Has difficulty following instructions
  Has difficulty understanding vocabulary
	Break down instructions into small chunks and allow time in between to respond
	Check that child has understood instructions
		Seek advice from speech and language therapist, advisory team for Asperger's syndrome

Teacher observations of the child	Practical strategies	Further advice
COMMUNICATION (Continued)		*Refer to Auditory processing Foundation Skills FS 1D page 23 and Language Foundation Skills FS 5, FS 5A–FS 5D page 101,103–109*
Has difficulty learning the meaning of concepts, e.g. same/different, first/last, big/little, some/all Has difficulty understanding time and sequence Has literal interpretation of language such as idioms, sarcasm Has understanding limited to explicitly stated information	Use written/pictorial support as appropriate, e.g. photos, symbols, written word, diagrams Give unambiguous instructions Encourage child to ask for clarification when necessary Use a variety of practical examples and visual support when introducing new concepts Make explicit links between how vocabulary is used in different subjects Use word webs to make links between vocabulary with similar meanings, e.g. subtract, minus, take away Use visual support to show time concepts and sequences, e.g. visual timetables, egg timers, digital timers, now/next boards, work system Clarify words that have a double meaning and explain metaphors	Refer to A11 page 397, A14 page 405, Equipment Resources page 407

Expressive language
Has a range of difficulties in the area of using spoken language:
  Has little or no spoken language
  Uses learnt phrases and echoed language
  Has repetitive questioning
  Has difficulty retrieving known vocabulary
  Has poor organisation of spoken language
  Has formal/pedantic language
	Use signing, pictures, alternative and augmentative communication system, e.g. Picture Exchange Communication System (PECS) on advice from speech and language therapist
	
	Model use of language
	
	Teach vocabulary specific to school routine and curriculum subjects
	
	Use visual support to structure language, e.g. story telling
	
	Provide word banks
		Seek advice from speech and language therapist

Social communication Uses language well but has difficulty adjusting it to a social context Has difficulty approaching others and initiating communication	Promote turn-taking by small group Consider visual prompt cards Instigate role play for social situations	Seek advice from advisory team for Asperger's syndrome, speech and language therapist

Teacher observations of the child	Practical strategies	Further advice
COMMUNICATION (Continued)		*Refer to Auditory processing Foundation Skills FS 1D page 23 and Language Foundation Skills FS 5, FS 5A–FS 5D page 101, 103–109*
Finds turntaking difficult; may interrupt or talk over others Tends to talk on one topic with limited awareness of listener's interest level Makes irrelevant comments focusing on specific details Is insensitive or makes socially inappropriate comments	Use social skills training, e.g. Social Use of Language Programme Use social scripts Provide comic strip conversations Use social story™	Refer to A 9 page 389
Non-verbal communication Has difficulties making eye contact Has difficulties understanding and using facial expression and tone of voice Fails to recognise the subtleties of body language May have odd intonation Has difficulty understanding personal space	Encourage, but do not force, eye contact Use verbal reinforcement to explain non-verbal communication, e.g. I am feeling sad/cross Use visual support, e.g. emotion pictures Give specific teaching of non-verbal communication	Seek advice from advisory team for Asperger's syndrome, speech and language therapist Refer to A 9 page 389
SOCIAL AND EMOTIONAL ASPECTS		*Refer to Introduction to social and emotional aspects Foundation Skills FS 7 page 113*
Has difficulty forming and maintaining peer relationships: Has reduced awareness of personal space Demonstrates difficulty with empathy and demonstrating emotions Lacks subtlety and is frequently naive	Use friendships as a topic in circle time Encourage friendship groups Provide social skills training programme Facilitate Circle of Friends scheme Foster mentoring schemes Discuss with parent Facilitate attendance at after school clubs Use social story™	Refer to A 9 page 389
Is unable to cope with unstructured situations Becomes stressed due to inflexibility Is unable to tolerate making a mistake	Establish clear boundaries Ensure environment and task are as structured as possible Consider adult/paired working Implement approaches aimed at coping strategies	Seek advice from advisory team for Asperger's syndrome Refer to A 9 page 389

193

Teacher observations of the child	Practical strategies	Further advice
SOCIAL AND EMOTIONAL ASPECTS (Continued)		Refer to Introduction to social and emotional aspects Foundation Skills FS 7 page 113
Has problems working with others, e.g. team games, group work: Is unable to perceive that there may be different points of view, due to inflexible thinking Has difficulty separating fact from opinion, 'shades of grey'	Implement social skills training programme Consider choice of partner/group members carefully Heighten staff awareness Foster mentoring schemes Use social story™	Refer to A 9 page 389
Displays inappropriate behaviour, e.g. student may hum, tap, fiddle: Treats everybody equally, e.g. family or strangers Prone to teasing	Discuss situation with parents Undertake behaviour analysis to identify potential reasons Consider use of behaviour management programme Use time out cards and movement breaks Use social skills programme Allow student to 'fiddle' with an agreed object, e.g. Blu-Tack, stress balls and/or chew a pencil	Seek advice from advisory team for Asperger's syndrome, occupational therapist Refer to A 9 page 389 Refer to OTA 8 page 323
Lacks confidence, self-esteem and self-image: Becomes frustrated quickly Opts out of task Has limited self-awareness Is prone to teasing and bullying	Implement self-esteem programme Provide positive praise systems Foster friendship groups Facilitate Circle of Friends scheme Use social groups to build up esteem Liaise with parents Use social story™	Refer to A 9 page 389
Has emotional difficulties: Shows anxiety, sense of failure, frustration, anger Has poor emotional regulation, mood swings, rages, low mood/depression, feelings of persecution	Liaise with parents Lessen potential frustrations and anxieties Foster friendship groups Implement initiatives to foster self-esteem Implement social skills group Facilitate Circle of Friends scheme, circle time activities Implement anger/anxiety management, time out cards when under stress or overwhelmed Use social story™	Seek advice from school nurse/doctor, child and adolescent mental health service, educational psychologist Refer to A 9 page 389

![Teacher observations icon] Teacher observations of the child	![Practical strategies icon] Practical strategies	![Further advice icon] Further advice
SOCIAL AND EMOTIONAL ASPECTS (Continued)		Refer to Social and emotional aspects Foundation Skills FS 7 page 113
Exaggerated behaviour, due to constantly living in stressful situation	Provide safe environment for child to discuss issues Consider regular contact with designated pastoral support member of staff or mentor	Seek advice from school nurse/doctor, child and adolescent mental health service, educational psychologist
FURTHER CONSIDERATIONS		
Relationships within the family and parenting approaches can also influence how a child is performing within the school setting. It is therefore essential to consider all aspects of the child's life rather than just seeing school life in isolation. Sometimes a parent will also have elements of the condition—they too may be disorganised and take things literally.	Provide regular contact with designated pastoral support/mentor so that family and school have consistent approach and can review priorities together as well as note how child may present differently at home and school. Ensure family have sufficient support and advice from key professionals.	

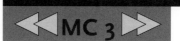
Cerebral palsy

 How does the condition impact on the child?

Children with cerebral palsy can vary enormously; no two children are the same. Some will go on to university; others may have learning difficulties. Some will be independent; others may need full-time support for learning, leisure and self-care. While some children are mildly affected, others will have difficulty talking, walking, using their hands, eating, going to the toilet and sitting without support. However mildly or severely they are affected, the school curriculum needs to ensure maximum participation and inclusion.

Many children with cerebral palsy may present with a combination of the following features, in varying degrees of severity. Children may be able to make specific movement, but the quality and fluidity of the movement may be affected.

Gross motor

The child:

- Displays spasms in muscles/increased or decreased postural tone
- Makes slow, awkward or jerky movements
- Experiences an associated reaction upon movement/activity; one movement often results in unwanted movements in another part of the body
- Has reduced stamina/fatigues, as has little reserves of energy
- Has reduced movement at some joints
- Experiences muscle weakness
- Walks in an uncoordinated pattern
- Uses a walker, stick, crutches or wheelchair for mobility; or uses a combination of aids
- Is wheelchair dependent, uses a self-propelling or powered chair
- Has specialist equipment, e.g. standing frame, supportive seating
- Finds transitional movements hard, e.g. getting up from chair or from sitting to standing

Fine motor

The child:

- Displays abrupt, jerky hand movements
- Experiences tightness of upper limb(s), fisting of hands, bending of elbows/low tone floppy limbs, loose joints

- Experiences muscle weakness
- Has spasm in muscles
- Is unable to manipulate equipment appropriately
- Is unable to perform self-help tasks at an age appropriate level
- Finds eye-hand coordination tasks difficult
- Has problems using both hands together

Perception

The child:

- Has reduced concentration/is easily distracted from task
- Has underdeveloped or disordered visual perceptual skills, problems learning letter shapes
- Has problems distinguishing or comparing shapes/size and visual sequences
- Has poor body and spatial awareness, finds sitting on carpet for circle time is difficult
- Is unable to follow a sequence of verbal or visual instructions
- Has impaired visual/auditory processing skills
- Has no visual perceptual difficulties

Cognition

The child:

- Displays poor memory skills
- Shows poor problem solving skills
- Is of average or above average intelligence
- Experiences learning difficulty (mild, moderate, severe) making learning slower
- Has a specific learning difficulty with a particular activity, e.g. reading, writing, drawing

Sensory

The child:

- Has disturbed sensory processing/perceptions—can be at risk of hurting herself as she shows less awareness of pain, often does not recognise extremes in temperature, may be over or under sensitive to noise, light, touch or taste
- Is unable to filter out extraneous noises, movements, excessive visual stimuli
- Is easily distracted by everyday sensory stimulation, e.g. radio, TV in background, interactive whiteboards, 'busy' displays on walls
- Reacts adversely to different textures/clothing/materials/carpet pile, e.g. labels, seams, fur fabrics, prickly floor covering

Social/emotional

The child:

- Has reduced concentration
- Shows low self-esteem

- Is tolerant of adult support
- Has learnt dependency on others
- Likes to be treated similar to peers
- Displays temper tantrums, anger
- Finds coming to terms with disability difficult, becomes frustrated
- Has difficulty establishing relationships with peer group, becomes socially isolated

Other possible associated problems

The child:

- Has difficulty understanding and processing what is said to them
- Talks to others with lack of clarity and poor speech content
- Finds chewing and swallowing hard, needs extra time for eating and drinking
- Experiences constipation
- Has poor general toileting awareness/may suffer from incontinence
- Experiences poor sleep patterns
- Has visual difficulties, or visual field deficits

 What is this condition?

'Cerebral palsy describes a group of disorders of the development of movement and posture causing activity limitation . . .the motor disorders of cerebral palsy are often accompanied by disturbances of sensation, cognition, communication, perception and/or behaviour' (British Association of Bobath trained therapists newsletter, 2006).

 What is the cause?

Cerebral palsy is caused by damage to the brain before, during or after birth while the brain is still developing, although it may not become obvious until early childhood. 'It is often not possible for doctors to give an exact reason why part of a baby's brain has been injured or failed to develop, as there may be no obvious single reason why a child has cerebral palsy. The causes of cerebral palsy can be multiple and complex. Some studies suggest that cerebral palsy is mainly due to factors affecting the brain before birth. Possible causes include:

- Infection in the early part of pregnancy
- Difficult or premature birth
- Cerebral (brain) bleed; this is more common following premature or multiple birth
- Abnormal brain development' (www.scope.org.uk)

Where is the child affected?

There are three types of cerebral palsy, depending on which part of the brain is damaged: spastic, athetoid and ataxic. Many people with cerebral palsy have a combination of two or more types and may have additional complications/medical disorders/diagnoses, such as epilepsy or learning difficulties.

Doctors and therapists often find it difficult to predict the ways in which a child's life may be affected as they grow up. The complexity of cerebral palsy and its effects vary from one person to another. Different parts of the body can be affected:

- Hemiplegia—when one side of the body is affected
- Diplegia—when both legs are affected but the arms are minimally affected if at all
- Quadriplegia—total body involvement, including oral difficulties

Spastic cerebral palsy

Spastic cerebral palsy increases the postural tone in muscle groups, which results in tightness in the muscles and reduced range of movement in joints. This makes fluent and coordinated movement very difficult and causes particular difficulties when changing position or letting go of an object held in their hand. This tightness or stiffness, which can be increased by activity and excitation, is always present, so a child with spastic cerebral palsy has to work harder than peers when moving, walking or speaking.

Athetoid (or dyskinetic) cerebral palsy

Children with this kind of cerebral palsy make unwanted movements because their muscles rapidly change from floppy to tense in a way that they cannot control. They find it hard to maintain balance and postures, as movement in one part of the body influences control and posture in the rest of the body. These children may have trouble holding themselves in an upright steady position for sitting or walking, and often show many movements in their face, arms and upper body, which are not intentional. Their speech may be hard to understand because they have difficulty controlling their tongue, breathing and vocal cords. Hearing problems are common.

Ataxic cerebral palsy

Ataxia affects the whole body causing jerky, uncontrolled movements. Children with this kind of cerebral palsy find it very hard to balance, may have poor spatial awareness and are generally uncoordinated. They experience uncontrolled tremor the majority of the time, which can become more pronounced when trying to perform fine controlled movements such as turning the page of a book. Usually these children will be able to walk, but will probably be very unsteady, so may have frequent falls. They may also have jerky eye movements and laboured speech.

What treatment could be offered?

There is no cure for cerebral palsy, but depending on their needs, the child may be offered different types of intervention to help their physical, social and emotional development:

- Physiotherapy including hydrotherapy
- Occupational therapy
- Speech and language therapy
- Medication to control muscle spasm, e.g. Botulinum toxin A
- Orthopaedic intervention/surgery
- Lycra® dynamic splinting
- Counselling/emotional support
- Specific treatment approaches, e.g. Bobath, conductive education

How will the child be affected in the future?

Cerebral palsy is not a progressive condition but the effects of the condition can be progressive. The ability of a child to reach their maximum potential is strongly influenced by early and consistent intervention and treatment. Children can benefit from a well-structured team approach with the child and their family at the centre. In addition, the child and family's motivation is a key component. It is important to remember that a child's skills will be developing throughout their primary school years, so careful monitoring will be necessary to 'fine tune' their progress. A child's abilities and skills may vary throughout their primary schooling. Staff should be aware that although a child may obtain a skill, e.g. walking or handwriting, the demands of the curriculum and life in general might make this impractical, so they may prefer to use a wheelchair or computer. As children get older their physical skills may decrease, e.g. a child who was walking may need to use a wheelchair for some or all of the time. This may be due to an increase in height and weight, compliance with programmes and/or the demands of the curriculum.

Further information

ACE Centre Advisory Trust

92 Windmill Road, Headington, Oxford OX3 7DR. Tel 01865 759800; Email: info@ace-centre.org.uk; Website www.ace-centre.org.uk

ACE Centre North

Hollinwood Business Centre, Albert Street, Hollinwood, Oldham OL8 3QL. Tel 0161 684 2333; Email enquiries@ace-north.org.uk; Website www.ace-north.org.uk. Isle of Man, Wales and N. Ireland Advice Service.

Capability Scotland
11 Ellersly Road, Edinburgh H12 6HY. Tel 0131 3135510; Email: ascs@ capability-scotland.org.uk; Website www.capability-scotland.org.uk

Bobath Centre
250 East End Road, London N2 8AU. Tel 020 8444 3355; Email info@bobathlondon.co.uk; Website www.bobath.org.uk

Bobath Children's Therapy Centre, Wales
19 Park Road, Whitchurch, Cardiff CF14 7BP. Tel 02920 522600; Email info@bobathwales.org; Website www.bobathwales.org

Bobath Scotland
Children's Cerebral Palsy Therapy Centre, Garscadden House, 3 Dalsetter Cresent, Drumchapel, Glasgow G15 8TG. Tel 0141 949 0022; Email info@bobathscotland.org.uk; Website www.bobathscotland.org.uk

Cedar Foundation Children and Young Peoples Service
1 Upper Lisburn Road, Belfast BT10 0GW. Tel 028 9062 3382; Email cse@cedar-foundation.org; Website www.cedar-foundation.org

Communication Aids Centre for Language and Learning (CALL) Centre
University of Edinburgh, Paterson's Land, Holyrood Road, Edinburgh EH8 8AQ. Tel 0131 651 6235/6. Email: info@callcentrescotland.org.uk; Website www.callcentrescotland.org.uk

Hemi Help
Camelford House, 89 Albert Embankment, London SE1 7TP. Tel 0845 120 3713. Helpline 0845 123 2372; Email support@hemihelp.org.uk; Website www.hemihelp.org.uk

National Institute of Conductive Education
Cannon Hill House, Russell Road, Birmingham B13 8RD. Tel 0121 449 1569; Email info@conductive-education.org.uk; Website www.conductive-education.org.uk

SCOPE Response
PO Box 833, Milton Keynes, Buckinghamshire MK12 5NY. Tel 0808 800 3333; Email: response@scope.org.uk; Website www.scope.org.uk. Requests from England and Wales only.

 References

British Association of Bobath trained therapists' newsletter (2006), *53*, p. 19 (quoted in part). London, British Association of Bobath trained therapists.

Further reading

Anderson, M.E. (2000) *Taking Cerebral Palsy to School*. New York, Jay Jo Books.

Bunnett, R. (1995) *Friends at School*. New York, Star Bright Books.

Cogher, L., Savage, E. & Smith, M. (1992) *Cerebral Palsy: the Child and Young Person*. London, Chapman and Hall.

Dalton, A. (2005) *Ferris Fleet the Wheelchair Wizard*. Middlesex, Tamarind.

Diamant, R.B. (1992) *Positioning for Play—Home Activities for Parents of Young Children*. Tucson, Arizona, Therapy Skill Builders.

Fassler, J. (1987) *Howie Helps Himself*. Morton Grove, Illinois, Albert Whitman and Company.

Finnie, N. (1997) *Handling the Young Child with Cerebral Palsy at Home*, 3rd edn. Oxford, Butterworth-Heinemann.

Geralis, E. (1998) *Children with Cerebral Palsy—a Parent's Guide*. 2nd edn. Bethesda, MD, Woodbine House.

Hinchcliffe, A. (2007) *Children with Cerebral Palsy—a Manual for Therapists, Parents and Community Workers*, revised 2nd edn. London, Sage Publishing.

Hollins, S. & Barnett, S. (1997) *Michelle finds a Voice*. Oxford, Communication Matters.

Lobel, G. (2005) *The Day Ravi Smiled*. Middlesex, Tamarind.

Miller, F. & Bauchrach, S.J. (1995) *Cerebral Palsy—a Complete Guide to Caregiving*. Baltimore, MD, The Johns Hopkins University Press.

Neville, B. & Goodman, R. (2000) *Congenital Hemiplegia*. Cambridge, Cambridge University Press.

Palmer, B. (1998) *Hands Up for Andie*. London, Hemihelp.

Pickles, P. (1998) *Managing Curriculum for Children with Severe Motor Difficulties: a Practical Approach*. London, Fulton.

Reed, C.L. (2001) *Quick Reference to Occupational Therapy*. 2nd edn. Baltimore, MD, Aspen Publishers.

Sullivan, J. (1999) *Two Left Feet*. Llandysul, Wales, Pont Books.

Yates, S. (1992) *Can't You be Still*. Manitoba, Canada, Winnipeg.

Further resources

A good selection of books and leaflets written for children who have cerebral palsy and their peers as well as resources for parents and teachers can be found on www.scope.org.uk and www.hemihelp.org.uk

Teacher observations of the child	Practical strategies	Further advice
Children diagnosed with cerebral palsy will present with varying areas of need depending on the severity of their condition. The teacher observations mentioned below may not all be relevant.	Practical strategies should be targeted for the individual child after analysis of the teacher's observations. It will then be important to decide whether the behaviour needs to be managed or changed.	To implement the further advice it may be necessary to discuss the concerns and issues with the special educational needs coordinator.
GROSS MOTOR COORDINATION		Refer to Gross motor coordination Foundation Skills FS 2, FS 2A–FS 2E page 31, 35–51
Lacks mobility: experiences reduced mobility due to physical difficulties and delay	Consider school environment before child starts school and make appropriate physical adaptation/alterations, e.g. install ramp or provide low level coat peg	Seek advice from occupational therapist, advisory teachers, LEA building surveyor, health and safety rep, refer to OTA 11 page 349
	Allow extra time for child to move around school/within class	Discuss timetable planning
	Ensure classroom is 'clutter free' in area where child is moving	
	Timetable physiotherapy programme into daily routine	Seek advice from physiotherapist, wheelchair service, occupational therapist, advisory teacher
	Give time and opportunity to practise skills	
Has changes in mobility—increase/decrease depending on prognosis	Monitor carefully and frequently liaise with physiotherapist/ occupational therapist	Seek advice from physiotherapist, occupational therapist
	Ensure mobility aids provided are used, e.g. wheelchair, walking frame, crutches, sticks	
	Ensure walking practice is part of timetable if recommended	
Spends time in wheelchair	Develop independent wheelchair skills, e.g. transfers	Seek advice from occupational therapist, physiotherapist, wheelchair service
	Ensure wheelchair training/ wheelchair proficiency scheme is part of child's timetable	
	Ensure classroom areas have wheelchair access	
	Ensure child can wheel up to and get under table, pull out drawers, sharpen pencil, etc.	
	Consider role of teaching assistant to be supportive whilst encouraging independence	

Teacher observations of the child	Practical strategies	Further advice
GROSS MOTOR COORDINATION (Continued)		Refer to Gross motor coordination Foundation Skills FS 2, FS 2A–FS 2E page 31, 35–51
	Discuss individual situations with child's peer group so help/space is appropriate Discuss classroom layout with physiotherapist/occupational therapist	
Displays poor spatial awareness	Provide adequate space when playing/working Use coloured mats on floor for carpet time Mark workspace on desk, with coloured tape Heighten peers awareness to child's inability to control movements accurately Consider child being first person in and out of classroom to minimise risk of accidents—create other turn taking opportunities that can happen in school environment Give child in wheelchair opportunities to develop spatial awareness skills by accessing the curriculum from a variety of positions	Seek advice from occupational therapist, physiotherapist, advisory teacher
Demonstrates reduced stamina	Plan task to enable child to have maximum output with minimum effort Timetable activities to conserve energy—spread tasks with high level of physical activity throughout school day Consider delivering activities requiring physical effort and concentration in the morning as the child will have more energy earlier in the day Ensure child positioned correctly to enable energy to be used on the task, rather than maintaining posture/position	Seek advice from physiotherapist, occupational therapist Refer to OTA 4 page 271
Difficulty participating in PE/games	Discuss with physiotherapist PE/games options that are appropriate and attainable Modify PE lessons to ensure child is integrated, consider alternative roles, e.g. refereeing	Seek advice from physiotherapist, occupational therapist, LEA PE advisor

Teacher observations of the child	Practical strategies	Further advice
GROSS MOTOR COORDINATION (Continued)		Refer to Gross motor coordination Foundation Skills FS 2, FS 2A–FS 2E page 31, 35–51
	Consider alternative activities e.g. horse riding, boccia, swimming 1:1 in school time Consider desired outcome of lesson—accept approximate movements from child rather than precise therapy requirements	
Has poor posture, affecting functional performance in sitting/standing	Refer to occupational therapist/physiotherapist for assessment of seating and positioning needs Ensure supportive seating is used regularly and training of staff has been provided Check chair/wheelchair height in relation to work surfaces especially for practical subjects—it may be helpful to have an adjustable height table Use standing frame as directed by therapist; incorporate use into classroom activities, e.g. assembly, artwork, story time	Seek advice from occupational therapist, physiotherapist, wheelchair service Refer to OTA 4 page 271 Refer to Equipment Resources page 407
Requires regular slot for physiotherapy exercises in school timetable	Ensure physiotherapy programme is regularly timetabled within school day Provide room and privacy for exercise programme Ensure manual handling and risk assessment is carried out in collaboration with physiotherapist and local authority representative	Seek advice from physiotherapist, advisory teacher Refer to LEA manual handling policy and undertake risk assessment
Has difficulty obtaining access into buildings, including classrooms, toilets, library, canteen, hall, including all fire exits	Check height/numbers of steps/stairs and consider ramps/rails Check positions of door handles, lockers, pegs, taps, plugs and alter if necessary Look at space in rooms and consider rearranging furniture Consider need for structural alteration, e.g. ramps, toilets with changing area Consider weight of doors and whether child is able to push them independently	Seek advice from physiotherapists, advisory teachers, occupational therapist, LEA surveyor, LEA manual handling advisor

Teacher observations of the child	Practical strategies	Further advice
GROSS MOTOR COORDINATION (Continued)		Refer to Gross motor coordination Foundation Skills FS 2, FS 2A–FS 2E page 31, 35–51
Requires access around external school facilities	Consider the need for ramps/rails or alternative route around site	Seek advice from occupational therapist, advisory teacher, LEA surveyor
Needs to travel safely to and from school	Carry out manual handling risk assessment with child and all adults involved with transport	Refer to LEA transport department, advisory teacher, occupational therapist
	Use appropriate seating/wheelchair which meets LEA safety requirements	
	Use appropriate equipment on transport complying with LEA safety regulations, e.g. car seat/ seat belts/safety harness/ ramps/wheelchair clamps/ head support	
	Ensure adequate and appropriate parking space available for parent/ taxi to park near school and get child into building	
Requires transport and access to venue when participating in school trips/field trips	Plan ahead, consider appropriateness of venue and activity; organise extra support and equipment/seek alternatives if needed	Refer to school trips policy and seek advice from advisory teacher
	Pre-check access and facilities, e.g. toilet, dining area, parking area	
	Arrange suitable transport so child can safely travel as part of the group	
	Use of appropriate transport, e.g. lift on bus/coach, wheelchair clamps	Refer to LEA transport department
	Request portaramps or fixed ramps if needed	Refer to Equipment Resources page 407
	Discuss with parents possible use of buggy/wheelchair for child who is ambulant but unable to walk long distances	
	Undertake risk assessments prior to school trips, especially when they are residential	Refer to LEA manual handling policy

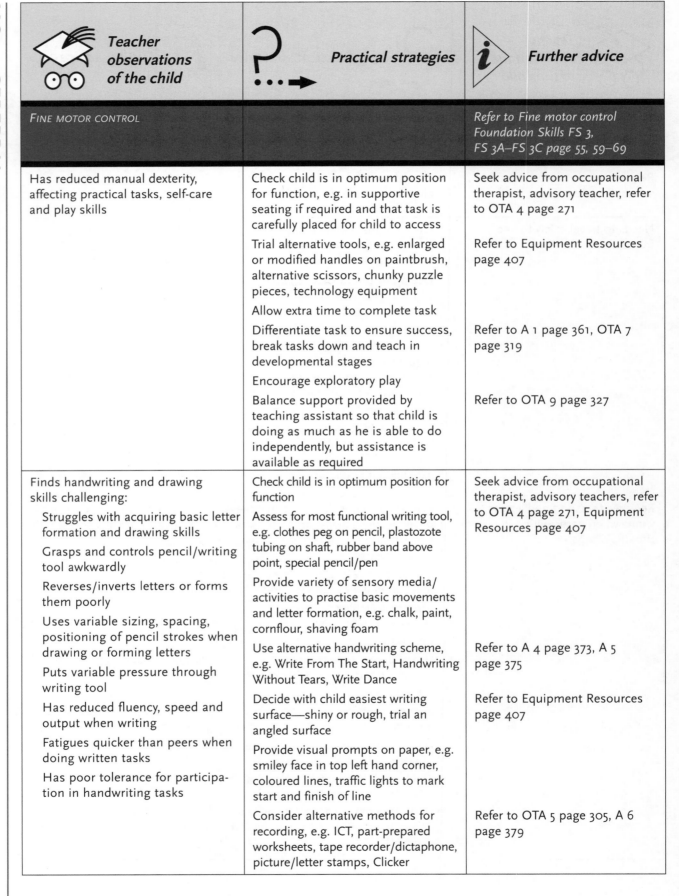

Teacher observations of the child	Practical strategies	Further advice
FINE MOTOR CONTROL		Refer to Fine motor control Foundation Skills FS 3, FS 3A–FS 3C page 55, 59–69
Has reduced manual dexterity, affecting practical tasks, self-care and play skills	Check child is in optimum position for function, e.g. in supportive seating if required and that task is carefully placed for child to access	Seek advice from occupational therapist, advisory teacher, refer to OTA 4 page 271
	Trial alternative tools, e.g. enlarged or modified handles on paintbrush, alternative scissors, chunky puzzle pieces, technology equipment	Refer to Equipment Resources page 407
	Allow extra time to complete task	
	Differentiate task to ensure success, break tasks down and teach in developmental stages	Refer to A 1 page 361, OTA 7 page 319
	Encourage exploratory play	
	Balance support provided by teaching assistant so that child is doing as much as he is able to do independently, but assistance is available as required	Refer to OTA 9 page 327
Finds handwriting and drawing skills challenging:	Check child is in optimum position for function	Seek advice from occupational therapist, advisory teachers, refer to OTA 4 page 271, Equipment Resources page 407
Struggles with acquiring basic letter formation and drawing skills	Assess for most functional writing tool, e.g. clothes peg on pencil, plastozote tubing on shaft, rubber band above point, special pencil/pen	
Grasps and controls pencil/writing tool awkwardly		
Reverses/inverts letters or forms them poorly	Provide variety of sensory media/ activities to practise basic movements and letter formation, e.g. chalk, paint, cornflour, shaving foam	
Uses variable sizing, spacing, positioning of pencil strokes when drawing or forming letters	Use alternative handwriting scheme, e.g. Write From The Start, Handwriting Without Tears, Write Dance	Refer to A 4 page 373, A 5 page 375
Puts variable pressure through writing tool		
Has reduced fluency, speed and output when writing	Decide with child easiest writing surface—shiny or rough, trial an angled surface	Refer to Equipment Resources page 407
Fatigues quicker than peers when doing written tasks	Provide visual prompts on paper, e.g. smiley face in top left hand corner, coloured lines, traffic lights to mark start and finish of line	
Has poor tolerance for participation in handwriting tasks	Consider alternative methods for recording, e.g. ICT, part-prepared worksheets, tape recorder/dictaphone, picture/letter stamps, Clicker	Refer to OTA 5 page 305, A 6 page 379

Teacher observations of the child	Practical strategies	Further advice
FINE MOTOR CONTROL (Continued)		*Refer to Fine motor control Foundation Skills FS 3, FS 3A–FS 3C page 55, 59–69*
	Provide regular breaks during writing tasks, use hand relaxation/stretching exercises as advised by child's occupational therapist or physiotherapist Allow extra time to complete task so child can work at his own speed or break task into stages and complete at different times of the day	Refer to OTA 3 page 259
Needs help accessing ICT equipment	Check child's position in relation to equipment to ensure maximum efficiency especially when using keyboard and monitor Consider ICT assessment for alternative access, e.g. roller ball mouse, ergonomic keyboard Use appropriate software to assist child, e.g. Clicker, Penfriend, voice activated software	Seek advice from LEA ICT advisor, occupational therapist, refer to OTA 4 page 271 Refer to A 6 page 379, OTA 5 page 305
ORGANISATION		*Refer to Introduction to organisation Foundation Skills FS 6 page 111*
Has problems hanging coat on peg, placing books in bag, putting things in tray	Provide peg on end of row at correct height, clearly marked Attach larger loop to coat, possibly in a contrasting colour to coat and peg Ensure cloakroom floor is 'clutter free' Position base unit where child can readily access drawer in class Consider adult support	Refer to OTA 9 page 327 Refer to OTA 6 page 315
Finds sequencing dressing hard—putting clothes on in appropriate order, cannot orientate clothes/inside-out/back to front	Use a visual timetable depicting dressing sequence—plan in conjunction with home for consistency Practise dressing skills and allocate time, record progress—star/achievement charts Liaise with parents regarding strategies, e.g. coloured label in back of all clothing, stickers in shoes which make a picture when shoes the right way round	Refer to OTA 6 page 315, A 11 page 397

![Teacher observations icon] Teacher observations of the child	![Practical strategies icon] Practical strategies	![Further advice icon] Further advice
ORGANISATION (Continued)		*Refer to Introduction to organisation Foundation Skills FS 6 page 111*
Has difficulty organising equipment in preparation for task: Starts task without having all equipment required	Ensure all necessary equipment is easily accessible. Provide visual checklist for equipment needed for each task	Refer to OTA 9 page 327, A 11 page 397

Forgets homework or submits incomplete work to teacher:
   Records task inaccurately in homework diary
   Becomes tired after school, due to physical exertion required to manage all daily tasks
   Takes much longer to complete task than expected
	Discuss strategies with child and parent, e.g. use of computer, parent to scribe, Dictaphone
	Set attainable goals with child and parents, confirm time spent on homework and quantity expected
	Allow time for out of school activities when setting goals
	Use homework planner, visual/work system
	Use homework club in school
		Refer to OTA 5 page 305, A 6 page 379
		
		Refer to OTA 9 page 327 A 11 page 397
		
		Refer to A 14 page 405

SENSORY PROCESSING		*Refer to Sensory processing Foundation Skills FS 1, FS 1A–FS 1E page 5, 11–27*
Auditory Becomes distractible with noise Is unable to identify relevant information through background noise Is over or under sensitive to noise	Limit unnecessary background noise if possible Provide quiet area where child can work Use headphones if appropriate Reinforce verbal instructions with visual reminders/ timetable Ensure child not sitting close to bell when it rings	Seek advice from occupational therapist, speech and language therapist Refer to FS 5 page 101, FS 5A page 103, A 11 page 397, OTA 8 page 323
Visual Becomes distracted by extraneous visual information, e.g. wall display, own or other children's work on table, cloakroom, interactive whiteboard	Limit distractions, ensure desk area is as uncluttered as possible Provide worksheets/books with small amounts of key information clearly presented/highlighted Provide designated work area/station, e.g. booth with enclosed sides and no visual distractions, but balance with whole class participation to reduce isolation	Seek advice from occupational therapist, behavioural optometrist Refer to FS 5A page 103, OTA 8 page 323

Teacher observations of the child	Practical strategies	Further advice
SENSORY PROCESSING (Continued)		Refer to Sensory processing Foundation Skills FS 1, FS 1A–FS 1E page 5, 11–27
Tactile Dislikes getting messy/does not notice mess on hands or face Has less awareness/heightened awareness of pain sensations Has less awareness/heightened awareness of extremes in temperature	Gradually build up tolerance for messy activities Heighten awareness of food around mouth Raise child and staff awareness of potential hazards during practical tasks or outside activities, e.g. may quickly become cold in winter	Seek advice from occupational therapist
Oral Has reduced tolerance for certain food textures	Recognise difficulty and discuss possible solutions and strategies with speech and language therapist/occupational therapist	Seek advice from occupational therapist, speech and language therapist
Proprioception Lacks body awareness Knocks into peers or furniture Shows poor ability to grade movements and judge force Ignores arm on affected side (hemiplegia) Bumps into furniture, peers as has poor organisation of herself in space	Provide postural cushion or use supportive seating as directed by therapist Weight bear through affected arm when sitting on floor, following advice from physiotherapist/ occupational therapist Encourage child to use affected arm wherever possible Use weighted wrist band/weighted pencil to increase sensory awareness as directed by therapist Sit by affected side when working with child to encourage awareness Use body awareness activities if therapist agrees Ensure there is adequate room for child to manoeuvre himself or his wheelchair	Seek advice of occupational therapist, physiotherapist Refer to Equipment Resources page 407 Refer to FS 2C page 43, OTA 1 page 249
PERCEPTION		Refer to Visual perception Foundation Skills FS 4, FSA–FS 4F page 73, 77–97
Has specific difficulties with certain aspects of perceptual tasks	Refer to specific sheet in Foundation Skills chapter once visual perceptual area has been identified	Refer to A 13 page 403

Teacher observations of the child	Practical strategies	Further advice
VISION AND OCULAR MOTOR CONTROL		*Refer to Vision and ocular control Foundation Skills FS 3B page 63 and Visual processing Foundation Skills FS 1E page 27*

Has difficulty with visual tracking and controlling eye movements:
 	
  Is unable to maintain focus on teacher/board
 	
  Finds copying from board hard
 	
  Cannot follow text in book/paper
 	
  Is unable to make directional changes quickly
 	
  Perceives print as fuzzy or blurred
	Provide regular breaks
	
	Consider providing extra time for child to complete task
	
	Sit child centrally directly facing teacher/board
	
	Check if child has glasses and should be wearing them
	
	Enlarge print
	
	Provide visual breaks
	
	Give paper copy or use small individual whiteboard on desk
	
	Use overlay with window or line tracker to minimise visual text
		Seek advice from behavioural optometrist, occupational therapist
		
		Refer to A 10 page 395
		
		Refer to Equipment Resources page 407

COGNITIVE	Where possible ensure child works on a task that motivates, is achievable and provides opportunities for success. When differentiating work ensure child is learning with others of the same ability.	Seek advice from educational psychologist, advisory teacher Refer to A 1 page 361
Becomes easily distracted in task due to poor attention span Appears distracted whilst listening or may appear to listen but is unable to respond appropriately	Break task down into small attainable targets Provide visual cues/timetable, work system Use thinking strategies	Refer to A 11 page 397
Has difficulty with short-term memory and sequencing tasks Is able to remember information but cannot always select the most relevant part upon request	Use visual schedules/timetables Encourage mind mapping, writing frames Use multi-sensory approaches to learning	Refer to FS 2B page 39, FS 5D page 109, A 4 page 373 Refer to A 11 page 397 Refer to OTA 4 page 271
Has specific learning difficulties with particular learning skills, e.g. reading, writing, drawing	Assess which early learning skills are in place Allow plenty of time to learn skills, frequent reinforcement will be necessary Implement specialist learning programmes as indicated/directed by professionals	Seek advice educational psychologist, advisory teacher Refer to A 11 page 397

Teacher observations of the child	Practical strategies	Further advice
SELF-CARE	Ensure privacy and time to develop abilities—respect the child's dignity and discuss self-care programme with child and parent	
Has problems accessing and transferring onto toilet	Undertake risk assessment Ensure adequate space for wheelchair, child and helper Consider rails, hoist, changing table Consider height of toilet	Refer to school manual handling policy Seek further advice from physiotherapist, occupational therapist, advisory teacher

Has difficulty managing in the toilet:
 	
  Cannot manage clothing
 	
  Is unable to use toilet paper
 	
  Has reduced awareness of needing to use toilet/incontinence
	Allow child extra time for toileting
	
	Assess toileting needs of child in conjunction with occupational therapist and provide support appropriately
	
	Discuss abilities with parents to promote consistent management at home and school
	
	Be aware that throughout primary years child is gaining independence in toileting skills
	
	Encourage child's participation and independence as much as possible, provide support as required
	
	Use wet wipes for wiping and/or toileting aids/bleeper system
	
	Instigate regular, timetabled trips to toilet; use star chart/reward system
		Seek further advice from physiotherapist, occupational therapist, advisory teacher, LEA manual handling advisor
		
		Seek advice from occupational therapist

Finds dressing challenging:
 	
  Has difficulty managing clothing, fastenings, laces, tying tie
 	
  Dresses slowly
 	
  Relies heavily on adult for help, thus reducing use of own initiative
	Assess for most functional position, e.g. low stool, sitting in corner against wall
	
	Play games incorporating dressing movements, e.g. quoits up arms, hoops over head
	
	Practise dressing skills and allocate time, record progress on star/achievement charts
	
	Break down task for dressing—start with easier items of clothing and leave more complex tasks until last
	
	Discuss with parent and child possibility of adapting clothing/fastenings, e.g. attach loops on waistbands to help pull up skirt/trousers/pants, Velcro® fastenings, elastic tie, elastic laces
		Seek advice from occupational therapist
		
		Refer to OTA 6 page 315
		
		Refer to Equipment Resources page 407

213

	Teacher observations of the child		Practical strategies		Further advice

SELF-CARE (Continued)	Ensure privacy and time to develop abilities—respect the child's dignity and discuss self-care programme with child and parent	

Teacher observations of the child	Practical strategies	Further advice
	Discuss with parent and child possibility of wearing alternative clothing which child can manage independently, e.g. polo shirt, trousers/skirts with elasticated waist band	
	Provide adult help as required, encourage child to do as much as can. If child wears a splint or special shoes she is unlikely to be able to manage without help	
	Ensure child is not penalised for dressing slowly. Allow extra time, e.g. changing for PE	
Needs help at mealtimes: Grasps and controls cutlery inappropriately Is unable to cut up own food Uses a cup/glass with poor grasp/control Spills contents Spills food/messy eater	Realise child may still be learning to eat independently Allow extra time—start meal early to enable playtime with peers Remember correct sitting posture will aid independence Provide appropriate cutlery, cups, plate guards, mirror, non-slip mats following discussion with child/parent/therapist Liaise with parents/speech therapist/occupational therapist for advice on feeding programme	Seek advice from occupational therapist, speech and language therapist Refer to OTA 4 page 271 Refer to Equipment Resources page 407
Has reduced mobility, so requires adequate space around dining hall	Ensure clear pathways to allow for wheelchair manoeuvrability and child's mobility. Consider where child's walking aid is placed during meal for safety and to enable easy retrieval after meal finished Position child at front or back of lunch queue Include child on a table with friends and not on a separate table Provide adult/peer support to help carry lunch box, food tray as required	Refer to school health and safety policy and undertake risk assessment

 Teacher observations of the child	 Practical strategies	 Further advice
SELF-CARE (Continued)	*Ensure privacy and time to develop abilities—respect the child's dignity and discuss self-care programme with child and parent*	
Has difficulty obtaining meal from serving hatch/carrying tray	Trial of alternative trays Arrange for meal to be collected by friend/helper Get child to choose meal which is carried to the table by someone else	Refer to Equipment Resources page 407
Is unable to open packets/ lunch-box/cartons	Provide adult support Liaise with family on choice of packaging	
COMMUNICATION		*Refer to Auditory processing Foundation Skills FS 1D page 23 and Language Foundation Skills FS 5, FS 5A–FS 5C page 101, 103–109*
Receptive language Has a range of receptive language skills linked to level of cognitive impairment	Give clear concise instructions in small steps and check child has understood, Provide written prompts Use visual cues/timetables Break down activity into small steps	Seek advice from speech and language therapist Refer to A 11 page 397
Expressive language Has a range of expressive language skills linked to level of cognitive impairment	Use home/school book to support child during news/circle time. Encourage teachers to ask targeted questions and support the child to give the answer Use alternative and augmentative communication systems (AAC) such as voice output communi-cation aids (VOCA) for child with severe learning difficulties and/or severe developmental verbal dyspraxia as recommended by speech and language therapist Practise using important curriculum vocabulary in sentences Model correct use of language rather than correcting child Expand on the child's language by modelling how to add another word	Seek advice from speech and language therapist

Teacher observations of the child	Practical strategies	Further advice
COMMUNICATION (Continued)		*Refer to Auditory processing Foundation Skills FS 1D page 23 and Language Foundation Skills FS 5, FS 5A–FS 5C page 101, 103–109*
	Allow time for child to formulate his response without fear of being interrupted	
Speech Has a range of difficulties in the area of speech production: Has a range in clarity of speech depending on level of oro-motor dysfunction. May experience difficulty with variation in pitch and intonation of voice. May have slow and laboured speech	Implement use of high or low tech communication aid as recommended by speech and language therapist (see AAC above) Heighten teachers' and peers' awareness of child's difficulty Allow extra time for child to respond Allow child to finish sentence without interrupting flow Prompt and teach child to stop and think Encourage child to slow down and take time	Seek advice from speech and language therapist
Non-verbal communication Has physical difficulties and poor muscle control which affect use of facial expression, hand gesture and posture	Heighten teachers' and peers' awareness	
SOCIAL AND EMOTIONAL ASPECTS		*Refer to Social and emotional aspects Foundation Skills FS 7 page 113*
Has difficulty establishing and maintaining relationships with peer group: Becomes socially isolated from peers	Use friendships as a topic in circle time Encourage friendship groups Facilitate Circle of Friends scheme Foster mentoring and buddy schemes Discuss friendship issues with parent Facilitate attendance at after school clubs Implement social skills training programme	Refer to A 9 page 389
Displays learnt dependency on adult support, poor at initiating independence	Consider paired working Break down task and practise specific skills Gradually increase independence in tasks as child achieves success and consider adult withdrawing after initial support	Refer to OTA 9 page 327, FS 6 page 111

Building Blocks for Learning. © 2008 John Wiley & Sons Ltd.

Teacher observations of the child	Practical strategies	Further advice
SOCIAL AND EMOTIONAL ASPECTS (Continued)		Refer to Social and emotional aspects Foundation Skills FS 7 page 113
	Regularly evaluate where support is needed and when to withdraw to enable independent learning Discuss with parents and agree on task to be targeted at home and school	
Has problems working with others, e.g. team games, group work	Consider carefully choice of partner/group members Foster mentoring schemes, Circle of Friends scheme Implement social skills training programme Implement initiatives to foster self-esteem	Refer to A 9 page 389

Lacks confidence, has poor self-esteem and self-image:
 	
  Displays shyness
  Has feelings of being different
  Has an increased awareness of own limited physical abilities
  Finds accepting disability difficult
	Consider use of self-esteem programme
	
	Provide positive praise systems
	
	Break down task and practise specific skills
	
	Provide frequent opportunities for child to experience success and improve his abilities
	
	Foster friendship groups
	
	Facilitate Circle of Friends scheme
	
	Use social groups to build up esteem
	
	Liaise with parents
	
	Investigate support groups and clubs for children with similar needs
		Refer to A 9 page 389

Demonstrates emotional difficulties:
 	
  Shows anxiety, sense of failure, frustration, anger,
  Displays jealousy towards peer group as becomes increasingly aware of own disability
	Liaise with parents
	
	Provide safe environment for child to discuss issues, regular contact with designated member of staff
	
	Work to lessen potential frustrations and anxieties
	
	Foster friendship groups
	
	Establish self-esteem and social skills group
	
	Facilitate Circle of Friends scheme
		Seek support from educational psychologist, child and adolescent mental health service, occupational therapist
		
		Refer to A 9 page 389

Teacher observations of the child	Practical strategies	Further advice
SOCIAL AND EMOTIONAL ASPECTS (Continued)		*Refer to Social and emotional aspects Foundation Skills FS 7 page 113*
	Implement anger/anxiety management, use time out cards when stressed or overwhelmed	
	Identify skills which motivate child, adapt and practise skills to facilitate integration with peer group	
	Enhance emotional literacy of all children within class	

Shows poor emotional regulation:
    Emotionally labile, cries easily, over reacts
    Mood swings, temper tantrums
	Discuss management with parent	Refer to A 9 page 389

	Heighten staff awareness	
	Implement initiatives to foster self-esteem, mood management and friendships	
	Implement self-esteem programme	
	Enhance emotional literacy	
	Identify skills which motivate child, adapt and practise skills to facilitate integration with peer group	
	Focus on child's strengths and abilities	
	Provide safe environment for child to discuss issues, regular contact with designated member of staff	
HEALTH		
Has poor posture, which could lead to deformities (e.g. curvature of the spine, mal-alignment of hips, flexion contractures of upper limbs) or impact adversely on internal organs (e.g. breathing, urinary and bowel function)	Discuss correct seating and positioning with occupational therapist/physiotherapist and use as directed	Seek advice from physiotherapist, occupational therapist Refer to OTA 4 page 271
	Ensure regular time spent in standing frame as directed by physiotherapist	
	Ensure physiotherapy programme is timetabled	
	Liaise with physiotherapist/ occupational therapist when splints require review	
Takes time out of school for hospital appointments, e.g. surgery, physiotherapy	Ensure child is given class work she has missed	Seek advice from advisory teacher
	Discuss strategies with parents to help complete work	
	Arrange home tutor if required	

Teacher observations of the child	Practical strategies	Further advice
HEALTH (Continued)		
Dribbles and has a sore mouth due to poor swallowing ability—in severe instances children may be offered surgery	Encourage child to consciously swallow and/or wipe mouth regularly Use towelling wristband to wipe mouth or buzzer to alert child to swallow Always encourage child to pat firmly rather than wipe face Encourage child to look in mirror as a way to promote self-checking and to maintain dignity	Seek advice from speech and language therapist, occupational therapist
Has increased weight due to reduced mobility	Follow advice on mobility and exercise given by physiotherapist Use wheelchair so child can propel herself around school building rather than be pushed or stay in classroom Allow time for child to propel self around school, rather than being pushed, to develop increased cardio-vascular exercise Undertake risk assessment to heighten staff awareness and look at manual handling implications Monitor dietary intake in discussion with family	Seek advice from physiotherapist Refer to school health and safety policy, LEA advisor Refer to manual handling policy and undertake risk assessment Seek advice from school nurse/doctor, dietician
Has reduced mobility of joints—pain can increase on activity	Seek advice from physiotherapist/ occupational therapist incorporate regular breaks in activity Use prescribed splints as directed Use standing frame as directed Include child in negotiations	Seek advice from physiotherapist, occupational therapist
FURTHER CONSIDERATIONS		
Relationships within the family and parenting approaches can also influence how a child is performing within the school setting. It is therefore essential to consider all aspects of the child's life rather than just seeing school life in isolation.	Provide regular contact with designated pastoral support/mentor so that family and school have consistent approach. Regularly review priorities together as child may present differently at home and at school. Ensure family have sufficient support and advice from key professionals.	

It is essential that:

1 A risk assessment is carried out prior to the child entering school and repeated in accordance with the school or county manual handling policy

2 Staff receive regular training in manual handling in accordance with the manual handling policy

3 Staff liaise with the physiotherapist/occupational therapist, since inappropriate activities may lead to increased problems and/or injury

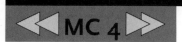
Developmental coordination disorder including dyspraxia

 How does the condition impact on the child?

The manifestations of developmental coordination disorder (DCD) vary with age and development. For example, younger children may display clumsiness and delays in achieving developmental milestones (e.g. walking, crawling, sitting, tying shoe laces, buttoning shirts, zipping trousers). Older children may display difficulties with many functional and daily living tasks and have significant difficulties with organisational skills. The motor aspects of assembling puzzles, building models, playing ball, manipulating equipment and printing or handwriting may also prove problematic. In moderate and severe cases DCD will significantly impact on social skills.

Children's skill development is impaired, so they are unable to perform some tasks at an age appropriate level. This often labels them as clumsy or disorganised as they may be unable to generalise skills to similar tasks. However, when taken out of class for work on a one-to-one basis they are often able to achieve more, although this needs to be weighed up against what a child is missing by not participating in the class activity.

The child may experience some or all of the features described below.

Gross motor

The child:

- Falls, trips and bumps into things
- Is awkward on stairs, lacks reciprocal pattern
- Looks awkward when walking, running, hopping, skipping
- Has difficulty coordinating and maintaining swimming strokes, riding a bicycle, hopscotch
- Lacks stamina/seeks support
- Pushes and shoves peers as unaware of personal space and own force
- Dislikes sitting on carpet and chairs, fidgets and bumps into others
- Shows low quality muscle tone and seems weak

- Has problems joining in PE activities, e.g. jumping, balancing, apparatus work
- Finds bat and ball games, trampolining challenging
- Has difficulty planning and carrying out a sequence of movements

Fine motor

The child:

- Displays difficulty with all pen and paper tasks
- Writes slowly, lacks flow and has untidy and laborious presentation, is often late to develop writing skills
- Has poor fine motor coordination, manipulation and dexterity, which is noticeable when playing with toys
- Is reluctant to undertake construction tasks
- Has delayed self-care skills, e.g. using cutlery, fastening buttons, tying laces
- Manipulates tools awkwardly, e.g. scissors, rulers, compass
- Carries out fine motor tasks slowly and has impaired quality of finished work

Sensory

The child:

- Displays over or under sensitive reactions to a range of sensory stimulation including noise, light, touch, taste, movement or smell
- Is unable to filter out extraneous noises, movements, excessive visual stimuli, etc., so may react adversely to different textures/clothing/materials/carpet pile, e.g. labels, seams, fur fabrics, prickly floor covering
- Is easily distracted by everyday sensory stimulation, e.g. radio, TV in background, interactive whiteboards, 'busy' displays on walls
- Has poor emotional self-regulation—swings easily from being very passive to excitable
- Demonstrates difficulties with sensory modulation

Cognitive

The child:

- Has poor attention span
- Finds short-term memory and sequencing tasks difficult
- Demonstrates poor problem solving—is unable to learn instinctively
- Finds it hard to listen, think and carry out task (physical action) at the same time, e.g. creative writing, taking notes
- Compensates for difficulties with organising and sequencing by self-talking through tasks

Organisation

The child:

- Has difficulty generalising learnt skills to other areas
- Finds it difficult to plan and carry out a sequence of movements, both gross and fine
- Has poor organisation of self, and within own environment
- Has poor sequencing and timing skills
- Demonstrates difficulties with problem solving
- Finds spatial/perceptual tasks challenging
- Struggles with self-care skills, e.g. has an untidy appearance
- Loses/forgets things, e.g. parent letters given out at school
- Becomes muddled

Social/emotional

The child:

- Lacks confidence, has learnt failure therefore is unwilling to try
- Uses compensatory strategies, e.g. may be class clown or withdrawn
- Has awareness of difficulties, leading to low self-esteem
- Suffers frustration, anger or anxiety as unable to complete task
- Shows adult dependency—'learnt helplessness'
- Is generally immature, prefers to play with younger children or adults
- Has difficulty establishing relationships with peers—child may feel 'no-one likes me, I don't get asked to friend's houses, I'm rubbish', etc.
- Finds making and keeping friends difficult, risks isolation as unable to keep up with peer group
- Prefers to be a loner or dominate play situation

▷▷ What is this condition?

Developmental coordination disorder is a marked impairment in the development of motor coordination, which significantly interferes with academic achievement, or activities of daily living.

In order to be given a medical diagnosis of developmental coordination disorder the child must meet certain criteria as outlined in the *Diagnostic and Statistical Manual of Mental Disorders* (DSM IV) or *International Classification of Diseases*, 10th edition (ICD10), where it is called specific developmental disorder of motor function.

Developmental coordination disorder is the current term now commonly used to describe children with motor coordination difficulties. It has also been known as perceptual motor dysfunction, clumsy child syndrome, minimal brain dysfunction or motor learning difficulty. It is an umbrella term that includes developmental dyspraxia (difficulty with motor planning), sensory integrative dysfunction and DAMP (this is a combination of developmental coordination disorder and attention deficit hyperactivity disorder, as there are deficits in attention, motor control and perception).

 ## What is the cause?

The exact cause of developmental coordination disorder is currently unknown.

 ## What treatment could be offered?

The child may be offered different types of intervention depending on local policies and availability of resources:

- Perceptual motor training
- Sensory processing advice
- Motor skills training
- Sensory integration therapy and/or sensory diets/programmes
- Cognitive approach using the Cognitive Observations of Occupational Performance (CO-OP)
- Biomechanical approach
- Organisational strategies
- Social/emotional support
- Advice on learning approaches in school
- Adaptation of environment
- Specific skill training

How will the child be affected in future?

Development coordination disorder is not progressive; it does not become more severe as the child becomes older. However, the organisational and social/emotional factors can have more impact on the child's well-being than their coordination difficulties. As functional demands at home, in school and in the wider community increase, the child's problems may become more marked. Lack of coordination may also become more apparent at times of stress or during excessive growth spurts. It may continue through adolescence into adulthood.

Further information and support groups

Can Child
Centre for Childhood Disability Research, Institute for Approved Health Studies, McMaster University, 1400 Main Street West, Room 408, Hamilton, Ontario L8S 1C7 Canada. Tel (905) 5259140 ext 27850; Email canchild@mcmaster.ca; Website www.fhs.mcmaster.ca/canchild

Dyscovery Centre
Allt yr ynn Campus, University of Wales, Newport NP20 5DA. Tel 01633 432330; Email dyscoverycentre@newport.ac.uk; Website www.dyscovery.co.uk

Dyspraxia Foundation
8 West Alley, Hitchin, Hertfordshire SG5 1EG. Tel 01462 455016; Helpline tel 01462 454986; Email dyspraxia@dyspraxiafoundation.org.uk; Website www.dyspraxiafoundation.org.uk

Highland Developmental Coordination Disorder Group
Unit 6, 15 Lotland Street, Inverness IV1 1ST. Tel 01463 709907; Email hdcd.org@tiscali.co.uk; Website www.hdcd.org.uk

Sensory Integration Network UK and Ireland Ltd, Registered Office
c/o Phillips & Co., Sullivan House, Widemarsh Street, Hereford HR4 9HG. Email info@sensoryintegration.org.uk; Website www.sensoryintegration.org.uk

 Further reading

Addy, L. & Barnes, R. (2004) *How to Understand and Support Children with Dyspraxia*. Cambridge, LDA.

Boon, M. (2000) *Helping Children with Dyspraxia*. London, Jessica Kingsley.

Chu, S. (1995) *Children with Developmental Dyspraxia—Information for Parents and Teachers*. Hitchen, Dyspraxia Foundation.

Chu, S. (1998a) Developmental dyspraxia 1: the diagnosis. *British Journal of Therapy and Rehabilitation*, 5 (3), 131–38.

Chu, S. (1998b) Developmental dyspraxia 2: evaluation and treatment. *British Journal of Therapy and Rehabilitation*, 5 (4), 176–80.

Drew, S. (2003) *Jack and the Disorganised Dragon*. University of Wales, Newport, Monmouthshire, Dyscovery Press.

Drew, S. (2005) *Including Children with Developmental Coordination Disorder (Dyspraxia) in the Foundation Stage*. Lutterworth, Featherstone Education Limited.

Jones, N. (2005) *Developing School Provision for Children with Dyspraxia: a Practical Guide*. London, Paul Chapman.

Kirby, A. (1999) *Dyspraxia—the Hidden Handicap*. London, Souvenir Press.

Kirby, A. & Drew, S. (2003) *Guide to Dyspraxia and Developmental Coordination Disorders*. London, Fulton.

Kirby, A. & Peters, L. (2007) *100 Ideas for Supporting Pupils with Dyspraxia and DCD*. New York, Continuum International Publishing Group Limited.

Koomar, J. & Friedman, B. (1998) *The Hidden Senses Your Muscle Sense*. Minnesota, PDP Press.

Koomar, J. & Friedman, B. (1998) *The Hidden Senses: Your Balance Sense*. Minnesota, PDP Press.

Kranowitz, C.S. (1998) *The Out of Sync Child: Recognising and Coping with Sensory Integration Dysfunction*. New York, Perigee Book.

Kranowitz, C.S. (2006) *The Out of Sync Child has Fun: Activities for Kids with Sensory Processing Disorder* (revised edition. New York, Perigee Trade.

Kurtz, L. (2003) *How to Help a Clumsy Child: Strategies for Young Children with Developmental Motor Concerns*. London, Jessica Kingsley.

Macintyre, C. (2001) *Dyspraxia 5–11: a Practical Guide*. London, Fulton.

Macintyre, C. & McVitty, K. (2004) *Movement and Learning in the Early Years Supporting Dyspraxia (DCD) and other difficulties*. Thousand Oaks, CA, Sage Publications.

Penso, D.E. (1993) *Perceptuo-motor Difficulties. Theory and Strategies to Help Children, Adolescents and Adults*. London, Chapman and Hall.

Poustie, J. (2001) *Identification Solutions for Dyspraxia/DCD*. Taunton, Next Generation.

Reed, C.L. (2001) *Quick Reference to Occupational Therapy*, 2nd edn. Baltimore, MD, Aspen Publishers.

Ripley, K. (2001) *Inclusion for Children with Dyspraxia/DCD—a Handbook for Teachers*. London, Fulton.

Ripley, K., Daines, B. & Barrett, J. (1997) *Dyspraxia—a Guide for Teachers and Parents*. London, Fulton.

Sugden, D.A. & Chambers, M.E. (2005) *Children with Developmental Coordination Disorder*. London, Whurr.

Velleman, S. (2002) *Childhood Dyspraxia Resource Guide*. Clifton Park, NY, Delmar Learning.

Yack, E., Aquilla, P. & Sutton, S. (2006) *Building Bridges Through Sensory Integration: Therapy for Children with Autism and other Pervasive Developmental Disorders*. Las Vegas, Sensory Resources.

Teacher observations of the child	Practical strategies	Further advice
Children diagnosed with developmental coordination disorder will present with varying degrees of need depending on the severity of their condition. The teacher observations mentioned below may not all be relevant.	Practical strategies should be targeted for the individual child after analysis of the teacher observations. It will then be important to decide whether the behaviour needs to be managed or changed.	To implement the further advice it may be necessary to discuss the concerns and issues with the special educational needs coordinator.
GROSS MOTOR COORDINATION		Refer to Gross motor coordination Foundation Skills FS 2, FS 2A–FS 2E page 31, 35–51
Displays low muscle tone: Has reduced stamina and fatigue Lacks balance, 'earthbound' Props or flops between activities Lacks strength and stability as joints are more flexible than peers Has difficulty maintaining postures against gravity	Ensure child uses a supported functional posture Where possible minimise amount of time required to stand Allow to prop/lean against furniture or wall Consider using chair when peer group sitting on floor or change positions frequently Use movin'sit cushions or gym balls when sitting Practise graded motor activities	Refer to OTA 4 page 271 Refer to Equipment Resources page 407 Refer to OTA 10 page 333, A 7 page 381
Lacks coordination/balance: Lacks fluency of movements Appears awkward and uncoordinated Has difficulty executing precise controlled movements Lacks the control to sustain balance postures	Use carefully graded programme to improve balance Develop coordination skills Ensure adequate space in work area Check sitting posture is correct and monitor frequently	Refer to OTA 10 page 333, A 7 page 381 Refer to OTA 4 page 271
Finds bilateral skills challenging: Has difficulty coordinating movements requiring the use of both sides of the body, e.g. swimming, cycling, bat and ball games, hopscotch, playing musical instruments	Break down activity and practice individual component parts Encourage use of both hands to establish a bilateral working pattern Practise midline crossing activities Use thinking skills	Refer to OTA 10 page 333, A 7 page 271 Refer to OTA 3 page 259 Refer to A 11 page 397
Has difficulty with sequencing and organising movements: Finds moving around school challenging Is unable to plan tasks	Encourage child to pre-plan task Provide verbal and physical prompts and reduce amount of prompts as child's abilities improve Use visual supports/timetable Use strategies to develop thinking skills—stop/think/do	Refer to OTA 9 page 327 Refer to A 11 page 397

Teacher observations of the child	Practical strategies	Further advice
GROSS MOTOR COORDINATION (Continued)		*Refer to Gross motor coordination Foundation Skills FS 2, FS 2A–FS 2E page 31, 35–51*
Lacks ability to anticipate, plan and respond whilst participating in an activity	Develop coordination skills Heighten staff awareness to importance of giving clear, detailed yet concise instructions	Refer to OTA 1 page 249, OTA 10 page 333, A 7 page 381
Shows reduced sense of danger: Runs out of class/playground Lacks awareness of car, especially speed and distances Is not safe using PE apparatus Uses equipment dangerously, e.g. holding scissors in hand whilst moving Is unable to anticipate force and movement of others and self Has poor ability to anticipate and judge consequences of behaviour	Heighten awareness of safety issues and undertake health and safety risk assessment Use social stories/pictures or photographs to visually demonstrate road safety Provide adult supervision Provide good role models when planning group work Teach thinking skills, e.g. goal-plan-do-check Practise road safety awareness	Refer to school health and safety policy Refer to A 9 page 389 Refer to A 11 page 397
FINE MOTOR CONTROL		*Refer to Fine motor control Foundation Skills FS 3, FS 3A–FS 3C page 55, 59–69*
Has poorly developed general grasps: Demonstrates reduced manipulative skills affecting all practical tasks Has impaired grasp when holding equipment, e.g. scissors, writing tools, cutlery	Request a hand assessment to clarify which hand skills need developing Break task down and teach in developmental stages Work on programme to develop mature hand skills Improve manipulative skills through a fine motor programme, e.g. hand gym Ensure that child uses correct grasp for activity Ensure that activity is graded at correct level so child does not revert to immature pattern Practice skill at level of child's ability Adapt grasp as necessary— work from large to small grip Use alternative/adapted equipment	Seek advice from occupational therapist or advisory teacher Refer to A 1 page 361, OTA 4 page 271, OTA 7 page 319 Refer to OTA 3 page 259, A 3 page 371 Refer to Equipment Resources page 407

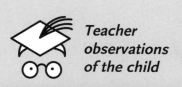 *Teacher observations of the child*	*Practical strategies*	*Further advice*
FINE MOTOR CONTROL *(Continued)*		*Refer to Fine motor control Foundation Skills FS 3, FS 3A–FS 3C page 55, 59–69*
Finds handwriting challenging: Has undecided hand dominance Takes longer than his peers to learn basic skills Has difficulty acquiring basic letter formation Reverses/inverts letters and has poor letter formation Writes letters in variable sizes, with poor spacing and positioning Is unable to write letters sitting on the line Has untidy work due to excessive crossing out and correcting Puts variable pressure through writing tool Has reduced quantity of output Finds creative writing hard Has not fully established handwriting as an automatic skill	Use a specific handwriting programme and practise daily to reinforce skills learnt Teach through a multi-sensory approach Teach correct pencil grasp/use pen grips Use visual prompts, e.g. coloured lines, traffic lights to mark start and finish of line Ensure 'building blocks' are fully learnt before moving onto next stage of writing Consider alternative recording methods, e.g. ICT, part prepared worksheets Teach touch typing and provide regular daily practice	Refer to OTA 2 page 253, OTA 4 page 271, A 2 page 369, A 4 page 373, A 5 page 375 and A 12 page 401 Refer to Equipment Resources page 407 Refer to A 1 page 361 Refer to A 6 page 379, OTA 5 page 305 Refer to Equipment Resources page 407
Demonstrates slow execution of task due to inconsistent hand dominance for practical tasks: Is constantly changing hands Leaves work unfinished Has difficulty with pressure	Work on establishing laterality, use hands to identify right/left Encourage midline crossing Use visual cues, e.g. stickers on hand to reinforce preferred hand or sticker on page as positional reference Provide suitable equipment if left handed Use part prepared work Encourage consistent hand use for older children Allow extra time for completion of task, set realistic attainable goals Use adult support	Refer to OTA 1 page 249, OTA 2 page 253 Refer to OTA 4 page 271, Equipment Resources page 407
Shows reduced proprioception and tactile awareness, resulting in awkward hand function: Is unable to grade pressure of movement Presses hard on pencil, flattens or squashes craft activities, Exerts insufficient pressure on pencil so faint marks on paper	Give heavy work at start of task to increase proprioceptive awareness Adapt task, use alternative equipment Use multi-sensory approaches when presenting work/task Allow more time for tasks Include warm up activity at start of lesson Use Hand gym activities	Refer to OTA 8 page 323, FS 1B page 15, FS 1C page 19 Refer to Equipment Resources page 407 Refer to OTA 4 page 271 Refer to OTA 3 page 259

Teacher observations of the child	Practical strategies	Further advice
ORGANISATION		*Refer to Introduction to organisation Foundation Skills FS 6 page 111*
Has difficulty hanging coat on peg, placing books in bag, clearing lunch box away	Provide peg on end of row, pack books in class, develop routine for lunch time	Refer to OTA 9 page 327
	Use visual timetable with pictures or photographs demonstrating task and sequence	Refer to A 11 page 397
Changes slowly for PE	Allow extra time, start before rest of class	Refer to OTA 6 page 315
	Practise self-care skills	
	Use visual timetable to identify sequence of clothing and raise child's awareness if clothes on back to front or inside out	Refer to A 11 page 397
	Discuss with parents possibilities for alternative clothing within constraints of uniform policy	Refer to Equipment Resources page 407
Is unable to recognise personal space when sitting on the carpet	Talk to peer group and explain reasons for child's difficulties	Refer to Equipment Resources page 407
	Use visual cue, e.g. cushion, mat to mark child's area	
	Use movin'sit cushion or sit child on edge of circle so she does not disturb peers	
	Work on body and spatial awareness programme	Refer to OTA 1 page 249
	Teach and reinforce 'rules' for personal space	Refer to A 9 page 389
Finds organising equipment in preparation for tasks hard:	Ensure all equipment is easily accessible for task	Refer to OTA 9 page 327
Makes several journeys to collect equipment needed to start task	Provide a visual checklist, work system identifying equipment needed for each task	Refer to A 11 page 397, A 14 page 405
Starts task without having all equipment required	Plan for paired working	
Intrudes on neighbour's work area	Encourage an uncluttered work space	
Is unable to organise self in personal space:	Teach personal space rule, refer to social skills training programme	Refer to A 9 page 389
Bumps into people and furniture constantly knocks things over	Prepare child physically by using graded resisted activities prior to task to increase sense of body awareness	Refer to FS 1C page 19, OTA 8 page 323

Teacher observations of the child	Practical strategies	Further advice
ORGANISATION (Continued)		*Refer to Organisation Foundation Skills FS 6 page 111*
Has a cluttered work area Is unaware of environment	Develop body and spatial awareness Talk to peer group and explain reasons for child's difficulties Work out strategies to help performance with child Encourage uncluttered work area Provide adult prompt	*Refer to FS 2C page 43, OTA 1 page 249*
Lacks awareness to break down components of task when problem solving	Use task analysis approach Use cue cards Give clear, concise, step-by-step instructions Give checklists and reduce prompts as child masters skill Practise task by using visual sequencing/backward chaining techniques Practise task using high interest or favourite equipment	*Refer to FS 2A page 35, A 11 page 397, OTA 9 page 327*

Finds formulating a plan of action when attempting new task hard:
  Knows what is required but unable to complete task
  Is unsatisfied with end result
  Starts task slowly and work is often incomplete
  Becomes muddled and frustrated with own performance
	Use activity analysis approach and breakdown task into easy stages
	Encourage child to pre-plan activity before he starts task
	Talk through ideas, formulate a plan of action
	Give written plan as well as verbal instructions
	Provide written or visual step by step instructions
		Refer to FS 2A page 35, OTA 9 page 327, A 11 page 397

Has difficulty coping with changes in routine:
  Becomes anxious, upset and agitated
  Has temper tantrums as unable to predict new task
  Becomes rigid in outlook, unwilling to 'give it a go'
	Use visual timetable to inform child of predicted changes
	Prepare child for change before it happens
	Adhere to established routines as much as possible and where not possible, give extra preparation
	Encourage child to pre-plan change and reinforce by talking it though
	Rehearse changed routines, e.g. how to get to new location in advance
		Refer to A 11 page 397, A 9 page 389

Teacher observations of the child	Practical strategies	Further advice
ORGANISATION (Continued)		*Refer to Organisation Foundation Skills FS 6 page 111*
Submits incomplete homework: Lacks understanding of task before going home Does not record task properly in homework diary Has excessive tiredness once home due to extra physical exertion at school for all tasks Takes much longer than allotted time Has unrealistic task set by teacher Has difficulty balancing home/school life	Set realistic goals, e.g. confirm with child the amount of time spent on homework and/or the quantity expected, allow time for out of school activities and play Discuss strategies with child and parent, e.g. use computer, parents to scribe, reduce amount acceptable, quality versus quantity Draw up a contract with child and parent Ensure parent understands homework tasks set Use alarms, watches, timers, timed checklist	Refer to OTA 9 page 327, A 11 page 397 Refer to OTA 5 page 305, A 6 page 379
Has reduced sense of time and urgency: Becomes absorbed in activity and finds it hard to stop Is desperate to complete task before doing next activity	Agree with child amount of work to be completed in given time frame Use visual support to show time concepts and sequences, e.g. visual timetables, egg timers, digital timers, timed checklist, now/next boards. Use work system, visual timetable Introduce start, finish boxes/now, next boards as in TEACCH Introduce behavioural strategies, e.g. star chart, reward charts	Refer to A 11 page 397, A 14 page 405 Refer to Equipment Resources page 407
Inability to generalise skills: Is unable to transfer skills to competently achieve similar task Becomes very frustrated and aware that she is unable to keep up with her peers, although cognitively able Requires longer to learn skill for task, but once learnt able to competently perform, e.g. catching a ball	Teach each new task separately Break down task and work on specific skill areas, then link skill with similar tasks Encourage pre-planning Provide extra adult support to practise skill Teach 'splinter skills' Ensure child is working on a task which motivates them	Refer to FS 2A page 35, A 11 page 397

Teacher observations of the child	Practical strategies	Further advice
SENSORY PROCESSING		*Refer to Sensory processing Foundation Skills FS 1, FS 1A–FS 1E page 5, 11–27*
Auditory Is unable to identify relevant information through background noises: Has difficulty understanding and responding to instructions Becomes distracted with noise Has difficulty filtering out relevant information Is sensitive to noise	Provide a quiet area where child can work Limit unnecessary background noises if possible Use headphones if appropriate Speak slowly and use simple phrases Allow extra time when communicating with child Provide cue cards to support spoken word Use visual timetables, written text to support verbal instructions	Seek advice from speech and language therapist, occupational therapist Refer to FS 5A page 103, FS 1D page 23 Refer to A 11 page 397
Visual Is unable to identify relevant visual information from background: Becomes distracted by extraneous visual information within his field of vision, e.g. wall displays, other children's work on table, children walking across room Has difficulty working in certain lighting conditions, e.g. fluorescent lighting, glare from sun, interactive whiteboard Becomes overloaded by a lot of visual information	Heighten staff awareness Provide books/worksheets with small amounts of information clearly presented Ensure desk area is uncluttered Provide designated work station, e.g. booth with no distracting visual information and enclosed sides	Seek advice from occupational therapist, behavioural optometrist Refer to FS 1E page 27, FS 5A page 103
Tactile Hates getting messy Does not notice mess on hands or face Dislikes being touched Always seeking physical contact from others Wriggles constantly as unable to tolerate clothing/materials/textures Prefers loose/baggy clothing	Gradually build up tolerance for messy activities Heighten awareness of food around mouth, paint on hands, etc. Respect child's need for personal space and be aware of consequences of personal contact Be aware that deep pressure is more easily tolerated than light touch Increase child's sensory input by providing 'fiddle' item, or warm-up exercises before starting activity	Seek advice from occupational therapist Refer to OTA 3 page 259, OTA 8 page 323, FS 2 page 31

Building Blocks for Learning. © 2008 John Wiley & Sons Ltd.

◊ Teacher observations of the child	? ...➔ Practical strategies	ⓘ▷ Further advice
SENSORY PROCESSING (Continued)		*Refer to Sensory processing Foundation Skills FS 1, FS 1A–FS 1E page 5, 11–27*
Oral Constantly needs to seek out something to chew, e.g. cuff/collar of sweater, finger nails, thumbs, pencils, water bottle tops: Dribbles and has a wet shirt front Licks lips constantly, so has soreness around mouth	Discuss with child appropriate and acceptable strategies Be aware that child is seeking oral input to help him to organise himself and concentrate Provide and allow child to have something suitable to chew throughout the day, e.g. tubing on pencil, sports water bottles, tubing, wrist band	Seek advice from3 occupational therapist Refer to OTA 8 page 323
Proprioception Has excessive movement/is fidgety in an attempt to gain extra feedback about her own body awareness: Lacks smooth controlled movements Is unable to negotiate own body through space—knocks into peers or furniture Is unable to sustain correct posture—slumps over desk/table Has difficulty grading movement or judging force, e.g. barges into people, knocks things over	Acknowledge need for physical movement at playtimes to enable her to sit and concentrate more readily later Increase body awareness through graded resisted activities/activities that involve deep pressure Use gross motor activity programmes Allow plenty of opportunity for 'heavy' muscle work Allow 'fiddle' items Give opportunities to have regular movement breaks Use movin' sit cushions	Seek advice from occupational therapist Refer to FS 2C page 43, OTA 1 page 249 Refer to A 7 page 381, OTA 10 page 333 Refer to OTA 8 page 323 Refer to Equipment Resources page 407
PERCEPTION		*Refer to Visual perception Foundation Skills FS 4, FS 4A–FS 4F page 73, 77–97*
Has specific problems with certain visual perceptual tasks	Refer to specific sheet in Foundation Skills chapter once area has been identified	Refer to A 13 page 403
VISION AND OCULAR MOTOR CONTROL		*Refer to Vision and ocular control Foundation Skills FS 3B and Visual processing Foundation Skills FS 1E page 27*
Has difficulty with visual tracking and controlling eye movements: Is unable to maintain focus on teacher/board Finds copying from board hard	Ensure child is seated centrally in class facing the front Give individual paper copy of instructions/work written on board	Seek advice from behavioural optometrist, occupational therapist Refer to A 10 page 395

Teacher observations of the child	Practical strategies	Further advice
VISION AND OCULAR MOTOR CONTROL (Continued)		Refer to Vision and ocular control Foundation Skills FS 3B page 63 and Visual processing Foundation Skills FS 1E page 27
Cannot follow text in book/paper Is unable to make directional changes quickly Perceives print as fuzzy or blurred	Use reading guide or ruler below line of print/figures in columns Expect less fluency in PE activities which require continual turning/ visual checking (team games) Consider use of individual coloured overlays	Refer to Equipment Resources page 407
COGNITIVE	Ensure child works on a task which motivates, is achievable and provides opportunities for success Ensure child is learning with her cognitive peer group	Seek advice from educational psychologist, advisory Refer to A 1 page 361
Shows discrepancy between cognitive ability and practical skills, verbal skills often better than non-verbal skills	Provide alternative recording methods, e.g. use of tape recorders, parents to scribe, part prepared worksheets, word processors Find alternative ways of demonstrating child's knowledge, use creative approach Use writing frame, part prepared worksheets and mind mapping techniques Reduce copying from board, produce table top copy of information written on interactive whiteboard with key information high-lighted	Refer to OTA 5 page 305, A 6 page 379 Refer to A 11 page 397 Refer to OTA 4 page 271
Has poor attention span	Break task down into small attainable targets Provide visual cues/timetable, work system Use strategies to develop thinking skills Consider sensory issues	Refer to FS 5A page 103 Refer to A 11 page 397, A 14 page 405 Refer to FS 1 page 5, OTA 8 page 323
Has difficulty with short-term memory and sequencing tasks	Use visual cues/schedules, support verbal instructions with written text Implement thinking strategies and skills, e.g. stop/think/do	Refer to FS 4F page 97, FS 5D page 109 Refer to A11 page 397

Teacher observations of the child	Practical strategies	Further advice
COGNITIVE (Continued)	Ensure child works on a task which motivates, is achievable and provides opportunities for success Ensure child is learning with her cognitive peer group	Seek advice from educational psychologist, advisory teachers Refer to A 1 page 361
	Encourage mind mapping, writing frames	Refer to A 11 page 397
	Pre-plan tasks and provide adult support	Refer to OTA 9 page 327
	Use multi-sensory approaches to learning	Refer to OTA 4 page 271
Is unable to learn instinctively or generalise skills	Ensure child has relevant foundation skills in place	Refer to FS 1–FS 7 page 5–113
	Teach 'splinter' skills	
	Break task down into small attainable targets	Refer to A 11 page 397, A 14 page 405
	Break down task and work on specific skill areas and link with similar tasks	
	Encourage pre-planning for tasks	
	Use multi-sensory approach to ensure consolidation of learnt skill	Refer to OTA 4 page 271
	Provide extra adult support to practise skill	
Has difficulty thinking, listening and carrying out tasks simultaneously	Help child to break task down into manageable/achievable chunks that he can think about planning and doing	Refer to FS 1D page 23, FS 5 page 101, OTA 9 page 327
	Use thinking skills, e.g. stop/think/do, writing frames, mind mapping	Refer to A 11 page 397
	Use visual checklist	
	Gain child's attention before starting task	
	Ensure child has understood instructions accurately before he begins task	
	Encourage adult monitoring	
Has immaturity of early learning skills Has lots of ideas but finds it difficult being selective	Assess which foundation skills are in place and which need to be developed	Seek advice from educational psychologist, occupational therapist

Teacher observations of the child	Practical strategies	Further advice
COGNITIVE (Continued)	Ensure child works on a task which motivates, is achievable and provides opportunities for success	Seek advice from educational psychologist, advisory teachers
	Ensure child is learning with her cognitive peer group	Refer to A 1 page 361
	Allow plenty of time to practise skills in small group or individual sessions	
	Ensure that child has learnt one stage before moving onto next	Refer to A 1 page 361
	Beware of need for constant reinforcement and over learning	Refer to OTA 4 page 271
Has difficulty accepting new ideas and abstract concepts	Provide concrete examples	Seek advice from educational psychologist
	Set clear expectations	
	Give plenty of time to acquire skill	
	Use multi-sensory approach, as child consolidates and learns skill more readily when all senses are engaged	Refer to OTA 4 page 271
SELF-CARE		
Finds dressing challenging: Has problems with small fastenings, laces, zips	Provide help when necessary and allow extra time when changing for PE	Seek advice from occupational therapist
		Refer to OTA 6 page 315
Orientates clothes incorrectly/ inside out and back to front	Practise individual skills, e.g. buttons, tying laces, tying tie	
Is unable to tie school tie	Check shoes on right feet, clothes right way round and tucked in	Refer to Equipment Resources page 407
Has a dishevelled appearance and poor general presentation	Use alternative fastenings, e.g. Velcro®, elastic laces, elasticated tie	
Dresses slowly for all dressing tasks	Use visual timetable to identify sequence of clothing and raise child's awareness if clothes on back to front or inside out	Refer to A 11 page 397
	Discuss with parents and child the possibility of wearing alternative clothing, e.g. polo shirts, trousers with elasticated waist	
	Remind child to check appearance after changing	
	Implement activities to develop manipulative skills	Refer to FS 3C page 69, OTA 3 page 259, A 3 page 371

Teacher observations of the child	Practical strategies	Further advice
SELF-CARE *(Continued)*		
Needs help at mealtimes: Has poor grasp and cutting action when using cutlery Spills food down shirt and is messy Has difficulty opening packets, yogurt tops, etc.	Raise awareness of need for child to cut up own food where possible Trial Caring Cutlery Use plate with lip and non-slip mat	Seek advice from occupational therapist, speech and language therapist Refer to Equipment Resources page 407
Has difficulty with personal hygiene	Remind child of hygiene, provide wet wipes instead of toilet tissue Check problem is not caused by reduced physical skills, i.e. poor reach or balance, and if so implement programme to improve balance	Seek advice from occupational therapist Refer to FS 2B page 39, OTA 10 page 333, A 7 page 381
Is unable to tell the time	Use visual support to show time concepts and sequences, e.g. visual timetables, egg timers, digital timers, timed checklist, now/next boards Use large plastic clock with moveable hands	Refer to A 11 page 397, Equipment Resources page 407
COMMUNICATION Developmental verbal dyspraxia can occur as part of a generalised developmental coordination disorder, or in isolation		*Refer to Auditory processing Foundation Skills FS 1D page 23 and Language Foundation Skills FS 5, FS 5A–FS 5D page 101, 103–109*
Receptive language Has a range of difficulties in the area of understanding spoken language: Has delay in the development of verbal comprehension Has greater ability to understand language than use language	Break down instructions into small chunks and allow time in between to respond Check that child has understood the instructions Use written/pictorial support as appropriate, e.g. photos, symbols, written word, diagrams Give unambiguous instructions Encourage child to ask for clarification when necessary Use a variety of practical examples and visual support when introducing new concepts Give instructions and allow child to verbalise back to check that she has heard and understood Withdraw child to quiet area and give simplified instructions	Seek advice from speech and language therapist Refer to A 11 page 397, A 14 page 405

Teacher observations of the child	Practical strategies	Further advice
COMMUNICATION (Continued)		*Refer to Auditory processing Foundation Skills FS 1D page 23 and Language Foundation Skills FS 5, FS 5A–FS 5D page 101, 103–109*
Expressive language Has a range of difficulties in the area of using spoken language: Has little or no spoken language, or very chatty but very difficult to understand Has spontaneous use of gestures and pointing to communicate Displays poor syntax, i.e. the way in which phrases, clauses and sentences are formed by combining words Omits grammatical function words such as 'is', 'are' and 'the' Has difficulty sequencing words in sentences shows poor organisation of spoken language due to difficulties sequencing events Demonstrates jumbled thoughts when speaking/writing Is often misunderstood and frequently frustrated	Use home/school book to support child during news/circle time Encourage teaching staff to ask targeted questions and support the child to give the answer Use a recognised signing system such as Signalong to encourage language development and reduce frustration for child and listener. Use an alternative means of communication such as PECS (picture exchange communication system) or voice output communication aids (VOCA) for child with severe learning difficulties and/or severe developmental verbal dyspraxia Practise using important curriculum vocabulary in sentences Model correct use of language rather than correcting child Expand on child's language by modelling how to add another word Allow time for child to formulate his response without fear of being interrupted Use pictures, story boards, spider diagrams and word webs to generate ideas for creative writing and practical activities Give choices if child is experiencing difficulty thinking of a word Heighten child and staff awareness of the difficulty	Seek advice from speech and language therapist

Refer to A 11 page 397 |
| **Phonological/speech sound development** Has a range of difficulties in the area of speech sound development: Has considerable difficulty developing a normal speech sound system Uses speech which is unintelligible or very unclear | Give extra time to allow child to process her thoughts and speech Use home/school book to note key names and events which the child may speak about | Seek advice from speech and language therapist |

Teacher observations of the child	Practical strategies	Further advice
COMMUNICATION (Continued)		Refer to Auditory processing Foundation Skills FS 1D page 23 and Language Foundation Skills FS 5, FS 5A–FS 5D page 101, 103–109
Produces articulation which is inconsistent and imprecise Is sometimes able to imitate sounds or words but not able to initiate them Has difficulty producing multi-syllable words May have difficulty with non-speech oral motor control	Model correct production of difficult words rather than correcting child	
Social communication Shows reluctance to take part in group discussions	Use a 'talking prompt' such as a stick or a teddy for younger children Gradually build up the size of the group, starting with more supportive peers	Seek advice from speech and language therapist
SOCIAL AND EMOTIONAL ASPECTS		Refer to Social and emotional aspects Foundation Skills FS 7 page 113

Shows low confidence/poor self-esteem:
   Demonstrates shyness, isolation from peers
   Is unwilling to volunteer for tasks
	Provide frequent opportunities for child to experience success and personal improvements
	
	Set realistic, attainable goals in tasks and praise for effort as well as achievement
	
	Implement initiatives to foster self-esteem
	
	Facilitate Circle of Friends scheme, circle time approaches
	
	Use social groups to improve self-esteem
	
	Discuss situation with parents
	
	Investigate clubs and groups which are prepared to accommodate child's need
		Refer to A 9 page 389

Uses diversion techniques in an attempt to avoid difficult tasks, e.g. sharpening pencil, going out to use toilet: Becomes class clown to cover up fact that skills are not at a similar level to peers	Break down task into achievable stages and practice stages Discuss with child and parent, agree on goals and produce a contract Implement system for praising effort Choose peers carefully when planning group work	Refer to FS7 page 113, A 11 page 397

![Teacher observations icon] Teacher observations of the child	![Practical strategies icon] Practical strategies	![Further advice icon] Further advice
SOCIAL AND EMOTIONAL ASPECTS (Continued)		*Refer to Social and emotional aspects Foundation Skills FS 7 page 113*
	Discuss with child and parent alternative coping techniques Facilitate Circle of Friends, use circle time approaches	Refer to A 9 page 389
Prefers company of younger peers or adults	Implement initiatives to foster self-esteem Circle of Friends scheme, circle time approaches Encourage friendship groups Provide frequent opportunity for child to experience success and personal improvement Develop performance in task to improve confidence and willingness to integrate with peers	Refer to A 9 page 389
Has difficulty reading non-verbal cues and emotional expressions	Facilitate circle time approaches Implement initiatives to foster emotional literacy and social skills Use verbal reinforcement to explain non-verbal communication, e.g. I am feeling cross/sad	Refer to A 9 page 389
Experiences frustration, anger and lowering of mood, possibly due to an increase in awareness of own limitations	Liaise with parents Facilitate circle time activities Set up 'whole school environment' to enable child to achieve Provide safe environment for child to discuss issues, and regular contact with designated member of staff Lessen potential frustrations and anxieties Enhance emotional literacy Implement initiatives to foster self-esteem, mood management and friendships Break down task into achievable stages and practice stages	Refer to A 9 page 389 Refer to relevant Foundation Skill

Teacher observations of the child	Practical strategies	Further advice
SOCIAL AND EMOTIONAL ASPECTS (Continued)		Refer to Introduction to Social and emotional aspects Foundation Skills FS 7 page 113

Finds regulating emotional responses difficult:
 	
   Is emotionally labile
 	
   Cries easily, is easily hurt
 	
   Over reacts to other children
 	
   May use physical force to express pent-up emotions
	Discuss management with parents
	
	Heighten staff awareness
	
	Facilitate Circle of Friends scheme, circle time activities
	
	Implement initiatives to foster self-esteem, mood management and friendships
	
	Enhance emotional literacy
	
	Identify tasks which motivate and are achievable and practise skills to facilitate integration with peers
		Refer to A 9 page 389

Relies on others in activities, poor at initiating independence	Gradually increase independence in tasks as child achieves success Discuss with parents and child, agree on skills to be targeted at home and school	Refer to A 11 page 397, OTA 9 page 327
FURTHER CONSIDERATIONS		
Relationships within the family and parenting approaches can also influence how a child is performing within the school setting. It is therefore essential to consider all aspects of the child's life rather than just seeing school life in isolation. Children may be reluctant to take part in activities due to anticipated difficulties based on past failure. Often a parent will also have elements of the condition—they too may be disorganised.	Provide regular contact with designated pastoral support/mentor so that family and school have consistent approach and can review priorities together Ensure family have sufficient support and advice from key professionals	

Building Blocks for Learning. © 2008 John Wiley & Sons Ltd.

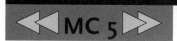
Physical disabilities

There are a variety of reasons why children may have physical difficulties whilst attending primary school. Some of the conditions that are more likely to be seen in the classroom are explained more fully in this chapter. Since the list is limitless, and it is probable that professionals are already involved (e.g. physiotherapist/occupational therapist/speech therapist, school nurse, teacher advisor), the following information provides suggestions for further research about less frequently seen conditions, rather than specific advice about an individual condition.

It is essential that staff are fully briefed on the salient points about the condition prior to the child entering school and when moving up to the next class. Some conditions are degenerative and therefore regular liaison with professionals and parents is essential. Parents are usually well informed about their child's condition and will therefore be able to point you in the right direction for relevant information, e.g. websites, support groups for specific advice and reading material.

The following questions may provide a framework when collating information to give to staff.

 ## How does the condition impact on the child?

- How much is the child able to do in relation to the expectation of their peers?
- How independent is the child?
- How much help will they need?
- How much is the child physically affected?
- How does the condition impact upon their cognitive ability?

What is the child's condition?

- Is it achondroplasia, arthrogryphosis, juvenile arthritis, head injury, limb deficiency, muscular dystrophy, spinal muscular atrophy, a specific syndrome or other condition?
- Is the condition degenerative?
- Are there specific activities which are not recommended for the condition?
- What is the prognosis?

Where is the child affected?

- The whole body
- Specific limb
- Specific parts of body, e.g. right hand/left knee

 When did it start?

- Was it at birth (congenital)?
- Did it occur following an accident (acquired)?
- Was the onset gradual, e.g. initial normal development?

 Who is already involved with the child?

- Parents/carers
- Medical team—occupational therapist/physiotherapist/speech and language therapist/doctor/school nurse/clinical psychologist
- Education team—educational psychologist/advisory teacher/behaviour support
- Voluntary sector staff—Portage worker/Sure Start/family centre/specific support group/after school activity clubs

 What does the school need to consider?

- How can school staff best support the child to reach their potential?
- Modify the curriculum
- Adapt the environment

 Possible physical conditions and sources of further information

Achondroplasia

Restricted Growth Association
RGA Office, PO Box 4008, Yeovil BA20 9AW. Tel 01935 841364; Email office@restrictedgrowth.co.uk; Website www.restrictedgrowth.co.uk

Arthrogryphosis

TAG
Beak Cottage, Dunley, nr Stourport-on-Severn, Worcester DY13 0TZ. Tel 01299 825781. Email taguk@aol.com; Website www.tagonline.org.uk

Down's syndrome

Down's Syndrome Association
Langdon Down Centre, 2a Langdon Park, Teddington TW11 9PS. Tel 0845 230 0372; Email info@downs-syndrome.org.uk; Website www.downssyndrome.org.uk

The Down Syndrome Educational Trust
Sarah Duffen Centre, Belmont Street, Southsea PO5 1NA. Tel 02392 855330; Email enquiries@downsed.org; Website www.downsed.org

Down's Syndrome Scotland
158/160 Balgreen Road, Edinburgh EH11 3AU. Tel 0131 313 4225; Email info@dsscotland.org.uk; Website www.dsscotland.org.uk

Head injury

Headway
4 King Edward Court, King Edward Street, Nottingham NG1 1EW. Tel 0115 9240800; Email enquiries@headway.org.uk; Website www.headway.org.uk

Juvenile idiopathic arthritis

Arthritis Care
18 Stephenson Way, London NW1 2HD. Helpline 0808 800 4050; Helpline for young people and parents 0808 808 2000; Email info@arthritiscare.org.uk/thesource@arthritiscare.org.uk; Website www.arthritiscare.org.uk

Muscular dystrophy

Muscular Dystrophy Campaign
61 Southwark Street, London SE1 0HL. Tel 0207 8034800; Email info@muscular-dystrophy.org; Website www.muscular-dystrophy.org

Hand and arm deficiencies

Reach
Association for Children with Hand or Arm Deficiency, PO Box 54, Helston, Cornwall TR13 8WD. Tel 0845 1306225; Email reach@reach.org.uk; Website www.reach.org.uk

Spinal muscular atrophy

The Jennifer Trust for Spinal Muscular Atrophy
Elta House, Birmingham Road, Stratford upon Avon, Warwickshire CV37 0AQ. Tel 01789 267520; Email jennifer@jtsma.org.uk; Website www.jtsma.org.uk

Specific syndromes and other conditions

Contact a Family
209–211 City Road, London EC1V 1JN. Tel 020 7608 8700; Helpline 0808 808 3555; Email info@cafamily.org.uk; Website www.cafamily.org.uk

Occupational Therapy Approaches

 Introduction to occupational therapy approaches

Occupational therapists use many different approaches when working with children. The choice will depend upon the therapist's initial assessment, the child's area of difficulty, their learning style and the resources available. Both teachers and parents will be aware of the areas of difficulty that are hindering the acquisition of the building blocks required to establish the firm foundations needed for successful learning.

It is important to realise that children learn through play and the 'little and often' approach, spending a few minutes each day targeting a particular skill area, will be more beneficial than one longer session weekly.

Teachers will need to:

- *Prioritise the area of need*—do the children need to learn a particular skill, e.g. cutting with scissors, using a compass, writing fluently or using a keyboard accurately?
- *Be flexible in their approach*
- *Be realistic* in the amount of time and resources children will need to master a skill effectively
- *Provide consistent adult support*
- *Realise that children need to 'over learn' the skill* so that when the support is withdrawn they can still succeed
- *Recognise that success* is often not sustained until skill is fully mastered

Children will need:

- *Constant and frequent encouragement* to practise tasks which they find challenging
- *Tasks broken down* into small attainable stages and presented through a multi-sensory approach
- *Visual feedback/positive reinforcement* to monitor and record their improvement

- *Consistent adult support,* reducing the amount of help given as the skill improves

Included in this section are ideas and activities to help develop, build up and consolidate some of the basic skills that form the foundation building blocks for learning:

- OTA 1 Building firm foundations for spatial and body awareness page 249
- OTA 2 Building firm foundations for left/right awareness page 253
- OTA 3 Building firm foundations for fine motor control page 259
- OTA 4 Building firm foundations for handwriting page 271
- OTA 5 Building firm foundations for alternative methods of recording page 305
- OTA 6 Building firm foundations for dressing skills page 315
- OTA 7 Building firm foundations for scissor development page 319
- OTA 8 Sensory strategies page 323
- OTA 9 Self-organisation approaches page 327
- OTA 10 Consolidating foundation skills through group activities page 333
- OTA 11 Consolidating foundation skills for transition from primary to secondary school page 349

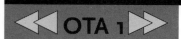

Building firm foundations for spatial and body awareness

Although it is important to help a child name his body parts, it is essential that he can move them independently of each other and feel how movements affect his balance and control. The child must also be aware of his own body size as well as the size and force of his movements. He later learns the relationship of his body to space and other objects.

 Teaching strategies

- Reinforce the names of a specific body part whilst the child moves it, to help develop 'body map' of self.
- Provide weighted arm/ankle bands or carry heavy objects to heighten awareness of weighted body parts.
- Place visual/auditory clues (ribbon, bell) on body part to give sensory feedback.
- Encourage child to close her eyes to eliminate visual inputs and aid concentration.
- Start with large body parts (head, leg) progress to small parts (hand, toes, eyes, ears).

 Activities to improve spatial and body awareness

- *Songs and rhymes* including:
  - Head shoulders, knees and toes
  - Hokey Cokey
  - If you're happy and you know it
  - This is the way we wash our face, comb our hair, clean our teeth
  - Peter Pointer

- *Dressing up games*, especially with heavy clothes, hats, shoes, mittens, necklaces.
- *Face paints*—let the child paint her own face and someone else's. Ensure that she paints both right and left sides. Do body painting with coloured soap paints.
- *Simon Says*—this game can be played with eyes open or closed. Demonstrate action if the child has difficulty with verbal directions:
  - touch right hand to left ear
  - touch toes, shoulders, knees
  - put hands on ankles, hips, knees
  - bend sideways, forwards, backwards at the waist
  - swing arms
  - point toes

- *Dressing dolls*, teddy bears, mannequins.
- *Food*—make gingerbread men, ice faces on biscuits, make sandwiches using people cutters.
- *Art and craft*—using many different media:
  - draw people using finger paints
  - make hand and foot prints
  - draw round child and make drawing into a collage,
  - make models of people using play dough or clay
  - draw people in shaving foam, corn flour, thick paint, sand tray
  - make people with junk modelling

- *Games with beanbags, sponges, ribbons, brushes*:
  - rub different body parts with a sponge/brush—how does it feel?
  - put a ribbon over your left hand
  - put a beanbag on your toe
  - sandwich a beanbag/sponge between your elbow and knee
  - brush/bandage different parts of your body
  - pick up a beanbag/sponge using only your chin/feet/teeth/toes

- *Make shapes with body*:
  - make your whole body into a circle/square
  - which parts of your body can you make touch the floor?—knees, stomach
  - which parts of your body can touch each other?—elbows touch knees
  - make body into animal shapes (frog, fish, worm), explore how they move
  - make body as small as possible/big as possible
  - move through tunnel/bounce on trampette
  - 'Angels in the Snow'

- *Exploring how a body moves*:
  - move forwards, sideways, backwards like animals
  - move quickly, slowly, quietly, loudly
  - symmetrical movements—raise both hands, feet
  - alternating movements—raise left foot then right foot
  - two different movements—raise one leg and one arm
  - moving around room with different parts of the body leading

- *Awareness of specific body parts*:
  - alternate between stretching body part then going 'floppy'
  - become aware of specific body parts without moving them
  - relaxation techniques—tighten/relax different body parts

Further resources

Refer to Foundation Skills

- FS 1 Introduction to sensory processing page 5
- FS 1A Vestibular processing page 11
- FS 1B Tactile sense and tactile processing page 15
- FS 1C Proprioceptive processing/sense page 19
- FS 2 Introduction to gross motor coordination page 31
- FS 2A Motor planning page 35
- FS 2B Postural stability and balance page 39
- FS 2C Spatial and body awareness page 43

Refer to Occupational Therapy Approaches

- OTA 2 Building firm foundations for left/right discrimination page 253
- OTA 10 Consolidating foundation skills through group activities page 333

Refer to Appendix

- A 1 Ages and stages of development page 361
- A 7 Movement programmes and gross motor resources page 381

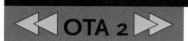

Building firm foundations for left/right awareness

Left/right discrimination

Children who experience confusion about the right and left side of their own bodies are also confused about the directions of right and left. This creates difficulties for them when performing everyday skills and they are unable to perform a specific task involving sidedness or giving directions. This may also result in reversal and inversion in writing.

Work to establish right /left 'discrimination' is designed to help children internalise the knowledge of right and left, so that any response concerning these directions becomes instantaneous and automatic.

Throughout all activities, tactile feedback will help the child identify the body part or direction to be travelled. However, it is important to be consistent and gradually withdraw the tactile stimuli as the child shows progress in internalising directional awareness. For example, if the left arm is grasped firmly to draw attention to it, contact with the right arm should be different—maybe touch with a finger.

Outlined below are selections of activities to help children become familiar with right/left on themselves, other people, in relation to objects and as it relates to writing skills. It is very important that the child verbalises what he is actually doing so he needs to identify whether he is using his right or his left side, whether he is putting a bean bag on his right foot or his left foot and in which direction his body is moving.

General activities

- *Draw around hands*—put the child's hand flat on the table on a piece of paper with the four fingers together and the thumb out at right angles. Draw around each hand and look to see which hand makes the letter 'L'. Reinforce to the child that that hand is her left hand.

- *Put a watch/bracelet/ring or other identifying marks on the dominant or writing hand* (if established). If dominance is not established, put them on the *right* hand.
- *Bandage body parts*, e.g., right hand, right foot, or put small sticky dots on parts of the body. Ask the child to identify where the sticky dots have been put.
- *Put bean bag onto body part*, e.g. the left foot, right ear, or left knee, etc.
- *Sponge sandwich game*—use a sponge and ask the child to make a 'sponge sandwich' by placing the sponge between two body parts. The child is asked to make a sandwich, e.g. use her right knee and her left elbow, her left foot and her right hand.
- *Sing or play the Hokey Cokey* song involving the left and right sides of the body, emphasising which part of the body is being moved.
- *Simon Says* 'Put your shoe on your right foot and your glove on your left hand.' Simon Says 'Put your right hand in the air and your left foot forwards.'
- *Games with instructions* like, 'touch your right knee with your right hand', or 'put your left heel on the floor'.
- *Positioning of objects* to the left or right.
- *Throw bean bags* into designated targets, holding them in the right/left hand, e.g. throw bean bag into left hoop with right hand.
- *Roll a ball* to the right/left.
- *Draw a silhouette*—ask the child to lie down on a piece of lining paper on the floor. Draw round the child. Label right and left parts of their body. Make the picture into a collage.
- *Picture of hands*—get some pictures of the right and left hand, palm up or palm down. Ask the child to make your hand look like this and give her the picture. Ensure that the child is aware of the direction in which she is doing the activity.
- *Directed hand/eye activities*—patting/bouncing/catching, stepping in/out/over things, pushing bean bag forwards or sideways with alternate feet
- *Practice drawing lines from left to right* in different media (shaving foam, sand, finger paints, etc.). Start with large lines and gradually reduce size and thickness.
- *Using rope, make patterns and shapes* and ask the child to face the rope and walk along from left to right. Follow the pattern pushing a beanbag or quoit with a cane

⯈ Activities to help with left/right discrimination on oneself

- *Play games identifying and naming all body parts* on right side of body emphasising your words and touching parts as you say them, e.g. 'This is your *right* hand, this is your *right* ear.'
- *Activities involving turning to right and left*, e.g. jumping quarter turn to right or left, putting that arm out sideways and then turning to face that direction, saying, 'I am turning to the right.'

- *Following a planned circuit,* which includes instructions to turn to the right or left, responding to instructions such as, 'Walk forward four paces, turn right and walk forward three paces.' First, give one instruction, and then two, and then ask the child to do it with his eyes closed, to increase levels of difficulty.
- *Pile of hands*—working with an adult, put alternate hands on top of each other's so that you make a pile of four hands. Put the right hand of the child on the left hand of the adult and then put the left hand of the child on the right hand of the adult. Make sure the child knows which are his right and his left hand. Repeat working with another child.

▷▷ Activities to help with left/right orientation on others

- *Identify body parts*—ask a child to bandage her partner's right hand, left foot, right elbow, etc. An alternative would be to ask the child to put a sticky label on different parts of her partner's body. To upgrade task ask a child to, 'Touch your partner's right shoulder with your left hand, put your left heel on your partner's right knee.'
- *Ask two children to stand side by side.* Give each child a stick/ball/toy in the outside hand. Ask the children to turn and face each other—point out, 'Your right hand [indicate one child] is at the same side as your left hand [indicate other child].'

▷▷ Activities to help with left/right discrimination of objects

- Ask the child to *stand to the right/left of objects,* e.g. 'Stand to the right of the table then to the left of the stool.'
- *Place objects to the left/right of other objects,* e.g. 'Put the stool to the left of the table.'
- *Throwing bean bag with right/left hand into designated targets,* e.g. ask the child to throw the bean bag into the left hoop/box/basket with her left hand.
- *Mark the floor as shown in the diagram.* A book and shoe on either side of the vertical line. An empty square is placed by the side and a short distance away from the original pattern. Later the empty square can be moved to the other end of the room.

■ *The child stands in the footprints,* facing away from the equipment. On command, the child turns and picks up the equipment, one piece at a time, and runs to place it in the same position on the other floor pattern. Initially, the distance between the pattern is kept short so that the child does not have to retain the floor pattern image for too long a time. As the child progresses, the distance between the patterns can be made greater. Place two, then three pieces of equipment on either side of the vertical line. As progress is made, change the positions of the equipment frequently. As the child improves, use more complex floor patterns and many more pieces of equipment.

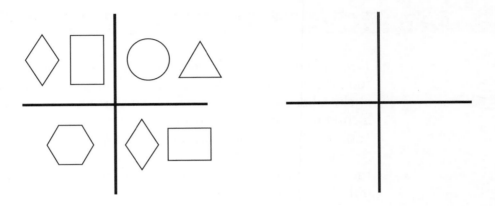

■ *Changing for PE*—ask the child to put his clothes on the chair to the left of the window and his shoes to the right of the door, etc.
■ *Constructional toys and games*—when the child is using Lego®, bricks, cars, etc., she can be asked to put the red brick to the right of the car or to build a garage on the left of the house.
■ *Block designs/positional referents*—place two different coloured blocks in various positions and ask the child to tell which is to the left of the other, to the right of the other. Add a block of another colour and discuss the relative positions of all three. Ask the child to place blocks to the left or right of each other.

▷▷ **Activities to help with left/right orientation and tracking when writing**

■ *Children who confuse and reverse 'b', 'd', 'p' and 'q'* can have smiley faces stuck onto the right or left side of the page. The child then has to remember that the 'b' goes towards the red smiley face and the 'd' goes towards the green smiley face. This helps some children.

- *Roll a ball from left to right*—ensure that the child realises that he always starts a line on the left hand side. When he has rolled the ball he can then draw a line from left to right in the same direction as the ball. Small marbles can be dipped in paint and rolled along the outside edge of a tray or baking sheet.
- *Lean quoits against a bench that is on its side*—the child stands facing the bench, holding a stick or cane. Moving from left to right, she inserts the cane into each quoit, lifting each one in turn and dropping it behind the bench. Once the child becomes proficient at working in this left to right pattern, she should be told it is the same as writing on a black-board or in a workbook.

References

Russell, J.P. (1988) *Graded Activities for Children with Motor Difficulties.* Cambridge, Cambridge University Press.

Further resources

Refer to Foundation Skills

- FS 1 Introduction to sensory processing page 5
- FS 1A Vestibular processing page 11
- FS 1B Tactile sense and tactile processing page 15
- FS 1C Proprioceptive processing/sense page 19
- FS 2 Introduction to gross motor coordination page 31
- FS 2C Spatial and body awareness page 43
- FS 2E Midline crossing and laterality page 51

Refer to Occupational Therapy Approaches

- OTA 1 Building firm foundations for spatial and body awareness OTA 1 page 249
- OTA 10 Consolidating foundation skills through group activities page 333

Refer to Appendix

- A 7 Movement programmes and gross motor resources page 381

Building firm foundations for fine motor control

 Warm up for the upper limb

The following ideas can be incorporated into an individual daily programme, a gross motor group or a whole class PE lesson. Children of all abilities enjoy working together on these activities to develop their postural stability and shoulder strength, which will assist with developing good handwriting posture, fluency when writing and accuracy for fine manual dexterity tasks.

Remember:

- *Quality of movement is more important than quantity.*
- *Alternate between extension (stretching) and flexion (bending) activities.*
- *Get children to shake their hands vigorously between activities.*

It may be helpful to have a small mat or carpet square as a visual cue to show the child where to place his hands/feet.

Wall press-ups

- Stand facing the wall an arm distance away, with the hands flat on the wall at shoulder height.
- Touch nose on the wall, and keeping the back and arms straight, use the fingers to push back from the wall to get to an upright position.
- Make press-up harder by moving the feet backwards, so there is greater angle when leaning against the wall.
- Repeat above but put a clap between each press-up and gradually build up speed.
- One-hand press-ups can be done standing sideways to the wall. Press using the right hand and then the left hand, realising that the further away from the wall the child stands the harder it is to push.

Bunny jumps

- Crouch down and place hands on floor a shoulder width apart, get child to kick her feet in the air.
- Ask her to keep her feet in the air for as long as possible.

Squat jumps

- Crouch down with knees bent placing hands on ground a shoulder width apart.
- Jump backwards to straighten legs and then forwards into crouch position again.

Crouch ball

- Place hands flat on the ground and get into a crouch position, with knees bent and apart.
- Place a ball slightly in front of the hands.
- Taking weight through the arms, try to keep the ball still whilst touching it with the forehead.
- Start with a large ball, progressing down in size to a tennis ball.

Chair dips

- Ensure that the chairs are stable—if necessary have another child sit on the chair.
- Place two chairs slightly apart, back to back.
- Either stand or kneel between the chairs and place one hand on each chair back.
- Push up with the hands to raise the body up onto the toes or jump up and hold a position of straight arms.
- Count the number of press-ups/jumps achieved in given time.

Chair pushes

- Choose a chair that allows the child to sit comfortably with feet on the floor when hands are placed either side of the seat.
- Perch on the edge of the seat and place hands on either side of the chair seat.
- Move forward and lower bottom towards the floor, keeping hands on the chair.
- Push up from the floor to get back onto the seat.

Coffee grinder

- Crouch down with knees bent and the hand used for writing flat on the ground to the side of the body.
- Ask the child to walk round the spread hand, repositioning to accomodate the movement.
- Count the number of complete circles done in a specified time.
- Make it harder by getting the free hand to guide or bounce a ball as the child moves round.

Modified crab walk

- Sit on the floor with hands placed behind the back, fingers flat and knees bent.
- Push up with arms straight, lifting the bottom off the floor.
- Count the number of times the child walks forwards/backwards/sideways between two points.

- Try rolling a ball under the child's bottom, starting with a small one and gradually increasing the size.
- Play crab football.

Air chair

- Stand upright against the wall, with feet slightly forward and apart.
- Bend knees and slide bottom down the wall until sitting comfortably on thin air.
- Keep back in contact with the wall.
- Maintain this position for as long as possible.

Skydiving

- Lie on tummy with arms out to side, elbows bent and palms of hands flat on the floor.
- Lift both arms in the air with head, chest, feet and lower legs off the ground to balance on the tummy.
- Gently lower back to ground and repeat or count the number of seconds the child can hold this position.

Seal moving

- Lie on tummy with arms bent and hands at shoulder level.
- Push the body up with extended arms.
- Keep legs straight behind body.
- Move forwards using the arms to propel body whilst dragging the feet behind.

Tray pushes

- Place a tray or board between two children so they can try to push each other backwards.
- Children face each other in a walk/standing position with one foot in front.
- Keep arms outstretched, hands spread and flat on the board to hold it between them.
- On command, each child tries to push the other backwards keeping arms straight.

Adapted from Russell, J.P. (1998) *Graded Activities for Children with Motor Difficulties*. Cambridge: CUP.

▷▷ Handwriting warm up

These exercises, which can either be used individually or combined into a routine, are designed to help those children who have cramped pencil hold and are an excellent 'warm up' to writing. They develop the small muscles of the hands that are important for manipulation of the pencil, i.e. mature pencil control. Poor pencil grasp and control results in difficulties with pressure, letter formation, fatigue and poor speed. In addition, these children probably dislike writing, as it is frequently seen as being very non-fluid, jerky and untidy. They may also become miserable because the results of their efforts do not match their expectations.

These activities can be used with the whole class in readiness for a hand-writing task. It is important to ensure that children are focused, so it may be helpful to select a piece of music and encourage children to establish slow rhythmical breathing. It may be helpful to use words that give the child a mental picture of relaxation, e.g. try and make your arms melt, or pretend you are a floppy rag doll. For the initial seated activities you may wish to ask the children to close their eyes to reduce distractions. The tasks can be modified depending on the gross motor abilities of the children.

Encourage ideas of releasing tension

- Start rolling the head slowly in a circular motion.
- Roll each shoulder as above.
- Ask the children to sway gently from side to side in their chairs.

Specific activities to encourage relaxation before writing

Standing behind chair

- Stand tall, back straight and feet apart.
  - Breathe in as arms are slowly raised in front of body.
  - Continue to reach up above head and stretch up onto toes.
  - Breathe out as arms are lowered down to sides.
  - Repeat five times.
- Hold onto back of chair whilst standing tall.
  - Go up on toes, then bend down to crouching position.
  - Come back up onto toes and place heels on ground.
  - Repeat five times.
- Stand with feet apart and fold arms behind back.
  - Rotate body to right—bounce 1, 2, 3.
  - Return body to centre.
  - Rotate body to left—bounce 1, 2, 3.
  - Repeat five times.
- Hold onto back of chair with left hand.
  - Bend right knee, lift right foot towards bottom and hold onto right ankle.
  - Stand up straight and concentrate on an object in front whilst breathing normally.
  - Emphasise normal breathing—do not hold breath.
  - Repeat using other side.
  - As balance improves, child can let go of the chair and raise that arm to side.

Seated exercises—check sitting position (feet flat on floor, bottom into chair and back straight)

- Rotate right shoulder—make a circle—repeat five times then shrug.
- Rotate left shoulder—make a circle—repeat five times then shrug.
- Rotate both shoulders—make circles—repeat five times then shrug.
- Hold sides of chair, straighten arms and push bottom up from chair.
- Repeat five times.

- Hold sides of chair and pull chair up towards body.
  - Repeat five times.
  - Shake arms and hands down by your sides.
- Place palms together with fingers spread and press together into 'prayer position'.
  - Push elbows out and heels of hands down to make a straight line.
  - Repeat five times.
- Interlock fingers, turn palms outwards and stretch arms out in front of body.
  - Repeat five times.
- Place heels of hands together with elbows on the table.
  - Curl fingers into palm keeping finger tips apart.
  - Uncurl and touch corresponding finger tips one at a time.
  - Repeat five times.
  - Work with eyes open and then eyes shut.
- Place heels of hands on table.
  - Play fast piano music lifting up each finger in turn.
- Place arms down by side.
  - Curl fingers into palm.
  - Tighten fingers into a fist then release.
  - Repeat five times.
  - Shake arms and hands down by side.

Relaxation period: 1–2 minutes

- Sit back into chair.
  - Let head and shoulders drop.
  - Close eyes.
  - Concentrate on breathing.
  - Come up to alert position slowly when signal given.

Adapted from Handwriting Workout by Karen Dyson, Paediatric Occupational Therapist, formerly of Child Development Centre, Portsmouth, Hampshire, Portsmouth City Primary Care Trust.

▷▷ Hand gym

The aim of the hand gym is to develop hand strength, in-hand manipulation and the fluid movements required for fine motor dexterity tasks. Many of the activities require the use of both hands, but emphasis is on the writing hand, since good control is required for fluency and speed when using a writing tool.

It is helpful to collect and store a variety of activities in a shoebox, which the individual child can personalise by decorating and taking responsibility for the contents. Alternatively, a class box could be assembled, which several children could use at certain periods throughout the school day. To achieve best results, the activities should be done for at least 5–10 minutes daily to improve fine motor function, which will assist in their development in all functional tasks, e.g. buttons, tying laces, and writing. Schools use these activities in a variety of ways during:

- Lunchtime groups or clubs
- Small group sessions led by a teaching assistant
- 'Golden time'
- The end of a lesson when the child has completed her work

It is advisable to discuss and plan the most suitable time/venue within the school day before starting to use the hand gym box. Parents should be encouraged to collect similar items and make a similar box for use at home.

The number and type of items placed in the box is dependent on the age and ability of the child or children. Some schools change the activities regularly, whilst others allow children to work on the same activities for several weeks. When using the activities with a small group of children at different developmental stages, a variety of activities (possibly six) can make up a fine motor circuit (see Appendix 3 page 371). The children attempt each task for a minute and record their scores on their score sheet. The next time they do the fine motor circuit they try to beat that score. In this way, they are competing against themselves rather another child.

When picking up small items the children should be encouraged to use a variety of grips, i.e. pincer, tripod, whole hand grasp, in-hand manipulation (see OTA 4 Hand development page 280). When two hands are required it is important that the assisting hand holds the equipment correctly, e.g. bottle.

Suggestion for items to include in a hand gym box

- *Length of Velcro®*—pull apart and use pincer grip to put it together again.
- *Bubblewrap in different sizes*—pop bubbles by placing thumb underneath a bubble and index/middle fingers on top or vica versa. Use each finger in turn. Try popping bubbles using both hands together.
- *Commercially available small toys*—squeezy toys, wind-up toys, jumping toys, 'press and go' cars, spinning top.
- *Finger puppets*—to isolate different fingers.
- *Nose/ear droppers or plastic bottles (of different sizes and diameters) and table tennis ball*—with partner play puff football by squeezing bottle/dropper to direct air on ball and shoot ball into goal.
- *Multi-link or Lego® bricks*—snap together and see how tall a tower can be made; then pull apart.
- *Sticklebricks/K'nex pieces/Popoids*—pushing together and pulling apart.
- *Clothes pegs/novelty pegs*—clip around the edge of a paper plate or cardboard box. Coloured pegs can be sequenced. Take off using thumb and each finger in turn.
- *Small tongs and cotton wool balls*—use tongs to transfer balls from one dish to another.
- *Pasta/beads and string/lace*—thread a variety of sizes and shapes of pasta/beads onto different laces/string. Does the child use the same hand for threading each time or does he swap hands?
- *Bulldog clips (with prongs flipped back for easy squeezing)*—make a chain by squeezing one clip onto the next.
- *Paper clips*—make a paperclip chain by linking one clip onto the next.

- *Pegboards and pegs of varying sizes*—put pegs in board or copy a pattern.
- *Posting box and coins or small jars with holes in lids*—post coins through hole using fingers; make it harder by holding coins in one hand and post by picking them up with clothes peg or tweezers held in the other hand. Post matchsticks through holes in small jar lid.
- *Small screw top jars in different sizes*—unscrew and fill with buttons, peas, beads, etc., and screw up again.
- *Nuts and bolts in different sizes*—unscrew and screw up, ensuring that the nut is twisted all the way up the thread using thumb and finger.
- *Thick elastic bands*—open with thumb and index finger. Try using other fingers. The thicker the band the harder the task.
- *Geoboards and assorted rubber bands*—place bands over pegs with thumb and fingers to make different shapes.
- *Hole punch and card*—make a pattern using the hole punch, or punch out pre-marked dots.
- *Stapler and card/paper*—make a pattern using the stapler or staple over pre-marked dots.
- *Lacing card and laces*—pull lace through hole to make pattern/shape or practise tying laces.
- *Coloured paper in variety of thickness*—make a paper fan, or fortune teller.
- *Origami paper and instruction book/card*—make object/aeroplane according to instructions.
- *Plain paper*—draw lines of different lengths on the paper and tear accurately, stopping at the end; tear into a spiral or square, either following pencil marking or tearing 'freehand'. Measure finished length; the closer the tears, the longer the length.
- *Paper*—place 'writing hand' flat onto paper. Screw up paper into tight ball without using other hand or pressing into body. When paper slightly screwed up place elbow on table to finish scrunching. Place forearm on table, make an 'O' with thumb and index finger and flick ball at target using each finger in turn.
- *Pebbles, assorted sizes and piece of foam*—pick up a handful of pebbles and drop onto foam one at a time, keeping the remaining pebbles in the palm of the hand.
- *Commercially available travel games with small parts*, e.g. Connect 4, Draughts, Jacks.
- *Play dough/Plasticene®/therapeutic putty.*

▷▷ Ideas for using therapeutic putty

Therapeutic putty is available in different strengths, identified by different colours. Always refer to the catalogue when ordering, as it is important that the child is given the correct strength, especially if he has hyper-mobile or lax joints. Since the putty softens with warmth from handling, it will also soften if left in the sun or over a heater. If left on a flat surface it will spread into a puddle and 'flow' along the surface. It is therefore essential that it is always put back in the storage container after use. If it drops onto the floor or gets onto clothes, take a small piece of putty and put it over the bit that needs to be removed and pull. It should come off the surface cleanly.

Work using putty in a sausage shape

- *Roll putty into a sausage*, using one or both hands. Use the fingers rather then the heel of the hand.
- *Push the pad of each fingertip and thumb into the sausage*, as in a piano exercise. Try doing each hand separately and then both together.
- *Tease up spines from the sausage using thumb and each finger in turn*, i.e. thumb and index finger, thumb and middle finger, thumb and ring finger, or thumb and little finger. Pull upright and let go.
- *Keeping sausage on the table, squeeze it with thumb and fingers to make it longer*. Fold sausage into thirds to make a 'dense' sausage. Place this between the hands. Press together to squash into flattened sausage, keeping the elbows out and pushing forearms down onto table.
- *Make an 'S' shape* and holding top and bottom in both hands squash together. Hold putty and twist in opposite directions to make a spiral sausage, then make into the 'S' shape and twist again. Pull down long strips with thumb and index finger of writing hand.
- *Holding putty at shoulder height in non-writing hand*, let it make a pattern whilst falling on the table in a heap. By changing the size of the piece being pulled and the strength of the pull, interesting patterns are formed, as the finished 'string' will vary in size and thickness.
- *Pull pieces off the sausage and roll* between the palms to make marbles, or use thumb, index and middle fingers to make into ball.
- *Make a long sausage into a small circle* and place outstretched fingers inside circle. Push fingers against the putty to make the circle bigger.

Work using putty in a round shape

- *Mould putty into a ball using one hand* by rolling it on the table, or two hands by placing it between the palms and using a circular movement.
- *Using two hands put the ball between the straight fingers*, extend the wrists, bring elbows out to the side and press hard, keeping the fingers straight. Remove the putty so that the vertical line imprints are now horizontal across the fingers. Repeat as above.
- *Make the ball into a 'burger'* by hammering it with the fist.
- *Put the 'burger' on the table* and with each finger try to press a hole through the putty.
- *Hold the 'burger' in the non-writing hand and crimp around the edge* (as when making pies) with the writing hand, using the thumb and each finger in turn.
- *Hold burger vertically in both hands*, placing thumbs on front of burger and fingers behind. Keeping elbows on the table pull sideways to enlarge, then turn burger around and repeat until pancake size.
- *Alternatively, hold and turn the 'burger' in the non-writing hand* and pull the putty, using thumb and finger(s) of the writing hand to make a 'pancake' large enough to cover one hand. Try and keep the shape round rather than oblong, triangular or like an octopus.

- *Place the 'pancake' over the palm of the writing hand*, prop the elbow on the table and put the other hand behind your back. Manipulate the putty into a ball, listening for the popping noises as the air is squashed.
- *Place hand on table* and put the pancake over the back of the hand, open the fingers and push the putty between the fingers. Squeeze the fingers together to squash the putty.

▷▷ Pencil aerobics

These exercises are designed to help children who have cramped grasp when holding a writing tool. They are designed to develop the small muscles of the hands that are important for manipulation of the tool. Keep your elbow on the table and last two fingers curled into the palm. Older children can use a chart to record their scores.

Push-ups

- Hold pencil horizontally with the fingers and thumb as if about to write on a wall in front of you.
- Pull your fingers towards your palm and keep the pencil horizontal as if pulling the pencil tip out of a crack in the wall.
- Then straighten the fingers and thumb to push the pencil back into the wall.

Jogging

- Hold the pencil and move your fingers and thumb along the shaft to the blunt end and back to the point as if walking or jogging.
- Try and keep the pencil straight.

See-saw

- Begin with jogging, but stop when fingers and thumb are in the middle of the shaft.
- Move the pencil like a see-saw up and down between index and middle finger.

Windmill

- Hold the pencil in the middle. Rotate the pencil like the blade of a windmill; only use the first two fingers and thumb to turn it.
- Change direction as the wind changes.

Helicopter

- As above, hold the pencil in the middle and rotate the pencil like the blade of a helicopter.
- Keep it horizontal using only the thumb, index and middle fingers.

Now try them all with closed eyes to increase awareness of the movements involved.

Disappearing dots

- Hold pencil with a rubber on the end and make a dot on paper.
- Using only the index and middle fingers, twist pencil round and walk fingers down to the rubber.
- Rub out the dot, twist pencil around, walk fingers to point and repeat.

▷▷ Doodle games

Doodle dots

- Prepare a piece of paper with a number of dots along a line, about two or three centimetres apart.
- Begin to make spikey stars or petal shapes with the pencil centred on the first dot and the hand firmly anchored (stress the notion of anchoring).
- Continue to repeatedly draw through the dot in a series of smooth, controlled movements to build up the shape.
- Move the hand onto the next dot and repeat.
- As the flexibility increases so should the area covered by the pattern. Particular emphasis should be placed upon passing *exactly* through the centre dot at each return.

Doodle pictures

- Draw an outline of an object or letter, e.g. car, cat, 'H'.
- Holding the paper still, go over the outline with a pen/crayon/coloured pencil/highlighter pen using one of the pre-writing patterns (see OTA 4 Handwriting page 287), keeping the writing tool in contact with the paper whilst changing direction.
- Change colour and repeat using the same pattern.

Doodle patterns

- Make shapes which are the constituents of handwriting patterns, e.g. circles and lines, aiming for speed, fluency and consistency of size.
- Each series of movements should last for only one or two seconds, but be as rapid as possible.
- *Circling to the left* (or anti-clockwise)—the basic movement for many letters: a, c, d, e, g, etc.
- *Circling to the right* (or clockwise)—needed for: b, h, m, n, etc.
- *A series of vertical lines drawn very rapidly* (between five and ten in two seconds), all nearly on top of each other or just touching, i.e. tightly bunched—needed for all ascenders and descenders in letter formations.
- As flexibility increases, a range of other more visually interesting patterns can be introduced.

Doodle alphabet

- Use the lazy eight pattern (eight on its side by forming two circles) as a basis for writing each letter of the alphabet.

- Start by taking pencil from centre up to the left and make a circle, follow through up to the right to make the other side of the eight.
- Draw the lazy eight several times, then, keeping the movment going, draw an 'a' in the left hand circle.
- Repeat process for each letter of the alphabet.

▷▷ Hand/finger relaxation strategies

Many children who experience pain and discomfort whilst writing will benefit from developing and using strategies to help them relax their hand and so enable them to continue the task. Younger children will need adult direction and support to achieve this, but older children can utilise strategies independently in preparation for secondary transfer. Since each child will have different muscle groups that are aching, they will need to experiment and find out which of the following exercises are helpful:

- If they are bending their fingers a lot they will need to stretch them.
- If they are stretching their fingers excessively they will need to bend them.

It is important that the child selects activities from the following exercises that she can do without disturbing her classmates.

- Hold onto the edge of the chair with both hands and push self up, lean to right and then to left.
- Sit on hands with palms uppermost.
- Shake hands up and down as if shaking water off hands.
- Shake one hand fast whilst holding the other still.
- Wiggle fingers.
- Rest forearm and wrist on table and tap each finger in turn as if playing the piano.
- Pull down length of each finger in turn as if pulling ring off.
- Screw hands into ball and then stretch out.
- Interlock fingers, turn palms outwards and stretch arms out in front of body.
- Place elbows on table with palms together and fingers spread; press together into 'prayer position'; slide elbows out and wrists down ensuring the heels of the hands stay together.
- Interlock fingers behind head and push elbows back.
- Interlock fingers and push above head with palms towards ceiling.
- Rub hands together.
- Make a fist and bring out each finger in turn.
- Place hands together with palms and fingers touching; maintain palms together and move fingers.
- Make interlocking hoops with fingers and thumbs; try to pull them apart. Try each finger in turn.

Adapted from Ann Markee and Maggie Wagstaff (1995) *Hands Up for Handwriting*, Rugby Handwriting Group, May 1995. Bicester, Oxon, Handwriting Interest Group, now National Handwriting Association (see Useful Addresses).

Further reading

Refer to Appendix

- A 5 Handwriting programmes and fine motor resources page 375

Further resources

Refer to Foundations Skills

- FS 1 Introduction to sensory processing page 5
- FS 2 Introduction to gross motor coordination page 31
- FS 2A Motor planning page 35
- FS 2C Spatial and body awareness page 43
- FS 2D Bilateral integration page 47
- FS 2E Midline crossing and laterality page 51
- FS 3 Introduction to fine motor control page 55
- FS 3A Visual motor integration page 59
- FS 3B Vision and ocular motor control page 63
- FS 3C Manual dexterity page 69

Refer to Occupational Therapy Approaches

- OTA 4 Building firm foundations for handwriting page 271
- OTA 7 Building firm foundations for scissor development page 319
- OTA 10 Consolidating foundation skills through group activities page 333

Refer to Appendix

- A 1 Ages and stages of development page 361
- A 3 Fine motor circuit page 371

Refer to Equipment Resources page 407.

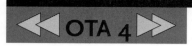
Building firm foundations for handwriting

 Handwriting

Handwriting is a very complex perceptual-motor skill, yet children are expected to achieve proficient handwriting early in their school career. It is assumed that they will have mastered the basics by the age of eight years and therefore be able to cope with the increasing demands of the Key Stage 2 curriculum.

Legible and fluent handwriting is the goal, as studies have shown that 'within a school day a child spends on average one third of their time on writing activities relating to language tasks, one quarter of their time on writing tasks relating to general studies including topic work, and a smaller proportion on writing related to mathematics'. Charles Cripps (2001) suggests that 'the majority of time children spend in the classroom is devoted to communication activities: listening, talking, reading and writing. Of these four, writing takes up the greatest amount of time'. He also indicates that 'children spend 55% of their communication time involved in writing related tasks in Key Stage 1, rising to 65% in Key Stage 2' (Addy, 2004). In addition, 'the development of writing ability is not only important in building a child's self-esteem, but is considered an essential ingredient for success in school' (Feder & Majnemer, 2007).

There are many components to handwriting 'encompassing a blend of visual-motor coordination abilities, motor planning, cognitive and perceptual skills as well as tactile and kinaesthetic sensitivities' (Feder & Majnemer, 2007). These can be further broken down:

- *Fine motor control* is required for:
  - *in-hand manipulation* when adjusting objects, e.g. pencil within the hand after initial grasp, in readiness for writing
  - *bilateral integration* to enable the child to stabilise the paper with the non-preferred hand whilst holding the pencil with the preferred hand
  - *motor planning* when the child needs to plan, sequence and execute letter forms and ordering of letters in words

- *Visual motor integration* is required to coordinate visual information with a motor response, thereby translating what the eye sees into finger/hand movements. This allows the child to reproduce letters and numbers for written tasks.
- *Visual perception* is required to accurately interpret what is seen in relation to its shape, size, position, orientation, closure, and spatial placing on the page, including where to start, how to track horizontally from left to right and where to finish. In addition, visual memory/sequencing, figure/ground discrimination and visual attention are needed.
- *Perception of kinaesthetic/proprioceptive input* is required as it provides the conscious awareness of the body position, movement and grading without auditory or visual cues. As the hand moves across the page, when using a writing tool, it provides perception to tell the child his hand/body movement and position. It lets the child know where to position and move his forearm, build a motor memory of the shape of each letter and helps him appreciate the rhythmic qualities of writing, as in joining letters for cursive script. It also influences pencil grip, the amount of pressure placed through the writing tool, the ability to write within boundaries and provides information about the direction of letters.
- *Auditory perception* is required to enable the child to register, transmit and interpret information given through aural input. It is important that she is able to discriminate sounds and retain what she has heard, so she can select and attend to relevant auditory stimuli whilst screening out irrelevant information.
- *Sensory awareness* in the fingers is required to provide information about grasp of the writing tool, eraser, paper and surface. Poor sensory awareness will require greater visual monitoring and therefore increase fatigue.
- *Sustained attention* is required to enable the child to perform a handwriting task for an extended period of time.
- *Postural stability* within the pelvic and shoulder girdles is required to sustain a good functional working position so that the child can concentrate on the written output without having to constantly adjust her posture.

According to the National Literacy Strategy Framework, by the end of Year 3 'it is expected that pupils should be able to do the following:

- Build up handwriting speed
- Increase fluency and legibility
- Be proficient in the implementation of the four basic joins introduced in Year 2. These include:
    - diagonal joins to letters without ascenders, e.g. ai, ar, un
    - horizontal joins to letters without ascenders, e.g. ou, vi, wi
    - diagonal joins to letters with ascenders, e.g. ab, ul, it
    - horizontal joins to letters with ascenders, e.g. ol, wh, ot

- Ensure consistency in size and proportions of letters and the spacing between letters and words.' (Addy, 2004)

Many children struggle to acquire the necessary handwriting skills in spite of having regular practice in the classroom. 'There is evidence to indicate that handwriting difficulties do not resolve without intervention and affect between 10 and 30% of school aged children' (Feder & Majnemer, 2007).

Before planning any intervention, it is essential *that a full assessment is given* to identify the specific areas of difficulty. There are many excellent handwriting programmes available (see A 5 page 375), and the following pages are designed to help start the remediation process.

▷▷ Development of pencil grasp

The child's tool grasp may affect the control efficiency, flow and speed of written output. An incorrect grasp may hinder the amount of recording a child is able to achieve before experiencing discomfort in the writing hand or forearm.

'Between the ages of three-and-a-half to six years a child's grasp should develop from a static tripod grip, where there is more than one finger on the barrel, to the dynamic tripod grip, where the tool is held between the pads of the thumb and the index finger' (Taylor, 2001). The overall aim is to achieve a dynamic tripod grasp, since in this hold the pencil is fully supported for fluent letter formation. Once a child has the necessary hand dexterity a dynamic tripod posture can be encouraged. It is important to have an awareness of the developmental stages, as it would be unrealistic to change a child directly from a palmar-supinate grasp to a dynamic tripod grasp.

Pencil hold is closely related to the development of fine motor skills, with the general pattern being as follows:

1–1½ years: palmar-supinate grasp—arm moves as a unit.

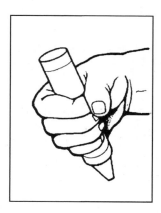

2–3 years: digital-pronate grasp—forearm moves as a unit.

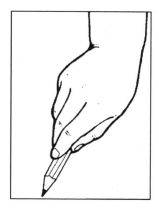

3½–4 years: static tripod posture—hand moves as a unit.

4½–6 years: dynamic tripod posture—thumb and index finger isolated.

Illustrations from *The Erhardt Developmental Prehension Assessment*, 2nd Edition, copyright © 1994 by Rhoda P. Erhardt. Published by Erhardt Developmental Products. 2379 Snowshoe Court, Maplewood, MN 55119. Reprinted by permission.

 ## Efficient and inefficient grasps

An efficient grasp, commonly referred to as a tripod grasp, consists of:

- Holding shaft of pencil between pads of index finger and thumb, 2 cm above point (2.5 cm for left-handed children)
- Supporting underside of tool shaft on side of middle finger, with ring and little finger slightly curled into palm to provide stability
- Resting outer surface of hand, i.e. side of the little finger, on writing surface
- Resulting in opening the 'web space' to form an open 'C' shape with thumb and index finger
- Wrist in extended position, which allows the side to side movement used both in letter formation and moving the hand across the page

A combination of thumb, finger and wrist movements allow the child to control the tool and regulate the amount of pressure exerted. (See Figures OTA 4.1 to OTA 4.4 for other efficient grasps).

An inefficient grasp does not allow the tool to be held comfortably and securely to enable a fluid and smooth writing action.

Adults observing these children writing will often notice that the child:

- Stops writing and shakes his hand due to pain
- Uses whole hand and arm movement to manipulate pencil, instead of isolating fingers and thumb movements

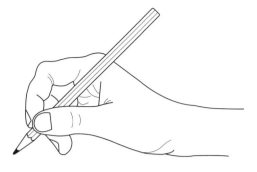

Figure OTA 4.1 Tripod grasp

Figure OTA 4.2 Low developed tripod grasp

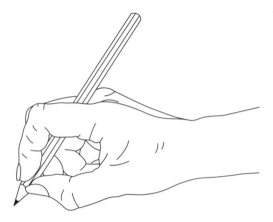

Figure OTA 4.3 Adapted tripod

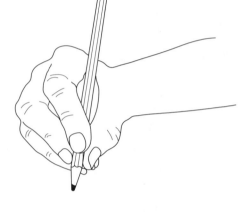

Figure OTA 4.4 Quadrupod

Figures OTA 4.1–4.4 Efficient grasps

- Looks very tense and the hand is often white around the knuckles as she has lost the open 'C' shape and flattened the natural arches of the hand which enable fluid movement
- Hyperextends (bends back) tip of index finger to compensate for her lack of control of writing tool
- Frequently lifts pencil off paper as she is unable to maintain fluid and efficient movements
- Has poorly developed writing skills compared to her peers
- Has a greatly reduced written output which is not commensurate with her verbal ability
- Adopts a very rigid posture or collapses across the table, in an attempt to gain more stability
- Tires quickly, becomes frustrated so wants to give up writing task

Some inefficient grasps are illustrated in Figures OTA 4.5 to OTA 4.9.

It is worth remembering that for some children an adapted grip, if functional and comfortable is appropriate. Since changing or improving a pencil grasp once it has become fully established can be extremely difficult, the success of this is often dependent upon the motivation of the child wanting to attempt the task. When undertaken, it is essential that teachers

Figure OTA 4.5 Inefficient grasp

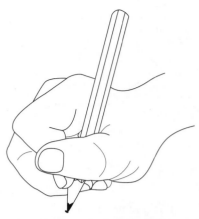

Figure OTA 4.6 Thumb wrap

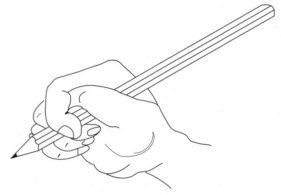

Figure OTA 4.7 Thump tuck grasp

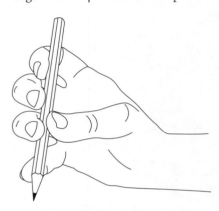

Figure OTA 4.8 Index grip

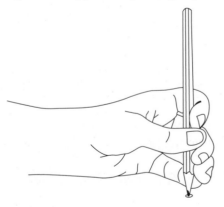

Figure OTA 4.9 Left hand index grip

Figures OTA 4.5–4.9 Inefficient grasps

and support staff are aware that the child is attempting to improve her pencil grasp and to provide positive help and feedback as required.

▷▷ Improving pencil grasp

Children who are trying to improve or change their pencil grasp may be helped by:

- *Sitting down with an adult* to discuss the reasons why they may want to change their pencil grasp and how that could be achieved

- *Trial of alternative pens* to determine the most comfortable and efficient, with particular reference to:
  - *shaft/barrel size*—larger barrels open the child's web space and reduce tension
  - *integral/cushion grip*—to help with placement of finger and thumb on shaft
  - *weight*—a heavy weight pen can increase sensory feedback
  - *flow*—investigate properties of different pens, e.g. roller pens, fountain pen, felt tip, biro, calligraphy pen
- *Trial commercially available pencil grips* to re-educate the child's finger/ thumb placement on the shaft. It is important to ensure the child uses this correctly and for a time limited period
- *Review posture*
- *Trial angled writing surface*
- *Provide regular opportunities to practice hand and upper body strengthening activities* (see OTA 3 page 259)

> ## Three easy stages for teaching pencil grip

These activities are designed to improve the child's pencil grip from an inefficient grasp to an efficient one by changing the motor memory. Before starting this exercise regime, it is important to decide which grasp the child is trying to achieve for maximum function, i.e. tripod or adapted tripod. The child should not be encouraged to use the new pencil grasp until it is firmly established, which may take several months. This is not a quick fix approach; it will take a considerable time as well as requiring motivation of both child and adult overseeing the programme.

- *Pick up*—get the child to pick up a pencil and hold it in the air with the thumb and fingers correctly placed. Make a few circles in the air with the pencil and then drop it down. Start with five pick-ups per day and build up in fives or tens until child can do 100 pick-ups of the pencil automatically.
- *Scribble-wiggle*—give the child a piece of paper that has a small coloured dot marked in the centre. Get the child to pick up his pencil, hold it correctly and place the point on the centre of the dot. Ensure the outer edge of the little finger rests on the paper. Get the child to make wiggly marks through and around the coloured dot without lifting his hand or the pencil. Build up as above.
- *Write*—get the child to pick up the pencil, hold it correctly and write the first letter of her name. Gradually add other letters until she is able to write all her letters using the correct grip. Initially, ask the child only to write her name using this new grip and gradually build up the amount of work to be done using it. It is likely that by this stage the child will be using the grip automatically for the majority of her work.

Adapted from Olsen (2003).

Equipment to help develop pencil grasp and fluency

Careful assessment of the child's difficulties is essential so that the aid or grip meets the child's needs, rather than thinking that every child requires the standard grip. Often a 'low tech' aid may solve the problem, although there are a huge variety of pencil grips, pencils and pens commercially available that may help the child gain greater control while encouraging correct grasp of the writing tool. Whilst many commercially available grips have clear indicators of the correct thumb position (L for left hand, R for right hand), it is essential to consider the position of the grip on the pencil, especially when working with a child who is left-handed.

'Low tech' ideas

To provide an efficient and effective way of problem solving and helping a child achieve a tripod grasp, teachers may find it helpful to have a box containing a variety of 'low tech' ideas available in the classroom. The box may include clothes pegs, small 'air' balls, foam, tape, coloured spots, stickers, rings, Micropore tape, insulating tubing or Plastazote®, small cardboard tube, Blu-Tack, rubber bands in various thickness and sizes, permanent coloured felt tip pens, and a variety of commercially available pencil grips, pencils in different degrees of hardness and pens with integral grips.

*If the child is **pressing heavily** (e.g. paintbrush/pencil/felt tip pen)* open the web space to reduce tension on the finger joints:

- *Try an alternative tool* with a larger, thicker and softer shaft/barrel.
- *Thread a writing tool through small plastic 'air ball'* and get the child to place the palm of his hand on top of ball and fingers/thumb around the shaft.
- *Enlarge the shaft* by pushing pencil through a piece of pipe insulating tubing or Plastazote®.
- *Pad up the pencil shaft* using foam and tape.
- *Use a softer pencil* (2B) rather than the standard (HB).
- *Place a strip of Micropore tape* along the back of his slightly bent index finger, to improve joint awareness and stability.

*If the child cannot **achieve stability*** by placing her fingers on the writing tool (with the ring and little finger curled into the palm and thumb, index and middle fingers moving freely):

- *Clip a clothes peg around the shaft above the point of pencil,* so it sticks out at right angles. Get the child to hold the peg by wrapping her middle, ring and little fingers around it and then holding the pencil with the thumb and index finger. The shaft then rests against side of the middle finger.
- *Curl ring and little finger around a small ball, cardboard tube or eraser* whilst holding pencil.

*If a child cannot **place his fingers in the correct position*** on the shaft:

- *Use a rubber band to provide tactile feedback* by wrapping the band around the pencil and telling him that his fingers must stay on the band.

- *Place adhesive tape or paint* around the pencil to give a visual cue for the correct positioning of fingers/thumb.
- *Colour code fingers and pencil* (using coloured dots or stickers) to indicate which finger holds the pen at a particular spot.
- *Place a ring* over the child's index finger to remind him that this finger needs to be placed on the pencil grip.
- *Mark a spot on the pencil or grip* to remind the child that the index finger needs to cover the spot.

*If a child cannot **hold the pencil at the correct angle**—pencil shaft may be upright or pointing away from the wrist:*

- *Put a thick rubber band* or pony tail hair band round the child's wrist.
- *Loop another band* to the first one, so joining them together.
- *Get the child* to place the top of the blunt end of the pencil shaft into the loop of the second rubber band.
- *Hold the pencil normally* with a tripod grasp, ensuring that the loop knot allows the pencil shaft to lean towards the web space.

Commercially available equipment

Some of the more common grips and pens include:

- *Triangular pencil grips*—both in hard rubber and softer sponge (place sticker/spot on both the pencil grip and the child's finger/thumb to act as a visual prompt for correct placement).
- *Tri-go pencil grips*—lets fingers touch pencil and controls fingers in tripod gasp.
- *Grippy/Stubbi/Stetro*—small pencil grips.
- *Ultra* pencil grips—available in two sizes, is a larger, softer pencil grip offering more control and support.
- *Cross-guard Ultra pencil grip*—has a finger guard, which prevents the fingers crossing over, so encourages correct placement.
- *Grotto* grips—have a partition and covered fingertips, which makes it virtually impossible to use incorrectly.
- *Comfort pencil grips*—either plain foam or ridged, provide visual and tactile cues on the pencil.
- *Ring fitting over index finger* with pencil grip hold to encourage angle of pencil backwards to thumb web space.
- *Noodle Doodle grip*—extends over the length of the pencil and scrunches up to fit right where the fingers need to be placed.
- *Hand hugger/Lyra Ferby/Write Start*—triangular pens/pencils with shaft in different thickness.
- *Textured pencil*—rubber spots up shaft to prevent hand slipping.
- *Integral cushioned grip* incorporated into pencil shaft—available in different diameters.
- *Angled pen nibs* raised from paper, e.g. Yoropen.
- *Alternative shaped pens*, e.g. Ring pen, Pen Again, Stabilo S'Move.

- *Moulded splints with integral pencil grips* for those children who cannot hold a writing tool could be made by an occupational therapist.
- *Dexball*—the ball is made of high-density foam and a special fixture, which allows the pencil to be held with a whole hand grasp. It slides easily over the paper so the whole arm can make the movement for writing or drawing.

Some children require additional sensory feedback to enable them to concentrate on their writing. Many different pens and writing aids are available including:

- *Wake up! Pencil grips*—textured grips for children with poor touch discrimination.
- *Tran-Quille pen*—provides a small vibration in fine, even stages which helps raise awareness of where the hand is in space and the way letters are formed, without making the writing 'squiggle'. The ends of the pen are chewable, which may prove a useful calming strategy.
- *Squiggle Wiggle Writer*—vibrating pen, which enables children to become aware of their hand movement and encourages fine motor control.
- *Star light-up pens*—good for grading pressure as when too much pressure is applied the pen lights up.
- *Light-up Jelly pens*—motivate children to hold the pen correctly when writing.
- *Propelling pencils*—lead breaks when excessive pressure is exerted.
- *Weighted pens*—can help dampen a child's tremor.
- *Lightweight pens*—can be useful for a child with muscle weakness.

Hand development for handwriting

It is important that children are encouraged in activities to promote the development of mature manipulation needed in preparation for writing. *Development of the palmar arches* gives the ability to maintain the curve in the palm whilst holding the writing tool.

Development of wrist extension is necessary for making skilled finger movements and changing direction fluently with the writing tool.

The separation of two sides of the hand through stabilisation of the ulnar (little finger) side allows skilled use of thumb, index and middle fingers. When writing, the ring and little finger should be curled into the palm to provide stability for making directional movements with the writing tool.

Development of the web space (the open/curved space between thumb and index finger) allows refined movement of the writing tool. The aim is to have an open 'C' space rather than a closed 'U' shape when holding a writing tool.

Development of intrinsic muscles of the hand allows fine push and pull movements of the fingers and thumb (flexion/extension). This often requires the tips of thumb, index and middle fingers to be touching, as required in a tripod grasp.

Adapted from Reeves (2005).

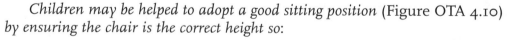

▷▷ Ergonomics

Functional sitting position

Children need to sit correctly so that they can concentrate on the classroom task without having to be constantly aware of their physical position. If they have to use increased effort to maintain good sitting balance, the precision for fine motor or cognitive tasks will be compromised. As a quick rule of thumb, seat heights should be at least one third of the child's height or above the hollow of the knee when the child is standing. Ideally, seats should have a forward sloping angle and the table should be at least half the child's height.

   Children may be helped to adopt a good sitting position (Figure OTA 4.10) *by ensuring the chair is the correct height so:*

- *Feet are supported*—flat on the floor or on a footrest
- *Knees are at 90°*
- *Chair seat depth* will fully support thighs; chair seats should not tip backwards
- *Lower trunk is touching the back of chair*
- *Child leans slightly forward*—optimum position 30° from upright
- *Forearms placed on the table*
- *Head is up*—approximate distance from table is elbow joint to the middle knuckle
- *Chair is pulled into the table/desk*
- *Table height*—approx 5 cm above the level of child's bent elbow when seated as above

- *Elbows are resting on the table* in a comfortable position (at least 30° from body)
- *An angled writing surface* may be required (see Equipment Resources page 407)
- *A wedge cushion* helps those children who tip their chair forwards (see Equipment Resources page 407)

Figure OTA 4.10 Correct sitting position when handwriting

Functional working position in standing

Children who have difficulty maintaining an upright standing posture will find fine motor tasks hard since they need to focus and concentrate on maintaining working posture.

Children who cannot maintain an upright position may be helped by:

- *Allowing child to work in an alternative position*—lying on wedge or roll, high kneeling, half kneeling on hands and knees, side lying
- *Allowing child to lean (prop)* against an appropriate fixed work surface
- *Enlarging child's workspace* to allow for propping and excess movements
- *Sitting for task* or providing a raised table if table/bench is too low
- *Adapting task* to enable child to sit throughout
- *Alternating standing with sitting*

 Table surface

It is essential that the writing surface is relatively clear so that the child can concentrate on the task without distractions (Figure OTA 4.11). The table surface may need to be angled to provide:

- More efficient position
- Stability of shoulders to increase handwriting flow
- Easier visual focus

Figure OTA 4.11 Working at an angled surface.

Children may be helped to work in a more efficient position by:

- *Experimenting with the gradient of working slope* required to achieve child's optimum working position. The recommended angle is 20°; however, some children may prefer more or less of an incline (see Equipment Resources page 407).
- *Using commercially available angled surfaces* (see Equipment Resources page 407) or homemade model designed to the child's requirements.
- *Improvising angled surface* with a lever arch file or clipboard resting against pencil case/book.
- *Ensuring use of drawing board/easel* in appropriate lessons.
- *Sitting appropriately.*
- *Working on a non-slip surface.*

 Texture of writing paper or surface

When children are first exploring with writing tools it is important to realise that the writing surface and paper texture will affect the movement of the writing tool, e.g. crayon, felt tip pen, pencil, paint-brush, chalk:

- A *white board* will provide a quick and easy result with little pressure.
- A *chalkboard* will provide a resistive surface, requiring more effort and control but giving greater feedback.
- *Shiny and glossy paper* will increase the fluency of the tool so is useful for children who have difficulty with smooth movements.
- *Matt and textured paper* provides more friction giving children greater control of the writing tool.
- *Raised lined/Stop-Go paper* allows the writer to see as well as feel the base and top lines (see Equipment Resources page 407).

Paper position

The position of the paper in relation to the child may affect the flow and speed of handwriting. Some children can produce good handwriting with paper in a variety of positions. The hand should be placed below the base line so that the child can see what is being written (Figure OTA 4.12). A strip of tape can be placed on the table to reinforce the correct position of the paper:

- *Right-handed children*—angle paper to the left or leave it vertical.
- *Left-handed children*—it is essential that paper is angled to the right and placed slightly to the left of midline, as the left-hander has to push the writing implement across the paper and the arm moves inwards.

An optimum position for paper is an angle between 35°–45°. An easy method for achieving this is to get the child to:

- Sit straight at table (check posture).
- Clasp hands together in line with both head and midline of body.
- Place elbows on edge of table so forearms make a triangle.
- Lay paper inside the formed triangle, parallel to writing hand.

Figure OTA 4.12 Left and right hand paper position

Position in class

Class teachers are faced with many challenges as they seek to present the changing curriculum in a variety of interesting and innovative ways. Children who experience problems with recording their learning through conventional means require greater consideration regarding their position in class for each activity.

It is important that children are seated so they:

- *Sit facing the board* without needing to turn their body
- *Have minimal visual distractions* between them and the board
- *Have room for their bookstand* if they require one for copying work
- *Have access to as much natural lighting as possible*; writing should not be obscured by shadow from the head or hand

- *Can move their writing arm with ease*—do not sit a left-handed child close to the right of a right-handed child as they will bump 'writing arms'; place a left-handed child on the left side or end of the table

 Development of pencil skills

Progression of pencil skills

It is important to understand the general development of handwriting skills so that the appropriate activities can be practised. Handwriting emerges from scribbling and as the child develops, design patterns evolve into more precise shapes and then letters. A child first learns to imitate geometric shapes and these can often be seen in early drawings beginning with vertical strokes, then progressing to horizontal strokes and circles. Children imitate before being able to copy freehand, but a good indication of writing readiness is the ability to make an oblique cross as this involves crossing the body midline. The diamond movement is found in zigzag 'v' and 'w'.

The developmental stages of pencil skills are as follows:

1 year—imitative scribble

1¼ years—*incipient* imitative stroke

1½ years—spontaneous scribble

imitates stroke obliterated by scribbling

2 years—imitates vertical stroke

imitates circular stroke

2½ years—imitates horizontal stroke

imitates two or more strokes for cross

3 years—copies circle

imitates cross

3½ years—traces diamond, angles rounded

4 years—copies cross

4½ years—copies square

traces cross

5 years—copies triangle

6 years—copies diamond

Illustrations from *The Erhardt Developmental Prehension Assessment,* 2nd Edition, copyright © 1994 by Rhoda P. Erhardt. Published by Erhardt Developmental Products. 2379 Snowshoe Court, Maplewood, MN 55119. Reprinted by permission.

Pre-writing skills, based around using your senses

Children often need help to develop a variety of skills prior to formalised writing activities. Many children are not ready to sit and do 'formal' activities at a table, so a variety of positions need to be incorporated into a programme. Regular practice for short periods each day is more beneficial than longer, infrequent sessions. Practice short 'word' length samples as well as working longer 'strings' across the page (Figure OTA 4.13). These activities are based around exploring the senses.

Patterns of movement that need to be included:

- Working from left to right
- Working from top to bottom
- Circles—clockwise and anticlockwise
- Diagonal lines in both directions
- Curved lines
- Zig-zag lines

Pre-writing patterns can include:

Figure OTA 4.13 Handwriting patterns

Visual media—looking

- Write/draw on aluminium foil.
- Write/draw on different coloured sugar paper, plain paper or in colouring books.
- Write/draw using a variety of coloured tools including chalk, felt pens, wax crayons, pencils; draw with paint using fingers or brush, try joining gummed stars to make shapes.
- Rub over stencils with wax crayon, or draw round with pencil.
- Colour within boundaries.
- 'Draw' pattern on wall with torch beam in a darkened room.

Tactile media—touching

- Write on resistive materials, e.g. sandpaper, bubble wrap, chalkboard with a variety of crayons, paintbrushes or chalks.
- Draw in sandpit or sand tray using finger, sticks, toy cars, etc.
- Draw in pasta, peas, flour on table or tray.
- Draw in shaving foam or cornflour on table, tray or mirror using brush, fingers.
- Make shapes with play dough, string, wool, lolly stick, wikki sticks.
- Walk, skip, creep along string or rope—place shapes, bean bag, etc., at beginning and end for start and finish.

Gustatory media—tasting

- Draw on an iced cake to decorate it.
- Draw using cheese spread tubes on crackers or bread.
- Ice biscuits.
- Roll out dough to make letter shapes.
- Pick out letters from alphabet spaghetti.
- Warm spaghetti lengths to make letter shapes.

Proprioceptive media—feeling body position

- Use a weighted paintbrush.
- Use a paper towel roll as a 'wand' and draw in the air with both hands.

- Use a ribbon/dance sticks to draw patterns or letters in the air.
- Wipe a table using vertical, horizontal and circular movements.
- Paint on a wall using a large brush and water.
- Make letter shapes with body.

Auditory media—listening

- Use a wristband with bell attached and paint.
- Attach bells to the end of a paintbrush.
- Make patterns in the air with shakers.
- Fill empty jars/milk bottles with varying amounts of water and hit with paintbrush or pencil from left to right.
- Play triangle looking at shape.
- Sing alphabet song while painting.

Olfactory media—smelling

Many children can be sensitive to smell so these ideas need to be used with great caution:

- Draw with scented markers, soap crayons.
- Draw in icing which has been flavoured with a strong essence.

Adapted from Klein (1982).

 ## Multi-sensory handwriting approach

Normal child development starts with exploration through gross motor development, which in turn provides foundations for learning. The multi-sensory handwriting approach works on the premise that children first need to experience gross motor activities prior to developing fine motor skills. Any handwriting programme therefore needs to begin with a gross motor approach.

Handwriting is a complex task made up of many different skills that become integrated to such an extent that an automatic response is achieved. The skills required for handwriting include:

- Gross motor control
- Postural stability
- Body awareness
- Bilateral integration
- Left/right discrimination
- Ocular motor control
- Fine motor control
- Manual dexterity
- Eye/hand coordination
- Spatial relationships
- Visual discrimination
- Visual figure ground discrimination
- Visual memory
- Visual closure

If any of these skills are poorly developed and poorly integrated, for whatever reason, problems with handwriting are very likely to occur. Handwriting does not become a useful skill until it is an automatic process, enabling the child to concentrate on the content and output without having to think about the ergonomics and physical movements needed to put pen to paper.

Since many children are confused over letter names and sounds it is important to identify exactly what they know and can do to develop a baseline before starting a programme.

Listed below are some activities to assist in the development of prerequisite foundations skills.

When devising a multi-sensory handwriting programme it is important to:

- *Give a variety of tools*—wax crayons both fat and thin, chalks, chunky pencils, felt tip pens, paint brushes, roll-on holder filled with paint, sponge pieces, charcoal (draw and smudge with fingers), shaving foam mixed with paint or food colouring, paint mixed with glitter, sand or other textures.
- *Work on variety of surfaces*—paper (white, coloured, black), blackboard, whiteboard, shiny card, textured wall coverings, tracing paper, paper over textured surfaces (corrugated card/sand paper).
- *Use a variety of PE equipment*—canes, ropes, beanbags, quoits, hoops, skittles.
- *Adopt a variety of exploratory positions*—lying on tummy, on all fours, standing, kneeling, sitting at a table: standing at a table, or at a vertical easel, with large sheets of paper pinned to wall, on blackboard, whiteboard flat on the floor, to assist in integrating and establishing patterns of orientation.
- *Write in a variety of sizes*—big blackboards/whiteboards, huge pieces of wallpaper, etc., tiny bits of card, squares or cash till rolls in various sizes.

During each activity it is essential to:

- *List and explain orientations* of up/down, over/under, beside/above/below.
- *Work from left to right and from top to bottom.*
- *Work on vertical surfaces* so the child understands 'up/down'.
- *Work from large to small.*
- *Learn to trace round circles* in an anticlockwise direction.
- *Provide constant reinforcement* to ensure good sensory feedback through touch, smell, sight and sound.
- *Encourage child to talk through the movement pattern* of an activity or letter formation, e.g. 'For "h" I start at the top, go down to the bottom, back up half way and jump over.'

Gross motor activities

Always have a variety of visual aids to reinforce each letter shape—work on either upper or lower case letters depending on the school handwriting policy.

Using the child's body to help develop and visualise an idea of a letter shape in their mind:

- *Make letter shapes with body, join with a partner and work in a small group; make a letter shape 'sculpture'.*

- *Make letter shapes with rope/beanbags/canes/hoops/quoits.*
- *Walk/hop/jump/skip*, etc., over/on the letter
- *Make 'pre-writing' patterns* on floor with canes/ropes/beanbags, chalk (Figure OTA 4.14). Walk along pattern or hold stick in writing hand and trace round shape. Push bean bag or quoit along pattern, verbalising movement, e.g. up, down and round. Always work left to right.

Figure OTA 4.14 Prewriting patterns.

- *Spot letter shapes around the room*, etc.
- *Orientation of letter shapes*—make letters of different material and sufficiently large, so that child can crawl on them, lie on them, hop round them etc.;
- *Place letters along a garden cane or skipping rope* to give child the idea that letters are usually written along a straight line.
- *Draw letter shapes* in the air using cardboard tubes/stick with ribbons or bells attached.
- *Draw letter shapes* on partner's back; use as a team game so last child selects correct letter from a pile and holds it up.

Hand activities

- *Draw pre-writing patterns/letters in shaving foam*, or move car/paintbrush through shaving foam if child is tactile defensive and unable to place hands/fingers in foam.
- *Colour within boundaries* to encourage wrist control.
- *Make pre-writing patterns* using variety of writing tools—multi-coloured crayons, chalk, highlight pens, felt tip pens, vibrating pens, lighting up pens.
- *Make pre-writing patterns on whiteboard* before tracing over with finger to erase it—accuracy can be assessed by seeing if there is any of the original pattern left on the board. Ensure child is standing in the middle of the board so she has to cross the midline of her body.
- *Rainbow pre-writing patterns*—using felt tip pen make pattern and then use another colour alongside previous one to make a 'rainbow'. Repeat using several colours.
- *Change colour of pre-writing pattern*—using blue highlight pen make pattern, then go over line in another colour (yellow will make green, red will make purple, etc.). Child can assess his accuracy as the colour will only change when he goes exactly over the top of the first line.
- *Write with fingers* in pasta, rice, peas, paint, shaving foam, cornflour, flour, etc.
- *Write using small finger paint brushes.*
- *Make large letter shapes* out of pipe cleaners, wikki sticks, lolly sticks, string, play dough, pasta, fir cones, etc.
- *Draw letter shapes in play dough/Plasticene®* using a knitting needle or small stick.

- *Finger tracing round large tactile letters*, e.g. sandpaper, raised wallpaper, furry material, scrunched up paper, etc.
- *Cut out large letters drawn on card or paper*—reinforce shapes by putting peas or string around them—make into a mobile, thread on string to make a message.
- *Roll 'n' write activities*—select letter, place marble in position and visually track pathway, reproduce on blackboard/white board/paper.
- *Recognise letter shapes through touch* using sticky letters/fuzzy felt/magnetic letters, letters placed in bag asking child to find specific letter or identify the letter they have found.

Fine motor activities

When the child is able to hold a thicker writing tool competently, work towards using finer equipment. As the child is learning to relate to top/bottom/up/down, etc., he needs to experience writing in both the horizontal plane, i.e. table/floor and in the vertical plane, i.e. wall/blackboard/whiteboard. It is important that children can recognise and internalise individual letters of the alphabet before they are expected to become proficient reproducing them:

- *Pre-writing patterns* using crayons/paint/pens/felt tips, etc., gaining experience working horizontally and vertically and producing fluent movements for cursive script. Initially make longer patterns and as fluency improves aim for shorter 'word' lengths.
- *Make 'doodle' pictures*—draw a large outline of an object or letter and go over this using a pre-writing pattern, making sure that the writing tool does not leave contact with the paper. Change colour and go over the outline again.
- *Write with stencils*; draw round plastic letters; tracing activities using letters.
- *Cut out and colour* in letters; make a letter mobile; peg sentence on line.
- *Thread beads to make letters*—set in play dough, modelling clay, stick on thick card.
- *Make letter design* using template and Hamma beads.
- *Sew or bake letter shapes.*
- *Group plastic or tactile letters* according to shape of letter features/'families', e.g. rounded letters, stick letters, high letters, low letters, letters with diagonals and mixed letters. When proficient try sequencing the alphabet using a visual prompt, which is gradually removed as the child learns her alphabet.
- *Place letters on three-lined paper* to sort into 'families', making sure they are in the correct zone, i.e. ascending, descending or mid-zone.
- *Use work sheets*—to reinforce accurate letter formation or develop flow for writing fluency.
- *Give paper with visual prompt*—use four-lined paper/three coloured lines for sky/grass/earth—graded from large to small line size to work on letter formation, i.e. high letters, mid-zone, low letters, diagonals, etc., to develop accurate positioning, relative sizing, and correct spacing.

Establishing correct pressure

A child's pencil pressure affects her control, efficiency, flow and output. Children should never write on a single sheet of paper on the table or desk. They should have a laminated sheet of card as part of their equipment.

The results of heavy pressure

- Excessive strain on thumb, finger joints and forearm leading to pain
- Increased force on the end joint of index/middle finger causing an excessive dipped appearance (see Figure OTA 4.15)
- Increased tension in forearm and wrist
- Loss of fluency
- Difficulty writing for a sustained period of time
- Imprinted paper
- Pencil lead breaking, making holes in paper

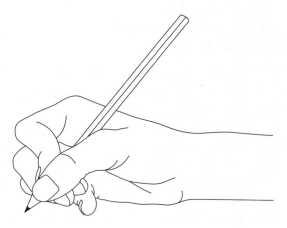

Figure OTA 4.15 Hyperextension

Children who display heavy pressure may be helped by:

- *Using an angled surface.*
- *Using pencil/pen with larger barrel* to reduce strain on finger joints.
- *Using commercially available pens with a cushioned grip* incorporated into the barrel.
- *Investigating nib type and flow of pen on paper*, e.g. fountain pen, roller ball, fibre tip.
- *Writing in an exercise book* rather than on a single sheet of paper on desk.
- *Placing card under paper* to prevent imprint of text onto next page.
- *Placing carpet tile/mouse mat or fleece under paper* so that the child can learn to adapt the amount of pressure exerted.
- *Using hand relaxation techniques* (see OTA 3 page 259).
- *Using two carbon sheets between three sheets of paper* and trying not to mark through to lower sheets.
- *Pressing lightly on tissue* paper resting on a carpet tile or towel and drawing or writing with a felt tip pen or sharp pencil. If the child presses too hard, the instrument makes a hole.
- *Using a pop-up propelling pencil*, trying not to break the lead.

- *Using Micropore tape* to get feedback through index finger. Slightly bend the index finger and fix the tape from the tip of the finger to the knuckle. If the finger hyper-extended due to pressing too hard the child will feel the tape pulling and be able to adjust pressure accordingly.
- *Use large felt tip pens*, which are made to retract when too much pressure is exerted.

The results of light pressure

- Poor pencil control
- Inability to make consistent marks on paper
- Illegible, spidery script
- Difficulty writing for a sustained period of time

Children who press lightly may be helped by:

- *Using an angled surface* to improve functional posture.
- *Investigating nib type and flow of pen on paper*, e.g. fibre tip, roller ball, fine flow, soft pencils.
- *Using hand strengthening activities* (see OTA 3 page 259).
- *Using two sheets of carbon between three sheets of paper* and try making marks through all of the sheets.
- *Pressing hard on paper when using wax crayons*, placing one colour on top of another to make a 'scraperboard' type picture base, before scraping away the colour with a sharp instrument. Talk about the pressure needed to colour and scrape.
- *Using felt pens/gel pens*, as they are sometimes easier to make marks with than a pencil.
- *Using a softer pencil* (2B) instead of an HB.
- *Using vibrating pens* and talking about the feeling when holding them.

▷▷ Consolidation for efficient handwriting

The amount of writing which a child has to complete in school varies tremendously, but 'in an average school day a child spends over half of his time engaged in writing tasks of some kind' (Addy, 2004). It is presumed that by the time a child is ready to transfer to secondary he will be able to write fluently, comfortably, legibly and quickly. 'The ability to produce legible handwriting at speed has been shown to make a significant contribution to achievement'. Researchers (Charter, 2000) concluded that 'continued attention to handwriting throughout the school years is essential and an early start with joined writing will aid a process that is far more than purely a physical activity' (Addy, 2004).

It is therefore important to help children consolidate their early skills, increase their speed and improve their legibility so they do not have to think about the actual physical movements required to produce each letter. There are a variety of handwriting speed tests available to calculate the number of words a child is writing a minute, and it is important that a recognised assessment is always made when extra time is being sought for external examinations. As a rough guide, the following table may be helpful as it gives a suggested number of words copied per minute for each age group:

AGE	6	7	8	9	10	11
WORDS/MIN	3.6	5.6	7.2	9	10.4	12

Handwriting speed test. *Chu, S.* (1999) Assessment and Treatment of Handwriting Difficulties, *11th edn. Self-published when he was working for Hounslow and Spelthorne Community and Mental Health NHS Trust; available as a course handbook.*

▷▷ Rules for writing tasks—preparation/success (P/S rules)

These strategies are aimed at giving children the tools they need to evaluate their own handwriting and set goals to improve it where necessary. They should be used in conjunction with the Handwriting self-evaluation checklist (see A 4 page 373).

Preparation for my writing task—preparation rules—'P' rules

Before starting any written work, think about the following:

> **Posture**
>> **Pencil**
>>> **Paper**
>>>> **Pressure**
>>>>> **Presser**

Posture: how am I sitting? Check if my:

- Bottom is at the back of the chair
- Knees are at right angles
- Feet are flat on the floor
- Chair is well pulled in
- Head and trunk are leaning slightly forward
- Hands and forearms are resting on the table; my elbows are fairly close to my body
- Non-writing hand is supporting the paper
- Head is at the right distance from the desk (knuckles to elbow)

Pencil: how am I holding my pencil? Do I have a:

- Functional grasp on the coloured part of the shaft?

Paper: how is my paper angled? Have I:

- Angled the paper to the left if my pencil/pen is in my right hand?
- Angled the paper to the right if my pencil/pen is in my left hand?

Pressure: how hard am I pressing with my pencil/pen? Have I got:

- Even pressure—not too light nor too heavy?

Presser: have I got something under my sheet of paper? Am I:

- Using a presser (laminated card) to rest my paper on, or am I writing in an exercise book?

Success of my writing task—success rules—'S' rules

Look at each letter carefully
Have I written my letters correctly? Think about the following:

Shape

    Slope

        Size

            Spacing

                Sitting on the line

Shape: ask myself—what shape are my letters?

- Are all the letter shapes formed correctly?

Slope: look to see if the long lines are the right length

- Are all the ascending strokes (sticks) and descending strokes (tails) straight and parallel?

Size: have I got the size right?

- Are all the similar letters the same size and height (mid-zone, ascenders, descenders)?

Spacing: what is my spacing like?

- Are the letters, within the word, evenly spaced?
- Are the words, within the sentence, evenly spaced?

Sitting on the line: do some of my letters 'float in the air' and others 'sink under the line'?

- Are the bodies of the letters touching the line?

When you have checked your finished writing—ask yourself

- What did I do well?
- What do I need to improve?

■ What realistic SMART (specific, measurable, achievable, realistic, timed) goal can I set myself?

Activities to encourage self-evaluation of handwriting

All these activities should be done in conjunction with the preparation/ success (PS) rules for writing. Children should be helped to acquire correct posture/preparation for the writing task before taking *one* aspect of their writing to evaluate and seek to improve. Frequently, working on one aspect will improve another. When they become more proficient, they can work on two or more aspects, until they are able to look at all five areas for one piece of written work to monitor their success.

Using role play to reinforce 'P' rules (this works best with a small group of children)

   Provide a suitable table and chair, with paper, pencil and piece of thick card available:

■ *Talk about each of the 'P' rules*—posture, pencil, paper, pressure and presser.
■ *Ask for a volunteer* to sit at the table incorrectly.
■ *Get the rest of the group to say what is wrong* and then one child goes to the table and tells her how to sit properly.
■ *Repeat the above, looking at each area outlined on the 'P' rules in turn*— make sure that all the children contribute and know how they should sit, hold their pencil, stabilise and angle their paper, exert pressure through their writing tool and rest their paper on a card, rather than directly onto the table surface.
■ *Repeat the 'P' rule* before and after each task, so the children learn it by rote.
■ *Display the 'P' rule* in an appropriate place in the classroom.
■ *If necessary, make a visual prompt*—either written or drawn—to be stuck on their desk.

Using lined paper (four lined, three coloured lines or two lines) (see Equipment Resources page 407) to provide visual cues to reinforce the 'S' rules:

■ *Ask child to copy short four-line poem* onto lined paper.
■ *Look at writing with reference to 'S' rules*—size, slope, shape, spacing and whether the letters are sitting on the line. Talk about the particular aspect that is being targeted.
■ *Choose two coloured felt tip pens* or pencils.
■ *Select one colour for all the 'good' letters* (blue).
■ *Select one colour for all the letters which are not formed correctly* (red).
■ *Encourage the child to underline* each letter with the appropriate pen, according to whether it is written well or badly.
■ *A visual pattern will emerge* so the child will be able to see instantly whether there is more blue or red on the page.
■ *Go through the piece of work discussing* with the child why she used the different colours. When she used red ensure that she knows the reason (the 'a' is too big, the 'p' is not sitting on the line, the 'h' stick is too short, etc.).

- *If necessary, make a visual prompt*—either written or drawn—to be stuck on their desk reminding them of the aspect being targeted.

Using ordinary lined paper

- Repeat as above, but the child will not have the visual cues to help when evaluating.

Copying off the board

- Repeat as above, but the child will have to recall the sentence whilst concentrating on the presentation of the work.

Dictation

- Repeat as above, but the child will have to process the auditory material before writing.

Using Handwriting self-evaluation checklist (see A 4 page 373)

- When the child no longer requires the visual cues of coloured pens use the checklist on a regular basis so that the child can monitor her improvement.
- Keep dated samples so that change is monitored and due praise given.

Follow-up to session

As the child needs continuity, encourage teachers/teaching assistants to use lined paper in every lesson for a defined period so that the child is able to build on the success of having visual cues. Handwriting books can be taken apart or lined paper downloaded from the computer. Alternatively, an extra line can be drawn on regular paper.

Children should be encouraged to use the coloured pens for evaluation. They will soon become very critical of their own work and be able to identify why a letter is correct/incorrect. This is a positive approach and is so much better than being told that their writing is illegible and being asked to repeat the task.

▷▷ Copying from the board

The ability of copying from the board becomes a necessity for children early on in their school career. Today, with the increasing use of interactive white boards, children are expected to be able to look up at information presented on the board or screen (a vertical plane) and transfer it to their book or paper (horizontal plane).

Children who experience visual perceptual difficulties or have problems with visual tracking and ocular motor control may find transferring information from the board to paper extremely challenging. The additional stress of using a writing tool whilst trying to maintain the place on the board/paper may make the task particularly slow. As well as working on the particular problem areas, the following strategies may be helpful:

- *Teacher writes every fifth word in red* and gets the child to use this word as a clue for checking the number of words he has copied. The child should also write that word in red.

- *Teacher writes each line* on the board with a different coloured pen (three minimum).
- *Teacher writes a small paragraph or poem* on the board so that it forms a specific pattern. Indent every other line as a visual clue for the pattern.
- *Provide a paper copy of the material* that can be placed on the table, rather making the child continually look up at the board. Ensure that the paper is placed correctly, possibly using a book holder, according to her visual tracking ability and handedness:
  - straight in front of the child so she only has to look up and down
  - to the left of the child, so she scans left to right
  - to the right of the child, so she scans right to left
- *Stick the teacher's pre-prepared notes* directly into the child's book.
- *Adapt the board material* to make a work sheet that only requires the child to write single words or short phrases.
- *Use highlight pens* to get the child to mark the main points or create a mind map using the information given on the board.

▷▷ Specific advice for left-handed children

Writing tool and grasp

Children who write with their left hand need to hold the pencil/pen at least 2.5 cm from the point (see Figure OTA 4.16) so that they can see the text as they write and prevent smudging when they start using a pen. This correct position for their fingers and thumb can be indicated by a small elastic band twisted around the desired area, by using a pencil grip or by having a pen with an integral grip. A left-handed child often pushes the pen/pencil across the paper and holds the barrel more tightly. If this occurs children should be reminded to stop the writing task and relax the muscles in their hand by shaking and bending the hand, wrist and fingers (see OTA 3 page 259).

Ballpoint, Berol or fibre tip pens produce less friction, whilst specially made left-hander pens, with a broader and more flexible nib, are available from commercial stationers. Sharp pointed pencils are not helpful for young left-handed children, as they tend to jab or pierce the paper. Soft pencils (2B) are more beneficial as they allow smooth movements across the paper.

Figure OTA 4.16 Correct grasp for left-handed student

Seating position in the classroom

It is important that teachers do not sit a left-handed child close to the right of a right-handed child, as they will bump 'writing arms':

- *Place a left-handed child on the left side of two children* or at the end of the table.
- *Sit child on a higher chair* if he finds it easier to write, but it is essential to check that his feet are supported on a footrest if he cannot reach the floor.
- *Check the table height,* because if the table surface is too high the child will be unable to see the letters over his hand when writing.
- *Ensure that natural light is coming over his right shoulder* so that there are no shadows from the child's head or hand when writing.

Paper position and the supportive hand

The paper should be positioned:

- *With the right side to the left of the child's midline* (centre of the body), so she can rest her elbow and swing the forearm in a complete arc without crossing her body.
- *To allow the elbow to move back,* so that the arc of the movement of the forearm is parallel to the next line down, whilst the child is writing.
- *To ensure that the left hand is always lower or to the left of the writing line* as the child writes from left to right across the page. If the writing line goes under the hand, vision will be blocked and a hooked grip is likely to develop. The paper may need adjusting during the writing task.
- *At a slant of up to 45°,* so that the left side of the paper is parallel to the child's forearm as she writes across the line. A useful way to achieve this is to:
  - sit straight at table
  - clasp hands together in line with both head and midline of body
  - place elbows on edge of table so forearms make a triangle
  - move the whole triangle to left of midline so hands are in front of the left shoulder
  - lay paper inside the formed triangle, parallel to left hand
- *Using a visual cue*—tape or draw a line on the writing surface to indicate the angle until the child becomes accustomed to writing with the paper slanted.

The position of the paper in relation to the child will affect the flow and speed of handwriting. There are two coping strategies frequently seen within the classroom:

- The child turns the paper completely sideways or writes down towards the body, which can cause smudging and puts strain on the shoulder joint (see Figure OTA 4.17).
- The child places paper vertically in front of the body, which cramps the left hand into the side (see Figure OTA 4.18).

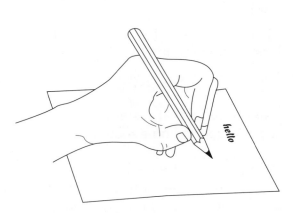

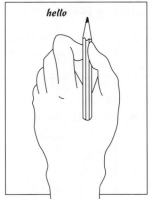

Figure OTA 4. 17 Paper position, sideways

Figure OTA 4. 18 Paper position, vertical

Children who have already developed a hooked grip (see Figure OTA 4.19) are likely to experience:

- *Reduced fluency of arm and finger movements* resulting in having to move the whole arm across the page
- *Jerky effortful movements* causing reduced speed of written output
- *Pain and fatigue in wrist and fingers* for extended periods of writing
- *Smudging of completed work* due to covering up the previous lines of text
- *Difficulty achieving neat writing* and satisfactory presentation of work

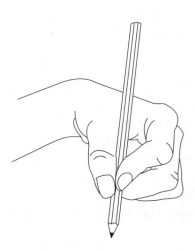

Figure OTA 4. 19 Hooked grasp

Children may be helped by:

- *Using a sloping desk top/angled board,* resting work on a lever arch file or a clipboard
- *Implementing relaxation techniques* (see OTA 3 page 269)
- *Experimenting with alternative tools,* pens or softer pencils
- *Ensuring paper is angled* correctly for a left-handed child
- *Sitting on a higher chair*

References

Addy, L. (2004) *Speed Up. A Kinaesthetic Programme to Develop Fluent Handwriting*. Wisbech, LDA.

Charter, D. (2000) Poor handwriting can cost a GCSE grade. *The Times* 5 June 2000. p. 4.

Chu, S. (1999a) *Handwriting Speed Test*. London, Community Occupational Therapy—Children's Services, West London Healthcare NHS Trust.

Chu, S. (1999b) *Assessment and Treatment of Handwriting Difficulties*. 11th edn (course handbook, self-published). London, Hounslow and Spelthorne Community and Mental Health NHS Trust.

Cripps, C. (2001) Getting it write from the start. Study day notes St John College, York, 28 February 2001.

Erhardt, R.P. (1994) *The Erhardt Developmental Prehension Assessment (EDPA)*. Maplewood, MN: Erhardt Developmental Products. (Original work published 1982).

Feder, K. & Majnemer A. (2007) Handwriting development, competency and intervention. *Developmental Medicine and Child Neurology, 49*, 312–317.

Henderson, S., Markee, A., Scheib, B. & Taylor, J. (1999) *Tools of the Trade*. Bicester, Oxon, National Handwriting Association (see Useful Addresses page 417).

Klein, M.D. (1990) *Pre-writing Skills—Revised*. Tucson, AZ, Therapy Skill Builders.

Olsen, J. (2003) *Handwriting without Tears*. Cabin John, MD, Jan Olsen.

Reeves, J. (2005) *Hand Development for Handwriting*. Dorchester, Dorset, Children's Therapy, Dorset County Hospital Foundation NHS Trust.

Shirley, M. (1996) Why Look at School Furniture? *Handwriting Review 1996, 10*, 55–65. Bicester, Oxon, Handwriting Interest Group, now National Handwriting Association.

Taylor, J. (2001) *Handwriting: a Teacher's Guide—Multi-sensory Approaches to Assessing and Improving Handwriting Skills*. London, Fulton.

Further reading

Alston, J. & Taylor, J. (2000) *Teaching Handwriting: a Guide for Parents and Teachers*. Lichfield, QED.

Barnett, A., Henderson, S. & Scheib, B. (2007) *DASH—Detailed Assessment of Speed of Handwriting*. Oxford, Harcourt Assessment.

Brown, B. & Henderson, S. (1989) A sloping desk? Should the wheel turn full circle? *Handwriting Review, No. 3*. Bicester, Oxon, Handwriting Interest Group, now National Handwriting Association (see Useful Addresses page 417).

Chu, S. (2000) The effects of visual perception dysfunctions on the development and performance of handwriting skills. *Handwriting Today, 2*, 42–55.

Levine, K. (1991) *Fine Motor Dysfunction—Therapeutic Strategies in the Classroom*. Tucson, AZ, Therapy Skill Builders.

Penso, D. (1990) *Keyboard Graphics and Handwriting Skills*. London, Chapman and Hall.

National Handwriting Association (formerly Handwriting Interest Group) works to improve handwriting standards and support children with difficulties. Website www.nhahandwriting.org.uk

The following are available from National Handwriting Association (see Suppliers' Addresses page 413):

- *Writing Left-handed . . .Write In, Not Left Out* (2007)
- *Which Handwriting Scheme?* (2005)
- *Developing a Handwriting Policy* (2005)
- *Tools of the Trade* (1999)
- *Handwriting—Are You Concerned? A Guide for Parents NHA*
- *Hands Up for Handwriting* (1995)

The following resources are available from Anything Left Handed (see Suppliers' Addresses page 413):

- *Writing Left-handed*
- *Helping Left-handed Children to Enjoy Handwriting*
- *Left-handed Children—a Guide for Teachers and Parents*
- *The Left-hander's Handbook*

Left 'n' Write Ltd provides resources, training and support for practitioners working to improve the handwriting of left-handed children (see Suppliers' Addresses page 413).

 Further resources

Refer to Foundation Skills

- FS 1 Introduction to sensory processing page 5
- FS 1B Tactile sense and tactile processing page 15
- FS 1C Proprioceptive processing/sense page 19
- FS 2 Introduction to gross motor coordination page 31
- FS 2B Postural stability and balance page 39
- FS 2D Bilateral integration page 47
- FS 2E Midline crossing and laterality page 51
- FS 3, FS 3A–FS 3C page 55–72 Fine motor control page 55–72
- FS 4, FS 4A–FS4F Visual perception page 73–97

Refer to Occupational Therapy Approaches

- OTA 2 Building firm foundations for left/right awareness page 253
- OTA 3 Building firm foundations for fine motor control page 259
- OTA 5 Building firm foundations for alternative methods of recording page 305
- OTA 8 Sensory strategies page 323
- OTA 10 Consolidating foundation skills through group activities page 333

Refer to Appendix

- A 2 Alphabet ABC sentences page 369
- A 3 Fine motor circuit page 371
- A 4 Handwriting self-evaluation checklist page 373
- A 5 Handwriting programmes and fine motor resources page 375
- A 6 ICT checklist page 379
- A 10 Teacher's checklist for visual signs page 395
- A 12 Twelve rules of legibility page 401

Refer to Equipment Resources page 407

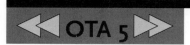

Building firm foundations for alternative methods of recording

At home, many children begin engaging with simple toys that teach cause and effect from an early age, such as games that play a tune when a button is pressed. They then progress to more complex games that require accurate control of a joystick, or mouse, or the depression of an arrow on a keyboard. Classrooms are frequently equipped with interactive whiteboards, digital cameras, laptops, computers and other technology to make the learning environment exciting and challenging, whilst providing the teacher with opportunities to use the wide range of teaching aids.

 ## Complexity of handwriting

Writing is a very complex task for children. 'First they have to figure out what direction the letters go, then they have to link those letters together in a particular sequence to spell words. Then they have to link those words together in a particular order to make sentences. Then they have to link those sentences in a particular order to make paragraphs. Then they have to link those paragraphs together to make reports, stories and essays' (Silverman, 2003).

Children with handwriting difficulties, which may include muscle weakness or associated movements, frequently find the additional visual input used during classroom presentation helpful, but struggle when they have to record on paper what they have learnt and consequently hate writing. Many are unable to 'think and do' simultaneously and so often have many ideas but cannot sequence and organise their thoughts to produce work of an acceptable standard.

Low-tech alternatives

Some children will be able to record work using a writing tool in the long term, but initially an alternative may need to be sought, as they are unable to write down their thoughts as quickly as they are forming in their mind. These alternatives are particularly helpful when children are being assessed for their knowledge gained rather than their handwriting competence. Alternatives may include using:

- *Concrete objects* for number work (teddy bears, cubes, peg boards)
- *Ink stamps* for number and literacy work
- *Plastic letters* to make words/sentences
- *Magnetic letters* on a magnetic board
- *Word banks* for literacy work
- *Bullet points* for taking notes
- *Pictures rather than words* to note/record information such as diagrams, stories, instructions
- *Mind mapping/writing frames* for creative writing
- *Part-prepared* photocopied work sheets
- *A writing buddy*
- *Digital camera*
- *Printout from interactive whiteboard*
- *Voice recognition software*

Interactive whiteboards

An interactive whiteboard is a presentation device that interfaces with a computer. Computer images are displayed on the board by a digital projector via a connection to a computer. Low-noise projectors are available and are essential for children with hearing impairments and for those who are sensitive to constant low-level noise, for instance children with Asperger's syndrome.

The projected images can be seen and manipulated on the whiteboard and a variety of software can be used from projecting video clips, using specialist software for mathematics and other curriculum areas, to using the board as a whiteboard, but inputing the information using specialist toolbars. These toolbars enable teachers and children to write on the board using a variety of colours and highlighting tools, including their fingers. Applications can be run from the board via the connected computer. Notes can be printed from the whiteboard in order to give a copy to children who find it difficult to take notes or process the information from the whiteboard.

The whiteboard is a colourful tool and it is important to use the pen and highlighting tools effectively for the class. Some children may find reading certain colours more difficult than others; at the same time, by effectively using the different coloured fonts on the whiteboard it is possible to draw attention to different instructions or information. For a child who is colour blind extra care needs to be taken when using colours, as the child may find certain colours difficult to discriminate. Line width can also be adjusted to increase the ease with which information displayed on the board can be read.

The interactive whiteboard may be helpful to those who learn visually, providing a stimulating visual environment; however, for children with perceptual difficulties the 'exciting' visual animations may be difficult to follow and too much information on each screen may cause them to turn off altogether. Kinaesthetic learners may be stimulated by the ability to interact with the whiteboard, touching areas to produce answers, for instance to maths or comprehension questions.

Children with motor difficulties may find tapping on the whiteboard easier than clicking on a mouse or finding a key on a computer keyboard. Young children and those with motor difficulties usually find using their finger to write and navigate the board easier than using the stylus.

It is important to plan the use of the interactive whiteboard carefully, taking into account any difficulties that the class members may have. It is an exciting educational tool but may cause problems for children who find visual processing difficult.

 ## Digital cameras

Increasingly, small digital cameras (for instance Digiblue by Tag) are used in the classroom throughout the curriculum. These small cameras enable children to take up to two minutes of video at a time and enable them to edit their shots through a computer programme, adding sound and visual effects. They can be used in almost all primary lessons to capture, for instance, specific moves in PE, to make advertisements and dramas in literacy, or to record a mathematical investigation.

To operate the camera a button needs to be continually pressed while videoing; at the same time the shot can be viewed through the small camera or via a computer screen. It requires dexterity to hold down the button and keep the camera steady focusing on the target shot. Children with fine motor skill difficulties have problems keeping the pressure on the 'on' button and operating the camera in order to record the correct pictures. For these children it may be necessary to hold down the button for them so they only need to concentrate on framing the shot. Some children will find it easier to operate the camera while looking at the picture via the computer screen rather than the viewfinder, which is small, so it requires a certain amount of dexterity to look through the viewfinder and operate the 'on' button at the same time.

Once the shots are downloaded onto the computer they can be edited together and various visual and sound effects added via an editing programme. The editing screens can be complex and difficult for children with visual perceptual difficulties to navigate. It is important for these children that instructions on how to use the system are clearly shown stage by stage. For some children it may help if instructions can be clearly written down so that they have something to refer to and go back to while using the programme, rather than just recalling a demonstration. For other children one demonstration may not be enough and they will need to be shown the various ways of using the programme several times.

 Word processing as an alternative

Using a keyboard and typing provides the opportunity for children to create neat and legible written work quickly through depressing keys, rather than having to think about, and then reproduce, the physical movements of each letter to make up the individual words. There are three stages to learning to type:

- Knowing the keyboard layout
- Typing accurately
- Typing quickly

Therefore, before word processing can be used as an effective alternative to writing by hand, children need to have regular designated time within their school timetable for working through an appropriate word processing/typing package. Establishing these skills takes time, but using a programme, which will possibly have both visual and auditory feedback and simple step-by-step instructions, will help children reinforce their learning so they can quickly and accurately locate keys. Children learn at different speeds and through different styles, so the programme should be selected to reflect the needs of the child rather than having a standard programme for all children in the class.

Generally, children need to be able to type as fast or faster than their handwriting speed before a keyboard is an effective means of regularly recording their work. 'As a rule of thumb, a child needs to have a spelling age of around a seven-year-old and up to progress well with learning to touch type (by which we mean not having to look at the keyboard). However, children with literacy difficulties may then find that learning to type, particularly with a system that uses real words may be beneficial to spelling' (Keyboarding and Touch Typing for Children AbilityNet Factsheet (2007) accessed through the website www.abilitynet.org.uk).

Classroom checklist

To enable children to have maximum output with minimum effort when producing work using word processing, the ergonomics need to be carefully assessed and recorded on a checklist (see A 6 ICT checklist page 379). The class teacher, SENCO and/or ICT specialist, in consultation with the occupational therapist, should complete this. Many areas need to be considered as described below.

Ergonomics

- Chair/stool
- Table/trolley

- The room
- The laptop
- The classroom computer
- Acquisition of keyboarding skills

Whole school awareness of the child and his needs

- Does everyone understand why the child is using the computer?
- Has the child got a contract detailing when the computer is to be used?
- Is the child able to move the laptop to other locations in school if needed?
- Is the child able to take the laptop home for homework?
- Has the family had training and been shown how to use the machine?
- Does the child need additional equipment, e.g. wrist support, book rest, tracker ball, etc.?
- Have safety and storage issues been addressed?
- Are arrangements for monitoring and assessment included in the child's individual education plan?
- Who is responsible for the equipment and the supervision of its use?
- How are staff kept informed and up-to-date?
- How are the child's changing needs addressed?
- Who is responsible for the storage of files on the memory stick, etc.?
- Who will save pictures or icons on the laptop in readiness for the child to use in lessons?

Other considerations when a child is using keyboarding as an alternative method of recording

- Does the ICT suite need adapting?
- Is a suitable touch-typing programme available?
- For which lessons will the child be using the computer/laptop to record work?
- Has a definite regular time been allocated in her timetable for work on developing skills?
- How will the child be prepared for using this ICT as she moves up the school and later in secondary school?
- Which lessons will need specific graphics packages?
- What amount of word processing is expected each day/week?
- How/where is this work being stored?
- What records are being kept to track the child's improvement?
- Are timed tests given regularly to monitor progress—initially aim for accuracy not speed?

ICT resources

It is essential that a multidisciplinary approach is adopted when a child is assessed for any ICT equipment. Seek advice from your LEA ICT advisor, occupational therapist and other personnel involved.

Suggested equipment

- *Rise and Fall computer tables* can improve a child's working posture
- *Wrist rest/support* can help to reduce user fatigue
- *Key guards* fit onto the keyboard and help children to press one key at a time
- *Screen filters* can help to reduce glare
- *Copyholders* can support work when children copy information
- *Key board letter stickers* are available in a variety of lower case letter styles and contrasts
- A range of *alternative access devices* are available such as switches, mouse, joysticks, big key keyboards

Software

There is a wide variety of keyboard awareness software using different approaches. It is essential that a child uses the same software at home and school when he is learning his way around the keyboard. Popular programmes, details of which can be found on the Internet, include:

- Adventures in Typing (Timon and Pumba)
- BBC Schools Dancing Mat Typing
- Easi Keys
- Englishtype Junior
- First Keys to Literacy
- Five Finger Typist
- Kaz (Keyboarding A–Z)
- Quicktype
- SpongeBob Squarepants Typing
- 2Type
- Ten Thumbs Typing Tutor
- Type to Learn Junior
- Type to Learn 3
- Ultra Key 5

Alternatively, a typing programme from a book may be preferable, e.g. Easy Type and Easy Type 2.

A variety of software/programmes with word lists/word banks are available, which enable the teacher to type in keywords relevant to the topic being studied so the child can click and select that word to put within her sentence. Programmes include:

- Clicker 5
- Find Out and Write About Series

A variety of software/programmes with prediction utilities, which display wordlists based on a combination of initial letters, are available, such as:

- Penfriend XP

A variety of voice activated software is available such as:

- Dragon Naturally Speaking version 9

 ## Adaptations/strategies to try

- *Double spacing of text* by setting in default.
- *Dampen keys auto-repeat facility* can be adjusted to stop letters repeating themselves across the screen if key is depressed for too long. On PC go to control panel and select keyboard then change rate of repeat keys to slow.
- *Text to speech facility* can be set to read back what has been written. Consider use of an earpiece.
- *Use consistent styles* if child has difficulty reading information presented in different font styles by setting a default font.
- *Use the On Screen keyboard* instead of the normal keyboard, if finger movements are impaired.

References

AbilityNet Factsheet (2007) *Keyboarding and Touch Typing for Children.* Website www.abilitynet.org.uk

CEA@Islington—*ICT Scheme of Work: Digital Blue Features Skills Guidelines* Website www.islingtonschools.net

Cottier, C., Doyle, M. & Gilworth, K. (1997) *Functional AAC Intervention—a Team Approach.* Bisbee, AZ, Imaginart International Inc.

Penso, D. (1999) *Keyboarding Skills for Children with Disabilities.* London, Whurr.

Silverman, L. (2003) *Poor Handwriting: a Major Cause of Underachievement*, compiled from excerpts of Silverman, L.K. *Upside-Down Brilliance: The Visual-Spatial Learner* (2002). Denver, DeLeon Publishing.

ACE Centre Advisory Trust
92 Windmill Road, Headington, Oxford OX3 7DR. Tel 01865 759800; Email info@ace-centre.org.uk; Website www.ace-centre.org.uk

ACE Centre Advisory Trust North
1 Broadbent Road, Watersheddings, Oldham, OL1 4U. Tel 0161 6271385; Email enquiries@ace-north.org.uk; Website www.ace-north.org.uk

Communication Aids Centre for Language and Learning (CALL) Centre
University of Edinburgh, Paterson's Land, Holyrood Road, Edinburgh EH8 8AQ. Tel 0131 651 6235/6; Email info@callcentrescotland.org.uk; Website www.callcentrescotland.org.uk

The ACE and CALL centres provide a focus for specialist expertise in technology with the communication and educational needs of young people who have speech, communication or writing difficulties. A wide variety of services are available, including assessment, information, specialist training. A variety of information sites is available on the websites.

Ability Net
Freephone 0800 269545 (if you call from home) or 01926 312847 (if you call from work, minicom accessible).

Ablenet is a national charity, helping disabled adults and children use computers and the Internet, by adapting and adjusting their technology. Email enquiries@abilitynet.org.uk; Website www.abilitynet.org.uk

AVP
School Hill Centre, Chepstow, Monmouthshire NP16 5PH. Tel 01291 625439; Email sales@avp.co.uk; Website www.avp.co.uk

Becta
Millburn Hill Road, Science Park, Coventry CV4 7JJ. Website www.becta.org.uk (leads the national drive to improve learning through technology)

IANSYST
Fen House, Fen Road, Chesterton, Cambridge CA4 1UN. Tel 01223 420101; Website iansyst.co.uk

Inclusive Technology Ltd
Riverside Court, Huddersfield Road, Delph, Oldham OL3 5FZ. Tel 01457 819790; Email inclusive@inclusive.co.uk; Website www.inclusive.co.uk, www.inclusive.net for downloads of 'cribsheets' and checklists

Keytools Ltd
PO Box 700, Southampton SO17 1LQ. Tel 023 8058 431114; Email info@keytools.com; Website www.keytools.com

REM Somerset
Great Western House, Langport, Somerset TA10 9YU. Tel 01458 254700; Email sales@r-e-m.co.uk; Website www.r-e-m.co.uk

RM

New Mill House, 183 Milton Park, Abingdon, Oxon OX14 4SE. Tel 0800 0197982; Email primarysales@rm.com; Website www.rm.co.uk

Semerc

Granada Learning Centre, The Chiswick Centre, 414 Chiswick High Street, London W4 5TF. Tel 0845 602 1937; Email sis@granadamedia.com; Website www.semerec.com

Refer to Appendix
- A 6 ICT checklist page 379

Refer to Equipment Resources page 407

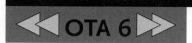

Building firm foundations for dressing skills

All children are learning to refine dressing skills during the primary school years. However, there will be some children who find it harder than their peers to learn or achieve these skills. There is a variety of reasons why a child may have difficulty acquiring the necessary skills for dressing. The most common reasons at primary school age are:

- Developmental, e.g. immature development in foundation skills
- Gross motor coordination, e.g. physical limitations, poor postural stability, reduced bilateral integration, immature spatial and body awareness and poor motor planning
- Fine motor control, e.g. reduced manual dexterity, immature visual motor integration affecting hand-eye coordination
- Sensory, e.g. poor or disturbed tactile feedback, slow visual processing
- Perceptual, e.g. poor processing, sequencing, memory, spatial awareness, shape and form
- Organisation, e.g. immature sequencing and memory

 General advice and considerations

- *Identify abilities and difficulties* in the following skill areas:
  - Developmental level
  - Gross motor coordination
  - Fine motor control
  - Sensory processing
  - Perceptual
  - Organisation
- *Discuss with parents and child* and agree on specific tasks to be targeted.
- *Agree on approach to be used,* e.g. activity analysis, verbal rehearsal, visual schedule/timetable, backward chaining.
- *Ensure a consistent approach* is used, as this is essential in the learning process. Practice each stage in the process in the same way every time.

▷▷ Practical strategies

- *Consider positioning of the child*: ensure that the child is in a stable position before starting any dressing or undressing. A younger child may prefer to sit in the corner on the floor with back and shoulders supported, whereas an older child may find sitting on a low stool or chair with feet resting on the floor more comfortable.
- *Provide a visual timetable/schedule.* This aid can assist the child by giving a pictorial sequence of the stages involved in a dressing sequence.
- *Consider alternative fastenings on clothes*: some children find it difficult to manage fastenings such as buttons, zips, poppers and tying shoelaces, so work on developing manipulative skills and manual dexterity to improve ability to manage fastenings. It may be necessary to consider adapting fastenings by using Velcro®, larger buttons/poppers, ring pull on a zipper and elasticated/curly laces.
- *Adapt style of clothing*, e.g. loose fitting clothing, larger sizes and clothing with an elasticated waist can be easier to manage. As the child's ability to manage dressing improves, try tighter fitting clothing and clothing with standard fastenings.
- *Use specific clothing* that has been adapted to meet a particular need. For example, a wheelchair user may wear back opening clothing or clothing with side zips. The child's occupational therapist will be able to advise on specialised clothing and clothing adaptations.

▷▷ Further reading

Ball, F. (2002) *Hints and Tips for Activities of Daily Living*. London, Jessica Kingsley.

Klein, M.D. (1995) *Pre-dressing Skills*. Tucson, AZ, Therapy Skill Builders.

Turner, L., Lammi, B., Friesen, K. & Phelan, N. (2001) *Backward Chaining*. A Dressing Workbook for Parents. Hamilton, Ontario, Canada. Can Child Centre for Childhood Disability Research. Website www.fhs.mcmaster.ca/canchild

Websites for visual symbols
  www.do2learn.com
  www.ispeek.co.uk

▷▷ Further resources

Seek advice from the child's occupational therapist

Refer to Foundation Skills

Refer to Occupational Therapy Approaches

Refer to Appendix

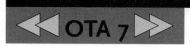

Building firm foundations for scissor development

Children are often fascinated by scissors from an early age. However, the task of using them proficiently is acquired over several years, as gross and fine motor skills are developed and refined. The following chart shows the developmental stages for acquiring accuracy when using scissors. It is important to have a clear understanding of each stage, so that the child can be given appropriate activities to practise.

 The 14 steps in scissor skill development

1. Child enjoys tearing paper during play activities.
↓
2. Child shows an interest in and understands the use of scissors.
↓
3. Child able to maintain correct grip when positioned by an adult.
↓
4. Child able to hold scissors appropriately without assistance.
↓
5. Child begins to open and close scissors.
↓
6. Child able to open and close scissors using a controlled action.
↓
7. Child able to hold paper and make random cuts.
↓
8. Child able to make consecutive cuts with a forward movement.
↓
9. Child able to cut in a straight line avoiding unintentional lateral movement.
↓
10. Child able to cut out simple shapes involving one change of direction.
↓

11. Child able to cut out simple shapes involving more than one directional change.

↓

12. Child able to cut along curved lines.

↓

13. Child able to cut out circles.

↓

14. Child able to cut more complicated shapes with straight and curved lines.

Source: Mahoney & Markwell (2004). Used with permission.

▷▷ Activities to develop pre-scissor skills

Controlling tools with open-and-close hand movements

- Use kitchen or salad tongs to pick up objects, move them from one place to another and release them.
- Punch holes with a handheld paper punch.
- Squirt water from one container to another to mix coloured water or aim at a target, using a turkey baster or small ear drop bottle.
- Commercially available tweezers, e.g. Fish Sticks/one piece chopstick.

Using the two sides of the hands for different functions

- Hold the pads of the ring and little fingers against the palm, whilst using any of the tools mentioned above.
- Open and close tools whilst holding a small object (e.g. cottonwool ball) in the palm with the ring and little fingers.
- Press the trigger on a squirt gun.
- Pick up and release objects between thumb and first two fingertips whilst holding the ring and little fingers against the palm.

▷▷ Activities to help with scissor skills

- Use snips to cut across rolled up play dough or Plasticene®.
- Make single snips on a drinking straw to thread as beads for a necklace.
- Go over the cutting line in highlight pen to make it more visible.
- Cut along thin card as it is easier than paper; cut on wide lines across short strips of card/paper before attempting narrow lines on longer pieces of card/paper.
- Cut between lines of glued straws, lollipop sticks, wool, sandpaper, etc.
- Cut to a target, e.g. to a sticker.
- Cut straight pieces to make paper chains.

- Cut through holes made by a hole punch—straight line, wavy line, circle.
- Cut out large squares, rectangles, triangles before attempting smaller shapes.
- Cut along wide to narrow mazes.
- Cut along a spiral to make a snake/mobile.
- Cut out large pre-drawn letters or numbers.
- Cut out pictures from a magazine to make a scrapbook.
- Photocopy cutting tasks onto card.

Adapted from Levine (1991).

Equipment to help with scissor control

Easy grip loop scissors—these are self-opening lightweight scissors, which allow the child to hold the loop without having to place fingers/thumb in smaller holes. Children who find it difficult to control their thumb and index fingers, or who have not mastered opening the scissors yet, will find them easier since they require less effort to make a cut.

Dual control training scissors—these allow the child to experience the motor movements involved in cutting, as an adult and child can cut simultaneously.

First scissors—these allow a child to learn the correct technique for using scissors as there is an extra loop for the ring finger.

Self opening scissors—these can be used with/without the spring. They make cutting less effortful, so that more concentration can be applied to accurate cutting.

Left-handed scissors—these are essential if left-handed children are to achieve success with cutting skills.

Roll Cut scissors—these have no sharp blades or points, making them very safe to use. Hold the paper 15 mm from the line to be cut, and pull the paper towards the body. The built in guide will enable the user to follow the line to be cut. The Roll Cut incorporates specially manufactured roller bearings, which cut the material, and its handle is designed on ergonomic principles.

Low-tech solution—put a coloured dot on the scissors to remind the child where her thumb needs to go so she can hold it upwards.

References

Levine, K.J. (1991) *Fine Motor Dysfunction, Therapeutic Strategies in the Classroom.* Tucson, AZ, Therapy Skill Builders.

Mahoney, S. & Markwell, A. (2004) *Developing Scissor Skills—a Guide for Parents and Teachers.* Revised edition. Dunmow, Peta UK. http://www.peta-uk.com.

Further Reading

Hill, M. & Hill, K. (2002) *Cutting Skills*, photocopiable activities to improve scissor technique. Wisbech, LDA.

Johnson, P. (2001) *Copy and Cut—My Family and Friends*. London, A & C Black.

Klein, M. (1996) *Pre-Scissor Skills*, 3rd edn. Tucson, AZ, Therapy Skill Builders.

Further resources

Refer to Foundation Skills

- FS 1B Tactile sense and tactile processing page 15
- FS 1C Proprioceptive processing/sense page 19
- FS 2A Motor planning page 35
- FS 2D Bilateral integration page 47
- FS 3A Visual motor integration page 59
- FS 3B Vision and ocular motor control page 63
- FS 3C Manual dexterity page 69
- FS 4B Visual spatial relationships page 81
- FS 4D Visual figure ground discrimination page 89

Refer to Occupational Therapy Approaches

- OTA 3 Building firm foundations for fine motor control page 259
- OTA 10 Consolidating foundation skills through group activities page 333

Refer to Appendix

- A 5 Handwriting programmes and fine motor resources page 375

Refer to Equipment Resources page 407

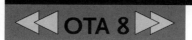 **OTA 8**

Sensory strategies

 ## Sensory diets

Sensory integration theory suggests that our sensory processing enables us to maintain alertness, attach meaning to experiences and learn. A 'sensory diet' is selected automatically and we are unaware of it. Where sensory processing and modulation are extreme or disrupted, it may be necessary to design a sensory diet in order to fulfil physical and emotional needs, so helping development of self and learning. 'A balanced sensory diet is defined as a planned and scheduled activity program that an occupational therapist develops specifically to meet the needs of the child's own nervous system. Its purpose is to help the child become more focused, adaptable and skilful' (Kranowitz, 1998). A sensory diet is like a nutritional diet that requires meals and snacks throughout the day in order to ensure a balance in the body's blood chemistries and sugar levels. Similarly, sensory diets require the right combination of sensory activities and stimulation throughout the day to keep an optimal level of alertness/arousal for learning and settled behaviour. As snacks do, some sensory-based activities can change our mood or level of alertness for a short period, while others (like meals) have a longer lasting effect on behaviour and performance (Paris & Murray-Slutsky, 2005). Wilbarger & Wilbarger (1991) developed the approach to provide the 'just right' combination of sensory input to achieve and maintain optimum levels of arousal in the nervous system.

A sensory diet provides the child with a combination of alerting, organising and calming input through the senses. When developing sensory diets occupational therapists will consider how much (intensity), how often (frequency) and how long (duration) a child needs specific input to help them focus and maintain attention.

We all have different sensory preferences to maintain our sense of alertness and therefore be more efficient at making adaptive responses. Activities that help one child may be inappropriate for another. In addition, how much, how long and how often the input is needed will also vary from child to child and referral to an occupational therapist is recommended. It is important to remember that for many children the phrase 'sit still and listen' is extremely difficult, 'most children can *either* sit still *or* pay attention. They need to move to get the sensorimotor input *in order* to pay attention' (Williams & Shellenberger, 1996).

Sensory techniques for use in the classroom

The classroom environment is often busy and distracting and the child with sensory processing difficulties who has problems regulating arousal levels often displays regulatory behaviours such as wriggling, daydreaming, fidgeting and wandering. The following activities/strategies may be helpful within school to help the child maintain attention and concentration and so reduce distractibility and off task behaviour (see Equipment Resources page 407 for further details):

- *Fidget/fiddle items*—'legitimate fiddling'. Allow child to have something to fiddle with, such as Blu-Tack, stress ball, key ring, fidget pen, as long as this does not distract the other children or become the focus of attention.
- *Movin'sit cushion*—air filled wedge cushion, which improves child's posture and increases proprioceptive input.
- *Heavy muscle work*—provide opportunities for child to carry items, e.g. heavy bag/tray to the office. Allow child to carry/lift/move, e.g. equipment in readiness for games/PE. Encourage activities against resistance, e.g. push-ups on chair or against wall.
- *Movement breaks*—regularly allow child to get up and walk around room, run an errand to the school office/another classroom or take part in school movement programmes such as Huff and Puff, Take Ten, Wake and Shake, Golden Mile (see A 7 Movement programmes and gross motor resources page 381). Make transitions between activities more active, e.g. marching.
- *Work Station*—privacy boards, to exclude too many visual distractions. This can be set up as an 'office' at the side of the room and should be used for set periods of work so the child is not excluded from the class group.
- *Headphones/ear defenders*—these reduce the background noise and can be used with or without music, for specific periods of work.
- *Chewing*—pencil with tubing on the top which can be chewed instead of cuff or collar; drinking water from sports bottles or through straws.
- *Weighted vests or lap snake*—heavy cuddly toys, such as kitty cuddles, to increase sensory awareness, if placed on shoulders or lap.
- *Clear uncluttered desks*—reduce visual distractions by only having essential items on the table.
- *Behavioural strategies*—set clear targets, which may contribute to reduction of sensory overload (protective reactions) and give meaning to discriminative ability.
- *TEACCH* strategies—can provide order to the sensory environment. (Treatment of Education of Autistic and related Communication handicapped CHildren TEACH).

The sensory activities should be provided proactively, rather than reactively, to help best prepare the child's nervous system for optimum learning. It is important to allow the child to use the sensory strategies that are helpful to them on a regular basis as part of the school day, e.g. always sit on movin'sit cushion at desk or on the carpet; rather than using this as a 'privilege'. It is also important not to penalise the child by keeping them in at break times, as the physical activity will help concentration during lessons.

References

Kranowitz, C.S. (1998) *The Out-of-Sync Child: Recognizing and Coping with Sensory Integration Dysfunction.* New York, Perigee.

Oetter, P., Richter, E. & Frick, S. (1995) *MORE Integrating the Mouth with Sensory and Postural Functions*, 2nd edn. Hugo, Minnesota, PDP Press Inc.

Paris, B. & Murray-Slutsky, C. (2005) *Is it Sensory or is it Behaviour? Behaviour Problem Identification, Assessment and Intervention.* San Antonio, Psychological Corporation.

Wilbarger, P. (1995) The sensory diet: activity programme based on sensory processing theory. *Sensory Integration Special Interest Section Newsletter*, **18**, 1–4. Bethesda, MD, American Occupational Therapy Association Inc.

Wilbarger, P. & Wilbarger, J. (1991) *Sensory Defensiveness in Children Aged 2–12: an Intervention Guide for Parents and other Caretakers.* Santa Barbara, CA, Avanti Educational Programs.

Williams, M. & Shellenberger, S. (1996) *How Does Your Engine Run? A Leader's Guide to the Alert Program for Self-Regulation.* Albuquerque, Therapy Works Inc.

Yack, E., Aquilla, P. & Sutton, S. (2002) *Building Bridges Through Sensory Integration: Therapy for Children with Autism and other Pervasive Developmental Disorders*, 2nd edn. Las Vegas, Sensory Resources.

Further reading

Dewey, D., Kaplan, B., Crawford, S. & Wilson, B. (2002) Developmental coordination disorder: associated problems in attention, learning, and psychosocial adjustment. *Human Movement Science*, Dec. **21** (5–6), 905–918.

Dunn, W. (2007) Supporting children to participate successfully in everyday life by using sensory processing knowledge. *Infants and Young Children*, **20** (2), 84–101.

Heller, S. (2002) *Too Loud Too Bright Too Fast Too Tight—What to do if you are Sensory Defensive in an Over-stimulation World.* New York, Harper Collins.

Kranowitz, C.S. (2003) *The Out-of-Sync Child has Fun: Activities for Kids with Sensory Integration Dysfunction.* New York, Perigee.

Nackley, V. (2001) Sensory diet applications and environmental modifications: a winning combination. *Sensory Specialist Interest Section Quarterly*, **24** (1), 1–4.

Rotz, R. & Wright, S. (2005) *Fidget to Focus—Outwit your Boredom, Sensory Strategies for Living with ADD.* New York, I-Universe Inc.

Shield, B. & Dockrell, J. (2006) Acoustical barriers in classrooms: the impact of noise on performance in the classroom. *British Educational Research Journal,* **32** (3), 509–525.

Further resources

Refer to Foundation Skills

- FS 1, FS 1A—FS 1E Sensory processing page 5–30
- FS 7 Social and emotional aspects page 113

Refer to Occupational Therapy Approaches

- OTA 1 Building firm foundations for spatial and body awareness page 249
- OTA 3 Building firm foundations for fine motor control page 259
- OTA 10 Consolidating foundations skills through group activities page 333

Refer to Appendix

- A 5 Handwriting programmes and fine motor resources page 375
- A 7 Movement programmes and gross motor resources page 381
- A 9 Resources for developing social, emotional and behavioural skills page 389
- A 14 Work system page 405

Refer to Equipment Resources page 407

Self-organisation approaches

Children who experience difficulty organising themselves throughout the day may benefit from utilising a variety of strategies. It is important to discuss any management approach with both the child and her parents to ensure the strategies can be consistently used and therefore become automatic and useful for the child. Initially the child may need considerable adult support, but this guidance can be gradually reduced as the child's independence increases.

Teacher observation	Practical strategies
The child is unable to recognise personal space of self and peers when sitting on the carpet.	Use a visual tool, such as a cushion, mat, carpet square or movin'sit cushion, to help identify the child's position on the carpet.
	Sit child on edge of circle or group so she does not disturb peers.
	Work on a body and spatial awareness programme (see FS 2C page 43, OTA 1 page 249).
	Teach rules around personal space and consider implementing a social skills/awareness programme (see A 9 page 389).
	Talk to peer group and explain reasons for child's behaviour.
The child is disorganised and lacks awareness of personal space- constantly bumping into people and furniture, knocking things over.	Teach rules around personal space.
	Work on a body and spatial awareness programme (see FS 2C page 43, OTA 1 page 249).
	Provide frequent opportunities for graded resisted activities to help increase the child's body awareness (see FS 1C page 19, FS 2C page 43).
	Involve child and parent in agreeing strategies.
	Talk to peer group and explain reasons for child's difficulties.
The child has a cluttered work area, disorganised work space, lacks awareness of environment.	Encourage an uncluttered work area, mark out work area with tape.
	Reinforce clearing away and putting equipment back where it belongs.
	Provide adult prompts as a reminder.

Teacher observation	Practical strategies
Child intrudes on neighbour's work area.	Ensure a supported functional posture is used (see OTA 4 page 271). Consider use of cushion, movin'sit cushion, footrest. Teach rules around personal space, consider implementing a social skills/awareness programme (see A 9 page 389) Work on a body and spatial awareness programme (see FS 2C page 43, OTA 1 page 249). Provide regular breaks in task at agreed intervals. Consider child's position in class, ensure there is adequate space in work area.
The child appears disorganised when preparing for task—makes several journeys to collect equipment, starts task without having all equipment required.	Encourage child to repeat back instructions to ensure he has understood task. Help and encourage child to pre-plan task, ask child to list equipment needed before starting. Ensure all equipment is easily accessible for task. Provide visual checklist/cue cards listing equipment needed for each task. Provide child with a set of equipment and ask child to list each piece and identify its purpose. Arrange for paired working and adult support as required
The child has difficulty organising personal items in cloakroom—difficulty hanging coat and PE bag on peg.	Provide peg on end of row. Consider use of a colour coding system for pegs, coordinate colour on peg with hanging loop on coat and PE bag. Discuss with parents adapting loop on coat—enlarging loop, changing colour of loop. Use visual schedule, showing sequence of activities to be performed on arriving in class at beginning of day, after break times and end of the day.
Child has difficulty managing self at lunchtime—standing in queue, carrying tray of food, messy eater, clearing lunch box away.	Develop routine for lunchtime. Use visual schedule showing sequence of activities. Position child at front or back of the queue. Consider position in dining hall, sit child at end of table. Make sure wet wipes are available throughout the meal and encourage child to routinely check face/hands are clean.
Child changes for PE slowly, has difficulty with fastenings and orientation of garments.	Allow extra time for dressing, start changing before rest of class. Practise dressing skills (see OTA 6 page 315). Discuss with parents possibilities for alternative clothing, e.g. elasticated waist trousers, polo shirts, Velcro® for fastening shirts. Use visual timetable to identify sequence of clothing and raise child's awareness if clothes are on back to front or inside out. Use timers and timed checklists, introduce behavioural/star charts to reward achievements. Provide adult support if required.

Teacher observations	Practical strategies
Child has difficulty coping with changes in routine.	Use visual timetable to inform child of predicted changes.
	Implement consistent system for preparing child for change before it happens, such as giving a five-minute verbal warning, use of a timer.
	Adhere as much as possible to established routines, and where not possible give extra preparation time and rehearse changes.
	Encourage child to pre-plan change and reinforce by talking it through.
	Rehearse changes to routine and what might happen next, e.g. how to get to new location in advance.
Child has difficulty formulating a plan of action when attempting new task—knows what is required but unable to complete task, slow to start task, work is often incomplete.	Use activity analysis approach to break down task into stages.
	Provide written or visual step-by-step instructions, as well as verbal instructions.
	Encourage child to pre-plan activity before he starts task, use mind mapping, writing frames, work system, Goal, Plan, Do, Check, approach (see A 11 page 397).
	Talk through ideas and what might happen next.
	Set attainable goals to be achieved within an agreed time period.
	Consider peer and adult support.
Child is unable to break down components of task when problem solving.	Break down task into stages, use Goal, Plan, Do, Check, approach (see A 11 page 397).
	Use cue cards and written checklists showing sequence for task.
	Practise breaking down task into component parts using a favourite, achievable task and reinforce each stage with visual reminder.
	Talk through ideas and what might happen next.
	Give clear, concise, step-by-step verbal instructions.
	Consider peer and adult support.
Child is unable to remember important information and items, packing school bag.	Ask child to repeat back or read aloud instructions to ensure he has understood, highlight instruction on paper with a marker or write on whiteboard.
	Make lists of things to do and cross things off when they are done.
	Use transparent pencil cases for ease of visual checking.
	Use rough book/small pocket-sized notebook/post-its, to jot down important things to remember.
	Highlight specific information.
	Encourage child and parents to use a diary/calendar at home with writing, pictures/symbols to transfer essential information to bring into school, e.g. days needed to bring in library book, musical instruments, homework (see A 11 page 397).

Teacher observations	Practical strategies
	Discuss with parents possibility for child and parent to pack bag together using diary/calendar, packing bag the night before often helps reduce pressure on time in the morning.
	Write simple checklists in 'link book' to remind child of items he regularly needs to take home, e.g. lunch box, PE kit, musical instrument.
Child has difficulty generalising skills—unable to transfer skills competently to achieve similar task, takes longer time to learn new skills.	Break down task and work on specific skill areas, then link skills together with similar tasks.
	Practise breaking down task into component parts using a favourite, achievable task, reinforce each stage with visual reminder.
	Encourage child to pre-plan activity before starting task, use mind mapping, writing frames, work system, Goal, Plan, Do, Check, approach (see A 11 page 397).
	Talk through ideas and what might happen next.
	Be aware that child will need to learn task as a new skill and need to practise each stage of the learning process. Provide extra adult support to practise skill.
Child has a reduced sense of time and urgency—becomes absorbed in activity and finds it hard to stop, desperate to complete task before doing next activity.	Use alarms, watches, timers, timed checklist to provide cues.
	Use work system, visual timetable (see A 14 page 405).
	Introduce behavioural strategies, e.g. star/reward chart.
	Agree with child the amount of work to be achieved in a specific time.
	Agree on a time in the day when child can finish a task, and write this on child's daily planner/timetable.
Child does not complete homework, homework forgotten, takes child much longer to finish homework than expected.	Consider quality of work versus quantity when setting goals and discuss with child.
	Set realistic goals and with child and parent, agree on the amount of time child should spend on homework.
	Discuss strategies with child and parents, e.g. use of computer, parents to scribe.
	Ask child to repeat back or read aloud instructions to ensure she has understood task.
	Ensure homework instructions are clearly explained in homework diary, link book. If necessary, provide adult/peer support (see A 11 page 397).
	Use a homework diary/folder/box file.
	Attend homework club if available.
	Use wall planner with blank spaces to write on homework and completion date.

Teacher observations	? •••➤ *Practical strategies*
Child is unable to follow instructions for a task.	Ask child to read instructions aloud twice to make sure he has understood.
	Ensure child reads instructions fully.
	Encourage child to highlight instructions with a marker pen to ensure all instructions are read, cross off highlighted instructions as work completed.
	Encourage child to 'self-talk' through each stage and check off each stage when completed.
Child is unable to organise a written task.	Ensure table and chair are at correct height and size and that lighting is good (see OTA 4 page 271).
	Ensure work area is clear of all but essential equipment.
	Use paper with dark blue or black lines as work will be neater.
	Consider writing on alternate lines.
	Keep alphabet and number charts nearby for easy reference.
	Record ideas using mind mapping, spider grams, tape recorders (see A 11 page 397).

Building Blocks for Learning. © 2008 John Wiley & Sons Ltd.

▷▷ Further resources

Refer to Foundation Skills

- FS 2A Motor planning page 35
- FS 2C Spatial and body awareness page 43
- FS 4, FS 4A—FS 4F Perception page 73–97
- FS 6 Organisation approaches page 111

Refer to Occupational Therapy Approaches

- OTA 1 Building firm foundations for spatial and body awareness page 249
- OTA 11 Consolidating foundation skills for transition from primary to secondary school page 349

Refer to Appendix

- A 9 Resources for developing social, emotional and behavioural skills page 389
- A 11 Thinking skills page 397
- A 14 Work system page 405

Refer to Equipment Resources page 407

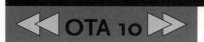
Consolidating foundation skills through group activities

The increasing demands of the National Curriculum often leave little time for children to consolidate the new skills they are acquiring. Whilst opportunities are given in Reception and Year 1 for a lot of 'hands on' exploratory play, by the time children are moving onto Key Stage 2 work it is expected that their skills are developing well and they are ready for the more formal learning. Children who learn quickly are able to integrate their new skills into the tasks they are set, whilst others struggle and frequently require an adult to give additional support.

Since children develop their skills at different rates, some will acquire certain tasks more quickly and easily than others. It is natural that a child who finds working with shape and form hard will opt for an easier task when left to choose his own activity. Unless opportunities are provided to teach and consolidate skills these children will always be building on a vacuum, as the foundation skills are not in place.

Generally, children need to establish and consolidate their gross motor skills first, as these provide a good foundation for all fine manual dexterity and perceptual tasks. Working within a small group provides children with the opportunity to raise their skill level, self-confidence and self-esteem as they realise that others also find the acquisition of certain skills difficult.

Many schools are now running very successful activity clubs that provide children with additional opportunities to work on basic skills and practise them in a non-threatening and 'fun' environment. Children may already be following a therapy programme at home and in school, or the classroom teacher may have identified certain areas of difficulty with some of the basic skills needed to access the curriculum. There are many commercially available movement programmes (see A 7 page 381) which are easy to implement and may meet the children's needs, or it may be helpful to 'mix and match' with a variety of gross and fine motor tasks and perceptual activities.

Establishing groups

It is essential to consider the following when establishing any activity group or club:

Why run a group? (aims)

- *To provide opportunities for children to practise skills* they find difficult in a fun and non-threatening environment.
- *To increase children's confidence and self-esteem* as they realise that other peers have similar problems.
- *To raise awareness* and stress the importance of implementing and integrating therapy principles more fully into classroom activities.
- *To identify one 'therapy' target* to be included in the child's individual education plan.

Who will run the group? (staffing implications)

- *Which member(s) of staff* will have overall responsibility for the group?
- *Who will be involved in setting up* the group initially?
- *Who will help run the group?*—there should be at least two adults for each session. Will the same two people work each week or will there be a rota?
- *Will adults have time,* away from their main classroom timetable, to prepare, run, record progress, clear up and liaise with other staff after the group?
- *Will additional help be forthcoming,* if necessary—voluntary helpers, parents?
- *Who will be responsible for reviewing* the group and making any changes?
- *How often will this review happen*—each half term/each term or annually?

Where will the group happen? (venue and equipment)

- *Which room is available* for both gross and fine motor activities—classroom, quiet room, hall, playground?
- *Is the space large enough* for gross motor activities/are tables available for fine motor tasks?
- *Is equipment easily accessible* or will it have to be moved for each session?
- *Is the equipment* colour coded for easy clearing up and storage in boxes/bags?
- *Is storage available* between sessions for work in progress/therapy equipment/activity boxes between sessions?
- *Will funding be available* for additional specific equipment/resources?

When will the group meet? (time and duration)

- *Will it be 'extra' to the school day* and meet before or after school?
- *Will it meet in the lunch hour*—thereby not putting extra constraints on parents to arrive early or pick up children late?
- *Will it be integrated into the school day*—small groups taken out as timetabled, or on a specific afternoon?
- *How often will the group happen*—daily, two times weekly, three times weekly?
- *How long will it run*—regular shorter sessions or one longer weekly session?

How will the children be referred and their progress recorded? (administration)

- *Will there be 'open' referral* by any class teacher or is it restricted to children on the Special Needs Register?
- *Will a referral form* need to be compiled for completion by the class teacher?
- *How many children will attend at any one time*—will numbers be limited?
- *How long will the children be eligible to attend*—a specific number of sessions or until their skills are satisfactory?
- *Will Key Stage 1 and Key Stage 2 children work separately* or are sessions 'skill based', e.g. scissor activities for all ages?
- *How will their progress be recorded* and reported back to their class teacher—after each session/after a block of sessions/each term?
- *Will class teachers be expected to follow up the group work* in between sessions?
- *Will a digital camera or cam recorder be available* to show the children their progress?

What are the training implications? (whole school awareness)

- *Consider liaising with the local children's therapy services* to help highlight the importance of secure gross and fine motor coordination skills in young children.
- *Arrange in-service training* for the whole school to raise awareness.
- *Attend any training courses* that target the skills being covered in the group.
- *Ensure integration of 'therapy' recommendations* into classroom setting, e.g. correct height table and chair, use of angle board, wedge cushion, pencil grip.
- *Outline the principles of the sessions* and relate therapy skills to classroom performance.
- *Ensure that all staff are aware of the aims and objectives of the group* and how attendance at the sessions will need to be followed up in class.
- *Always relate pre-writing activities* to school handwriting policy.
- *Raise awareness of the many resources* already available in school—identify and collate activities that can be kept in boxes in the resources cupboard and used by class teachers to follow up group sessions, e.g. scissor activities, hand gym, shape and form games.

How will the whole school benefit? (whole school philosophy)

- *Encourage the children to choose their own name* for the group/club so that they feel it 'belongs' to them, e.g. On Target, Pirates, Dinosaurs Group, Cool Club, Challenge Club, Fun Club, Play Movement.
- *Use the parent newsletter* to ask parents to contribute toys, games, equipment, etc. no longer required at home.
- *Invite parents to an 'open session'* to watch their child working on the activities. Explain the importance of regular practice.
- *Involve parents* by asking them to practise one activity with their child at home between sessions. Set this as a SMART goal each week.
- *Use a home/school book or communication sheet* to record progress with family.

- *Designate a display board/notice board* in the corridor to show the children's work or to issue challenges to other staff and children, e.g. how many paperclips can you join in one minute?
- *Hold a special assembly* and let the children tell the whole school about the activities they do in their group.
- *Consider a governor's challenge.*

> Think 'outside the box' and be creative.

Which activities could be used in the group? (programme)

- *Gross motor activities* including those targeting postural stability and balance, body and spatial awareness, bilateral integration and midline crossing, right/left discrimination, eye-hand/eye-foot coordination, motor planning and organisation, visual tracking and ocular motor control, ball skills.
- *Fine manual dexterity activities* including construction tasks, art and craft, modelling, origami, cutting and sticking, cooking, gardening.
- *Pencil and paper activities* using pre-handwriting multi-sensory activities, drawing and colouring, handwriting and using writing tools—ruler, compass, protractor.
- *Perceptual activities* targeting visual, auditory, tactile and kinaesthetic processing.
- *Social interaction/emotional well-being* through turn-taking, team games, projects.

▷▷ Non-themed activity groups

Once children have been identified as needing intervention through group activities the groups can be planned using:

- Published handwriting/movement programmes (see Appendix 5 page 375 and Appendix 7 page 381)
- A specific piece of equipment, e.g. balls, hoops, benches, skipping ropes
- Specific foundation skills or movements, e.g. motor planning, balance, body awareness, (see FS 2A page 35, FS 2B page 39, FS 2C page 43)
- Specific core skills being taught to the whole class, e.g. gym balance, basketball, scissor skills, threading.

▷▷ Themed activity groups

These activities are designed for a small group of children to develop gross and fine motor control and enhance their perceptual skills. If the school hall is available the wall bars, ropes and PE apparatus provide additional challenges. Children enjoy working around a theme, as it provides a good talking point, gives continuity over the sessions and offers many opportunities for a lot of creative thinking. There are many resources within the classroom and school library, and children willingly rise to the challenge of finding out about the particular theme for 'show and tell' activities. The following ideas provide suggestions for three topics.

Pirate group activities

Activities are based loosely around the theme of pirates, so by the end of the final session each child can dress up as a pirate with his own:

- *Hook hand*—twist pipe cleaners and shape into a hook, before fastening to the bottom of an upturned plastic flowerpot.
- *Eye patch*—draw round a template onto black card, cut out and make two holes each side and attach with sheering elastic.
- *Pirate hat*—fold black paper into a hat shape before drawing round templates of a skull and two bones. Cut these out, place on front of hat and stick them down.
- *Telescope*—use a cardboard tube or rolled up newspaper. Draw handwriting patterns on paper; roll these around the tube and stick, before threading string through tube so it can hang from the shoulder.
- *Bottle with a message in it*—use lemon juice for writing the message on paper and roll it up to put in a bottle. Later use a wax crayon to rub heavily over the paper to reveal message.
- *Pieces of eight*—use Hama beads to make a shape on a template and iron in place when pattern completed, or rub over a textured surface and cut out shape.
- *Sword*—cut round a template, roll up paper or use a cardboard tube for the length of the sword. Take another smaller roll or tube placed at right angles across the top of the roll to form a handle. Flatten out, cut end to shape, paint and decorate with glued shapes.
- *Parrot*—follow instructions from Internet/book for folding paper to make an origami parrot.
- *Skeleton*—use pre-drawn skeleton templates, cut around individual bones and put them together with split pins so that the skeleton moves.

In addition, the gross motor tasks are all related to physical activities suitable for exploring an island. Over the sessions an obstacle course is set up and another activity is added each day. The children are asked to remember the layout and assemble it themselves in the following session. During the final session, the children 'escape' from the 'baddies' by breaking a code and finding their own pieces of eight.

A detailed breakdown of each activity for the pirate group is given at the end of this section, together with instructions, list of equipment and skill areas targeted. The format and ideas can be easily modified for a treasure island and knights and castles themed group. The only limitation is the creativity of the leader.

Treasure island activities

These activities are based loosely around the theme of treasure island, so by the end of the sessions each child has made her own island with the following features stuck in place:

- *Island*—use a large piece of hardboard or thick cardboard and draw an outline of a large island. Paint the island green and the sea blue. When the paint is dry, stick sand around the coastline using a glue stick and sand on a teaspoon, or pick up sand and sprinkle between the fingers.
- *Trees*—roll up paper into a tube, cut down tube to make branches (the longer the cut, the bigger the branches) then pull up from the middle to make tree. Cut up the bottom of the tree trunk, fold outwards and stick onto the board.
- *Tent*—place rectangular template on stiff card, draw round it and cut out. Fold in half, open out and use cocktail sticks as tent poles.
- *Flag pole and flag*—make flag, twist pipe cleaners for flagpole and attach.
- *Mountain*—cut large triangular wedge of foam, pull and pinch out bits to make undulating surface. Paint in appropriate colour. Use silver glitter to emphasise craters. Stick in place on island.
- *Flowers*—screw up tissue paper, arrange in patterns and stick in appropriate places.
- *Boat*—follow origami instructions from book or internet.
- *Whale*—follow origami instructions from book or internet.
- *River*—cut out curved shapes from blue paper and stick onto island.
- *Lake*—cut shape from bubble wrap and paint blue before sticking on island.
- *People*—make from pipe cleaners, bend into shapes and distribute appropriately.
- *Treasure chest*—use a box with a lid, paint or cover with paper and decorated with 'jewels'.

In addition, the gross motor tasks are all related to physical activities suitable for exploring an island. Over the sessions an island is created and another activity is added each time. The children are asked to remember the layout and assemble it themselves the following session. During the final group the children 'escape' from the island by breaking a code and finding hidden treasure in their own treasure chest.

Knights and castles group activities

These activities are loosely based around the theme of knights and castles, so by the end of the sessions each child can dress up as a knight with his own:

- *Tunic*—cut out from a black plastic bin liner, with holes for head and arms.
- *Belt*—thread pieces of pasta on a string, and paint, either all the same colour or in a coloured sequence.
- *Shield*—draw around a template onto a large sheet of thick card; divide shield into four sections and draw a small circle in the middle of the shield. Decorate with the child's initial or make a coat of arms. Write different handwriting patterns in each section.
- *Sword*—cut round a template, roll up paper or use a cardboard tube for the length of the sword. Take another smaller roll or tube placed at right angles across the top of the roll to form a handle. Flatten out, cut end to shape, paint and decorate with glued shapes.

- *Helmet*—draw round a template, cut out and decorate.
- *Cannon balls*—screw up pieces of paper into tight round balls.

In addition, the gross motor tasks are all related to physical activities suitable for exploring a castle. Over the sessions an obstacle course is set up and another activity is added each time. The children are asked to remember the layout and assemble it themselves each session. On the final day, the children 'escape' from the castle by breaking a code and firing cannon balls.

Further resources

Refer to Foundation Skills

- FS 1, FS 1A–FS 1E Introduction to sensory processing and all sheets within section page 5, 11–27
- FS 2, FS 2A–FS 2E Introduction to gross motor coordination and all sheets within section page 31, 35–51
- FS 3, FS 3A–FS 3C Introduction to fine motor control and all sheets within section page 55, 59–69
- FS 4, FS 4A–FS4F Introduction to perception and all sheets within section page 73, 77–97
- FS 5, FS 5A–FS 5D Introduction to language and all sheets within section page 101, 103–109

Refer to Occupational Therapy Approaches

- OTA 1 Building firm foundations for spatial and body awareness page 249
- OTA 2 Building firm foundations for left/right awareness page 253
- OTA 3 Building firm foundations for fine motor control page 259
- OTA 4 Building firm foundations for handwriting page 271
- OTA 7 Building firm foundations for scissor development page 319
- OTA 11 Consolidating foundation skills for transition from primary to secondary school page 349

Refer to Appendix

- A 5 Handwriting programmes and fine motor resources page 375
- A 7 Movement programmes and gross motor resources page 381
- A 9 Resources for developing social, emotional and behavioural skills page 389
- A 13 Visual perception resources page 403

Refer to Equipment Resources page 407

Gross motor activities for pirate groups			
Activity	**What to do**	**Materials needed**	**Skills targetted**
Parachute games e.g. Waves in sea Pirate cave Whales and fish	Spread parachute on floor Get children to stand around outside and hold parachute in both hands Gather parachute in hands by 'creeping' fingers to bring material into palm Lift and lower parachute Place ball(s) in middle and make 'waves' to pass ball(s) around circle Change positions by running under parachute when names called Push ball out from middle Chasing child moving under parachute whilst another child on top of parachute tries to 'catch' him	Parachute Selection of balls of different sizes	Core stability—shoulder and pelvic girdle Finger strengthening and dexterity Body and spatial awareness Auditory processing
'Captain Says' based on Simon Says game	Play 'Captain Says' using the hook on the hand to practise left/right discrimination	Hook made in fine motor activity session	Left/right discrimination Auditory processing Postural stability Balance Body and spatial awareness
Captain's coming	Action game following commands Captain's coming—salute Man overboard—lie on back Hoist the sail—hands in air pulling down halyard Scrub the decks—mime action of sweeping	Adult to give commands	Auditory processing Postural stability Body and spatial awareness
Exploring pirate ship	Rolling along mat Commando crawling on 'all fours' keeping bottom low Bottom walking—forwards/ backwards Walking in high kneeling Stepping/jumping over rods from Gymkit	Gymkit Mats	Prone extension Shoulder stability Pelvic stability Balance Body awareness Spatial awareness Rhythm and sequencing Right/left discrimination
Walking the plank	Practise balance activities using the bench, beam and wobble board	'Off ground' PE equipment, e.g. bench, box, trampoline	Agility Balance

Gross motor activities for pirate groups			
Activity	**What to do**	**Materials needed**	**Skills targetted**
Moving around ship without getting wet feet	*Moving between equipment/apparatus* without touching the floor	Bench Beam Wobble boards Foam shapes	Balance Agility Body awareness Spatial awareness
Target practice	*Use bean bags* as cannon balls, children lie over moving rolls or wooden bench and throw into barrels. Vary distance and size of barrel	Large roll/wooden bench Barrels Bean bags Mat	Prone extension Eye-hand coordination Grading and force Timing and rhythm Spatial awareness
Hitting moving target	*Use bean bags* as cannon balls *Children stand side-by-side* on mats in line *Adult rolls barrel* in front of each child to another adult at other end of room *Children throw bean bag* into moving barrel Vary: speed of barrel, throwing hand, colours of bean bags, number thrown at once, etc.	Bean bags Mats Barrel	Prone extension Shoulder strengthening Body awareness Spatial awareness Eye-hand coordination
Stepping stones when get ashore	*Jumping* on 'stepping stones' *Walking* along raised surfaces	Coloured shape mats (circle/square/rectangle/triangle) or carpet squares Wooden blocks Tumble form foam shapes	Balance Postural stability Body awareness Spatial awareness Organisational skills
Finding snakes	*Jumping side to side* along rope *Jumping over 'wiggly' rope* as moved by adults, both along floor and in vertical plane *Running into/under rope* arc as it is turned by adults	Long rope Two adults to turn rope	Bilateral integration Timing and rhythm Judging distance, speed
Crawling along tree trunks	*Pulling along* upturned bench	Wide bench	Pelvic stability Bilateral integration Shoulder girdle strengthening Hand strengthening

Gross motor activities for pirate groups			
Activity	What to do	Materials needed	Skills targetted
Jumping into puddles	Jumping into coloured hoops placed around room Jump from hoop to hoop in sequence: forwards/backward, right/left	Coloured hoops in different sizes	Spatial awareness Bilateral jumping Grading movement Rhythm and timing Sequencing
Quicksand	Spread large sheets of bubble wrap onto floor Walk over bubble wrap making as little noise as possible	Bubble wrap	Body awareness Spatial awareness Proprioception Grading movement
Transferring treasure from boat to island	Position child on scooter board Pull along rope anchored at both ends Transfer treasure from one end of rope to other	Scooter board Rope Treasure (bean bags, pieces of eight, etc.)	Upper body strengthening Body awareness Spatial awareness Force and direction
Crossing ravine	Lying on bench with arms stretched in front Bench may be hooked over another piece of equipment to make a slope Pulling along/up bench	Upturned bench Rail or another piece of equipment to hook bench over Mat to place at end when jumping off	Shoulder strengthening Pelvic stability Motor planning and organisation
Crawling in undergrowth/ along path	Spread parachute out on floor Commando crawling using reciprocal pattern of movement Crawl under material from one side to the other	Parachute Mat	Body awareness Spatial awareness Pelvic stability Shoulder stability Proprioception
Planning an escape from the ship	Put together an obstacle course of activities practised so far, e.g. walk the plank, crawl along the deck, throw cannon balls at enemy, Introduce extra activities each session and get children to remember and set up escape route next session	Parachute Bench Beam Climbing bars Ropes Apparatus Bean bags and targets Coloured sequencing mats Gym kit	Auditory processing and recall Balance Motor planning and organisation Shoulder strengthening Pelvic stability

Gross motor activities for pirate groups			
Activity	What to do	Materials needed	Skills targetted
Auditory games	*Clapping hands or shaking shakers* or musical instruments to make rhythms/drumming sticks/sending secret messages *Sing pirate songs/rhymes.* *On the pirate ship we had . . .*	Musical instruments, e.g. drums, shakers Words for songs	Auditory processing
Kim's game	*Play Kim's game* using objects relating to pirates. Either add or remove objects one at a time or try and remember all objects on tray.	Tray for objects Objects brought in by children or chosen by adult Cloth to cover objects Paper and pens if recording	Visual memory Visual sequencing

Fine motor activities for pirate groups

Activity	What to do	Materials needed	Skills targetted
Making pirate hat	Draw around hat template Cut out hat Draw around skull and crossbones template Cut out skull and crossbones Stick on front of hat	Template for hat Cardboard/thick paper Pencil/felt tips Scissors Stapler	Pencil control Bilateral integration Eye-hand coordination Visual motor integration
Making sword	Draw around template Cut out Make handle Decorate sticking shapes in patterns	Cardboard/cardboard tubes Template for sword Scissors Glue Decorative materials	Eye-hand coordination Spatial awareness Bilateral integration Visual motor integration
Making an eye patch	Draw round template Cut out shape Make two holes for elastic Thread elastic through hole Tie knot when size correct	Template for eye patch Black sugar paper Scissors Thin elastic	Pinch grasp Fine manual dexterity Hand strength Bilateral integration
Making a pirate hand hook	Make hook from pipe cleaners by twisting two together and making 'hook' shape Thread pipe cleaner through bottom of pot Secure tightly Place hand inside pot	Small plastic flower pots Pipe cleaners	Bilateral integration Eye-hand coordination Motor planning and organisation Visual motor integration
Making pieces of eight	Select template for pattern Place Hamma beads on template in desired shape Iron into place	Templates for Hamma beads Hamma beads Dishes for beads Paper for ironing Iron	Motor planning Organisation Fine manual dexterity Sequencing
Making message to put into bottle	Write message on paper using wax candle or lemon juice Roll up paper Unscrew bottle Post rolled message into narrow necked bottle	Paper Candle/lemon juice Writing tool/stick Plastic drink bottles with lids	Manual dexterity Pencil skills

344

Fine motor activities for pirate groups			
Activity	**What to do**	**Materials needed**	**Skills Targetted**
Making parrot to sit on shoulder	Follow directions on making parrot Cut out parrot Stick Place on shoulder	Photocopied parrot sheet Coloured paper Felt tip pens Scissors Glue	Bilateral integration Dexterity Eye-hand coordination Pencil skills
Making a skeleton	Stick skeleton onto card Cut out each part of skeleton Colour Assemble skeleton using split pins so it can move	Skeleton outline on paper Card Glue Scissors Split pins	Bilateral integration Eye-hand coordination Fine manual dexterity
Making a telescope	Copy pre-writing patterns onto coloured paper Wrap the completed paper sheet around a cardboard tube Stick open edge Thread string through tube	Coloured paper Felt tip pens Cardboard tubes Sellotape® Glue stick String	Bilateral integration Pencil control/fluency Motor planning and organisation Eye-hand coordination
Dressing up as pirates using accessories made during the group activities	Pirate hat Eye patch Telescope Hook hand Sword/dagger Parrot to sit on shoulder Pieces of eight Message in bottle to throw in sea	Own child's work, i.e. Pirate hat Eye patch Telescope Hook hand Sword/dagger Parrot to sit on shoulder Pieces of eight Bottle with message	Bilateral integration Spatial awareness Body awareness Motor planning Organisation Eye-hand coordination Fine manual dexterity
Making targets and fire cannon balls at them	Cut out pirate shapes Stick against a wall or bench using Blu-Tack Screw paper into balls Use as targets for 'flicking' activity (lie on tummy with eight balls in front, four for each hand) Flick at target by opposing each finger and thumb in turn—initially each hand separately and then both together	Pictures of pirates Scissor Felt tip pens Blu-Tack Paper to screw up into balls Mats for children to lie on Wall or bench turned on side to attach target and 'fire' balls	Bilateral integration Pencil control Motor planning and accuracy Organisation Fine manual dexterity Hand strengthening

Fine motor activities for pirate groups			
Activity	**What to do**	**Materials needed**	**Skills targetted**
Making model using clay or play dough	Pinch, poke, pull, squeeze, roll, etc. to make models	Easy modelling clay Play dough Modelling tools Slabs/plates for completed models	Hand strengthening In hand manipulation Thumb-finger opposition Fine manual dexterity
Making models from paper	Select origami shapes (boat, whale, fish, etc.) Fold paper step by step, Flatten paper with tips of fingers Decorate finished object	Photocopied instructions Appropriate paper Pens for colouring Decorative materials	Shape and form Spatial awareness Hand strengthening Finger dexterity
Making pirate mask	Colour mask Stick onto cardboard Cut out Make two holes for elastic Thread elastic through holes Tie in knot when correct size	Paper mask picture Cardboard Felt tips Scissors Elastic	Eye-hand coordination Visual motor integration Bilateral integration
Pencil and paper tasks	Dot-to-dot activity sheets on appropriate island topics Find the hidden . . . Word searches Pictures to colour Scrambled words Paint by numbers Matching shapes, e.g. fit key into treasure chest	Activity sheets Pencils/felt tips Paints Scissors	Eye-hand coordination Visual motor integration Sequencing Pencil grasp Pencil pressure Tracking and flow Visual perceptual skills
Therapeutic putty activities	Give putty in appropriate grade to each child Pinch, poke, pull, squeeze, roll, to make putty change shape	Selection of putty, as it is sold in different strengths from very soft (yellow) to extra hard (blue)	Hand strengthening In hand manipulation Thumb-finger opposition Fine manual dexterity

Fine motor activities for pirate groups			
Activity	**What to do**	**Materials needed**	**Skills targetted**
Circuit training—fine manual dexterity tasks These activities are done for one minute and the score recorded on a score sheet (see A 3 page 371). Each child is working on her own, trying to beat her previous score rather than challenging her neighbour. The children complete all activities in sequence.	*Threading pasta* on lace/string *Posting pennies* in box with clothes peg or tweezers *Clipping clothes pegs* around a box or plate *Putting pegs into holes* on pegboard *Holding bottle* with one hand and *posting peas* through narrow opening *Making necklace* with paper clips/bulldog clips *Squeezing sponges* to transfer water from one pot to another *Squirting water* from squeezy bottle to hit target, e.g. ping pong ball in bowl	Pasta in bowl and lace Pennies, clothes pegs, tweezers, box with slit in lid Clothes pegs, paper plates or box Pegs and pegboard Plastic bottle with narrow neck and peas in bowl Paper clips/bull dog clips in bowl or on plate Sponges and pot(s) Plastic bottles of different sizes, bowl and ping pong ball Score sheets Pencils	Fine manual dexterity Hand strengthening Bilateral integration Eye-hand coordination In hand manipulation Counting and recording

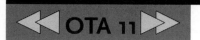

Consolidating foundation skills for transition from primary to secondary school

Leaving primary school and moving to secondary school is a time of change and mixed emotions, such as excitement, sadness and apprehension. It can also provide opportunities for new beginnings and friendships, as well as a wider range of facilities, subjects and clubs. It is a time of considerable change, facilitating development from childhood through adolescence and into adulthood. The expectations for children at this time can be high; they generally leave a small close-knit school where they are the eldest to become the youngest member of a larger community.

As children progress through the school system the content of the curriculum increases in complexity at a time when they are expected to have already developed the necessary underlying skills. Children are required to work independently in a more demanding and social environment, which can be overwhelming if earlier skills, are not well consolidated. This may be an extremely challenging time for children, who continue to have trouble as they watch their peer group move ahead with seeming ease. Children are particularly vulnerable at this time to teasing, bullying, low self-esteem and anxiety.

To ensure smooth and successful transition it is essential to spend sufficient time on preparing children who have additional needs. It is essential to liaise closely with key staff at the new school and transfer all relevant information detailing children's needs well in advance of the end of year six. Discuss with the secondary school staff whether other arrangements are available to assist children needing additional support, such as extra visits in the last term of Year 6 and attendance at a summer school.

The following observations and comments have evolved through partnership working with children, parents and teaching staff during transition from primary to secondary school.

Observations	Children comment	Practical strategies
Larger school environment, buildings spread over bigger area; different lessons held in different parts of school site.	How do I find my way around and what do I do if I get lost? Do I need to carry all my books with me all the time? What happens if I am late for lessons? How will I manage the stairs and crowds at lesson change over? What happens if I get too tired and use too much energy getting from lesson to lesson? How will I know where my lessons are?	Arrange additional visits to new school at various times of the day. Provide a map of new school site and practise finding way around. Practise map reading, e.g. town plans and site maps. Assess for access to secondary school site and ensure recommendations are in place in advance of the start of term. Practise reading timetables and finding way around school with the site map. If possible, provide a copy of actual timetable prior to the start of term. Discuss strategies with child, parents and new school staff, which can be used if child gets lost or is late for a lesson. Consider use of lockers or specified areas to store equipment/ books safely. Practise negotiating stairs without crowds initially, consider the option of leaving lesson slightly earlier or later than the rest of the class if this is helpful. Discuss possible options with person responsible for timetable planning well in advance of timetables being set, if fatigue or mobility is an area of concern.
More children in the school, no longer with a familiar peer group that has become supportive of their needs, peer group might change in different lessons so children may not necessarily be with friends in all lessons.	Will I make new friends? Will I be teased? Who will be in my tutor group and lessons? Will anybody help me? How will I know where my next lesson is? Will I be bullied?	Arrange early liaison with secondary school to look at groupings of children for form groups and lessons. Plan extra visits to prepare child for the volume of children and crowded situations. Discuss with advisory teachers, therapists and parents any necessary considerations for training/advice for teachers or peer group about the child's presentation/condition.

	Observations	Children comment	Practical strategies
			Consider use of mentoring and buddy schemes with secondary school staff, parents and child.
			Ensure child knows who she can go to for help and practise using the system, e.g. scenarios, role play.
			Suggest to parents the possibility of the child joining clubs and activity schemes in the secondary school catchment area prior to the start of term to help establish new friendships.
Teachers are subject based, children will be taught by a variety of teachers with varying teaching styles.		Will teachers help me? How will the teacher know how to help me? Will I be told off? What if the teacher does not like me? Will I be able to keep up with the writing? Can I take my laptop with me?	Ensure good handover of information regarding child's presentation and learning styles. Discuss with secondary SENCO and parents key information that is essential to be circulated to teaching staff, summarise needs and considerations onto one side of A4 paper if appropriate. Promote effective multidisciplinary handover. 'Train' children in how to deal with different adults and learning styles, e.g. if Mr X insists on hands up, provide a reminder/cue card for that specific lesson. Practise interactions through scenarios/role play.
Teaching assistant (TA) support can often be allocated differently in secondary schools. TA can be subject based rather than specific to an individual child.		Will I get any help in lessons? How will the TA know how to help me? Will the same TA help in all lessons I do not want to be different. Will the TA be with me all the time? Will somebody be there to write for me?	Ensure good handover of information regarding child's presentation and learning styles. Provide opportunities for TAs and child to meet prior to start of school term. Discuss with secondary school SENCO options for limiting the number of TAs supporting child.

Building Blocks for Learning. © 2008 John Wiley & Sons Ltd.

	Observations	Children comment	Practical strategies
			Develop child's independence by experimenting with level and timing of TA support.
			Label timetable to show who will be supporting the child and when.
			Increase child's awareness of their own abilities, by reducing frequency of support to enable child to ask for help when it is required, when in the familiar environment of the primary school.
	Emphasis on greater independence in learning and self-organisation	Will I remember what I need? Will I remember my homework? Will I get a detention? What happens if I lose things? Will I be able to do the work? Will I be able to keep up with the writing and will it still be legible? When will there be help? I can't tie a tie or do my shoelaces. How will I know what I need to do?	Practise study and thinking skills, e.g. mind mapping, writing frames, thinking skills. Ensure learning expectations are increased, but the targets set are still attainable. Consider alternative recording methods, provide regular touch typing practice sessions. Involve parents in developing independence and self-care skills. Practise self-care tasks, work towards completing task within a time limit, e.g. shoelaces, tie, fastenings. Practise reading timetable and preparing all books, equipment required for the school day. Encourage child to take responsibility for packing school bag each day and completing homework during Year 6. Discuss with parents benefits of packing school bag the night before. Consider introducing visual timetables/schedules and colour coding of timetables.

352

Observations	Children comment	Practical strategies
Greater distance from home to school; use of school bus, community transport, walking to and from school.	How will I know what time and where to catch the bus? What happens if I forget or lose my bus pass/ticket? How will I manage the bus on my own? Will I find my way to school? What happens if I miss the bus? Will I be bullied on the bus?	Liaise with parents and recommend trip to school and back is practised prior to starting school. Consider using a TA or mentor to escort child on trial journeys. Liaise with parents over timetable reading and packing school bag so that essential items for the day are the only things carried in school bag. Talk to parents about whether children transferring up to the same school could initially travel on transport or walk together. Make arrangements for practicing road safety awareness. Recommend parents implement an agreed system for keeping bus pass in designated place in school bag, in pocket and arrange for a back-up system, e.g. copy bus pass, provide money for bus ticket in case of emergencies. Recommend to parents that child has a list of phone contact numbers in case of emergencies and that child carries mobile phone.

The following group plan has been used to run an occupational therapy transition group in the summer holidays prior to starting secondary school for children with developmental coordination disorder (DCD) at The Occupational Therapy Service, Children's Centre, Royal United Hospital, Bath. The group is run over four days for three and a half hours each day, with a maximum of ten children and a minimum of three staff. The transition group has focused on meeting the needs of children with DCD; however, similar ideas could be used for any children at the transition stage.

The activities could be timetabled into the last two terms of Year 6, using worksheets from *Farewell and Welcome* (Cossavella & Hobbs, 2002) and *Arfur Moe* (2006).

Main aims of the group

To develop:

- *Self-organisation*, e.g. reading a timetable; packing a school bag; filing/ sorting papers/books at home.
- *Study skills/thinking skills*, e.g. using mind maps; problem solving techniques; memory aids such as colour coding, alphabet strip and Post-it notes.
- *Self-care and dressing*, e.g. tying shoelaces; management of ties; speed of dressing/changing.
- *Use of school equipment*, e.g. using compass, protractor, and ruler; trying alternative equipment; using a dictionary and looking things up alphabetically.

Transition group 2006

Day 1

- Ball game warm up
- Introduction: why we are here?
  - rough outline of the day
  - record cards to check progress with practical tasks
  - rules for the week

- Hand out folders, form filling (of name, etc.), record sheets to check progress with practical tasks. Give out dividers for folder filing and label: planning, organisation, time and tools.
- Sort worksheets into alphabetical categories.
- Obstacle course.
- Make drinks, discuss menu plans for the week.
- Prepare and eat lunch.
- Practical circuit to include:
  - map reading
  - dictionaries/Yellow Pages searches
  - shoelace tying
  - managing school ties
  - managing small buttons

- use of alphabet strips
- use of acetate line tracker
- Give out homework sheets and explain.

Homework day 1

- Decorate folder.
- Bring school bag in tomorrow.
- Arfur Moe's work sheets iii and iv.
- Complete clutter control sheets from organisation book.

Day 2

- Project from *Art Attack*/parent talk (45 minutes).
- Feedback from homework.
- Make group hopes and fears mind map.
- Bullet point list of useful organisational strategies.
- Drink.
- School bag packing activity.
- Prepare and eat lunch.
- Scrap heap challenge exercise.
- Complete B/G Steem questionnaire. See further reading.

Day 3

- *Art Attack* activity.
- Making friends worksheets from *Farewell and Welcome* and discussion.
- Drink/feedback on homework, learning styles.
- Bag packing activity using colour coded timetable.
- Feedback on mind map.
- Make and eat lunch.
- Practical circuit:
    - protractors
    - compass
    - story telling with five-point thinking or mind maps

Homework day 3

- Plan a story using five-point thinking or a mind map.
- School rules sheet.
- Handouts from *Arfur Moe/Farewell and Welcome*, e.g.:
    - making friends
    - eye contact
    - asking for help
    - saying sorry
    - settling into school
    - five-point thinking

Day 4

- Practical circuit:
    - protractors
    - compass

- story-telling with five-point thinking or mindmaps
- dictionary
- ties
- ruler

■ Discussion group: talking to partner and finding out something you don't know about them and then feeding this back to the group.
■ Writing positive comments on each other's backs.
■ Drink/feedback of homework.
■ Bag packing activity—colour coded timetable.
■ Moving around to different rooms at the sound of a bell.
■ Prepare and eat lunch.
■ Questionnaire to feedback about the group.
■ Obstacle course.
■ Parents in for the last half hour to see equipment and strategies children found useful.

 Further references

Cossavella, A. & Hobbs, C. (2002) *Farewell and Welcome, a Neat Finish and a Good Start*. Bristol, Lucky Duck Publishing.

Freedman Spizman, R. & Daniels Garber, M. (1995) *Helping Kids Get Organised, Activities that Teach Time Management, Clutter Clearing, Project Management and More!* Carthage, IL, Good Apple.

Hanner, S. (2004) *Arfur Moe's Transition Workbook*. Manchester, Outreach Support Service for Mainstream Education. Website www.autismtoolkit.com/downloads.htm

Hyde, T. & Ahmad, S. (2005) Transition Groups for Children with Developmental Coordination Disorder. *National Association of Paediatric Occupational Therapists*, **9** (3), 11–14.

Jenkinson, J., Hyde, T. & Ahmad, S. (2002) *Occupational Therapy Approaches, for Secondary Special Needs, Practical Classroom Strategies*. London, Whurr Publishers.

Further reading

Buchanan, N. (1999) *Art Attack*. London, Dorling Kindersley.

Maines, B. & Robinson, G. (1988) *B/G Steem—User Manual and CD ROM. A Self-evaluation Scale with Locus of Control Items*. Bristol, Lucky Duck Publishing.

Further resources

Refer to Foundation Skills

- FS 3, FS 3A–FS 3C Introduction to fine motor control and all sheets within section page 55, 59–69
- FS 4, FS 4A–FS 4F Introduction to visual perception and all sheets within section page 73, 77–97
- FS 6 Organisation page 111
- FS 7 Social and emotional aspects page 113

Refer to Occupational Therapy Approaches

- OTA 5 Building firm foundations for approaches to alternative methods of recording page 305
- OTA 8 Sensory strategies page 323
- OTA 10 Consolidating foundation skills through group activities page 333

Refer to Appendix

- A 6 ICT checklist page 379
- A 9 Resources for developing social, emotional and behavioural skills page 389
- A 11 Thinking skills page 397
- A 14 Work system page 405

Appendices

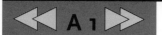

Ages and stages of development

Since each child develops in their own particular manner, it is impossible to tell exactly when or how they will achieve a given skill. These developmental milestones will give only a general idea of the changes you can expect as a child gets older. Do not be alarmed if their development takes a slightly different course. The important thing to be aware of is a steady progression of gaining skills.

 Developmental milestones 3–4 years (Nursery)

Movement

- Balances on one foot for 2–3 seconds.
- Jumps on the spot with two feet together.
- Runs easily, able to stop to avoid a collision.
- Able to run and kick a stationary ball.
- Kicks ball with direction.
- Demonstrates good posture when sitting or standing (at a desk/table, on a chair, in line).
- Able to jump up approximately 30 cm in the air.
- Able to jump along approximately 30 cm.
- Able to jump down approximately 30 cm.
- Attempts to hop, may manage two or three on dominant foot.
- Walks up and down stairs, alternating feet.
- Runs in a coordinated way.
- Stands on tiptoes and walks 3 m.
- Balances and walks on a 10 cm wide beam.
- Walks heel to toe along a line a short distance.
- Able to walk and run backwards with agility.
- Pedals tricycle.
- Bends over easily without falling.
- Catches a large ball from 1.5 m, possibly against body.
- Throws a small ball overhand in correct direction.
- Climbs well on and off furniture/toddler gym equipment.

Hand and finger skills

- Hand preference usually obvious.
- Forms letters, numbers, and basic shapes that are accurate and legible.
- Copies **O, V, H, T, +**.
- Picks up small objects with a pincer grip.
- Threads beads.
- Builds a tower of more than six blocks or copies three steps with six cubes.
- Draws a person with one or two body parts.
- Makes vertical, horizontal and circular strokes with pencil or crayon.
- Holds a pencil in writing position (may not use correct grip).
- Screws and unscrews jar lids, nuts and bolts.
- Turns rotating handles.

Language

- Understands positional relationships (on, in, under, up, down, front, back).
- Follows a two or three component command.
- Recognises and identifies almost all common objects and pictures.
- Understands most sentences.
- Uses four and five word sentences.
- Can say name, age and sex.
- Uses pronouns (I, you, me, we, they) and some plurals (cars, dogs, cats).
- Strangers can understand most words.

Cognitive

- Shows and repeats words for hands, feet, nose, eyes, mouth, shoes.
- Makes mechanical toys work.
- Matches an object in her hand or room to a picture in a book.
- Plays make-believe with dolls, animals and people.
- Sorts objects by shape and colour.
- Completes puzzles with three or four pieces.
- Understands concept of 'two'.

Social

- Imitates adults and playmates.
- Spontaneously shows affection for familiar playmates.
- Can take turns in games.
- Understands concept of 'mine' and 'his/hers'.

Emotional

- Expresses affection openly.
- Expresses a wide range of emotions.
- By three years old, separates easily from parents.
- Objects to major changes in routine.

Concerns should arise if a child continues to experience the following:

- Frequent falling and difficulty with stairs.
- Persistent drooling or very unclear speech.
- Inability to build a tower of more than four blocks.
- Difficulty manipulating small objects.

- Inability to copy a circle by age three.
- Inability to communicate in short phrases.
- No involvement in 'pretend' play.
- Failure to understand simple instructions.
- Little interest in other children.
- Extreme difficulty separating from mother.

 Developmental milestones 4–5 years (Reception)

Movement

- Uses playground/gym equipment (climbing frame with ladder slide, low balance beams, swings—may not be able to initiate the swing) independently.
- Jumps over/across low objects in play environment (blocks, low hurdles, ropes, etc.).
- Stands on one foot for five seconds or more.
- 'Gallops' along 4–5 metres.
- Hops on one foot for five or more times.
- Skips along on alternate feet four or more times.
- Runs around obstacles and turns corners with agility. Goes upstairs and downstairs without support and with one foot to each step.
- Kicks ball forward with good aim.
- Throws ball overhand with accuracy.
- Bounces and catches a football to self.
- Catches bounced ball most of the time with hands only—does not need to use a body grasp.
- Moves forwards, backwards and sideways with agility.
- Walks along a line heel to toe and backwards six or more steps.
- Walks sideways on a 10 cm beam without stepping off.

Hand and finger skills

- Copies square.
- Draws a person with two to four body parts, includes head, legs, trunk and usually arms and fingers.
- Holds instrument with proper tension and grasp (scissors, pencils, pen, paintbrush).
- Turns book pages one at a time.
- Hands out individual sheets from a stack of paper.
- Uses scissors.
- Draws circles and other simple shapes independently.
- Begins to copy some capital letters.
- Attempts to do buttons and other fastenings on self or dolls.
- Able to unscrew and screw up objects.

Building Blocks for Learning. © 2008 John Wiley & Sons Ltd.

Language

- Understands the concepts of 'same' and 'different'.
- Has mastered some basic rules of grammar.
- Speaks in sentences of five to six words.
- Speaks clearly enough for strangers to understand.
- Tells stories.

Cognitive

- Correctly names some colours.
- Understands the concept of counting and may know a few numbers.
- Approaches problems from a single point of view.
- Begins to have a clearer sense of time.
- Follows three-part commands.
- Recalls parts of a story.
- Understands the concept of same/different.
- Engages in fantasy play.

Social

- Puts on and takes off articles of clothing independently (shirt, sweater, socks).
- Shows ability in personal hygiene (wash hands, brush/comb hair).
- Interested in new experiences.
- Cooperates with other children.
- Plays 'mum' or 'dad'.
- Increasingly inventive in fantasy play.
- Negotiates solutions to conflicts.
- More independent.

Emotional

- Imagines that many unfamiliar images may be 'monsters'.
- Views self as a whole person involving body, mind and feelings.
- Often cannot distinguish between fantasy and reality.

Concerns should arise if a child continues to show the following:

- Cannot throw a ball overhand.
- Cannot jump in place.
- Cannot ride a tricycle.
- Cannot grasp a crayon between thumb and fingers.
- Has difficulty scribbling.
- Cannot stack four blocks.
- Still clings or cries whenever her parents leave her.
- Shows no interest in interactive games.
- Ignores other children.
- Does not respond to people outside the family.
- Does not engage in fantasy play.
- Resists dressing, sleeping, using the toilet.
- Lashes out without any self-control when angry or upset.
- Cannot copy a circle.

- Does not use sentences of more than three words.
- Does not use 'me' and 'you' appropriately.

> ## Developmental milestones 5–6 years (Year 1)

Movement

- Stands on one foot for ten seconds.
- Skips along for 4–5 metres.
- Walks around classroom/school avoiding collision with stationary objects/people.
- Carries objects around classroom/school avoiding collision with stationary objects/people.
- Hops on either leg 5–10 times or more.
- Swings and climbs with agility.
- Able to ride bicycle without stabilisers (girls can be a little slower to achieve).
- Dribbles a ball.
- Kicks a rolling ball with accuracy.
- Bounces and catches a tennis size ball.
- Throws a ball with accuracy.
- Able to skip with a rope (boys can be a little slower to achieve).

Hand and finger skills

- Cut/draw/trace with accuracy and precision.
- Uses blocks, beads, puzzle pieces to complete appropriate tasks.
- Copies triangle and other geometric patterns.
- Colours neatly.
- Draws person with body.
- Prints some letters.
- Dresses and undresses without assistance.
- Uses fork, spoon and (sometimes) a table knife.

Language

- Recalls part of a story.
- Speaks sentences of more than five words.
- Uses future tense.
- Tells longer stories.
- Says name and address.

Cognitive milestones

- Knows there is a right and left side to their body (not able to consistently name correctly).
- Can count ten or more objects.
- Correctly names at least four colours.
- Better understanding of the concept of time.
- Knows about things used every day in the home (money, food, appliances).

Building Blocks for Learning. © 2008 John Wiley & Sons Ltd.

Social

- Wants to please friends.
- Wants to be like friends.
- More likely to agree to rules.
- Likes to sing, dance and act.
- Shows more independence and may even visit a next-door neighbour by herself.
- Usually cares for own toilet needs.

Emotional milestones

- Aware of sexuality.
- Able to distinguish fantasy from reality.
- Sometimes demanding, sometimes eagerly cooperative.

Concerns should arise if a child continues to show the following:

- Exhibits extremely fearful or timid behaviour.
- Exhibits extremely aggressive behaviour.
- Is unable to separate from parents without major protest.
- Is easily distracted and unable to concentrate on any single activity for more than five minutes.
- Shows little interest in playing with other children.
- Refuses to respond to people in general, or responds only superficially.
- Rarely uses fantasy or imitation in play.
- Seems unhappy or sad much of the time.
- Does not engage in a variety of activities.
- Avoids or seems aloof with other children and adults.
- Does not express a wide range of emotions.
- Has trouble eating, sleeping or using the toilet.
- Cannot differentiate between fantasy and reality.
- Seems unusually passive.
- Cannot understand two-part commands using prepositions ('Put the cup on the table'; 'Get the ball under the couch').
- Cannot correctly give her first and last name.
- Does not talk about her daily activities and experiences.
- Cannot build a tower of 6–8 blocks.
- Seems uncomfortable holding a crayon.
- Has trouble taking off clothing.
- Cannot brush her teeth efficiently.
- Cannot wash and dry her hands.

▷▷ Developmental milestones 6–7 years (Year 2)

By this age children should have acquired most of their developmental milestones.

- Basic motor skills acquired; improvement in speed and skill of tasks should be observed.
- Able to use ball skills whilst running at speed and changing direction.

- Accuracy with aim and throw whilst on the move.
- Able to coordinate bat and ball activities.
- Skills can be incorporated into team games.
- Able to copy a diamond or rectangle.
- Able to tie a bow or do shoe laces. Mastering a tie usually takes a few more years.
- Emotionally confident and independent of adult.

Children are not expected to be consistent with identifying right and left until eight years.
Source: Compiled by Lou Wollard in Chapman (2007). Used with permission.

References

Chapman, G., Drew, S., Jenkinson, J. & Woollard, L. (2007) *Learn to Move, Move to Learn – How to Help Children with Coordination Difficulties.* Dorset County Council, West Dorset General Hospitals NHS Trust, Poole Hospital NHS Trust.

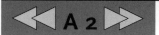
Alphabet ABC sentences

Children who need to practise with handwriting may find these sentences more interesting than copying words, as they contain every letter of the alphabet.

1. The five boxing wizards jump quickly.
2. Pack my box with five dozen liquor jugs.
3. Jail zesty vixen who grabbed pay from quack.
4. Dumpy kibitzer jingles as exchequer overflows.
5. Martin J Hixeypozer quickly began his first word.
6. Brawny gods just flocked up to quiz and vex him.
7. Jim just quit and packed extra bags for Liz Owen.
8. Many big jackdaws quickly zipped over the fox pen.
9. A large fawn jumped quickly over white zinc boxes.
10. Five or six big planes zoomed quickly by the new tower.
11. The exodus of jazzy pigeons craved by squeamish walkers.
12. Now is the time for all brown dogs to jump over the lazy lynx.
13. The vixen jumped quickly on her foe barking with zeal.
14. Picking just six quinces, the new farmhand proved strong but lazy.
15. Alfredo just must bring very exciting news to the plaza quickly.
16. Anxious Paul waved back his pa from the zinc quarry just sighted.
17. Venerable Will played jazz sax 'til 3 o'clock in the morning before he quit.
18. Travelling beneath the azure sky in our jolly ox-cart, we often hit bumps quite hard.
19. Someone just asking was quite pleased with our gifts of a zebra and a clever oryx.
20. As we explored the gulf of Zanzibar, we quickly moved closer to the jutting rocks.
21. Their kind aunt was subject to frequent dizzy spells, thus causing much anxiety and worry.
22. William said that everything about his jacket was in quite good condition except for the zipper.
23. The junior office clerks were quite amazed at the extra reward given by their generous employer.
24. The quick brown fox jumps over the lazy dog.

Source: Jarman. (1979). Used with permissions of The National Association of Primary Education.

369

References

Jarman, C. (1979) *The Development of Handwriting Skills.* Oxford, Blackwell Ltd.

A3 Fine Motor Circuit Score Sheet

NAME: ....

CLASS: ....

Child records the number of items used for task within designated time

FINE MOTOR TASK	Threading pasta	Posting pennies through slot	Clipping pegs onto box/paper plate	Placing pegs into pegboard	Squeezing sponges full of water	Making paper clip chain
Date						
Date						
Date						
Date						
Date						

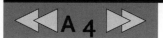

Handwriting self-evaluation checklist

Name .... Class .... Date ....

I am sitting correctly	YES [ ]	NO [ ]
My tool hold is correct	YES [ ]	NO [ ]
My non-writing hand is placed on the paper correctly	YES [ ]	NO [ ]
I need to use a tool grip	YES [ ]	NO [ ]

	ALL	MOST	SOME	NONE
1. My letters are formed correctly.	ALL [ ]	MOST [ ]	SOME [ ]	NONE [ ]
2. My tall letters are the correct height.	ALL [ ]	MOST [ ]	SOME [ ]	NONE [ ]
3. My letters with tails are the correct length.	ALL [ ]	MOST [ ]	SOME [ ]	NONE [ ]
4. My middle size letters are the same size.	ALL [ ]	MOST [ ]	SOME [ ]	NONE [ ]
5. My oval letters are closed.	ALL [ ]	MOST [ ]	SOME [ ]	NONE [ ]
6. The straight lines of my letters are straight.	ALL [ ]	MOST [ ]	SOME [ ]	NONE [ ]
7. The slant of my letters is regular (parallel).	ALL [ ]	MOST [ ]	SOME [ ]	NONE [ ]
8. My letters sit on the lines correctly.	ALL [ ]	MOST [ ]	SOME [ ]	NONE [ ]
9. The spacing between my letters is even.	YES [ ]			NO [ ]
10. The spacing between my words is even.	YES [ ]			NO [ ]
11. My capital letters are formed correctly.	ALL [ ]	MOST [ ]	SOME [ ]	NONE [ ]
12. I use my capital letters correctly.	YES [ ]			NO [ ]
13. I use full stops correctly.	YES [ ]			NO [ ]
14. I join letters correctly.	ALL [ ]	MOST [ ]	SOME [ ]	NONE [ ]
15. My horizontal joins are correct.	ALL [ ]	MOST [ ]	SOME [ ]	NONE [ ]
16. My diagonal joins are correct.	ALL [ ]	MOST [ ]	SOME [ ]	NONE [ ]
17. My numbers are formed correctly.	ALL [ ]	MOST [ ]	SOME [ ]	NONE [ ]

I need to work on:

1. _____

2. _____

3. _____

Source: Taylor, J. (2001) *Handwriting: a Teacher's Guide – Multisensory Approaches to Assessing and Improving Handwriting Skills*. London: Fulton. With permission.

References

Taylor, J. (2001) *Handwriting: a Teacher's Guide – Multisensory Approaches to Assessing and Improving Handwriting Skills*. London, Fulton Publishers.

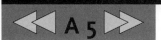

Handwriting programmes and fine motor resources

 Programmes

BBC Magic Pencil (2002) Window and pictures software—combines movement, sounds, clear speech and excellent graphics to help children develop their understanding of correct letter and number formation (available from BBC Worldwide (educational publishing) and Sherston Software Ltd).

Callirobics. Laufer, L. (1990) Charlottesville, VA, Callirobics. Uses handwriting exercises incorporating patterns of straight and curved lines set to music. Four books: *Pre-writing Skills with Music* (ages 4–7), *Handwriting Exercises to Music* (age 7–14), *Callirobics for Beginners: Basic Shapes to Music for Developing Pre-writing Skills*, and *Learning Letters to Music* (available from Special Direct).

Hands up for Handwriting: lively, fun and useful warm-up exercises to prepare the hands and arms for handwriting, devised by Ann Markee (available from National Handwriting Association).

Handwriting for Windows version 2.1. Balcombe, K. (2002) *Handwriting for Windows*—resource on CD ROM to make your own handwriting worksheets and resources (available from Special Direct).

Handwriting Without Tears. Olsen, J. (2003) *Handwriting Without Tears: a Systematic Developmentally Based Multi-sensory Programme*, 9th edn. Cabin John, MD, Jan Olsen (available from Pearson Assessment). HWT is a systematic, developmentally based system that assists children who have handwriting difficulties to improve their skills. This multisensory programme is suitable for use with individuals or groups.

Left-handed Writing Skills. Stewart, M. & Stewart, H. (2005) Stourbridge, Robinswood Press. A specially designed progamme to help left-handers, with 28 worksheets to aid motor-skill development initially. Available in three books or on CD ROM (available from Special Direct)

Loops and Other Groups. A Kinaesthetic Writing System. Benbow, M. (1995) San Antonio, CA, Psychological Corporation.

Pegs to Paper: a handwriting programme with a booklet of pegboard exercises for children who need to make a new start or have great trouble with size (available from National Handwriting Association).

Penpals for Handwriting. Budgell, G. & Ruttle, K. (2003) Cambridge, Cambridge University Press. The series covers each year group from Reception to Year 6 with lots of activities to support the development of gross and fine motor skills. It includes 36 teachers' books, audio CDs, and interactive CD ROMs for use with whiteboard, workbooks, etc.

Pre-writing Skills. Klein, M.D. (1990) *Revised Pre-Writing Skills—Skill Starters for Motor Development.* Tucson, AZ, Therapy Skill Builders.

Senter Series (2005) Special Needs Success (Leeds) publish three books and CD: *One a Day Letter Formation; One a Day Number Formation; Joint Exercises.*

Speed Up: Addy, L. (2005) *Speed Up—a Kinaesthetic Progamme to Develop Fluent Handwriting.* Cambridge, LDA. In just 8 weekly sessions Speed Up! provides a multisensory course of help for any child aged 8–13 whose handwriting is illegible, slow or lacking in fluency.

Structured Cursive Writing. Phillips, L. (1981) *Structured Cursive Writing—a Structured Multi-sensory Handwriting Programme.* Belford, Ann Arbor.

The Scoop on Letter Groups—OT on Hand: suggested mnemonics to teach printing by grouping similar letters. Capital Health, Edmonton, Canada. Website www.capitalhealth.ca/especiallyfor/otonhand/kits

Write Dance. Voors, R. (2000) *Write Dance—a Progressive Music and Movement Programme for the Development of Pre-writing and Writing Skills.* Bristol, Lucky Duck Publishing.

Write from the Start. Teodorescu, I. & Addy, L. (1996) *Write from the Start: the Teodorescu Perceptual—Motor Programme—Developing the Fine Motor and Perceptual Skills for Effective Handwriting.* Cambridge, LDA. A unique approach to developing fine motor and perceptual skills. It offers structured activities to develop the muscles of the hand - so that children gain the necessary control to produce letter forms - alongside the perceptual skills required to orientate and organise letter and words.

Handwriting assessment

Reisman, J. (1999) *Minnesota Handwriting Assessment.* San Antonio, Harcourt Assessment. This is designed to analyse handwriting skills, show how children are performing in relation to their peers and demonstrate the progress made through intervention programmes. The scores are based on legibility, form, alignment, size and spacing.

Handwriting speed assessments

Handwriting Speed Assessment: distributed by PATOSS. The Professional Association of Teachers and Students with Specific Learning Difficulties. Website www.patoss-dyslexia.org

Barnett, A., Henderson, S. & Scheib, B. (2007) *Detailed Assessment of Speed of Handwriting. DASH.* Oxford, Harcourt Assessment. There are five subtests each covering a different aspect of handwriting speed. It is designed to help identify children with handwriting difficulties and provide relevant information when planning intervention.

Handwriting screener for class teachers

Shore, L. (2004) *Shore Handwriting Screener for Early Handwriting Development.* Oxford, Harcourt Assessment. It is designed for use with young children and evaluates the major components of effective handwriting, including postural control, hand control, letter/number formation and environmental factors. There is also information about developmental handwriting milestones.

The following are available from Anything Left Handed (see Suppliers Addresses page 413)

- *Writing Left Handed*
- *Helping Left Handed Children to Enjoy Handwriting*
- *Left Handed Children—a Guide for Teachers and Parents*
- *The Left Hander's Handbook*

The following are available from National Handwriting Association (see Useful Addresses page 417)

- *Writing Left Handed . . .Write In, Not Left Out* (2007)
- *Which Handwriting Scheme?* (2005)
- *Developing a Handwriting Policy* (2005)
- *Tool of the Trade* (1999)
- *Handwriting—Are You Concerned? A Guide for Parents* (currently out of print)
- *Hands Up for Handwriting*—warm-up exercises in preparation for handwriting

Left 'n' Write Ltd provides resources, training and support for practitioners working to improve the handwriting of left-handed children (see Suppliers' Addresses page 413).

▷▷ Further reading/resources

Alston, J. & Taylor, J. (2000) *Teaching Handwriting: a Guide for Parents and Teachers.* Litchfield, QED.

Beery, K. & Beery, N. (2004) *My Book of Letters and Numbers: Instructor's Guide Visual Motor Integration.* USA, NCS Pearson.

Beery, K. & Evans, L. (2004) *The Developmental Teaching Activities: Visual Motor Interaction.* USA, NCS Pearson.

Beery, K. & Evans, L. (2004) *My Book of Shapes: Instructor's Guide Visual Motor Integration.* USA, NCS Pearson.

Chu, S. (1999) *Assessment and Treatment of Children with Handwriting Difficulties,* 11th edn (course book, self-published). London, Hounslow and Spelthorne Community and Mental Health NHS Trust.

Chu, S. (2000) The effects of visual perception dysfunctions on the development and performance of handwriting skills. *Handwriting Today, 2,* 42.

Klein, M.D. (1990) *Pre-Writing Skills* (revised). Tucson, AZ, Therapy Skill Builders.

Levine, K. (1991) *Fine Motor Dysfunction—Therapeutic Strategies in the Classroom.* Tuscon, AZ, Therapy Skill Builders.

Penso, D. (1990) *Keyboard Graphics and Handwriting Skills.* London, Chapman and Hall.

Taylor, J. (2001) *Handwriting. A Teacher's Guide.* London, Fulton.

Fine motor resources

Rainbow Road Programme is designed for children aged 4–12 who have specific learning difficulties. The programme box provides a set of colourful cards, grouped into various skill areas, each with a single activity or task to be performed. The children can record their progress along the 'Rainbow Road' on the chart supplied. Website www.rainbowroadresources.com.au/ products.html

Fine Motor Skills Box contains games and activities to develop fine motor skills. There are instructions for each activity, ideas for making each task easier or harder and a set of 15 activity cards (available from Special Direct).

Puzzle and Games Resource Packs contain a selection of graded activities to allow children to learn through play. Each game is coded to show which specific key skill areas are being targeted, e.g. fine motor skills, hand/eye coordination, visual perception, speed of thought, spatial awareness, problem solving (available from Happy Puzzle company).

The following companies supply equipment for a wide range of fine manual dexterity activities. See suppliers addresses page 413.

ASCO Educational Suppliers Ltd	NES Arnold
Bright Minds	Nottingham Rehab Supplies
Consortium	Peta UK Ltd
Galt Educational and Pre-school	Philip and Tacey
GLS Educational Supplies Ltd	Physio Med Services Ltd
Homecraft Ability One Ltd	Special Direct
Hope	Smart Kids
LDA	The Happy Puzzle Company
Mind Ware	

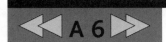

Information communication technology checklist

Seating, positioning and keyboarding skills

Name: .... Date of Birth: .... Class: ....

Completed by: .... Date: ....

TEACHER OBSERVATIONS

To ensure children are able to produce maximum output with minimum effort ask . . . .

	YES	NO
CHAIR/STOOL Is the chair the right height and size? Does the stool give adequate support? Does the child need postural seating or a cushion? Are the child's feet on the floor or appropriately supported? Is the chair pulled up to the table?		
TABLE/TROLLEY Is the table/trolley the right height and size? Is there enough support for the forearm? Is the mouse the right size and design and can the child manage it? Will the wrist roll fit in front of the keyboard? Is there room for the child to work around the keyboard? Can a book rest be placed beside the screen?		
ROOM Can the computer be easily accessed? Is there easy access to plugs? Is there good natural light without reflection? Will other children be distracted? Is there easy access to printer, etc?		
THE LAPTOP Is the position/angle/height correct? Does the font size/style/colour need changing? Are the keys an appropriate size for the child to use? Does the laptop have an integral mouse, and if so, can the child operate it? Is the screen definition clear? Does the child know how to access different functions? Is the child organised enough to open/close files, print out work and save it? Are there appropriate arrangements for saving, printing, recharging batteries, etc?		
THE CLASSROOM COMPUTER Is the screen at eye level? Is the screen far enough away? Is the screen in front of the child? Does the font size/style/colour need changing? Is the keyboard easily accessible?		
KEYBOARDING SKILLS Does the child have good hand skills/finger awareness? Will a key guard be required? Is the child using both hands? Is the child consistent about the fingers used? Does the child need keyboard prompts – dividing strips, lower case stickers or colour coding? Does the keyboard response time need adjusting? Is the child motivated to learn keyboard skills? Is the child following a keyboarding programme? Is there a keyboarding target in the child's individual education plan?		

Lisa Johnson, ICT Inspector
Jill Jenkinson, Paediatric Occupational Therapist

Adapted from September 2001 checklist

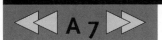

Movement programmes and gross motor resources

Any classroom will already have a variety of resources that can be used to enhance gross motor skills. When selecting equipment to run programmes and activities it will be helpful to consider the foundation skills and occupational therapy approaches, since these address specific skill areas. Since many of the skills are inter-related resources will frequently target several areas at one time. The list of equipment and activities is extensive so the suppliers are listed below and their details can be found under the Suppliers' Addresses page 413.

 Whole school movement approaches

Active Playtimes: Hurn, R. (2006) London, A&C Black Publishing. Offers over 70 practical, easy-to-follow activities and games to help teachers and school assistants introduce constructive, positive, physical play to playtimes.

Golden Mile is a simple walking, jogging and running initiative designed to help children become fit and active by completing 50 miles during a school year within the safety of their own school grounds. It is an award-based scheme encouraging children to exercise with their friends in both a competitive and non-competitive environment, whilst focusing on self-achievement and fun. www.goldenmileclub.com

Huff and Puff seeks to make sport exciting by creating a range of products that encourage inclusion in all aspects of physical activity regardless of ability or aptitude. The equipment is chosen to ensure that children have fun and are kept active, whilst developing the core skills needed to play sports later, such as hand-eye coordination, balance and core muscle stability. Website www.daviessports.co.uk

School Sports Partnership provide a variety of initiatives to encourage children of all ages and abilities to engage in sporting activities. Website www.healthyschools.gov.uk

Take Ten, Fit to Succeed

Active Every Day Key Stage 1. Kelly, L. & Seward, W. (2006) London, A&C Black.
Active Every Day Lower Key Stage 2. Kelly, L. & Seward, W. (2006) London, A&C Black.
Active Every Day Upper Key Stage 2. Kelly, L. & Seward, W. (2006) London, A&C Black.

These form a series of books and DVDs to help primary teachers encourage children to be physically active throughout the school day. There are six activity themes, including coordination and manipulative challenges, running and chasing games and activities for small spaces. Each page gives a ten-minute activity that requires minimal equipment.

Top Start has been designed to support achievement of the Early Learning Goals for Physical Development in the Foundation Curriculum. Training courses are organised by TOP Start training units that are based within local authorities. Website www.youthsporttrust.org

Wake 'n' Shake programmes encourage children to take active exercise at the start of each school day. Activities, which can range from classroom stretches to running round the school, increase children's confidence, self-esteem and their ability to learn and remain focused.

Wake Up and Shake Up is an initiative of the Youth Sports Trust, which works in partnership with schools. The programme is designed to build a brighter future for children and young people through sport, by encouraging fun, fitness and learning through daily physical activity. Website www.youthsporttrust.org

▷▷ Specific movement programmes

Astronaut Training: a Sound Activated Vestibular-visual Protocol for Moving, Looking and Listening. Frick, S. & Kawar, M. (2005) Madison, WI, Vital Links. Astronaut Training presents a long awaited protocol for improving function in the vestibular-auditory-visual triad (includes music CD).

BEAM—Balance Education and Movement. Movement Towards Learning for Reception Aged Children. Finlayson, A. & Rickard, D. (2002) Aylesford, Maidstone Weald NHS Primary Care Trust. Available from Mainstream Therapy Team, Foster Street Clinic, Maidstone, Kent ME15 6NH. A screening package for schools aiding identification of children with coordination difficulties.

Bend and Stretch with the Sticky Kids: Fun and Fitness Songs and Rhymes for Active Children (2004) Glasgow, Sticky Music. Website www.stickykids.co.uk

Core Concepts in Action. Frick, S. & Kawar, M. (2004) Madison, WI, Vital Links. Easily implemented movement activities for children of all ages to develop power, endurance and rhythmicity (includes music CD).

Fizzy Training Games: Targeting Balance, Ball Skills and Body Awareness and Coordination (1999) East Kent Community NHS Trust. Double page leaflet for differing levels of ability: 1 Beginner; 2 Intermediate; and 3 Advanced, complete with illustrations showing abilities, suggested targets and a box to record progress. Available from The Mary Sheridan Centre, 43 New Dover Road, Canterbury, Kent CT1 3AF.

Fun Fit Clubs. Davies, R. (2005) 2nd edn. Cornwall, Cornwall and Isles of Scilly NHS Trust, Cornwall County Council. A screening coordination questionnaire identifies children with movement difficulties and activities, based on typical motor skill development, who could benefit from regular Fun Fit Club sessions.

Get Physical! An Inclusive Therapeutic PE Programme to Develop Motor Skills. Addy, L. (2006) Cambridge, LDA. It contains 40 detailed lesson plans covering the PE curriculum for Key Stage 1 to support children who display specific motor problems. *Get Physical! PE Pack* contains equipment specially selected to support many of the activities outlined in *Get Physical!* (available from LDA).

Kids on the Move: Creative Movement for Children of All Ages. Schmutz Boyd, K. Schmutz Law, J. & Schmutz Chalk, M. (2003) Flower Mound, TX, Creative Publishing. Different aspects of movement are targeted in 45 lesson plans to help children develop physically, musically, socially and mentally.

Learn to Move, Move to Learn: Helping Children with Coordination Difficulties (2005) Dorset County Council, West Dorset General Hospitals NHS Trust and Poole Hospitals NHS Trust. Designed to provide early school-based intervention and support for children who have movement difficulties. A screening and assessment tool that targets gross and fine motor skills, by identifying deficit areas, linking them to activity sheets and suggesting goals to measure improvement. Details of the project are available from Dorset County Council Psychological Service, Cedar Road, Ferndown, Dorset BH21 7SB.

Making Moves: a Practical Guide for Primary School Teachers to Help Children with Motor Skill Difficulties. Ownership shared between Preston PCT, Blackpool, Wyre and Fylde PCT and Morecombe Bay PCT. This programme aims to help teachers recognise and work with children in class by providing individual information and techniques to work on situations encountered in the classroom. Email zenaproject@hotmail.com; Website www.nhselearningdatabase.org.uk/search.asp.

Motor Development Program for School-age Children. Shanks Sellers, J. (1996) Tucson, AZ, Therapy Skill Builders. Creates individualised programmes to assess the motoric development levels of children from 4–12 years old. Sequential activities assist children in building on each skill acquired.

Movement Stories for Children Ages 3–6. Landalf, H. & Gerke, P. (1996) Lyme, NH, Smith & Kraus, Inc. Contains ten movement stories that are active, imaginative tales to be told by a teacher as children act them out. During each story, children are given the opportunity to experience basic movement concepts such as level, direction or size of movement.

Planning a Motor Skills Programme (2004) Developed by Barnet Council in conjunction with Barnet Primary Care Trust through the Barnet Healthy Schools Scheme. The programme has a video and resource cards targeting Brain gym, warm-up ideas, key activities, skill development and cool down activities. Available from Christine Morris, Barnet Healthy Schools

Scheme, Building 5, North London Business Park, Oakleigh Road South, London N11 1NP.

101 Movement Games for Children: Fun and Learning with Playful Moving. Wiertsema, H. (2001) Alameda, CA, Hunter House Inc. Activities include concentration games, hiding and guessing games, reacting games, cooperating games, trusting games and music and movement games.

101 Dance Games for Children: Fun and Creativity with Movement. Rooyackers, P. (1996) Alameda, CA, Hunter House Inc. Activities include hand and meeting dances, cooperation dances, imagination dances, story and party dances

Sensory-motor Integration Activities. Fink, B. (1989) Tucson, AZ, Therapy Skill Builders. These activities are categorised into several basic sensory-motor areas for use with children who have sensory-motor integration difficulties. Each activity includes a performance or behavioural objective, basic method of procedure (or how to play the game), purpose and precautions.

Smart Moves: Motor Skills Development Programme. Drew, S. (2006) Usk, Monmouthshire, Smart CC Publishing. This programme provides simple screening tools which enable non-specialists to profile children aged 5–11 with motor coordination difficulties. It includes over one hundred PE activities and games (includes CD); Website www.specialdirect.com

The Core Workout: a Definitive Guide to Swiss Ball Training for Athletes, Coaches and Fitness Professionals. Elphinston, J. & Pook, P. (1998) Fleet, Core Workout, Rugby Science.

The following companies supply equipment for a wide range of gross motor coordination equipment and activities (see suppliers addresses page 413):

ASCO Educational Suppliers Ltd	NES Arnold
Davies Sport	Philip and Tacey
Galt Educational and Pre-school	Physio Med Services Ltd
Hope	Special Direct
Jabadao	TFH
LDA	Vidipro UK
Left n' Write	Winslow

>> Further reading

Benari, N. (1999) *Early Movement Skills.* Brackley, Speechmark Publishing Ltd.

Cocks, N. (1992) *Skipping not Tripping—How to Help Children Whose Motor Skills Seem Clumsy and Uncoordinated.* Sydney, Australia, Simon and Schuster.

Cocks, N. (1996) *Watch Me, I Can Do It!—Helping Children Overcome Clumsy and Uncoordinated Motor Skills.* Sydney, Australia, Simon and Schuster.

Macintyre, C. (2002) *Early Intervention in Movement: Practical Activities for Early Years Settings.* London, Fulton.

Nash-Wortham, M. & Hunt, J. (1997) *Take Time, Movements and Exercises for Parents, Teachers and Therapists of Children with Difficulties in Speaking, Reading, Writing and Spelling.* 4th revised edn. Stourbridge, The Robinswood Press.

Pointer, B. (1992) *Movement Activities for Children with Learning Disabilities.* London, Jessica Kingsley.

Russell, J. (1988) *Graded Activities for Children with Motor Difficulties.* Cambridge, CambridgeUniversity Press.

Shanks-Sellers, J. (1989) *Motor Development Program for School-aged Children.* Tucson, AZ, Therapy Skill Builders.

Sherborne, V. (2001) *Developmental Movement for Children.* London, Worth Publishing.

Sieglinde, M. (2006) *Teaching Motor skills to Children with Cerebral Palsy and Similar Movement Disorders. A Guide for Parents and Professionals.* Bethesda, Woodbine House Inc.

Welton, P. (1997) *Bright Ideas, Games for PE.* Whitney, Oxon, Scholastic.

Young, S. (1988) *Movement is Fun. A Pre-school Movement Program.* Torrance, Sensory Integration International.

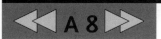
Individual child profile

The following profile has been developed to enable special needs coordinators or teachers to identify the key problem areas affecting a particular child's performance within the classroom or wider school environment. A blank proforma of the individual child profile has been provided for staff to complete.

The teacher's observations can be recorded in the first column and a realistic target set in the second column. Practical strategies can then be selected using the appropriate foundation skills or medical condition table. In the fourth column, a note can be made about who will implement the strategies and when they will be used. A final column has been included to evaluate the outcome.

INDIVIDUAL CHILD PROFILE

Name: ....   Date of birth: ....   Year: ....
Teacher: ....   Date: ....   Review date: ....

Teacher observation	Target	Practical strategies	Who will implement and when?	Outcome
Lacks strength and stability as joints more flexible than peers	Improve sitting position	Ensure child is supported in sitting, e.g. feet on floor/box	Teacher, daily	Child able to work for longer periods
	Provide alternative working position	Allow the child to sit when other children are standing	Teacher/teaching assistant (TA) daily	
Finds handwriting challenging Reduced amount/quantity of output	Complete work set within allotted time	Use part prepared worksheets Allow extra time for completion of task Set realistic goals for written work	Teacher/TA daily	
Difficulty using scissors	Cut along a curved line accurately	Break down task and teach in stages Ensure child has correct scissor grasp Ensure scissors are appropriate	TA small group twice weekly working on scissor skills	Able to cut along curved line accurately

A8 Proforma planning

Name: ....

Teacher: ....

Date of birth: ....

Date: ....

Year: ....

Review date: ....

Teacher observation	Target	Practical strategies	Who will implement and when?	Outcome

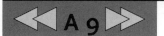

Resources for developing social, emotional and behavioural skills

The following are details of a range of resources that may be helpful in supporting the effective work that staff are doing to promote emotional health and well-being. Although the resources are grouped under specific headings it is recognised there are many overlaps between resources and materials so several areas of emotional health and well-being will be targeted.

Anger

Anger is a normal and healthy emotional response which helps cope with hurt, frustration, threat and if channelled carefully it can be an aid to survival. When children become angry, the body experiences a 'fight or flight' response caused by adrenaline, a hormone that helps the body to react instantly to stress.

Crouch, R. (2000) *Anger Management*—a ten-week small-group counselling programme for students in grades 3–6. Warminster, PA, Mar*co Products Inc.

Droost, J. (2004) *Bubble Gum Guy How to Deal with How You Feel*. Bristol, Lucky Duck Publishing.

Eastman, M. & Craft-Rozen, S. (1994) *Taming the Dragon in Your Child: Solutions for Breaking the Cycle of Family Anger*. Chichester, John Wiley & Sons Inc.

Faupel, A., Hernick, E. & Sharp, P. (1999) *Anger Management—a Practical Guide*. London, Fulton.

Rae, T. & Simmons, K. (2002) *The Anger Alphabet: Understanding Anger—an Emotional Development Programme for Young Children*. Bristol, Lucky Duck Publishing (Book and CD-ROM).

Rae, T. & Marris, B. (2006) *Teaching Anger Management and Problem Solving Skills for 9–12 Year Olds*. London, Paul Chapman Publishing.

Whitehouse, E. & Pudney, W. (1996) *A Volcano in my Tummy—Helping Children to Handle Anger*. Gabriola Island, Canada. New Society Publishers.

Anxiety

Anxiety is a feeling of fear and worry. It is a natural response to experiences, which are uncertain, new and even frightening. All children will feel anxious at times, but if everything goes well the anxiety tends to subside. However, some children can have more difficulty coping with worries, life events and the changes experienced in growing up.

Stallard, P. (2002) *Think Good-Feel Good: a Cognitive Behaviour Therapy Workbook for Children and Young People.* Chichester, John Wiley & Sons Ltd.

Sunderland, M. & Hancock, N. (2001) *Helping Children Who are Anxious or Obsessional.* Brackley, Speechmark Publishing.

Refer to Friends, listed under Miscellaneous resources page 392. Website www.friendsinfo.net/uk.htm

Behavioural strategies

Behaviour is contextual and interactive. Children's behaviour is considered to be underpinned by the stage of development they have reached in social and emotional development. A range of resources aimed at understanding, managing behaviour and promoting positive behaviour are available.

Dunn Buron, K. & Curtis, M. (2003) *The Incredible Five-point Scale.* Shawnee Mission, KS, Autism Asperger Publishing Company. Website www.asperger.net

Emery, C. (2005) *An Essential Guide to Social, Emotional and Behavioural Skills.* Milton Keynes, IncentivePlus.

Mosley, J. & Niwano, Z. (2007) *They're Driving Me Mad!* Nottingham, LDA.

Mosley, J. & Thorp, Georgia (2002) *All Year Around Exciting Ideas for Peaceful Playtime.* Cambridge, LDA.

Rogers, B. (2006) *Classroom Behaviour: a Practical Guide to Effective Teaching, Behaviour Management and Colleague Support,* 2nd edn. London, Paul Chapman Publishing Ltd.

Wallace, F. & Caesar, D. (2007) *Just Stop and Think: Helping Children Plan to Improve their own Behaviour,* 2nd edn. Bristol, Lucky Duck Publishing.

Bullying

Bullying is aggressive behaviour that is intended to intimidate or persecute other people through threats or superior force. Bullying can take many forms; it may include name calling, teasing, pushing, hitting and kicking. Anti bullying resources:

www.dfes.gov.uk/bullying
www.kidscape.org.uk
www.bullying.co.uk
www.childline.org.uk/bullying.asp
www.parentlineplus.org.uk
www.luckyduck.co.uk/approach/bullying

National Autistic Society (1999, revised and updated 2001) *Words Will Really Hurt Me: How to Protect your Child from Bullying.* London, National Autistic Society.

Circle time approaches

Circle time is a forum in which children speak to and listen to one another, express feelings and work on problems or issues together. Circle time sessions involve children sitting in a circle, sharing ideas and feelings on a variety of matters, including emotional, social and behavioural issues.

www.circle-time.co.uk
www.luckyduck.co.uk/approach/circletime
www.incentiveplus.co.uk

Collins, M. (2004) *Circling Safely: Keeping Safe Activities for Circle Time for 4 to 8 Year Olds*. Bristol, Lucky Duck Publishing.

Mosley, J. (1998) *Quality Circle Time in The Primary Classroom*. Nottingham, LDA.

Mosley, J. (2005) *Photocopiable Materials for use with Jenny Mosley Circle Time Model*. Arlington, USA, Positive Press.

Mosley, J. (2005) *Circle Time for Young Children*. London, Routledge.

Mosley, J. & Thorp, G. (2002) *All Year Around Exciting Ideas for Peaceful Playtime*. Cambridge, LDA.

Emotional literacy

Emotional literacy is considered as the ability to recognise, understand and express emotions in a healthy way. Emotional literacy programmes aim to enable children to learn the skills required to develop greater emotional awareness, emotional control and build effective relationships.

www.antidote.org.uk Antidote: Campaign for Emotional Literacy
www.nelig.com   The National Emotional Literacy Interest Group
www.kidsEQ.com   Kids EQ: the Children's Emotional Literacy Project

Antidote (2003) *The Emotional Literacy Handbook: Promoting Whole School Strategies*. London, David Fulton.

Maines, B. (2003) *Reading Faces and Learning About Human Emotions*. Bristol, Lucky Duck Publishing (Book and CD-ROM).

Rudd, B. (2001) *Talking for Us: Emotional Literacy for KS 2 Children*. Bristol, Lucky Duck Publishing.

Weare, K. (2004) *Developing the Emotionally Literate School*. London, Sage.

Mentoring

Mentoring is an approach that aims to provide children with support and advice from a peer.

www.nmn.org.uk   The National Mentoring Network

Clark, A. & Blades, J. (2007) *Mentoring Activities Box*. Brackley, Speechmark.

Self-esteem

Self-esteem is considered a primary factor in building and maintaining social, emotional and mental well-being. Generally, self-esteem is viewed as the product of evaluating oneself against a criteria and reaching expected standards on these criteria. Some children are identified as having low self-esteem and others as having inappropriately high self-esteem. Nurturing self-esteem in children can help to ease feelings of anxiety, sadness and prevent outbursts of anger. Children with healthy self-esteem are more able to handle anxiety, hurt and anger in positive and constructive ways. Helping children build and maintain healthy self-esteem requires an integrated approach incorporating specific classroom routines and the development of emotional literacy.

Burn, G. (2005) *NLP Pocketbook—a Pocket Full of Neuro-linguistic Programming Tips to Help You Succeed and Make a Positive Difference to Your Life*. Arlesford, Management Pocket Books.

Forster, J. (2004) *Target Self-esteem—Essential Reading for Effective Teaching*. Edinburgh, Barrington Stoke Ltd.

Leicester, M. (2006) *Special Stories for Disability Awareness: Stories and Activities for Teachers, Parents and Professionals*. London, Jessica Kingsley.

Plummer, D. (2006) *Self-esteem Games For Children*. London, Jessica Kingsley.

Plummer, D. (2007) *Helping Children to Build Self-esteem*. London, Jessica Kingsley.

Rae, T. (2000) *Confidence, Assertiveness, Self-esteem*. London, Paul Chapman Publishers.

Social skills

Social skills enable children to relate to others, take an active part in a group, communicate, negotiate and resolve differences.

Aarons, M. & Gittens, T. (2003) *Social Skills Training Programmes*. Bicester, Speechmark Publishing.

Adderley, A., Petersen, L. & Gannoni, A. (1997) *Stop, Think, Do Social Skills Training*. Camberwell, Melbourne, ACER Press.

Baker, J. (2003) *Social Skills Training—for Children and Adolescents with Asperger Syndrome and Social Communication Problems*. Shawnee Mission, Kansas, Autism Asperger Publishing Company.

Barratt, P., Border, J., Joy, H., Parkinson, A., Potter, M. & Thomas, G. (2000) *Developing Pupils' Social Communication Skills*. London, David Fulton.

Gray, C. (1998) *Social Stories and Comic Strip Conversations- Unique Methods to Improve Understanding* (video). Arlington, TX, Future Horizons.

Gray, C. (2002) *My Social Stories Book*. London, Jessica Kingsley.

Kiker Painter, K. (2006) *Social Skills Group for Children and Adolescents with Asperger's Syndrome: a Step-by-Step Programme*. London, Jessica Kingsley.

Maines, B. (2003) *Reading Faces and Learning About Human Emotions*. Bristol, Lucky Duck Publishing (book and CD-ROM).

Schneider, C.B. (2006) *Acting Antics: a Theoretical Approach to Teaching Social Understanding to Kids and Teens with Asperger Syndrome*. London, Jessica Kingsley.

Team Asperger (2000) *Gaining Faces*. CD-ROM for teaching people to interpret facial expression. Appleton, WI, Team Asperger. Gaining Faces has been purchased by Stone Mountain Software of Bel Aire, KS and is available from public@StonemountainSoftware.com

The Transporters™ (DVD) (2006) *Transporters Discover the World of Emotions*. Ashton under Lyne, UK, Catalyst Pictures Ltd. Commissioned by Culture Online, produced by Catalyst Pictures with the Autism Research Centre at Cambridge University.

>> **Other resources**

Circle of friends

Circle of friend is an approach that aims to enhance inclusion of a child who is experiencing difficulties. The circle of friends works by trying to build a relationships around the child.

Maines, B. & Robinson, G. (1998) *All for Alex. A Circle of Friends.* Bristol, Lucky Duck Publishing.

Taylor, G. (1997) Community building in schools: developing a circle of friends. *Educational and Child Psychology*, **14**, 45–50.

Whittaker, P., Barrett, P., Joy, H., Potter, M. & Thomas, G. (1998) Children with autism and peer group support: using circle of friends. *British Journal of Special Education*, **25** (2), 60–64.

Friends scheme

Friends scheme is a school-based anxiety prevention programme that aims to help children cope with feelings of fear, worry and depression by building resilience and self-esteem by teaching cognitive and emotional skills. www.friendsinfo.net/uk.htm

Social and Emotional Aspects of Learning (SEAL)

SEAL is a resource which aims to provide primary schools with an explicit, structured whole school curriculum framework for developing all children's social, emotional and behavioural skills and is intended for the whole school community.

The resource focuses on five broad social and emotional aspects of learning:

- self-awareness
- managing feelings
- motivation
- empathy
- social skills

DCSF (2005) *Excellence and Enjoyment: Social and Emotional Aspects of Learning: Guidance: Primary National Strategy.* Nottingham, Department for Children, Schools and Families.

Social Story™

Social Story™ describes a situation or skill in terms of relevant social cues, perspectives and common responses in a specifically defined style. The goal of a Social Story™ is to share accurate social information in a reassuring manner that is easily understood by the child and to improve the child's understanding of events and expectations. Social Stories™ were first developed for use with children with ASD, but the approach has also been successful with other social and communication delays.

Baker, Jed (2003) *Social Skills Training—for Children and Adolescents with Asperger Syndrome and Social Communication Problems.* Shawnee Mission, Kansas, Autism Asperger Publishing Company.

Fisher, R. (1999) *First Stories for Thinking KS1.* Oxford, Nash Pollock Publishing.

Gray, C. (1994) *Comic Strip Conversations: Colourful, Illustrated Interaction with Students with Autism and Related Disorders.* Jenison, MI, Jenison Public Schools.

Gray, C. (1997) *Social Stories and Comic Strip Conversations.* Arlington, TX, Future Horizons.

Gray, C. (1998) *Social Stories and Comic Strip Conversations—Unique Methods to Improve Understanding* (video). Arlington, TX, Future Horizons.

Gray, C. (2000) *The New Social Story Book*. Arlington, TX, Future Horizons.

Smith C (2003) *Writing and Developing Social Stories—Practical Interventions in Autism*. Bicester, Oxon, Speechmark Publishing Ltd.

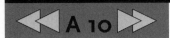

Teachers' checklist for visual signs

Child's name: .... Class teacher: ....

1) Please circle the special areas (if any) of difficulty this child has with reading:

Vocabulary	Word recognition	Oral reading	Silent reading
Rate	Interpretation	Attention	Comprehension

2) Four classifications of frequency of performance traits are given:

- A Meaning very often observed (many times/day)
- B Meaning regularly observed (daily)
- C Meaning sometimes observed
- D Meaning seldom observed

3) Please ring the letter you best consider indicates the child's performance

Does the child show any of the following?

a)	Skipping or rereading lines or words	A	B	C	D
b)	Reads too slowly	A	B	C	D
c)	Uses finger or marker as pointer when reading	A	B	C	D
d)	Lacks ability to remember what he has read	A	B	C	D
e)	Shows fatigue or listlessness when reading	A	B	C	D
f)	Complains of print 'running together' or 'jumping'	A	B	C	D
g)	Gets too close to reading and writing tasks	A	B	C	D
h)	Loss of attention to task at hand	A	B	C	D
i)	Distracted by other activities	A	B	C	D
j)	Assumes an improper or awkward sitting position	A	B	C	D
k)	Writes crookedly, poor spaced letters, cannot stay on ruled lines, excessive pressure used	A	B	C	D
l)	Orientates drawings poorly on paper	A	B	C	D
m)	Is seen to blink frequently	A	B	C	D
n)	Rubs eyes excessively	A	B	C	D

General observations

o)	Clumsiness and difficulty manipulating own body and other objects in space available, including problems with ball control	A	B	C	D
p)	Awareness of things around him in the classroom to point where he turns to look at stimulus	A	B	C	D
q)	Is this child able to maintain his involvement with your instruction?	A	B	C	D

Building Blocks for Learning. © 2008 John Wiley & Sons Ltd.

Scoring

Any scores of 'A', more than two scores of 'B', and more than three or four scores of 'C' suggests that prompt referral to an optometrist specialising in children's eye care is indicated. A copy of this checklist would also be helpful to the optometrist.

Source: Holland (1995). Used with permission.

 References

Holland, K. (1995) *Visual Skills for Learning in Topic*, Spring 1995, Issue 13, Nfer-Nelson.

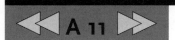

Thinking skills

The term 'thinking skills' is used to describe a wide variety of approaches designed to help with effective learning and problem solving. Information processing skills, reasoning skills, enquiry skills, creativity skills and evaluation skills are considered to be key components. The following are details of a range of resources and programmes designed to develop effective learning and problem solving. Although resources are grouped under specific headings it is acknowledged that there are many overlaps between resources.

Thinking skills

Thinking Skills Website www.standards.dfes.gov.uk/thinkingskills

Blagg, N., Ballinger, M. & Gardner, R. (1988) *Somerset Thinking Skills Course Handbook.* Oxford, Basil Blackwell Ltd.

Dawes, L., Mercer, N. & Wegerif, R. (2000) *Thinking Together– a Programme of Activities for Developing Thinking Skills KS2.* Birmingham, Questions Publishing Ltd.

Evans, A. (1992) *Looking and Thinking—Book 1.* Wolverhampton, Learning Materials Ltd.

Evans, A. (1992) *Looking and Thinking—Book 2.* Wolverhampton, Learning Materials Ltd.

Fisher, R. (1997) *Poems for Thinking.* Oxford, Nash Pollock Publishing.

Fisher, R. (1997) *Games for Thinking.* Oxford, Nash Pollock Publishing.

Fisher, R. (1999) *First Stories for Thinking.* York, York Publishing Series.

Fisher, R. (2006) *Starters for Thinking.* Oxford, Nash Pollock Publishing.

Fleetham, M. (2003) *Thinking Classroom.* Cambridge, LDA.

Jeffries, M. & Hancock, T. (2002) *Thinking Skills: a Teacher's Guide.* Leamington Spa, Hopscotch Educational Publishing.

Kite, A. (2000) *A Guide to Better Thinking—Positive, Critical, Creative.* Windsor, Nelson Publishing Company.

Kite, A. (2000) *A Guide to Better Thinking—Teachers' Guide.* Windsor, Nelson Publishing Company.

Petreshene, S. (1989) *Brain Teasers! Over 180 Quick Activities and Worksheets that make Kids Think.* West Nyack, NY, The Centre for Applied Research in Education.

Shapiro, S. (2002) *Thinking Skills—photocopiable activities.* London, A & C Black.

Wallace, B. (2001) *Teaching Thinking Skills Across the Primary Curriculum.* London, David Fulton Publishers.

Brain gym

Brain gym is an education, movement based programme which uses activities to integrate the whole brain, senses and body. The programme aims to enhance learning and ability through a series of physical exercises to develop neural pathways. Website www.braingym.org.uk

Dennison, P. & Dennison, G. (1989) *Brain Gym*, teachers' edition revised 1994. Oxford, Blackwell.

Cognitive Orientation to (daily) Occupational Performance (CO-OP)

CO-OP is a task orientated problem-solving approach that uses cognitive skills to improve the child's motor performance during daily occupations. Children learn this problem solving process by initially observing and modelling the process. This process can be easily learnt and applied by the child using Goal, Plan, Do, Check. In CO-OP, Goal is the activity identified by the child as something that he or she wants to do better. Plan refers to the ideas that enable the child to perform the activity better. Do is the execution of the activity and Check is the evaluation of the effectiveness of the Plan.

Polatajiko, H., Mandich, A., Miller, L.T., MacNab, J. & Kinsella, E.A. (2000) *CO-OP, The Therapist Training Manual*. London, Ontario, School of Occupational Therapy, University of Western Ontario.

Mind mapping

In mind mapping the idea is to create a picture or diagram of an idea or theme by writing down the words and recording the links between the ideas as branches. A typical mind map may look like a river or tree with lots of branches and sub-branches. The diagram structure or 'map' keeps track of the sub-ideas and related ideas, creating new 'branches' as the child works. In concept mapping the idea is to explore the relationship between the themes and ideas in more detail and the links between ideas are labelled. A typical concept map will look more like a web.

Mind mapping software: Inspiration and kidspiration www.inspiration.com

Buzan, T. (1989) *Use Your Head*. London, BBC Publications.

Buzan, T. & Buzan, B. (1993) *The Mind Map Book—Radiant Thinking*. London, BCA.

Buzan, T. (2003) *Mind Maps for Kids—the Shortcut to Success at School*. London, Harper Collins Publishers.

Buzan, T. (2003) *Mind Maps for Kids—Rev Up for Revision*. London, Harper, Collins Publishers.

Buzan, T. (2005) *Mind Maps for Kids—Max your Memory and Concentration*. Thorsons, London.

Buzan, T. (2006) *Brilliant Memory—Unlock the Power of your Mind*. Harlow, Essex, BBC Active.

Hoffman, E. (2001) *Introducing Children to Mind Mapping*. Brigg, Lincs, Learn to Learn.

Hoffman, E. & Handford, Y. (2004) *Mind Mapping in Primary Classrooms*. Brigg, Lincs, Learn to Learn.

Russell, P. (1984) *The Brain Book*. New York, Dutton.

Stop Think Do

Stop Think Do is a multi-purpose programme for improving children's social and learning skills devised by Lindy Peterson. The programme follows the traffic light symbols: STOP: urge children not to react but to clarify and reflect. THINK: Consider solutions and evaluate consequences. DO: choose best solution, act and follow up. Website www.stopthinkdo.com

Adderley, A., Petersen, L. & Gannoni, A. (1997) *Stop, Think, Do Social Skills Training.* Camberwell, Melbourne, ACER Press.

TASC: Thinking Actively in a Social Context

TASC is a model for the teaching of problem solving and thinking skills.

Wallace, B. (2001) *Teaching Thinking Skills Across the Primary Curriculum.* London, David Fulton Publishers.

Wallace, B. (2002) *Teaching thinking Skills Across the Early Years.* London, David Fulton Publishers.

Visual timetable/schedule: a visual way for describing the sequence of events involved in a task.
www.widgit.com/SIP/resources/classroom/timetables
www.schoolslink.co.uk/resources_displays
www.ispeek.com

Writing frames

Writing frames can provide valuable scaffolding to support children's writing. Children are asked to select, and think about what has been learnt. Writing frames also give an overview of the writing task and can employ both written and visual prompts.

Lewis, M. & Wray, D. (1998) *Writing across the Curriculum: Frames to Support Learning.* Reading, University of Reading.

Wray, D. & Lewis, M. (1997) *Extending Literacy: Children's Reading and Writing Non-fiction.* London, Routledge.

Work system

For details refer to Appendix 14 page 405

 ## Other resources

Hoffman, E. (2002) *Introducing Children to their Senses.* Brigg, Lincs, Learn to Learn.

Hoffman, E. (2003) *Introducing Children to their Amazing Brains.* Brigg, Lincs, Learn to Learn.

Hoffman, E. & Norman, S. (2004) *How Children Learn—Inspiring Teaching.* London, Saffire Press.

Toomey, M. (1994) *Teaching Kids of All Ages to Ask Questions.* Marblehead, Mass, Circuit Publications.

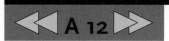

Twelve rules of legibility

Children sometimes find it helpful to have specific rules they can refer to when trying to establish neat handwriting.

1. Letters must be the correct height in relation to each other.
2. Letters that are meant to be closed must look closed.
3. Letters that are meant to be open must look open.
4. Straight strokes must look straight.
5. Curved strokes must look curved.
6. Parts of letters meant to be joined together must be joined, e.g. k not l
7. All parts of letters, such as loops and circles, must appear, also cross-bars and dots on i.
8. There should be a difference between over-curves and under-curves.
9. Letters must be spaced so that it is obvious where one letter ends and another begins.
10. Finish one letter before starting the next.
11. The joining strokes must be indicated, or enough space left, to show where one letter ends and the next begins.
12. The joining stroke must not distort a letter so that it looks like another or suggest an extra letter.

Reproduced by permission of SAGE Publications, London, Los Angeles, New Delhi and Singapore, from Sassoon, R. Handwriting Problems in the Secondary School, © Sassoon, R, 2006

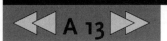

Visual perception resources

Any classroom will already have a variety of resources that can be used to enhance visual perceptual skills. When selecting equipment to run programmes and activities it will be helpful to consider the foundation skills, since these address specific skill areas. Since many of the skills are inter-related, resources will frequently target several areas at one time.

The list of equipment and activities are extensive so the suppliers are listed below and their details can be found under the Suppliers' Addresses page 413.

SUPPLIER	EQUIPMENT RESOURCE
Ann Arbor	Perceptual Activities, The Maze Book, Eye-Hand Coordination Boosters, Classroom Visual Activities, Sound Discrimination Series
ASCO	Kit Cubes, Pyramis, Pyramix, Giant Floor shapes, Formix, Blocolo, Geomag
Bright Minds	Blokus, Gizmos, Wild about Wildlife, Ntropy
Hope	Numicon, Polydron, Bead Sequencing, Marble Run
LDA	Stile, Story Card Sequences
Mind Ware	Quirkle, Blik Blok, Ultra Designs, Space Odyssey
NES Arnold	K'nex, Technicho, Brio, Octoplay, Isotiles
Philip and Tacey	Geonimoes, Constructor Corners, Geostruct, Jumbo Pattern Blocks, Activity Cards, Beads and Pattern Set, Tactile Numerals, Unifix
Tarquin	Altair Design, Look Twice, Dime Solids, Tricubes, Pentominoes, Tangrams
Taskmaster	Geostrips, Geoboards, Lonk-a-word, Floor Dominoes
The Happy Puzzle	Mandala Mosaics, Rush Hour, Shape by Shape, Legend of Landlock, Speedy
Company	Fingers, Bedlam Cube, Timeshock, Penguin Pile Up, Frame It
Winslow	Dotbot Language Activities, Sequencing game

   Further reading

Barsch, R. (1995) *Fine Tuning: an Auditory—Visual Training Program Book One.* Novato, CA, Adademic Therapy Publications.

Barsch, R. (1995) *Fine Tuning: an Auditory—Visual Training Program Book Two.* Novato, CA, Academic Therapy Publications.

Bullock, W. & Loveless, G. (1980) *ABC Mazes*. Novato, CA, Ann Arbor.

Chu, S. (1999) *Assessment and Treatment of Children with developmental Perceptual Dysfunction*, 8th edn (course book, self-published). London, West London Healthcare NHS Trust.

Edwards, J. (1996) *Visual Discrimination—Exploring and Solving Picture Patterns*. Nuneaton, Prim-Ed Publishing Ltd.

Edwards, R. (1993) *Number Activities and Games*. Tamworth, NASEN Enterprises Ltd.

Evamy, B. (2003) *Auditory and Visual Discrimination Exercises—a Teacher's Guide*. Bridlington, Yorkshire, BJE Publications. Email Barbara Evamy@aol.com; available from Dyslexia Action.

Evans, B. (1996) Visual Problems and dyslexia. *Dyslexia Review*, **8** (1), 4–7.

Gardiner, M. (1996) *Test of Visual Perceptual Skills* (non-motor), revised. Navoto, CA, Academic Therapy Publications.

Gentile, M. (1997) *Functional Visual Behaviour—a Therapist's Guide to Evaluation and Treatment Options*. Bethesda, MD, American Occupational Therapy Association.

Heimann, R. (2002) *Mind Munchers—Maze Puzzles and Problems for your Mind to Feast on*. London, Southwood Books Ltd.

Heller, E. (1992) *Half 'n' Half—a Visual Fine Motor Programme Design and Colour Book* (just complete the other half). Novato, CA, Ann Arbor.

Hill, M. & Hill, K. (2007) *Visual Perceptual Skills*. Cambridge, LDA.

Hutchinson, L. (1996) *Cue to Cloze 1*. London, Hodder & Stoughton.

Hutchinson, L. (1996) *Cue to Cloze 2*. London, Hodder & Stoughton.

Jarman, C. (1998) *False Teeth and Vampires. Cloze Procedure Stories*. Cambridge, LDA.

Jay Lev, L. (1992) *Eye Hand Coordination Boosters*. Novato, CA, Ann Arbor.

Lever, M. (2003) *Shape and Space: Activities for Children with Mathematical Learning Difficulties*. London, Fulton.

Levine, K.J. (1991) *Fine Motor Dysfunction, Therapeutic Strategies in the Classroom*. Tucson, AZ, Therapy Skill Builders.

McCreary, P. (1972) *Perceptual Activities (Level 2)*. Multitude of reusable perceptual activities. Novato, CA, Ann Arbor.

McCreary, P. (1997) *The Maze Book*. Novato, CA, Ann Arbor.

Merttens, R. & Kirkby, D. (2000) *Shape, Data and Measures*. Oxford, Ginn and Company.

Morris, C. (1993) *Fold your own Dinosaurs*. London, Collins.

Needham, K. (2005) *The Great Undersea Search*. London, Usborne.

Nilsen, A. (2005) *Famous Journeys—Twelve Incredible Journeys—Twelve Challenging Puzzles*. Sydney, Little Hare.

Scheiman, M. (1997) *Understanding and Managing Vision Deficits—a Guide for Occupational Therapists*. Thorofare, NJ, SLACK Inc.

Tansley, A. (1980) *Perceptual Training*. Tucson, AZ, Communication Skill Builders.

Williams, D. (1998) *Early Visual Skills*. Chesterfield, Winslow.

Williams, H. (1983) *Perceptual and Motor Development*. New Jersey, Prentice Hall.

Williams, L. (2004) *Target Motor and Perceptual Skills—Essential Reading for Effective Learning*. Edinburgh, Barrington Stoke Ltd.

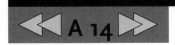

Work system

Children with autistic spectrum disorder (ASD) need visual information to help them understand what they have to do. This work system incorporates the TEACCH principles to enable teachers to provide children with clear guidelines.

It was developed for use with children with ASD in mainstream schools who were not completing tasks set by staff, both in lessons and for homework. It has a general application for children with other medical conditions presenting the same difficulties.

WORK SYSTEM

Name: ....   Date of birth: ....

Subject: ....   Task/topic: ....   Teacher: ....

What work?	How much work?	How will I know it is finished?	What next?
Details of content, e.g. written exercise? Essay? Questions to be answered? Independent reading? etc.	Quantity of work . . . amount of writing, number of questions, time allowed, etc.	Details of how it will be assessed . . . mark allocation, how will teacher monitor what I have done?	If work completed satisfactorily what will next 'work' be? If unsatisfactory what will happen?
Piece of creative writing titled '. . . . .' OR Worksheet on Queen Victoria. OR Reading book '. . . . .' (homework).	One side of A4 lined paper. Answer all the questions. Spend ½ hour this evening reading.	amount of writing satisfactory standard beginning middle and end all answered complete sentences for answers at least 15/20 correct check times (get witness?) be ready to say what you read about	Breaktime Start project on the 20th century Own choice

Source: Reevey 2007

> **REFERENCE**

Schopler, E., Mesibov, G.B. & Hearsey, K. (1995) 'Structured teaching in the TEACCH system. In: Schopler, E. & Mesibov, G.B. (eds). *Learning and Cognition in Autism*. New York, Plenium Press.

WORK SYSTEM

Name: ....   Date of birth: ....
Subject: ....   Task/topic: ....   Teacher: ....

What work?	How much work?	How will I know it is finished?	What next?

Source: Reevey 2007

A blank proforma of the work system has been provided to enable teachers to use this technique with children. This was designed by Alison Reevey, Fosseway School, Midsomer Norton, Bath and North East Somerset (January 2007).

Equipment Resources

Equipment	Supplier
ANGLED WORK SURFACES	
'Write Start' desk top	LDA, Left 'n' Write
'Write Angle' desk top	Philip and Tacey, Special Direct, Left 'n' Write, Nottingham Rehab
Posturite Angle	Posturite
Posturite Board	Posturite
Posture Pack™	Back In Action
Handwriting desk	Taskmaster
Ergo 20 writing slope	Consortium
Writing desk	Hope
CUSHIONS (WEDGE)	
Movin'sit	LDA, Homecraft-Rolyan, Nottingham Rehab, Vidipro
Posture Pack™ seating wedge	Back in Action
COMPASSES	
Safety drawing compass	Hope Educational
Gear headed safety compass	Consortium, GLS Educational Supplies, Hope Educational
Junior compass	Consortium
Berol rule tool	GLS Educational Supplies
Disc compass	Consortium
PAPER	
Visible exercise book	Philip and Tacey
Stop Go Right Line® paper with raised lines	Taskmaster
Right Line® paper with raised lines	Taskmaster
Heavily lined paper	Partially Sighted Society
PENCIL GRIPS	
Comfort grips	Special Direct, Taskmaster
Cross-guard ultra pencil grip	Consortium, Left 'n' Write, Special Direct, Taskmaster
Grotto Grip	Special Direct
Large ultra grip	Special Direct, Taskmaster
Noodle doodle grip	Special Direct
Ridged comfort pencil grip	Special Direct, Taskmaster
Stubbi/Grippy	Anything Left handed, ASCO, GLS Educational Supplies, Hope Educational, LDA, NES Arnold, Nottingham Rehab, Philip and Tacey, Special Direct, Taskmaster
Triangular	Anything Left Handed, Consortium, GLS Educational Supplies, Left 'n' Write, Hope Educational, Philip and Tacey, Special Direct, Taskmaster

Equipment	Supplier
PENCIL GRIPS (Continued)	
Tri-go pencil grip	ASCO, Homecraft-Rolyan, Hope Educational, Left 'n' Write, LDA, Smart Kids, Taskmaster
Solo pencil grip	GLS Educational Supplies, Special Direct, Taskmaster
Ultra grip	Consortium, Homecraft-Rolyan, Special Direct, Taskmaster
Wake Up! pencil grips	Special Direct
Furballz	
Textreme	
Kush-N-Flex	
PENCILS	
Write Start pencils	LDA
Hand huggers	Anything Left Handed, Bright Minds, Consortium, Galt Educational, GLS Educational Supplies, Homecraft-Rolyan, Hope Educational, NES Arnold, Nottingham Rehab, Philip and Tacey, Special Direct
Lyra 'Ferby' pencils	Consortium, Galt Educational, Hope Educational, NES Arnold, Philip and Tacey
Mini Yoro/Yoro pencil™	GLS Educational Supplies, LDA, Left 'n' Write
PENS	
Berol handwriting pen	Consortium, GLS Educational Supplies, Homecraft-Rolyan, Hope Educational, NES Arnold, Philip and Tacey
Berol hand hugger writing pen	Anything Left Handed, Consortium, GLS Educational Supplies, LDA, Hope Educational, NES Arnold, Special Direct
Light up pens	Homecraft-Rolyan, SEN Marketing
Pen Again™	Homecraft-Rolyan, Nottingham Rehab
Ring pen	Consortium, GLS Educational Supplies, Hope Educational, Left 'n' Write, Philip and Tacey, Special Direct
Stabilo S'Move	Homecraft, Special Direct
Squiggle Wiggle Writer™	Special Direct
Tran-quille pen set	Homecraft-Rolyan
Weighted universal holder	GLS Educational Supplies, Left 'n' Write
Yoro pen™	
PROTRACTORS	
Helix angle measure	Consortium, GLS Educational Supplies, NES Arnold, Philip and Tacey
SMP angle measure	Hope Educational
RULERS	
Alligator easy grip ruler	Hope Educational, LDA, NES Arnold, Smart Kids, Taskmaster
SCANNING	
Line tracker	Taskmaster
Reading window	LDA

Equipment	Supplier
SCISSORS	
Easi-Grip®	ASCO, Consortium, GLS Educational Supplies, Left 'n' Write, Homecraft-Rolyan, Hope Educational, NES Arnold, Nottingham Rehab, Peta UK, Philip and Tacey, Special Direct, Taskmaster
Free hand desk clamp and paper holder	BIME, Homecraft-Rolyan, Peta UK, Taskmaster
Mini Easi-Grip®	Left 'n' Write, Peta UK, Special Direct, Taskmaster
Self-opening scissors	ASCO, GLS Educational Supplies, Left 'n' Write, LDA, Homecraft-Rolyan, Peta UK, Taskmaster
Long loop scissors	Consortium, Peta UK, Taskmaster
Long loop self-opening scissors	ASCO, Consortium, Peta UK, Taskmaster
Teaching/dual control training scissors	ASCO, Consortium, Homecraft-Rolyan, Hope Educational, NES Arnold, Peta UK, Philip and Tacey, Taskmaster
Rollcut scissors	Homecraft-Rolyan, Nottingham Rehab, Taskmaster
SENSORY EQUIPMENT	
Fidget items	Hawkins Bazaar, Happy Puzzle Company, Special Direct
Blowing toys	Hawkins Bazaar, Special Direct
Chewy tubes	Winslow
Doodlebug book pad	Special Direct
Ear defenders	LDA
Fidget pencils	LDA, Special Direct
Focus on fidgets	Special Direct
Privacy boards	LDA
Tangle	Happy Puzzle Company, Special Direct
Weighted blanket	TFH
Weighted lap pad	LDA
Weighted wraps	LDA
HANDWRITING RESOURCES	
Roll 'n' Write	ASCO, LDA, GLS Educational Supplies, Hope Educational, NES Arnold, Philip and Tacey
ACE Spelling Dictionary aurally coded English	GLS Educational Supplies, LDA, Smart Kids
Alphabet pegboards	ASCO
Dexball, small and large	Homecraft-Rolyan,
Jumbo magnetic letters	ASCO
Eye-hand integration cards/writing activitycards	Special Direct, Taskmaster
Magnetic writing gel boards	Hope Educational, Special Direct
HandiWriter (wrist loop)	Taskmaster
TIMERS	
Time timer	ASCO, Davies Sport, GLS Educational Supplies, Hope Educational, LDA, NES Arnold, Special Direct, Taskmaster
Sand timers	ASCO, GLS Educational Supplies, Hope Educational, LDA, NES Arnold, Smart Kids, Special Direct, Taskmaster
Time tracker	ASCO, Bright Minds, Hope Educational, LDA, NES Arnold, Special Direct
Catch the clock	Special Direct

Equipment	Supplier	
INCLUSIVE SPORTS EQUIPMENT		
Giant fun football	Davies Sports	
Wheelchair football	Davies Sports	
Inclusive sports equipment	Davies Sports, Nottingham Rehab	
GROSS MOTOR EQUIPMENT		
Balance boards	ASCO, Davies Sports, GLS Educational Supplies, Homecraft-Rolyan, Hope Educational, LDA, NES Arnold, Physio Med, Posturite, Smart Kids, Special Direct, TFH	
Co-Oper™ blanket	Davies Sports, NES Arnold	
Co-Oper™ band	Davies Sports, Homecraft-Rolyan, Jabadao, NES Arnold, Winslow	
Dance sacs/body sox	Davies Sports, Hope Educational, Jabadao, NES Arnold, Winslow	
Lycra® material	Jabadao	
Disc 'O' Sit/Wobble cushion	Homecraft-Rolyan, Physio Med, Posturite, Special Direct, Videpro	
Gymball	widely commercially available	
Ball chair	Back in Action, Davies Sports	
MISCELLANEOUS		
Foot boxes/supports	BIME, Nottingham Rehab, Posturite	
Frenchay E-Tran frame	Winslow	
Porta Ramp	Homecraft-Rolyan, Nottingham Rehab	
Theraband™	Homecraft-Rolyan, Nottingham Rehab, Physio Med, Videpro	
Theraputty®	Homecraft-Rolyan, Nottingham Rehab, Physio Med	
Theraband™ tubing	Homecraft-Rolyan, Physio Med	
Rubazote/plastazote tubing	Homecraft-Rolyan, Nottingham Rehab	
SELF-CARE		
Caring cutlery (junior)	Homecraft-Rolyan, Nottingham Rehab	
(adult)	Homecraft-Rolyan, Nottingham Rehab	
Dycem® mats	Homecraft-Rolyan, Nottingham Rehab	
Dycem® rolls	Homecraft-Rolyan, Nottingham Rehab, Taskmaster	
Non-slip tray	Homecraft-Rolyan	
Curly/coiler laces	Homecraft-Rolyan	
Shoe buttons	Homecraft-Rolyan	
Lace locks	Homecraft-Rolyan	
ICT EQUIPMENT		
Rise and fall tables	Activate, Astor Bannerman, Atkinson Vari tech, Back in Action, Panilet, Posturite	
Wrist rest/support	Consortium, GLS Educational Supplies, Inclusive Technology, Posturite, REM	
Key guards	Inclusive Technology, REM	
Document/copy holders	Back in Action, Consortium, GLS Educational Supplies, Posturite	

Equipment	Supplier
ICT EQUIPMENT *(Continued)*	
Keyboard letter stickers	Granada Learning Ltd/SEMERC, Inclusive Technology, REM
Alternative access devices	Granada Learning Ltd/SEMERC, Inclusive Technology, Posturite, QED, REM, TFH
Big keys	Inclusive Technology, REM, Granada Learning Ltd/SEMERC, QED
Intellikeys	Inclusive Technology, REM, Granada Learning Ltd/SEMERC
Touch screens and monitors	Inclusive Technology, REM, Granada Learning Ltd/SEMERC

Suppliers' Addresses

Activate
Unit 2, Watt Road, Churchfields Industrial Estate, Salisbury SP2 7UD.
Tel 01722 340600; Email sales@activateforkids.com

Ann Arbor Publishers Ltd
PO Box 1, Belford, Northumberland NE70 7JX. Tel 01668 214460;
Email enquiries@annarbor.co.uk; Website www.annarbor.co.uk

Anything Left Handed Ltd
Head office/mail order, 18 Avenue Road, Belmont, Surrey SM2 6JD.
Tel 0208 770 3722; Email enquiries@anythingleft-handed.co.uk;
Website www.anythingleft-handed.co.uk

ASCO Educational Supplies Ltd
19 Lockwood Way, Parkside Lane, Leeds LS11 5TH. Tel 0113 270 7070;
Email sales@ascoeducational.co.uk; Website www.ascoeducational.co.uk

Astor-Bannerman Ltd
Unit 11F, Coln Park Industrial Estate, Andoversford, Cheltenham GL54 4HJ.
Tel 01242 820820; Email sales@astorbannerman.co.uk; Website
www.astorbannerman.co.uk

Atkinson Vari-Tech Ltd
Sett End Road North, Shadsworth, Blackburn, Lancashire BB1 2PT.
Tel 1254 678777; Email sales@vari-tech.co.uk; Website www.vari-tech.co.uk

Back in Action
(4 stores nationwide – contact website for details), 11 Whitcomb Street,
London WC2H 7HA. Tel 0207 9308309; Email info@backinaction.co.uk;
Website www.backinaction.co.uk

Bath Institute of Medical Engineering
The Wolfson Centre, Royal United Hospital, Combe Park, Bath, BA1 3NG.
Tel 01225 824103; Email info@bime.org.uk; Website www.bime.org.uk

Bright Minds
Unit A, Wellsway Works, Wells Road, Radstock, Bath BA3 3RZ.
Tel 0870 4422124; (customer service); Email info@brightminds.co.uk;
Website www.brightminds.co.uk

The Consortium
Hammond Way, Trowbridge, Wiltshire BA14 8RR. Tel 0845 330 7780;
Email orders@theconsortium.co.uk; Website www.theconsortium.co.uk

Davies Sports
Lee Fold, Hyde, Cheshire SK14 4LL. Tel 0845 1204515; Email
enquiries@daviessports.co.uk; Website www.daviessports.co.uk

Galt Educational and Pre-school
Johnsonbrook Road, Hyde, Cheshire SK14 4QT. Tel 08451 20 30 05;
Fax 08000 56 03 14; Email enquiries@galt-educational.co.uk;
Website www.galt-educational.co.uk

GL Assessment
The Chiswick Centre, 414 Chiswick High Road, London W4 5TF.
Tel 0845 602 1937; Email information@gl-assessment.co.uk;
Website www.gl-assessment.co.uk

GLS Educational Supplies Ltd
1 Mollison Avenue, Enfield EN3 7XQ. Tel 0208 344 4000;
Email sales@glsed.co.uk; Website www.glsed.co.uk

The Happy Puzzle Company
PO Box 586, Elstree, Hertfordshire WD6 3XY. Tel 0844 8482820;
Email sales@happypuzzle.co.uk; Website www.happypuzzle.co.uk

Hawkins Bazaar
The Old Aerodrome, Worlingham, Beccles, Suffolk NR34 7SP.
Tel 0870 4294000; Email sales@hawkin.com; Website www.hawkin.com

Homecraft-Rolyan
Nunnbrook Road, Huthwaite, Sutton in Ashfield, Nottinghamshire NG17
2HU. Tel 08702 423305; Email homecraft.sales@patterson-medical.com;
Website www.homecraft-rolyan.com

Hope Education
Hyde Buildings, Ashton Road, Hyde, Cheshire SK14 4SH. Tel 08451 20 20 55;
Fax 0800 92 91 39; Email enquiries@hope-education.co.uk; Website
www.hope-education.co.uk

Incentive Plus Ltd
70 Alston Drive, Bradwell Abbey, Milton Keynes MK13 9HG.
Tel 0845 180 0140; Email info@incentiveplus.co.uk; Website
www.incentiveplus.co.uk

Inclusive Technology Ltd
Riverside Court, Huddersfield Road, Delph, Oldham, OL3 5FZ.
Tel 01457 819790; Email inclusive@inclusive.co.uk; Website
www.inclusive.co.uk

JABADAO
National Centre for Movement, Learning and Health, The Yard, Viaduct
Street, Stanningley, Leeds, West Yorkshire LS28 6AU. Tel 0113 2363311;
Email info@jabadao.org; Website www.jabadao.org

LDA
Pintail Close, Victoria Business Park, Nottingham NG4 2SG. Tel 0845 120
4776; Email orders@ldalearning.com; Website www.ldalearning.com

Left 'n' Write/Wise Owl Toys
5 Charles Street, Worcester WR1 2AQ. Tel 01905 25798;
Email info@leftshoponline.co.uk; Website www.leftshoponline.co.uk;
www.wiseowltoys.co.uk

MindWare
PO Box 644, York YO30 4ZT. Tel 01904 696990; Website www.mindwareonline.co.uk

NES Arnold
Hyde Buildings, Ashton Road, Hyde, Cheshire SK14 4SH. Tel 0845 120 4525; Email enquiries@nesarnold.co.uk; Website www.nesarnold.co.uk

Nottingham Rehab Supplies
Findel House, Excelsior Road, Ashby-de-la-Zouch, Leicestershire LE65 1NG. Tel 0845 120 4522; Email customerservices@nrs-uk.co.uk; Website www.gl-assessment.co.uk

Panilet
Unit 17, Dragoncourt, Crofts End Road, St George, Bristol BS5 7XX. Tel 0117 951 1858; Email sales@panilettables.co.uk; Website www.panilettables.co.uk

Partially Sighted Society
7–9 Bennetthorpe, Doncaster, South Yorkshire DN2 6AA; Tel 0844 4774966; Email hls@partsight.org.uk

Pearson Assessment (formerly The Psychological Corporation)
Pearson Assessment, Halley Court, Jordan Hill, Oxford AX2 8EJ. Tel 01865 888188; Email info@pearson-uk.com; Website www.pearson-uk.com

Peta UK Ltd
Marks Hall, Marks Hall Lane, Margaret Roding, Dunmow, CM6 1QT. Tel 01245 231118; Email sales@peta-uk.com, Website www.peta-uk.com

Philip and Tacey
North Way, Andover, Hants SP10 5BA. Tel 01264 332171; Email sales@philipandtacey.co.uk; Website www.philipandtacey.co.uk

Physio Med Services Ltd
Glossopbrook Business Park, Glossop, Derbyshire SK13 7AJ. Tel 01457 860444; Email sales@physio-med.com; Website www.physio-med.com

Posturite (UK) Ltd
The Mill, Berwick, East Sussex BN26 3SZ. Tel 0845 3450010. Email support@posturite.co.uk; Website www.posturite.co.uk

QED (Quality Enabling Devices Ltd)
Unit D16, Heritage Business Park, Heritage Way, Gosport, Hants PO12 4BG. Tel 0239 258 0600; Email sales@QEDonline.co.uk; Website www.QEDonline.co.uk

REM (Rickitt Educational Media Ltd)
Great Western House, Langport, Somerset TA10 9YU. Tel 01458 254700; Email sales@r-e-m.co.uk; Website www.r-e-m.co.uk

Granada Learning Ltd/SEMERC
The Chiswick Centre, 414 Chiswick High Road, London W4 5TF. Tel 0845 602 1937; Email sales@semerc.com; Website www.semerc.com

SEN Marketing
618 Leeds Road, Outwood, Wakefield WF1 2LT. Tel 01924871697;
Email info@senbooks.co.uk; Website www.senbooks.co.uk

Smart Kids (UK) Ltd
5 Station Road, Hungerford, Berks RG17 0DY. Tel 01488 644644;
Email sales@smartkids.co.uk; Website www.smartkids.co.uk

Special Direct
TTS, Park Lane Business Park, Kirby-in-Ashfield, Nottinghamshire
NG17 9LE. Tel 0800 318686; Email sales@specialdirect.com; Website
www.specialdirect.com

Tarquin Publication
99 Hatfield Road, St Albans AL1 4JL. Tel 01727 833866;
Email orders@tarquinbooks.com; Website www.tarquinbooks.com

Taskmaster Ltd
Morris Road, Leicester LE2 6BR. Tel 0116 2704286;
Email info@taskmasteronline.co.uk; Website www.taskmasteronline.co.uk

TFH (Worcestershire) Ltd
5–7 Severnside Business Park, Stourport-on-Severn, Worcestershire
DY13 9HT. Tel 01299 827820; Email info@tfhuk.com; Website
www.specialneedstoys.com

Vidipro UK
Unit 6, Wilden Industrial Estate, Wilden Lane, Stourport-on-Seven,
DY13 9JY. Tel 01299 829400; Email info@vidipro.co.uk

Winslow
Goyt Side Road, Chesterfield, Derbyshire S40 2PH. Tel 0845 230 2777;
Email sales@winslow-cat.com; Website www.winslow-cat.com

Useful Addresses

Association of Paediatric Chartered Physiotherapists
see The Chartered Society of Physiotherapists

Bath Institute of Medical Engineering (BIME)
The Wolfson Centre, Royal United Hospital, Combe Park Bath BA1 3NG.
Tel 01225824103; Email info@bime.org.uk; Website www.bime.org.uk

Design and technology charity interested in developing devices that have a
general application but are not commercially available

The British Association of Behavioural Optometrists (BABO)
Christine Hancock (Secretary), Greygarth, Littleworth, Winchcombe,
Cheltenham GL54 5BT. Tel 01242 602689; Email admin@babo.co.uk;
Website www.babo.co.uk

Behavioural optometrists use lenses and vision training to facilitate
the development of a more efficient and complete visual process. Early
detection of visual difficulties is vital, but should not rely on simple
school eye tests, which are not designed to pick up these difficulties. A full
optometric or behavioural optometry examination should be carried out
wherever possible.

British Association/College of Occupational Therapists
106–114 Borough High Street, Southwark, London SE1 1LB. Tel 020 7357
6480; Website www.cot.co.uk

British Dyslexia Association
98 London Road, Reading RG1 5AU. Tel Helpline 0118 9668271; Email
helpline@bdadyslexia.org.uk; Website www.bdadyslexia.org.uk

The Chartered Society of Physiotherapy
14 Bedford Row, London WC1R 4ED. Tel 0207 3066666; Email
enquiries@csp.org.uk; Website www.csp.org.uk

Children Young People & Families (CYPF)
see British Association/College of Occupational Therapists' website
www.cot.org.uk/specialist/children/intro/intro.php

A specialist section of the College of Occupational Therapists

Contact a Family (UK Office)
209–211 City Road, London EC1V IJN. Tel 0207 608 8700; Helpline
0808 808 3555; Email info@cafamily.org.uk; Website www.cafamily.org.uk

A directory of specific conditions and rare syndromes in children, with
their family support networks. They also have a website and helpline.

CP Sport England and Wales
Unit 5, Heathcoat Building, Nottingham Science and Technology Park, Nottingham NG7 2QJ. Tel 0115 9257027; Email info@cpsport.org; Website www.cpsport.org

Disability Sport Events
Belle Vue Centre, Pink Bank Lane, Manchester M12 5GI. Tel 0161 9532499; Email info@dse.org.uk; Website www.disabilitysport.org.uk

ENABLE Scotland
Sixth Floor, 7 Buchanan Street, Glasgow G1 3HL. Tel 01412264541; Email enable@enable.org.uk; Website www.enable.org.uk

Inclusive PE for physically disabled users (Talin Skeels-Piggins)
Email tskeelspiggins@hotmail.com; Website www.solutions4accessibility.co.uk;

Talin is a PE teacher who is now a paraplegic and gives advice to schools on inclusive sports. He is in the GB disabled ski team from November to March but is contactable by email.

Mencap England
123 Golden Lane, London EC1Y ORT. Tel 020 7454 0454; Email information@mencap.org.uk; Website www.mencap.org.uk

Mencap in Northern Ireland
Segal House, 4 Annadale Avenue, Belfast BT7 3JH. Tel 02890 691351; Email mencapni@mencap.org.uk; Website www.mencap.org.uk

Mencap Cymru
31 Lambourne Crescent, Cardiff Business Park, Llanishen, Cardiff CF14 5GF. Tel 02920 747588; Email information.wales@mencap.org.uk; Website www.mencap.org.uk

National Handwriting Association
Rita Mechen, NHA Administrator, 12 Isis Avenue, Bicester, Oxon OX20 2GS. Tel 01869 600951; Email admin.nha@ntlworld.com; Website www.nha-handwriting.org.uk

Aims to raise awareness of handwriting as a crucial component of literacy; to maintain good practice in teaching of handwriting; to provide support for those working with children and adults who have handwriting difficulties.

National Organiser for REMAP Scotland
Mr David Reid, Forgue House, Forgue, Huntly AB54 6DA. Tel 01466 730254; Email davidreid@forgue.freeserve.co.uk

RDA Riding for the Disabled Association (incorporating carriage driving)
Norfolk House, 1a Tournament Court, Edgehill Drive, Tournament Fields, Warwick CV34 6LG. Tel 0845 658 1082; Email info@rda.org.uk; Website www.rda.org.uk

REMAP Head Office
D9 Chaucer Business Park, Kemsing, Sevenoaks, Kent TN15 6YU. Tel 0845 1300456; Email info@remap.org.uk; Website www.remap.org.uk

Covers England, Wales and Northern Ireland. Registered national charity who design and make technical equipment (which is not commercially available) for disabled people. Helps people with disabilities to achieve greater independence and enjoyment of life's opportunities.

RoSPA the Royal Society for the Prevention of Accidents
RoSPA House, Edgbaston Park, 353 Bristol Road, Edgbaston, Birmingham B5 7ST. Tel 0121 2482000; Email help@rospa.org.uk; Website www.rospa.com

Has details of wheelchair proficiency training.

Royal College of Speech and Language Therapists
2 Whiteheart Yard, London SE1 1NX. Tel 0207 3781200; Website www.rcslt.org

Scottish Disability Sport
Caledonia House, South Gyle, Edinburgh EH12 9DQ. Tel 0131 3171130; Email admin@scottishdisabilitysport.com; Website www.scottishdisabilitysport.com

Wheel Power
British Disability Sport, Stoke Mandeville Stadium, Guttmann Road, Stoke Mandeville, Buckinghamshire HP21 9PP. Tel 01296 395995; Email info@wheelpower.org.uk; Website www.wheelpower.org.uk

Further Reading

Condition specific information

Inclusive Education for Children with Muscular Dystrophy and other Neuromuscular Conditions—Guidance for Primary and Secondary Schools, UK: Muscular Dystrophy Campaign

Britton, C. (2006) *Kids with Arthritis: a Guide for Families*. Hove, East Sussex, Choices.

Hunsley, D. (2004 updated) (first published 1996) *A Day with Sam*. London, Arthritis Care.

Diagnostic criteria

American Psychiatric Association (1995) *Diagnostic and Statistical Manual of Mental Disorders: DSMVI: International Version with ICD 10 Codes*, 4th edn. Washington DC, The American Psychiatric Association.

World Health Organisation (1994) *International Statistical Classification of Diseases and Related Health Problems*, 10th revision (three volumes). Geneva, World Health Organisation.

Educational inclusion

Cheminais, R. (2003) *Closing the Inclusion Gap: Special and Mainstream Schools Working in Partnership*. London, David Fulton.

Cheminais, R. (2006) *Every Child Matters: a Practical Guide for Teachers*. London, David Fulton.

Farrell, M. (2000) Educational inclusion and raising standards. *British Journal of Special Education*, **27** (1), 35–38.

Gross, J. & White, A. (2003) *Special Educational Needs and School Improvements: Practical Strategies for Raising Standards*. London, Fulton.

Gross, J. (2007) *Special Educational Needs in Primary School: a Practical Guide*, 3rd revised edn, Buckingham, Open University Press.

Jenkinson, J., Hyde, T. & Ahmad, S. (2002) *Occupational Therapy Approaches for Secondary Special Needs: Practical Classroom Strategies*. London, Whurr.

Mackey, S. & McQueen, J. (1998) Exploring the association between integrated therapy and inclusive education. *British Journal of Special Education*, **25** (1), 22–27.

Mitler, P. (2000) *Working Towards Inclusive Education*. London, Fulton.

General development

Sheridan, M.D., Frost, M. & Sharma, A. (1997) *From Birth to Five Years; Children's Developmental Progress*. London, Routledge.

Government documents

Department for Children, Schools and Families (2005) *Every Child Matters Change for Children, Aims and Outcomes*. London, Department for Children, Schools and Families. Website www.everychildmatters.gov.uk/aims

Department for Children, Schools and Families (2006) *The Common Assessment Framework for Children and Young People: Practitioners Guide*. London, Department for Children, Schools and Families. Website www.everychildmatters.gov.uk/caf

Department of Health (2003) *Briefing Pack for Strategic Health Authorities: the National Service Framework for Children Young People and Maternity Services*. London, Department of Health.

The National Curriculum

Department for Education and Employment (1999) *The National Curriculum. Handbook for Primary Teachers in England; Key Stages 1 and 2*. London, Department for Education and Employment.

Glossary

asymmetrical	When one side of the body differs from the other.
ataxia	Movements are jerky, unsteady, walking with a wide base, imperfect balance and at times an intention tremor.
atrophy	Wasting of muscles or nerve cells.
backward chaining	A technique used for learning skills. The skill or task is broken down into small component parts and learnt or practised by starting with the last part in the sequence and gradually working backwards, as each part is fully established.
buddy scheme	A strategy to promote positive relationships between children. Buddies are 'trained' to listen to classmates and taught ways of dealing with other children's problems.
Child and Adolescent Mental Health Service (CAMHS)	This is a specialist service for children and families with a significant level of concern regarding emotional health and well-being. It is usually a multidisciplinary team, offering a variety of therapies and interventions for children and young people where there are emotional, behavioural, relationship problems and mental health concerns.
Common Assessment Framework (CAF)	The CAF is a standardised approach to conducting an assessment of a child's additional needs and deciding how these needs should be met. It can be used by practitioners across all children's services in all local areas in England. It aims to help early identification of need, promote coordinated service provision and reduce the number of assessments that some children and young people go through.
congenital	Existing at or before birth.
contracture	Permanently tight muscles and joints
dynamic balance	The ability to maintain balance as we are moving, e.g. walking, roller-blading.

dystonia	Fluctuating, variable tone.
extension	The process of straightening or stretching the body or a limb.
eye teaming	A term used to describe the general skills needed to ensure the two eyes work together when viewing a target; these skills include convergence, focus and eye movement (sometimes called tracking) skills as well as the perceptual skills needed to control these processes.
flexion	Bending or pulling in a part of the body or a limb.
hypertonia	High muscle tone, which often results in a degree of tightness.
hypotonia	Low muscle tone, which often results in a degree of floppiness.
ICT	Information, communication and technology.
kinaesthesia	'The sense of kinesthesia combines proprioception and tactile sensations to provide the brain with information about movements of body parts in relation to each other. Intact kinesthetic sensations are required for throwing balls, playing tennis or golf, climbing stairs, typing, writing, and riding a bike. The body needs sensory clues from its body parts to make continual, subconscious readjustments to the motor performance. For example if a toe is injured, the body automatically adjusts its standing position.' Tupper, L.C. & Klosterman Meisner, K.E. (1995) *School Hardening, Sensory Integration Strategies for Class and Home.* San Antonio, Texas, Therapy Skill Builders.
LEA	Local Education Authority (Education Library Boards in Northern Ireland).
lordosis	Forward curvature of the spine.
occupational therapy (OT)	Occupational therapy enables people to achieve health, well-being and life satisfaction through participation in occupation. Occupational therapists work with a range of people, including those who have physical, mental and/or social problems, either from birth or as the result of an accident, illness or ageing.

proximal	Nearest to the body.
scoliosis	A sideways curvature of the spine.
SENCO	Special educational needs coordinator (Learning Support Services in Scotland).
SMART target	Specific, Measurable, Achievable, Realistic, Timed target.
splint	A support made for joints that are inflamed, to rest and maintain them in a functional position.
splinter skills	An isolated activity that is developed with effort and cannot then be generalised for other purposes.
static balance	The ability to maintain balance while standing still, e.g. standing on one leg while putting on a shoe.
symmetrical	When both sides of the body are the same.
task analysis	A method for identifying the stages and components required in order to complete a task.
tone	The normal tensions of the muscles at rest.
tremor	A very fine kind of jerking spasm.

Index